Mark Beech is Editor at Bloomberg Television in London. He has worked for *Independent Television News*, *PA News* and the *Sunday Times*.

His own musical career was meteoric – it crashed to earth fast. It included a memorable spell with an infamous Oxford University punk group Marius And The Firebombers, who broke up after a concert during which the audience threw insults, jelly babies and bottles at the stage. He took the hint and tried writing poetry: however his first book was called *Passionfruit*, which meant it ended up on the cookery shelves in some shops ...

He has since interviewed many top musicians, as well as their families, friends, managers, concert promoters, roadies, groupies, and anyone else he could think of along the way.

He lives in London and Worcestershire and is working on several writing projects including a follow-up to this book.

THE A–Z OF NAMES IN ROCK
and the amazing stories behind them

by
Mark Beech

ROBSON BOOKS

First published in Great Britain in 1998 by Robson Books Ltd, Bolsover House, 5–6 Clipstone Street, London W1P 8LE

British Library Cataloguing in Publication Data
A catalogue record for this title is available from the British Library

ISBN 1 86105 059 3

Set by Columns Design Ltd., Reading
Printed in Finland by W.S.O.Y.

Nicely disparaging quotes

Rock journalism is by people who can't write, for people who can't read.

Frank Zappa

Don't take action because of a name! A name is an uncertain thing, you can't count on it!

Bertolt Brecht, *A Man's A Man*

We could have called ourselves the Vegetables or the Potatoes. ... What does a Led Zeppelin mean?

It doesn't mean a thing.

Jimmy Page

Names are but noise and smoke, Obscuring heavenly light.

Johann Wolfgang von Goethe, from *Faust Part One*

When you think about it, the whole concept of picking a name for a band is ridiculous.

Simon Armstrong, songwriter with the band BOB

It's what's on the record that counts. It's all that ever fucking counts.

Elvis Costello, asked about name and image

What's in a name? That which we call a rose, By any other name would smell as sweet.

William Shakespeare, *Romeo And Juliet*

... when asked t'give your real name ... never give it.

Bob Dylan, closing words of *Advice For Geraldine On Her Miscellaneous Birthday*

Acknowledgements

My sources, apart from my own interviews with stars, include many single and album covers, material from videos, radio and TV programmes, nearly every major rock reference book, an assortment of Web sites, biographies and autobiographies of bands and stars.

Another source of data was secondary material: interviews by other journalists in the national press plus *NME, Vox, Mojo, Rolling Stone, Melody Maker* and *Q* magazine.

I wish to thank all those record company press officers who lent their assistance. My journalistic colleagues and friends have chipped in with information too. Gratitude to Barry Oliver, Charles Edinger, Tim Evans and Chris Kirkham. Staff at the British Library and the National Sound Archive gave unfailing help.

Also while I'm in "without whom ... " mode, I must express thanks to Kazuyo Enomoto, for helping to print the first draft and much else. This book would never have appeared without literary agent Lisa Eveleigh and the Robson team, especially Kate Mills. Acknowledgements to my kind neighbours in both city and country for tolerating the occasional loud playing of records for "research purposes".

Preface

This work was born after conversations with three people: my granny, a newspaper columnist ... and Sting.

My grandmother on my father's side hated rock music – but she loved philology: the origin of words and names.

What I learned from her proved to be invaluable when I started work as a news reporter and the idea of a book came about during chats with my then-colleague Phil Hainey – with thanks and a tip of my hat to him, wherever he may be now. If I could answer his queries why not write them down?

Which brings us to the Sting interview. Another friend of mine suspected that, in keeping with Sting's serious image, his *alter ego* meant something deeply profound or pretentious. I'd heard it was something to do with a jumper. Sting confirmed that my version was correct: it was merely a silly nickname because of a black and yellow horizontally striped Breton-type top. It was a great story and made me realise there's a tale behind many aliases just waiting to be discovered. So one source of primary material was my own interviews with stars ranging from the sublime (The Smiths) to the ridiculous (Sigue Sigue Sputnik, Lemmy from Motörhead).

After Sting, I habitually included the question: "How did you and/or your band get the name?" I had certain impertinent "pay-offs", usually left to the end of the meeting – such as "How much are you worth?" and: "Do you mind if I ask how old you are?" (where I didn't know the answer or it was unclear). In other words, I knew they could produce irritation and were best kept until the main questions were in the can.

Many full-time music journalists rarely bother to ask exactly why identities come into being – even in initial articles about new acts, despite it being an obvious starting point. Maybe the reporters don't dare blow their cool. Sometimes fledgling talents are reluctant to reveal these origins or influences. Still, if asked, naïve groups will often happily explain.

In other cases the question comes up *ad nauseam*. Peter Hook of New Order says he's been asked "hundreds of times". He calls it "a dumb question". Still, it's often perfectly valid to ask – and it's perfectly valid to reply, too: "It means nothing" or: "I'm not going to tell you."

However, if fans can't find out from initial articles, what next? Generally, the explanation will come sooner or later in a feature, a fanzine, a biography, a radio interview or Internet profile – while the fact-hungry follower still might miss it. In many cases, listeners cannot solve the riddle even by having every record and going to every concert.

Why the excitement? Well, stars as varied as The Doors, NWA, U2, The Clash, Blind Faith, The Beginning of the End, UB40, Devo, Tears For Fears, The Levellers and The Beautiful South nuncupated after their intention, manifesto, interests or whole philosophy. To have this fully explained can be deeply insightful.

This book will annoy those people who don't want every mythology explained, categorised and defined. Mystery can make life more interesting, yes, and ignorance can be bliss – but how much people miss in their ignorance. This is far more than a book for trainspotters, anoraks or fact-freaks – it is for anyone who wants to understand music. In a non-mysterious way.

Introduction

This book should be of use and entertainment to all those interested in names, words and especially popular music. Rock is the main subject, as the title suggests, but there's also plenty on styles from pop to punk, jazz to soul, country to indie, heavy metal to folk, and rock 'n' roll to reggae. Artists from genres outside the mainstream are included, especially where they are well known or where there is a good story to tell.

The quick-reference guide runs from Aaliyah to ZZ Top. It covers the stars and groups of today, yesterday, and – in some cases – maybe even tomorrow. In short, it provides the answers to one of the great questions in contemporary music: "Why are they called that?"

We'll see the replies are sometimes iconoclastic, occasionally controversial, often hilarious, frequently revealing and usually fascinating. This book should solve many Trivial Pursuits arguments and satisfy the curiosity of those who are baffled at the variety of occasionally ridiculous tags that musicians insist on calling themselves.

Its goldmine of useless information will prove an education on subjects as varied as prehistoric dinosaurs (T Rex), Gaelic swear-words (Pogue Mahone), medieval torture machines (Iron Maiden), U.S. television comedy shows of the 1960s (The Lucy Show), birdwatching (The Nightingales), science fiction (The Human League) and bizarre sexual practices with rodents (allegedly, The Pet Shop Boys).

It has 2,440 entries but isn't a full encyclopedia of music. While the length of each entry isn't meant to reflect the importance of each artist, major stars generally get a fuller treatment.

Some superstars have simply kept their real cognomens. Elvis Presley, Michael Jackson, Mick Jagger and Bruce Springsteen are examples. This makes detail only worthwhile where, for example, they have dropped a prenomen, have interestingly christened backing bands or have used stage aliases for production work, session-playing and other projects. Many other bands, especially from the early 1960s and before, had designations which simply suited their style or image and don't warrant more than a few words at best.

Dates or personnel details are usually only added where they're clearly relevant to the nuncupation process. The entries are not intended to be full biographies and so often deal only with the start of a career, when the pseudonym was fixed.

On the other hand, this volume includes many other things that a conventional encyclopedia would exclude. For example, some entries give nicknames, billing names, anagrams and "unflattering derivatives" – used jokingly by radio disc jockeys and the music press. Some entries list the unusual, not to say whacky, prenomens rock stars are apt to give their offspring. Examples: Zowie Bowie, Rolan Bolan, Moon Unit Zappa, Fifi Trixibelle Geldof. And some give author's prize ratings for particularly good/bad/beautiful/ugly designations or for individual band members.

There are some origins of other music-related epithets included, such as companies and magazine titles. Plus a few record labels owned by the stars, managers and fan clubs – particularly those that relate to the stars' own real or assumed nominal identities.

There are also details of informal or contracted versions used by fans: The Rolling Stones to The Stones, The Wonder Stuff to The Stuffies. Plus there are album names which pun on the *nom de noise* of their authors. And entries like Sade and Björk offer helpful pronunciation tips.

Many entries give cross references to related or similarly named acts, shown by ▷. This book is made for browsing. A good strategy is to pick up on a cross reference, see where it leads and then go on from that.

Some of the more detailed stories are drawn from a composite of sources – maybe an interview; several book-length biographies; television and radio interview transcripts and many cuttings. The Bob Dylan, Beatles, Led Zeppelin and Oasis entries, for example, are already comparatively lengthy. They would be a maze of references if each fact was annotated like a a doctoral thesis. Source references are given only where essential or where accounts differ. Mischievous musicians in L7, The Jesus And Mary Chain and other acts have also fabricated many amusing explanations of their monikers, which are sometimes worth including purely for their entertainment value.

Wherever possible, then, multiple cross-checks of spellings and stories have been used. Readers who do discover mistakes can turn their irritation or dismissal to most productive use. You are warmly invited to write in with any corrections, suggestions and additional names/stories, plus documentary proof where possible. Write to the author, care of A.P. Watt Literary Agents, 20 John Street, London WC1 2DR.

All the information used will be appropriately acknowledged in future editions. Which will surely come: new bands and stars come into existence every day, and some are bound to have aliases even more noteworthy than those in this volume.

But that's for the future ... now, read on – and enjoy.

Mark Beech

Aaliyah

This first entry introduces a theme which we'll return to: the single name artist. The trend has become more common since the time of ▷ Sting and ▷ Madonna. This Detroit-born R&B star was born Aaliyah Haughton. She knew quite a few other Haughtons but no other Aaliyahs. *Hence the name.*

Abba

Swedish singer-songwriters Benny Andersson and Bjorn Ulvaeus had previously worked as The Hootenanny Singers and with The Hep Stars. They teamed with two girl singers to release their first single as "Bjorn, Benny, Agnetha and Frida" because all were already known recording acts in their country. This was clearly a bulky name and swiftly reduced to the initial letters of their Christian names. Agnetha was known as Anna, Frida was also called Anni-Frid. This made Abba an acronym, palindrome and later – with the second B backwards – a registered trademark.

This 1970s/early 1980s Eurovision-winning and commercially massive band spawned 1990s successful spoof acts: ▷ Bjorn Again and Fabba.

ABC

Why the name? "Because the first letters of the alphabet are known the world over," explained Martin Fry. A similar sort of reasoning produced the appellation ▷ The Police for another Northern England singer, Sting.

Fry also thought the choice would put the band's records "at the top of the pile in the alphabetical section of shops". So it did, apart from the likes of ▷ Aaliyah and ▷ Abba. He added: "It's vague enough not to be limiting."

Fry, the band's mainman, guiding light, vocalist and lyricist, teamed with the other original ABC members after interviewing them in Sheffield for his samizdat pop magazine *Modern Drugs.* The others were at that time – 1981 – in an abortive synthesiser group called Vice Versa, a name Fry deemed "not poppy enough".

ABC also said the designation stood for "Always Be Cool", perhaps to counter suggestions it was really "Awfully Boring Crap". There was concern at possible confusion with the now-defunct British ABC TV station and ABC of America – though how anyone could mix them up God only knows. Fry revived the act in 1997, declaring ABC stood for nothing at all.

AB/CB

Inspired by ▷ AC/DC.

Abraxas Pool

Comprising many members of ▷ Santana who played on the *Abraxas* and *Santana III* albums.

Abyssinians

It wasn't a statement of origin. It was from their Rastafarian beliefs. Abyssinia's the homeland of the religion's father-founder. Cf ▷ Ethiopians.

AC/DC

This band was formed in Sydney, Australia, in 1973, with a Scottish contingent. They intended their name simply to refer to the electrical term "alternating current/direct current", used for an instrument switchable to be used on AC or DC mains depending on the country. Because their music was *High Voltage* – the title of their first LP.

Guitarist Malcolm Young insists that even original vocalist Bon Scott didn't know it had a connotation meaning bisexuality: "It was not widely used as an expression then."

They found out soon enough after moving to Melbourne – and ended up playing in gay bars where Malcolm's brother Angus went down a storm by dressing as a schoolboy.

Mainstream success for such a moniker would seem impossible in Australia, never the most tolerant nation towards homosexuality. AC/DC made it with Scott's macho image – it was a brave journalist who dared to quiz him on the name – and their emphasising the electrical theme through later albums such as *Powerage* and *Flick Of The Switch*.

▷ AB/CB.

Ace

This U.K. band formed from pub-rock outfits Mighty Baby and Dust. The new name came from 1973 British street parlance derived from card games and terms like "flying ace". So "you're ace" translates as: "You're very good." And "ace high flush!" means: "Exceptionally good!"

Ace Of Base

Originally Tech Noir, the name of a disco in *The Terminator* film. These Swedes thought the alternative name was "more descriptive of our sound". The re-spelling of "bass" was deliberate.

A Certain Ratio

▷ ACR.

ACR

Originally A Certain Ratio, allegedly referring to the ratio between men and women in the population, this late 1970s-on Manchester, U.K. group renamed in abbreviated form ACR.

Action Painting!

Inspiration from the visual arts for this British 1990s band who liked performance art and were named after a technique which goes back to Leonardo da Vinci's blot drawings and popularised by Jackson Pollock and Mark Tobey from the 1930s. Take a large canvas and pots of paint. Chuck, dribble or daub latter on former.

Adam And The Ants

Londoner Stuart Goddard, born 1954, called himself "Adam", after Adam and Eve: "I'm the *first* man!"

His first musical experience was in ▷ Bazooka Joe And The B-Sides. After leaving Hornsey Art College in 1977 he formed the first version of The Ants, using alliteration with "Adam" and critical comments that the juvenile music would only suit those with ant-like brains. It also provided a pun on "adamant", someone determined and hard, and recalled Adam Adamant, the hero of a mid 1960s BBC TV science fiction series played by Gerald Harper.

It was ▷ Sex Pistols manager Malcolm McLaren who advised Adam to forget punk, put on the warpaint and use African tribal drums in the incarnation which brought him success, as the original Ants became ▷ Bow Wow Wow.

Fans called: Ant People.

Cannonball Adderley

U.S. alto-saxophonist Julian Adderley was called "cannibal" – because of the amount he ate. According to legend, the corruption of his nickname followed a mis-hearing during a long-distance phone conversation. Like ▷ Freddie Cannon later, it produced predictably "explosive" puns in record titles.

King Sunny Ade

This African singer reworked his name Sunday Adeniyi. Pronunciation: Ard-ay.

Ad Libs

Because they were always forgetting the words and having to improvise. The musical term *ad libitum* is often applied to any passage that is made up on the spur of the moment.

Adolf And The Casuals

▷ R.E.M. side-project. The name's a joke: recalling German dictator Adolf Hitler and 1950s-on U.S. bands such as Kenny And The Kasuals. Because Adolf isn't a casual sort of name.

Adrenalin O.D.

Only fans of this New Jersey neo-punk completely unsubtle crew need to be told adrenalin is a chemical released by the body during excitement or danger. The "fright, fight, flight" hormone stimulates muscular action, faster heartbeats and emotion. The rest of us know.

The Adult Net

A spin-off from ▷ The Fall and ▷ The Smiths. Led by American Laura Elise, AKA Brix, Smith. Brixie, the now former other half of Mark E. Smith, lifted the name from a line in one of his songs.

The Adventures

They began as punk band The Starjets in Belfast, Northern Ireland, which later disbanded with two of the founder members moving to London, U.K., in 1980, hoping to have adventures ... Cf ▷ The Ventures.

Aerosmith

Drummer Joey Kramer pieced together words Scrabble-style. Aerospace and songsmith were chosen. The result – Aerosmith, not Spacesong – was meaningless but sounded good. He denied any relation to Henry Sinclair Lewis's influential 1925 novel *Arrowsmith*.

▷ The Toxic Twins.

Trivia note: *Kerrang!* magazine said the band initially considered the provocative tag The Hookers – but guessed this choice would limit airplay.

A Flock of Seagulls

▷ Flock of Seagulls.

African Queen

Named after the 1951 film starring an Oscar-winning Humphrey Bogart, with Katharine Hepburn. The classic flick is about a dangerous river journey by a raffish trader and a reserved missionary.

Afrodiziak

African music band with afro haircuts, included here purely for their dreadful punning name.

AFT

Another abbreviation; no relation to ▷ ATF. This band's initials stood for Automatic Fine Tuning. No, not American Federation of Teachers.

After The Fire

There have been two bands of this name. One group, with Christian commitments, said it's a biblical reference to an inferno-style Apocalypse and the flames of hell for those sinners after Judgement Day. The other lot, a better known 1980s British act, were more reluctant to reveal the origin. They had a hit with *Der Kommissar* and later became ▷ ATF.

Don't confuse with ▷ AFT.

Aggrovators

From British street-patois "aggro", short for aggravation or trouble.

A-Ha

Norwegian 1980s pop phenomenon with a name chosen – from an early song title – by keyboardist/vocalist Mags Furuholmen because it would be remembered in many languages. Cf ▷ The Police, ▷ ABC etc.

Everywhere "aha" means "yes", "Eukeka" or "got you!", often uttered after the disclosure of incriminating evidence or something being kept hidden, especially being concealed intentionally.

It's often written as lower case a-ha, although their record sleeves and press releases were inconsistent.

Curious to note, they started off in a less commercial ▷ The Doors / ▷ Jimi Hendrix mould, called first Spider Empire and later The Bridge. Morten Harket admits once liking deeply unfashionable progressive rockers ▷ Uriah Heep.

Aints

Because they ain't the Saints. They were formed by songwriter Ed Kuepper who dropped the S after the Saints split.

Airhead

U.K. band jokingly reacting, in a very 1980s "breadhead" way, against 1960s "airhead" hippies. Hippy parlance: breadhead = someone concerned with money, a capitalist; airhead = someone concerned with nothing very much at all. They were for a while ▷ Jefferson Airhead, a name which satirised ▷ Jefferson Airplane. They changed to plain Airhead after the prospect of legal action.

Air Supply

… Because this soft rock group's music was seen as a counterattack – a breath of fresh air – to the growing popularity of heavy metal.

Alabama

Countless bands have named after their home: ▷ Black Oak Arkansas, ▷ Bush, ▷ East 17, ▷ Portishead and this lot to name but a few.

They started as Wild Country: their music is country. They renamed because of their strong regional following. The choice was controversial because of those who saw Alabama, the state, as synonymous with redneck conservatism. Check out the song dispute between ▷ Neil Young – *Southern Man* – and ▷ Lynyrd Skynyrd – *Sweet Home Alabama*.

The Alarm

Works on several levels: alarm for future, human emotion of alarm, alarm clock, striking as an alarm. For the record, ahem, they came from Rhyl, Wales, and started playing as punksters The Toilets: reference *The Spirit of '76*. This anti-commercial appellation didn't last long. They evolved into punk-mod band 17, named after the ▷ Sex Pistols song and a reference to their ages.

Alarm Alarm was the title of one of their songs. So good they named it twice. It was abbreviated because of fears of unfair comparisons to other double-barrelled names such as ▷ Duran Duran.

Also for the record, the 1980s rock stars stayed in Rhyl and became so familiar that their spiked haircuts no longer alarmed the natives there. Sad.

They have none the less made a career out of it, which would have been highly unlikely as The Toilets.

José Alberto

▷ (El) Canario.

Albert y Los Trios Paranoias

Spanish for Albert And The Three Paranoias. The members of this U.K. rock/comedy outfit, who never took life – or themselves – too seriously, masqueraded as Paraguayans. They got their name inspiration from several real bands who took themselves far too seriously. The Latin American music was also mercilessly parodied in ▷ Monty Python's song *Llamas*.

The Albion Band

Albion means Great Britain, it doesn't just relate to the well-known English football team West Bromwich Albion. It is from the European root word *albh*, or "white". *The Oxford English Dictionary* adds *albus* is Latin. It was probably chosen as a country name by Romans on their first sight of Britain, although it may also refer to the Celts.

This band was set up by bassist Ashley Hutchings after he quit ▷ Fairport Convention and ▷ Steeleye Span. He wanted to make music based on traditional English and Celtic folk. The act began as The Albion Country Band and then The Albion Dance Band, reflecting Hutchings's interests, later becoming Albion Band '89. Spin-off ▷ The Home Service.

Dennis Alcapone

Cf ▷ Dillinger. Another Jamaican star to name after a U.S. outlaw, in this case Al Capone. He was born Dennis Smith.

Alf

Nickname for a tomboy singer, not the most feminine of figures who was inappropriately called Genevieve. The new name, based on her punky nature, was a corruption of her other first name, Alison, which she preferred to Genevieve.

Later the Essex girl aimed for a slimmer-line serious sexy image, insisting she was a plain vocalist, not a singer. This was accompanied with hair, dress and name worn longer: she reverted to her full name Alison Moyet … (for it is she, the singer in ▷ Yazoo).

Alice In Chains

Originally, Alice In Chains was the name of a school band led by singer Layne Staley. He later joined with members of another amateur outfit, Gypsy Rose, to form the embarrassingly glammy unit called Diamond Lie, with Nick Pollock singing. Alice In Chains was resurrected as a joke name for a spoof time out project, an ▷ Alice Cooper-style group in punk-style bondage gear. Early Alice Cooper favoured drag; this U.S. ensemble favoured grunge clothing and music and used the Alice In Chains identity full time when they couldn't agree on anything better for their day-job performances. Pollock went on into My Sister's Clothes, which had similar Alice influences.

Alien Sex Fiend

U.K. singer Nick Wade created a science-fiction character as his *alter ego*, called Demon Preacher – the name of his first band. The character became the sex fiend, with Wade wearing weird make-up to complete the alien role. The rest of the band complemented the look with very pale faces and very black hair duly dyed and spiked in best pre-goth style.

Alisha's Attic

British pop hopefuls of the 1990s from Dagenham, Essex, Alisha's Attic comprises sisters Shellie and Karen. They are supported and produced by Dave Stewart, the former ▷ Eurythmics star.

The name comes from a fictional character, Alisha, who is an innocent and a devil simultaneously – "a woman like us who embraces her demons: she's good and bad in the same breath," they told the London *Evening Standard* in July 1996. Their lyrics put it like this: "She's an angel but she sins sometimes/ Dressed in white gets drunk on red wine." It's also a reference to their Dagenham loft which they use for writing.

All About Eve

Nostalgic/psychedelic name, harking back as far as you can go, to Adam and Eve and the heavy heady days of hippiedom. This London, group founded their own record label, appropriately enough called Eden.

All About Eve was an award-winning 1950 film with Bette Davis at her bitchy best, and it was from here they found the appellation.

The film's about a burning out, fading star who's in danger of being eclipsed by a new talent. Leader Julianne Regan thought this an apt plot line at the start of their career.

Part spin-off from ▷ Gene Loves Jezebel. Cf ▷ Adam Ant.

All Fall Down

This name becomes marginally less silly when it emerges it was inspired by a 1962 film of the same name. It comes from the end of the children's rhyme *I'm The King Of The Castle*. Nearly all the characters in the silver screen story fall from grace.

The Allisons

There are many "brother" and "sister" acts who are related; for example ▷ The Allman Brothers Band. There are many who aren't. An example of the latter is this 1960s British duo. John Alford and Bob Day's joint tag was adapted from Alford's surname in memory of a schoolgirl sweetheart called Alison.

The Allman Brothers Band

Well, yes; Duane and Gregg Allman, of course. The two interesting facets of the name story lie off the page.

First, the duo, from Georgia, went though tags The House Rockers, Allman Joys – a pun on the U.S.A. chocolate sweet – The 31st of February (with Butch Truck), Hour Glass For Liberty and Hour Glass – the last cutting three albums and more interesting than The Allman Brothers choice.

Second, the Brothers appellation stayed some time after the 1971 death of guitar virtuoso Duane in a motorcycle accident.

All Saints

The all-girl band, dubbed as the new ▷ Spice Girls, named after All Saints Road near their homes in London's Notting Hill.

Marc Almond

Mr Almond chose his second Christian name for the stage. Somehow, the camp, be-ringed, tatooed torch-singer – all agony, angst and androgyny – would never have seemed so convincing as an unpierced, stable-sounding Peter, his bourgeois first name ...

His lyrical interests in degeneracy, decadency and debauchery influenced the choices ▷ Soft Cell, Marc And The Mambas, ▷ The Immaculate Consumptives, The Willing Sinners, The Venomettes etc. His fan club, Gutter Hearts, is from another rejected band name. No relation to ▷ Mark-Almond.

Alone Again Or

The band evolved from ▷ The Shamen and made several singles for Polydor in the 1980s. Their psychedelic style was well to the fore. *Alone Again Or* was the lead-off track on ▷ Love's acclaimed album *Forever Changes*, which for many summed up the hippy ethos in 1967's summer of love.

Alphaville

This German act named from a 1965 movie, a chilling sci-fi tale about a clinically cold society where love has lost out to logic and law. Best known for their hit *Big In Japan*. No relation to ▷ Big In Japan.

ALT

1990s act consisting of:
A = Andy White;
L = Liam O'Maonlai of ▷ The Hothouse Flowers;
T = Tim Finn, once of ▷ Split Enz and ▷ Crowded House.

And we had hoped supergroup abbreviations like this died out years ago …

Altered Images

Glaswegian Claire Grogan, a star in the film *Gregory's Girl*, was discovered in the late 1970s – and discovered in the early 1980s *I Could Be Happy*. The name came from a graphics consultancy, Assorted Images which designed book covers and album sleeves. Grogan altered the name to avoid trademark disputes.

▷ Talulah Gosh named after Grogan's nickname for herself.

Altered States

From the 1980 science fiction film. The band thought it could also relate to the United States of America.

Alternative TV

▷ ATV.

Amazing Blondel

This 1970s U.K. band married rock with period music. The original Blondel was a French musician who was famous in England in the twelfth century.

The group later abbreviated to Blondel. The young Dave Stewart got involved with them en route to ▷ Eurythmics.

Amboy Dukes

Not the only band to name after a street gang because it sounded good: cf ▷ Sigue Sigue Sputnik. Actually, there have been several groups of this name. Of the best known, founder Ted Nugent said he appropriated the name in the 1960s from a well-known New Jersey gang of 20 years before.

Nugent also named ▷ Damned Yankees.

Ambrosia

Los Angeles art-rock band of the 1970s on. Their name was a reference to both food and music.

Food: originally Ambrosia was not a make of flavoured dairy products such as custard, but the reputed food of Greek mythological figures. Cf ▷ Elixir.

Music: ambrosian Chant is a church music plainsong introduced by St Ambrose which differs from Gregorian Chant.

AMC

American Music Club are a 1990s U.S. outfit who play loud guitar music. It's an ironic name. They are totally unlike the original AMC, a 1950s record club for lovers of high classical music.

Amen Corner

They came together in 1966 in Cardiff, Wales, moving up to London and taking their name from a district of the U.K. capital. There are two roads so named, in EC4 near St Martin's Church and in SW17.

The alias was a humorous comment on sanctimonious Welshmen. It was the title of play by U.S. activist James Baldwin (1924–87), although the group didn't know this at first.

After their 1970 break up, they re-formed as Judas Jump – a name inspired from Amen Corner – and ▷ Fair Weather.

America
Formed in 1967, this band contained three sons of American servicemen stationed in Britain. Ironically for their all-American sound and name, they hardly knew America at the time. They only went back there after chart success.

America's First Lady Of Song
Ella Fitzgerald. Also called The First Lady Of Jazz.

Tori Amos
This flame-haired American singer-songwriter has produced some of the most intriguing music of the 1990s but only has herself to blame for all the "kooky chick" and "ginger nut" headlines.

The author approached with care. Tori is known for pronouncements such as "I like making new flavours of ice-cream … you know, like chicken and telephone" (eh?) and "I believe in fairies … I just feel them in my stomach" (sorry?).

Tori sounds like a cute diminutive of Victoria. Her real name is Myra-Ellen. The answer is that she renamed herself after a tree because she has an affinity "with all things natural". Plants are "beautiful, so still".

Ampex
From the initials of Alexander M. Poniatoff and "excellence".

And All Because The Lady Loves
From the long-running Cadbury advertise-ments. A James Bond-type secret agent avoids sharks while swimming to a luxury yacht; parachutes from helicopters to a hilltop chateau; leaves a box of choccies with a silhouette card; vanishes into the night as he came. An elegant lady in her boudoir finds the choc box as a caption flashes up: " … and all because the lady loves Milk Tray".

This U.K. female duo took the slogan as a protest/comment. In recent years the advert has replaced its seriousness and sexism with a knowingly satirical stance.

And Why Not
Birmingham post-house-music three piece, also known as Black Bros. The name was chosen for a joke: why not "why not?" Variously seen as cavalierly daring, over casual or just careless. Cf ▷ Bros.

Horace Andy
Jamaican singer; no relation to Bob Andy but renamed in his honour by ▷ Coxsone Dodd, who thought him Andy's heir. Originally Horace Hinds.

Angelband
Named by Emmylou Harris in memory of ▷ Gram Parsons, and her work with him on the classic 1974 country album *Grievous Angel*.

Animal Nightlife
More club culture – ▷ Culture Club – and drugs references. Amyl nitrate, or poppers, were used by some U.K. clubbers as cheap way of achieving an ecstasy-like state.

The Animals
It was much more mild-mannered at the beginning. Back in 1962, in Newcastle, U.K., these musicians joined Alan Price. He had his own Alan Price Combo: coincidentally the new name echoed this title and used letters from it.

Singer Eric Burdon said they needed a name with impact. His choice was in honour of a then friend of his, "Animal" Hogg, a tough Army veteran, whose squatting-freewheeling lifestyle they wanted to emulate.

So the name did not, repeat not, come from their wild stage act. However, the choice was confirmed by comments made by an outraged audience after seeing an early frenzied performance by the new beat group: "Mad!" "No breeding!" "Disgusting!" "Well named – like wild animals!"

There is a dispute over how much this story is hype, how much genuine, while it makes for a good part of the legend. Predictably, the performers claimed they were far from upset at overhearing such remarks, which they took as complimentary. "Like animals, eh? The Hogg name's right then – fair enough!" But it is probably being unfair on animals.

For years interviewers reported the view

that the name came from audience reaction. This was partly because it was so creditable, partly to protect Hogg, whom Burdon had lost touch with, and partly because nobody was very interested in hearing about a near-hermit who was disturbed after seeing plenty of human suffering during his time in the armed forces.

They later became The New Animals and Burdon subsequently recorded with ▷ War.

Burdon's official name account came in his 1986 book *I Used To Be An Animal, But I'm All Right Now*, while he has since given fuller, more creditable explanations. See Andy Blackford's *Wild Animals* and Jeff Kent's *The Last Poet*.

The Animals featured Chas Chandler (1938-July 1996, born Bryan James Chandler), who went on to manage ▷ Jimi Hendrix and ▷ Slade.

Adam Ant
▷ Adam And The Ants.

Anthrax
Formed in New York in 1981, the only heavy metal group to be named after a rather unpleasant scourge of cattle and sheep. The infectious disease can spread to humans.

There is a convoluted theory which says it's homage to ▷ Curved Air, who took their alias from a ▷ Terry Riley's third album, *A Rainbow In Curved Air*. Riley's fourth album, with John Cale in 1971, was called *Church of Anthrax*. This theory can be denied: the band learnt about anthrax at college and just chose it for its sound as a word rather than its repulsive meaning involving throat inflammation, malignant pustules, boils, fever etc.

Also nothing to do with the 1979 ▷ Gang Of Four track *Anthrax*.

Anti-Nowhere League
Nowhere, as in ▷ Beatle ▷ John Lennon's *Nowhere Man*, said songwriter Animal, who was born Nick Karmer. His lyrics savaged "nowheres", "nobodies" and "no ones" such as moderate/mediocre/middle of the road/ married/middle-class mortgage payers with meaningless lives and mind-numbing nine-to-five jobs.

Aphrodite's Child
Band whose tongue-in-cheek name referred to the children of the Greek goddess of love, desire and procreation. Roman name: Venus. Featured ▷ Vangelis, *inter alios*.

The Apollinaires
This Leicester, U.K., band named after their idol, French cubist poet Guillaume Apollinaire (1880–1918), who invented the term Surrealism.

Apple
▷ The Beatles named their record company because of the pun. Apple Corps = "apple core". They also liked its simplicity and its echoes of the apple "first temptation" story. Yoko Ono had used apples as an image and the Japanese had long been amused by the name Ringo, which sounds like their word for "apple". Cf ▷ Ringo Starr.

No relation, of course, to Apple Computers, first marketed in 1977.

Apple Boutique
A group who paid tribute to ▷ The Beatles.

The ▷ Fab Four's ▷ Apple organisation was intended to cover a wide variety of fields, such as film-making, investments, publicity, publishing and retailing. Only the record business proved a success. The band opened two – then trendily tagged – "boutiques" selling knick-knacks, colourful clothes and trendy things to trendy things, and both proved spectacular failures. The first opened in London's Baker Street on 7 December 1967, the next on the King's Road in May 1968. Both crashed in July and the Baker Street store was wrecked by hundreds of fans when it gave away stock before closing down.

All of which goes to show, as this 1990s act said: "If you're a group, stick to playing music. *That's* what you're supposed to be good at."

Applejacks
Led by David Appel. "Applejack" is American for apple brandy, either drunk on its own, used in cooking or mixed as cocktail sours or rickeys.

Arcadia
When members of ▷ Duran Duran briefly

went their separate ways in 1985, two formed ▷ The Power Station. The rest, i.e., Simon Le Bon, Nick Rhodes and Roger Taylor, nearly called themselves So Red The Rose, while it instead became the title of their first and only album. "We wanted something that sounded *different*."

In a 1985 BBC radio interview, they said the name was nothing to do with an Oxford restaurant fashionable with foodies and the well-heeled university crowd. It was intended as another "heaven" name. Cf ▷ Ambrosia, ▷ Heaven 17, ▷ Nirvana etc.

The name came from Arcus, son of Zeus. Arcadia was a rural area of Greece; it came to mean a blissful place after Virgil's Arcadians, in *Eclogues*, who were skilled at "arcady" music. It was pushed into English after the play by Sir Philip Sidney; a French colony in Canada was named Arcadia.

The Archers

Tasmin Archer became famous in the 1990s as a solo artist, starting with the hit *Sleeping Satellite*.

Her band took her last name and paid tribute to the BBC radio soap opera *The Archers*. It started in 1951 and tells "an everyday story of country folk" in the fictional village of Ambridge, Borsetshire. The series is a favourite of disc jockey ▷ John Peel.

The Archies

From *The Archies* U.S. comics and TV cartoon series. They were a manufactured group of session players, launched in 1968 by producer Don Kirshner, one of the men behind ▷ The Monkees, who also had a TV tie-in. The name was meant to be simple, meaningless and inoffensive. Cf ▷ Soupy Sales.

Area Code 615

These top professional musicians from Nashville, Tennessee, were regarded with awe by many in the record business, including ▷ Bob Dylan, who used some of them for sessions. They played on his 1969 release *Nashville Skyline* and emphasised their origins by naming after the phone code for Nashville.

Argent

The French think it's funny
To have a band called "money" ...

U.K. 1970s band named after leader Rod Argent, previously of ▷ The Zombies. *Argentum* is Latin for silver plate and money and used in heraldry as a colour. Spin-off: ▷ Phoenix.

The Arizona Cowboy

Nickname for American country singer Rex Allen, who really came from a cowboy family in rural Willcox, Arizona.

Ar Log

Welsh band formed to play festivals; the name translated as On Hire.

The Armoury Show

Named after The Armory Show – note spelling. The event was staged in 1913 in a regimental armoury in New York. This important exhibition was the principal means of introducing post-impressionist art to the U.S.A.; the building has an international reputation for exhibitions.

It fits in well with the pretensions of founder, Scotsman Richard Jobson, who hoped to introduce his musical art to the States. It followed the far more prosaically named ▷ Skids. The contrast between aliases could hardly be greater.

Louis Armstrong

▷ Dippermouth, ▷ Satchmo.

Army Of Lovers

From a movie title. The band was less than a veritable army in size, but thought they qualified as lovers anyway.

Arnold Corns

Short-lived "band" formed by ▷ David Bowie, who wanted an off-putting, old-fashioned name.

Arrested Development

From their rap lyrical concern with police repressing free expression. Individual names: Headliner, who was born plain Timothy Barnwell, and Speech – who was Todd Thomas to his family and first known on stage as DJ Peech.

▷ D.L.R.

Ars Nova

Means "new art"; this group of U.S. students liked the Latin term from the Renaissance. It applied to all arts initially and has come to apply most specifically to music.

Art Of Noise

Luigi Russolo was one of the leaders of the Italian twentieth-century futurist movement in art. He urged a new view of music in a 1913 pamphlet *L'Arte De Rumori* or *The Art Of Noises*. His polemic said mechanical movement had a new beauty for visual art and "one day ... every factory will be transformed into an intoxicating orchestra of noises".

The name was coined in 1984 by ▷ ZTT Records boss, former rock journalist Paul Morley, for the near-anonymous instrumental band, consisting of three British producers working with Trevor Horn.

The Artwoods

Because they were led by the brother of ▷ Faces and ▷ Rolling Stones guitarist Ronnie Wood, Arthur "Art" Wood.

Ärzte

Berlin band best known for their song *Eva Braun*. *Ärzte* means the physicians. It's pronounced "arts" so gains a pun in translation. (One of many musical medical names: see under Doctors.)

ASAP

Not As Soon As Possible but Adrian Smith And Project.

Ashphalt Ballet

These bikers named from a poem about a high speed crash.

Asia

Contenders for the most Boring Band Name Of All Time. Short-lived (1981–85) U.K. supergroup consisting of players from by then lumbering dinosaurs such as ▷ Yes and ▷ ELP, or Emerson, Lake and Palmer. The four members wanted a short name, Abba style. The continent's name came from Assyrian for "dawn".

Cf ▷ U.K.

Asleep At The Wheel

This U.S. country act built up a following on the strength of non-stop concert travelling. They commemorated countless miles of cheap motels, drug-store diners, gasoline stop-overs and all-night drives. It's surprising they rejected the literary, Jack Kerouac-influenced, name On The Road. Kerouac's had his influence on plenty of other bands though: for example ▷ The Dharma Bums.

The Assembly

U.K. band founded by Vince Clarke, ex ▷ Depeche Mode, who wanted to show he'd assembled a few musicians. They laboured long and hard on a name ...

The Associates

They began in Dundee, Scotland, as The Ascorbic Ones.

Leader/singer Billy Mackenzie explained the name to a BBC interviewer. Anybody who wanted to join could be an associate band member, "even someone you met a bus stop or your mum who wants to play spoons or something". Ironically, the band shrank. Initially the fruits of the association of Mackenzie and keyboardist Alan Rankine, a further name change to The Associate seemed appropriate later. Sadly, Mackenzie committed suicide in early 1997.

One of a wide range of "corporate style names"; cf ▷ Public Image Ltd.

The Association

A flip through a dictionary yielded this. "A group of people with a joint purpose was the definition. It perfectly fitted what we were trying to do."

Fred Astaire

Anglicisation of Frederick Austerlitz.

Astralasia

They're from the U.K., not Australia or Asia. The name was astrological in origin.

Aswad

British reggae band from the 1980s on. *Aswad* means black in Ethiopia's Amharic language; it's an encapsulation of their politics.

A Taste Of Honey
▷ Taste Of Honey.

ATF
Stood for ▷ After The Fire.

Atilla, Atilla The Hun, Attila The Stockbroker
The real Attila (circa 406–443), invading King of the Huns from Asia, was a brutal tyrant with forces who specialised in rape, riot, mayhem, rape, pillage, rape, torture and yet more rape. He overran part of the Byzantine and west Roman empires. The name was a Gothic diminutive meaning "little father".

He inspired the following:

Three minor rock and heavy metal bands, two from the U.S. and one from the Netherlands, who all traded under the incorrectly spelled name Atilla.

Atilla The Hun – also wrongly spelled. Ironically used as a stage name by a gentle Trinidad calypso singer.

U.K.-born John Baine was on his way to a City career when he turned to performance poetry and became Attila The Stockbroker. He meant stockbrokers could be as dangerous in their way as one of mankind's most feared figures of terror.

Atlanta Rhythm Section
Because they were freelance studio musicians from Doraville, near Atlanta, Georgia, U.S.A.

Atomic Kandy
Like ▷ Ned's Atomic Dustbin, a nuclear name. From the book by Phyllis Burke.

A Tribe Called Quest
▷ Tribe Called Quest.

The Attractions
▷ Elvis Costello's sometime backing band, their name puns on sexual characteristics and showbusiness attractions. Cf the very different ▷ Fairground Attraction.

ATV
A very alternative act, the name was an abbreviation for Alternative TV. No relation to ATV, the former U.K. regional TV station for the English Midlands which was the predecessor to Central.

Au Go-Go Singers
Named after the New York venue at which they played, the Café Au Go Go. The Au Go-Gos were a 1960s act and its members went on into bands including ▷ Buffalo Springfield; no relation to 1980s popsters ▷ The Go-Gos.

Au Pairs
This 1990s U.K. band liked the multi-meaning French name. While au pairs are usually foreign, female child minders who receive a room, food and pocket money, the phrase also refers to the pairing up of couples.

The Australian Doors
▷ The Doors. Ersatz ▷ Lizard Kings from Down Under.

Auteurs
French for authors. U.K. band, authors of the impressive debut *New Wave*.

Auto Da Fe
Named after the 1935 novel by Austrian Elias Canetti, winner of the Nobel Prize for literature in 1981. His book tells of a great man's decline into madness. Canetti took the title from the phrase meaning "act of faith", describing the public burning of suspected heretics under sentence of the Spanish Inquisition.

Frankie Avalon
He was born in Philadelphia, U.S.A., as Francis Avallone. This was an anglicisation to make life easier. Cf ▷ Fabian.

Average White Band
The band fortunately rarely needed to counter ill-founded allegations of racism or excessive modesty. For this outfit, formed 1972 with musicians from Scotland, named after their obsession with black music. Their repertoire includes songs which are among the closest any white group has come to true soul music.

AWBH
▷ Yes.

Stands for (Jon) Anderson, (Rick) Wakeman, (Bill) Bruford and (Steve) Howe.

Beech's First Law Of Band Naming states most boring supergroups have boring appellations. This because there's a need to placate enormous egos; stars mistakenly believe their names alone attract interest; all the members' names have to be included. This usually results in group designations which sound like a partnership of estate agents; or which are stupid acronyms/meaningless abbreviations.

Charles Aznavour

Anglicisation of his real name Shahnour Aznavurjan.

Aztec Camera

A band appellation with all the surreal values of ▷ Prefab Sprout.

Leader, vocalist and lyricist Roddy Frame, from East Kilbride, Scotland, formed the group at 15 during an infatuation with psychedelia. He's given many whimsical explanations, depending on his mood, but the most common one is that Aztec "sounded right" and Camera came from a ▷ Teardrop Explodes single.

The group banner has always been illusory. Like ▷ The Pretenders, ▷ The Lightning Seeds and ▷ The The, to name just three, this is a catch-all name for solo projects. ▷ Neutral Blue.

Babe Ruth

All-British band, from Hatfield, Herts; they took their all-American name from the legendary U.S. baseball player George Herman "Babe" Ruth (1894–1948). First LP titled *First Base*.

More sport inspiration: ▷ The Bobby Charltons etc.

Babes In Toyland

1990s U.S. female rock band: the name is a pun on "babes" as in children and "sexy young women". "Happy as a babe in toyland" was a phrase taken by Victor Herbert for a musical suite, *Babes In Toyland*, which was made into films.

▷ Courtney Love was sacked from the band. She also failed the audition for ▷ Faith No More. She got out of the hole fast and made it big with ▷ Hole. Babes In Toyland are part of the ▷ Riot Grrrl movement.

Babyface

Kenneth Edmonds was nicknamed by Bootsie Collins from his youthful looks.

Babylon Zoo

Jas Mann shot to fame 1996 on the back of a number one song *Spaceman*, the fastest-selling debut single of all time.

Babylon Zoo is known as B. Zoo in the Middle East, where "Babylon" is liable to be misunderstood. Jas explained to *Q* magazine in 1996: "Babylon before the enslavement is a paradise thought, but in this present society we are Frankenstein and the monster is biting back at us, so it's become a zoo."

Baccara

Taken from the card game baccarat. (Also named after a game: ▷ *Hüsker Du*. Not named from a game: ▷ Bagatelle.)

Bachelors

This Dublin band started as The Harmony Chords. The ▷ DECCA company suggested a sexier image with a more enticing name: "What do girls like … bachelors!" Unfortunately, it produced plenty of poor jokes about being in the soup.

Bachman-Turner Overdrive

The band considered the name Brave Belt – the sort worn by American Indians to indicate success as a hunter. Their record company complained this was obscure and said they should play up links with ▷ The Guess Who.

Their surnames were Bachman (Randy, ex Guess Who; Robbie; and later Tim) and Turner (bassist C.F. "Fred" Turner). Still, they didn't want to sound like folky trio. They spotted Canadian truckers' magazine *Overdrive* which suited their top-gear rock, and carried the concept through with a logo of a gearwheel found on an old industrial site. The name was often abbreviated to BTO.

Spin-off: ▷ Ironhorse.

The Back Door Band

Mike Mills and Bill Berry were in this band after ▷ Shadowfax. It's named after *Back Door Man*, the Dixon-Burnett song famously covered by ▷ The Doors. The title came to have a gay connotation not intended by the lyric. Mills and Berry went on into ▷ R.E.M.

Back Street Crawler

Paul Kossoff, one of the forces behind ▷ Free, made a solo 1973 LP called *Back Street Crawler* and liked the name so much he used it in 1975 in assembling a touring band. Within a year he was dead after a heart ailment aggravated by drug problems. The band carried on for a while as Crawler.

B.A.D.

Abbreviation for ▷ Big Audio Dynamite.

Bad Brains

The band led the Washington, D.C. punk movement of the 1980s and named after a ▷ Ramones song on the 1978 album *Road To Ruin*. Another of self-disparaging appellation in the ▷ Simple Minds mode.

Bad Company

This British band named from a Stanley R. Jaffe and Robert Benton western – released a few months before their formation – about two youths on the run in the U.S. Civil War, who team up and become outlaws. They thought the plot line mirrored their careers – and said it was also a protest at faceless corporations. Related bands: ▷ Free, ▷ Mott The Hoople, ▷ King Crimson.

Badfinger

Started as ▷ The Iveys, Swansea, 1967, a corollary to then successful ▷ Hollies. They realised the alias sounded dated and there were other bands with similar choices.

In 1969 they signed with ▷ Apple, ▷ The Beatles' record company, and realised it was now or never to change before releasing ▷ Paul McCartney's song *Come And Get It* as a single: the Macca connection alone made it a guaranteed hit, and after that a new name would be out of the question.

Their style reminded Apple boss Neil

Aspinal of an obscure blues record he'd once heard called *Badfinger Boogie* – nobody involved in this tale has any idea who recorded it. Badfinger struck the group as ridiculous but they couldn't think of anything better ... and the record was about to be pressed. They'd been given a moniker and a Top Five song: few artists are so lucky.

Bad Manners

Suggested by the manic antics of the vocalist with this U.K. ska revival band, Fatty Buster Bloodvessel. He was born Douglas Trendle, in 1958. This bald-headed, 17-stone, extrovert, bovver-boot-wearing hunk's habits included dressing up as a ballet dancer and diving into vats of baked beans – showing bad manners, but not pure ▷ Madness. He knew he was getting well paid for it all.

Award for good individual band member name: harmonica player Winston Bazoomies.

Bad News

Deliberate irony by U.K. comedians ▷ The Young Ones for their intentionally terrible heavy metal band film. Cf another satire band, ▷ Spinal Tap.

Bad Religion

U.S. band with opinionated views and loud music. The name refers to their hatred for much conventional patriarchal religious teaching.

The Bad Seeds

Nick Cave led band named after a book called *The Bad Seed*. He also used literary inspiration for ▷ The Birthday Party.

Badu

Erykah Badu in full. She was born with the surname Wright. Badu is from scat *ad lib*.

Bagatelle

A bagatelle was, and is, a board game popular in the 1960s; a trifling matter; and a short, light piece of music. Beethoven wrote about 20 bagatelles. This U.K. band named after the musical term because "most pop music is a mere bagatelle".

Bakerloo

This 1960s band from the English Midlands were first called Bakerloo Blues Line. The Bakerloo Line on the London Underground originally ran from Baker Street to Waterloo. Its name was coined by a London newspaper and adopted by the railway company reluctantly; the line has since been extended. Cf ▷ Central Line.

Balaam And The Angel

They were from Scotland, so there was no link to the well-known districts of London, Balham in the south and Angel in the north.

This ▷ Cult-inspired power-rock band were named after an incident in *The Old Testament* involving the soothsayer Balaam, who cannot discern the divine messenger which even his donkey can see.

They later abbreviated to Balaam.

Long John Baldry

Singer from London, whose name recalled Long John Silver and relates to his 6 ft 7 ins height. His bands include ▷ The Hoochie-Coochie Men, and Bluesology, both christened from musical terms. Bluesology became The John Baldry Show and his first name was adopted by the group's keyboardist, who became ▷ Elton John.

Afrika Bambaataa

The name was adopted to tie in with his musical cohorts The Zulu Nation. The Jungle Brothers, another act, dub themselves as Baby Afrika Bambaataa in his honour. Spin-off: ▷ Time Zone.

Bambinos

This Italian female band get a mention only as an object lesson in how not to choose a *nom de noise*. They started as The Barbies. Fears of legal action followed from the doll makers. They became the similarly named Bambies – until they were told this could upset Walt Disney. Finally, they became Bambinos, the word for "children" or "babies". Because they were, after all, babes. Fame and fortune, in their case, beckoned. Not.

Bananarama

The U.K.'s most successful female band, until

▷ The Spice Girls.

Their first single was a Caribbean dance song called *Aie A Mwana*. This led to the not-very-original name The Bananas. The fruit has inspired many jokes about mentality and sexuality down the years: the latter gave them inspiration. They'd a jokey approach to life and liked ▷ Roxy Music's *Pyjamarama*. They hoped their fame would lead to plenty of Bryan Ferry-like types armed with bananas in pyjamas.

The trio later claimed it was a reference to the teenage TV series The Banana Splits and ▷ Archies-style spin-off group – an altogether safer thing to explain on children's television.

Their publishing company was called In A Bunch Music. Spin-off: ▷ Shakespears Sister

The Band

They were formerly ▷ The Hawks, the backing band of rockabilly Ronnie Hawkins. All of his frequently changing groups used this name. This Canadian ensemble later deserted Hawkins to become Levon And The Hawks – Levon being drummer/vocalist Levon Helm, The Levon Helm Sextet, The Crackers (really!), The Honkies (really!! – considered, not seriously used) and The Squires in 1965. The Crackers was a derogatory name, for poor white southern trash, which went over the record company's heads. The Hawks name was excessively warlike and meaningless when they moved from under Ronnie's wing.

They were simply and colloquially called "the band" soon after they started on their own, probably because no other appellation seemed right.

Robbie Robertson recalled, in the 1978 valedictory film *The Last Waltz*, that *everybody* called them "the band" when they started to back ▷ Bob Dylan: Dylan himself, their friends and neighbours. "That's all we were known as."

They kept the title because it was so simple and they liked its slight arrogance: *the* Band, as if no other mattered. It was justified because they were a *band*, able to switch instruments and without inflated egos hampering team work.

It was a simple choice which didn't limit their scope in the way contemporaries found with aliases such as ▷ Strawberry Alarm Clock. The Band were never psychedelic, never hippy:

their timeless music was reminiscent of the 1860s not 1960s.

However, they toyed with the longer identifier The Band From Big Pink. This was a reference to their communal base, which – surprise, surprise – was a large Woodstock house painted pink. Their home was finally immortalised with the title of their 1968 debut LP *Music From Big Pink*.

The Band as a designator did not actually become fully official until their second – eponymous – album of 1969, according to the biography *Across The Great Divide,* by Barney Hoskins. The 1993 book says the first album had no corporate name on it apart from a small "Band" on the spine so it could be filed in the shops. The front cover was a childlike daub by Dylan – sans name – and on the back there was a list of all five members. When *The Weight* was released as a single many reviewers listed all of them. "This is even worse than ▷ Dave Dee, Dozy, Beaky, Mick and Tich," complained one British writer.

Hence the name. Hence the low-key music.

Cf for similar name idea: ▷ The Pop Group.

A Band song was the cue for the naming of ▷ Nazareth.

Band Aid

▷ Boomtown Rat ▷ Bob Geldof's name for his supergroup which cut the three million plus sales 1984 single *Do They Know It's Christmas* to aid the starving in Ethiopia.

The appellation was preserved for the Band Aid Charity which organised the July 1985 Live Aid concerts. Reportedly, the choice produced problems with the manufacturer of Band Aid plasters – which many saw as petty, given the act's charity purpose. Geldof's autobiography, *Is That It?* explains he was concerned the designation didn't give the impression that they were simply trying to patch over the starvation problem. The hope was to cure it for good.

Not related to Arthur Lee of ▷ Love, who recorded a 1972 album which used backing musicians known as Band Aid, so called, he explained, "because the band helped me out".

Band Of Holy Joy

Leader Johnny Brown said he was not religious as such; the name described their early sound.

Cf Too Much Joy.

Band Of Susans

The band consists of three guys and two girls, only one of whom is a Susan. The explanation is their "Susan Content" has severely diminished. There were originally three of them in a sextet: Lyall, Stenger and Tallman: two left.

Band Of Thieves

Formed by Luke Goss, former drummer with ▷ Bros, who was watching the BBC real-life crime programme *Crimewatch U.K.*

Bangalore Choir

Explosive U.S. thrash-rock band, named after American military slang for a torpedo.

Ed Banger And The Nosebleeds

Links heavy metal "headbanging" with the nosebleeds sometimes produced as a result. Intended as a novelty name because this U.K. band scorned heavy metal. Without Ed Banger, the Nosebleeds searched around for a new vocalist, at one point famously considering ▷ Morrissey, later of ▷ The Smiths.

Bangles

Supersonic Bangs! screamed the headline above a U.S. magazine fashion article on retro hairdos. This Los Angeles female group loved it: the pun referred not to jet booms but bangs, as in long tresses of hair hanging in front of the ears. Beyond their own hairstyles, it assumed yet another dimension because bang is also American slang:

1. For pleasure ... as in "this'll give you a big bang";
2. Relating to drug-taking ... as in "they banged some heroin to get high";
3. And sexual intercourse ... as in "he banged her all night".

See Chapman's *American Slang* dictionary for more.

They discovered another band on the other side of America called The Bangs so went for a close alternative. U.K. television personality Paula Yates said on *The Tube* that they renamed partly because they thought The Bangs too outrageous: "Which just about sums them up."

Bankstatement

This nominal statement comes from ▷ Genesis co-founder Tony Banks, branching out for a part-time post with Alistair Gordon and Jayney Klimek.

This sort of pun doubtless appealed to Mr A. Banks's bank manager counting the takings from his time-out project.

The Banshees

▷ Siouxsie And The Banshees.

Barbecue Bob

Singer Robert Hicks used to work at a barbecue in Georgia, U.S.A.

Barclay James Harvest

Band from Oldham, Lancashire, who signed to EMI in 1968 and when the recording company launched its progressive rock label in 1969 it had such high hopes for them it named it ▷ Harvest. By 1990 they were called simply B.J.H.

According to a 1993 report by the U.K. Press Association news agency's then showbusiness correspondent: "One of rock's longest-surviving bands is coming up to its 30th anniversary with a bit of a problem – its members have forgotten how they got the name."

PA's Rob Scully quotes singer and bassist Les Holroyd: "We started in 1963 in pubs and clubs in the north playing blues under various names then in 1966 we changed our name again. It was probably because they needed the name for posters and we gave them the first thing that came into our heads."

Barenaked Ladies

This 1990s grungey band from Toronto, Canada, consists of five guys. Far from being naked they favour thick clothes of several layers. They've had to play down the nickname of "fat Canadian ▷ Housemartins".

According to *Time Out* magazine they said of the name: "It's a term we all used when we were kids of six years old. You looked at a picture of a nude woman, and said she was barenaked. It was the name which made us laugh the most." Which is a good reason for choosing some names: cf ▷ The Crickets.

Barmy Army

U.K. 1980s/1990s pub rock band, led by East London producer Adrian Sherwood. The name was based on the classic children's comic cartoon strip *Barmy Army*.

Barnstorm

Joe Walsh's 1973 album *Barnstorm* provided the eponymous name for the backing band who played on it and a number of his subsequent releases. It's just as well he didn't christen the band after these subsequent few albums, produced after further brainstorming: *The Smoker You Drink, The Player You Get; So What; You Can't Argue With A Sick Mind* or *You Bought It, You Name It.*

Basher

Nickname for ▷ Nick Lowe before his ▷ Rockpile days. Refers both to his studio slogan of "bashing it down and tarting it up later" and his interest in vintage planes, like Royal Air Force characters Biggles and Basher.

The Bash Street Kids

West London based collective named after a comic strip. ▷ Barmy Army.

Basia

Polish vocalist who wisely abbreviated her original moniker, Basia Trzetrzelewska.

Count Basie

U.S. bandleader Bill Basie got his name from deejays incessantly comparing him to jazz aristocrats *King* Benny Goodman, *Duke* Ellington and *Earl* Hines.

However Basie said he'd have preferred "Buck or even Fats".

Shirley Bassey

Her real name. Her real unflattering derivative nickname: Burly Chassis.

Bastard

This German heavy rock band picked up on an abortive choice by Lemmy Kilmister for his band which became ▷ Motörhead. ▷ Lemmy at least knew enough about the English language to know it wasn't the most commercial of choices.

Bauhaus

A reversal of the German *hausbau*. This turns "building of houses" into "house of building". It was the name coined by Walter Gropius for his school of radical design, founded 1919 and lasting until 1933. It aimed to simplify design and combine architecture and technology to create "the compositely inseparable work of art, the great building".

The Northamptonshire group at first were Bauhaus 1919: they thought it sounded stylish in 1978. The band's antecedents include punk outfits The Craze and The Submerged Tenth.

After the sky went out for Bauhaus in 1983, Peter Murphy went on into ▷ Dali's Car. Other members formed Tones on Tail and ▷ Love And Rockets.

Bay City Rollers

By the mid 1970s they were simply The Rollers to their teeny-bopper fans. But this Edinburgh band began in 1967 as The Saxons. Their manager, danceband leader Tam Paton, wanted an American handle.

In true *Coming To America* style, he blindly stuck a pin in a map and found Bay City. There's confusion on whether he hit the Bay City in Oregon, Texas or in Rochester, Michigan. It's most often said to be the latter, the birthplace of singer ▷ Madonna. Who of course only became famous later.

The name harped back to surf music and tied in with rock, while hinting at a ▷ Rolling Stones pun.

The tale's similar to how ▷ The Commodores were nearly called The Commodes: there's been speculation on where else Paton's pin could have landed: Queens, maybe, as in the film; or Alligator Swamp, Jackson Hole or even Ass Hole?

Bazooka Joe

From the kiddies' bubble-gum brand name. ▷ Adam Ant.

B.B.

▷ B.B. King.

BBA

This sort-of supergroup consisted of ex ▷ Yardbird Jeff Beck, and ▷ Vanilla Fudge members Tim Bogert and Carmen Appice. From their surnames.

The Beach Boys

An everyday story of the evolution of a California band who started by singing Four Freshmen style harmonies and using garbage cans as drums. The name changed, the beards grew, the drum kit got better, hair greyed, then went … the music stayed.

They began as The Wilson Brothers, then Carl And The Passions – suggested by Dennis Wilson 1961, and a identity later adopted for a 1972 LP. They metamorphosed into the similar-sounding Kenny And The Cadets – songwriter Brian Wilson being Kenny.

A growing interest in surfing led to the third alias The Pendletones. This was taken from the name of heavy Pendleton plaid top worn by surfers and beach nuts – the group wore similar matching shirts on stage – and with a pun in the "tones" recalling Dick Dale's Del-Tones.

Their first record, 1961 release *Surfin'*, was trial-pressed on Robert and Richard Dix's X Records label. Herb Newman of Era Records wanted to issue it on the Dix brothers' new Candix label, which had already had a surfing hit – *Underwater* by The Frogmen. But he hated the Pendletones appellation, which he thought was too obscure. In a round of phone calls which the Wilsons knew nothing about, Candix A&R man Joe Saraceno played the demo to a record distributor. Saraceno said he thought the group was called The Surfers. It turned out that this pseudonym had been done and Saraceno said he preferred something like, oh, say, The Beach Boys. Russ Regan of the local Buckeye Record Distributors took this as a cue. The moniker would also suit the image of the single, associate them with Jan and Dean – the song sounded like ▷ Jan and Dean – and was a nice echo of their West Coast origins, similar to ▷ The Coasters, who went through a Surf Boy period.

According to *The Nearest Faraway Place* by Timothy White, published in 1996: "It was not until the initial run of Candix singles had been pressed and released on 8 December 1961, that the group discovered their new name."

The first they knew about it was when promotional copies were delivered, according to

Brian Wilson's autobiography *Wouldn't It Be Nice – My Own Story*, co-written with Todd Gold. The young band members were scandalised and their father/self-appointed manager, the outspoken Murray Wilson, had a therapeutic shout down the telephone to the company – only to be told it was too late. Not only would it be expensive to reprint labels but they had already been sent out to shops. The youngsters shrugged it off because they were pleased to have a record out; their father worked hard to make it a local hit.

A press release by the band's bigger record company a few years later said: "They [the Wilsons] knew the name fitted in with what they wanted to do. The group went on to record some of the classic albums and singles of the era which could only have been recorded by The Beach Boys." In other words, they had designation, image, music and voices in perfect harmony.

Hindsight suggests The Beach Boys was a better handle than the obscure Pendletones, which would have quickly sounded dated. Similar choices by other acts such as The Silvertones and The Quailtones were soon confined to the dustbin of musical history.

Still, critics claim The Beach Boys choice has subsequently suited only song subjects such as *Endless Summers* of hot rods, girls, sex, sea, surf, and sun sun sun.

Only drummer Dennis was particularly interested in surfing – he died in a swimming accident in 1983 – and it became dated as the group aged well beyond boyhood. The Beach Men? Few bands have had their success or staying power regardless.

Hence the name. Hence the good vibrations.

The Beach Boys inspired the spoof band ▷ The City Surfers.

Brian Wilson's daughters Wendy and Carnie were two-thirds of ▷ Wilson Phillips.

The Bear
Bob Hite of ▷ Canned Heat; because of his size and weight. Cf ▷ Blind Owl.

Beastie Boys
These New Yorkers acted as repulsively as possible, like the ▷ Ramones and ▷ Sex Pistols rolled into one. The Beasties' antisocial

behaviour was celebrated on the B side of a 1983 single with a song called *Beastie Revolution*. The name was part of the hype.

King Ad-Rock, AKA Adam Horovitz, admitted they could have been The Beastly Boys or The Beasts. He discussed similar names with Mike D – or Mike Diamond; and MCA – Master of Ceremonies Adam – Adam Yauch, who liked their song *Bad Brains*, known as *BB*.

The Beat
This American group cut an album in 1979 before ▷ The (English) Beat came on to the scene. They claimed the legal right to the name and won but were handicapped because The (English) Beat were better and more widely known. They later tried renaming Paul Collins's Beat; their 1983 LP was called *To Beat Or Not To Beat*. A name's nothing without success.

The Beat
known in the U.S. as:
The English Beat
Singer David Wakeling was browsing "music" synonyms and antonyms in *Roget's Thesaurus*, divided into "discord" and "melody". The latter yielded ▷ Clash. The other began with "Beat" so was harmonious for a band with black and white members.

While it was like ▷ The Beatles, another name clash (see above entry) meant a change to The English Beat for an October 1980 American tour. Beat graduates founded ▷ General Public and help start ▷ Fine Young Cannibals.

The Beatles
The first version of the band, formed by ▷ John Lennon in 1957 in Liverpool, U.K., was a Teddy Boy/Skiffle outfit called The Quarrymen, after the local Quarry Bank High School which he attended. ▷ Paul McCartney and ▷ George Harrison joined later. By the time they briefly disbanded in 1959, the Quarrymen designation had become irrelevant anyway – John left the school for art college the year before and the others were at The Liverpool Institute.

The re-formed trio went through a series of monikers at parties and small concerts, for example christening themselves The Rainbows for one night because they all turned up for the gig in different coloured shirts.

The drummerless band entered one talent competition, selecting, on the spur of the moment, the handle Johnny And The Moondogs. This was possibly a reference to the origins of rock with the singer ▷ Moondog and Alan Freed's 1951 radio show *Moondog's Rock 'n' Roll Party*. Most acts in those days, such as ▷ Cliff Richard And The Shadows, had a leader – and John was then acknowledged as the prime mover.

It was he who suggested their final designation. He wanted to emulate ▷ Buddy Holly, idolised for his songwriting and guitar-playing. Holly died in 1959, but his music lives on to this day. John liked the double meaning of Holly's backing band ▷ The Crickets – as "cricket" = insect and "cricket" = game – and was annoyed someone had beaten him to it. John's love of word play, which emerged in books such as *In His Own Write* and *A Spaniard In The Works*, caused him to search around for a similar insect designator. He soon misspelled Beetle as Beatle to make the pun on beat music obvious. The term "The Beat Generation", coined by writer Jack Kerouac, was reaching its apogee. In time, he influenced the naming of many minor bands such as ▷ The Dharma Bums and ▷ Elmerhassell.

Still, there's another possible origin: John knew of *The Wild One*, the 1954 film which propelled Marlon Brando to greater stardom wearing the leather jacket look much favoured by the early Beatles. Brando led a motorcycle gang against Lee Marvin's rival faction who were called The Beetles: their black jackets made them look like beetles.

Lennon jokingly referred to "the Bootles" in several interviews, so he knew of another connection, with the Liverpool district of Bootle. However, there's no evidence this was an initial motivation for the choice of the moniker.

Liverpool friend Casy Jones, of Cass And The Casanovas, said the Beatles appellation was too short and, following the fifties trend for showbizzy long designations, suggested Long John And The Silver Beetles. The ▷ Baldry-style Long John alias was another reference to Lennon, still seen as the leader.

They changed it to The Silver Beatles, the billing they used for an audition in 1959 and until 1960. Even then they preferred its further-abbreviated form without the meaningless "Silver" tag. It was as The Beatles they evolved with Stuart Sutcliffe [left 1961, died 1962], Pete Best [sacked 1962] and ▷ Ringo Starr [replaced Best, 1962].

However, they made one demo record in 1961, backing pop singer Tony Sheridan as The Beat Boys because Beatles was thought to be too confusing.

Clearly, there was some resistance to the handle, revolutionary in its time – the band discovered during their Hamburg days that Germans often said it as Peedles, slang for cock or John (Lennon) Thomas. Top English promoter Arthur Howes, on first hearing of the band, merely thought "another group with a silly name!"

The Beatles often shrouded the choice in secrecy, claiming it was given to them by a man on a magic carpet and various other entertaining yarns. As John put it: "It came in a vision – an man appeared on a flaming pie and said unto us 'From this day on you are Beatles with an A'. Thank you, Mister Man, we said, thanking him." (In May 1997 McCartney released an album entitled *Flaming Pie*.)

Hence the name. Hence the reappearing graffiti outside London's Abbey Road studios.

There is more on all four individual Beatles' other pseudonyms in their separate entries. All four became household names, among the most famous people in the world, as their band's identifier passed into popular consciousness and into the language: Beatlemania, Beatlesque. They became colloquially known as The Fab Four or The Fabs. However, for perhaps their most famous album they became ▷ Sgt Pepper's Lonely Heart's Club Band.

For further details, see the following: *The Beatles Anthology*. Pete Best and Patrick Doncaster, *Beatle! The Pete Best Story*. Hunter Davis, *The Beatles: The Authorized Biography*. Bill Harry, *Mersey Beat: The Beginnings of The Beatles*. Philip Norman, *Shout! The Beatles in Their Generation*. Gareth Pawlowski, *How They Became The Beatles – A Definitive History of Their Early Years*. Billy Shepherd, *The True Story of The Beatles*. Derek Taylor, *As Time Goes By*.

Lennon and McCartney have sometimes

been referred to as ▷ The Nerk/Nurk Twins. Cf Jagger-Richards, ▷ The Glimmer Twins; Perry-Tyler, ▷ The Toxic Twins.

In January 1969 they toyed with the name ▷ Ricky And The Red Streaks, which like Sgt Pepper was a choice which could have allowed them to lay smaller venues until their cover was blown as inevitably would occur quickly.

The Beatles' soubriquet inspired the spelling of ▷ Little Feat; their work inspired ▷ The Glove's moniker; their ▷ Apple Corps inspired another bunch of musicians to call themselves ▷ Apple Boutique. Also ▷ Badfinger, ▷ Prefab Four, ▷ Revolution 9, ▷ Revolver and ▷ Yeah Yeah Yeah.

Tribute and spoof bands: ▷ The Bootleg Beatles and Sgt Pepper's Magical Mystery Trip, 1990s live acts; ▷ The Rutles, a 1970s film and album.

▷ The Smoking Mojo Filters.

The Beatnigs

Three San Francisco blacks brought together "beatniks" and "beatings", to remind everyone the problems of racial inequality still exist. Their intentions were frequently misunderstood, hindering radio play.

To quote from the liner notes of their 1988 debut album, "nig" is "a positive acronym ... it has taken on a universal meaning in describing all oppressed people who have actively taken a stand against those who perpetuate ethnic notions and discriminate on the basis of them."

Cf ▷ N.W.A.

Beau

Trevor Midgeley's French schoolteacher had problems. There were two Midgeleys in the class. One was small and ugly. The other big and handsome. The latter became Beau. It stuck.

The Beau Brummels

This 1960s American band from San Francisco remembered British dandy and fashion leader George Beau Brummell (1778–1840). (Note the differing spellings.)

Like the similar Santa Cruz harmony outfit ▷ Harpers Bizarre – which one Brummel joined after a 1967 line-up change – ▷ The Buckinghams and ▷ Sir Douglas Quintet, the name was a bid to counter the "British Invasion" of the time.

Beautiful Pea Green Boat

This ▷ Cocteau-Twins-bedfellows-band, made up of Ian Williams and Heather Wright, named from the nursery rhyme by Edward Lear (1812–88) which starts: "The Owl and the Pussy Cat went to sea/ In a beautiful pea green boat ... "

The Beautiful South

"The beautiful south" is a slogan for several U.S. states – still, this reference is strictly British. The band evolved from ▷ The Housemartins, whose patriotism for Northern England led to titles such as *Hull 4 London 0*.

Leader Paul Heaton said the previous image meant The Housemartins weren't taken seriously. They were seen as a ▷ Madness of the North.

Hence the serious debut album, *Welcome To the Beautiful South*, which featured a picture of a crazed woman with a gun in her mouth. This was changed after protests to show inoffensive fluffy toys – although restored to the CD release. The sarcastic moniker attacked all Britain south of Hull, and south London in particular.

Cf ▷ Hatfield And The North.

Beck

Late 1990s act named after singer-songwriter/ leader Beck Hansen. No relation to Jeff Beck of ▷ The Yardbirds.

Bedlam

From the loud sound of these 1970s rockers led by Cozy Powell. *The Oxford English Dictionary* says it means: "Any madhouse; scene of uproar. ... from the Hospital of St Mary of *Bethlehem*, used as a lunatic asylum."

The Beefeaters

▷ The Byrds.

Captain Beefheart

Another fairy story, of how once upon a time 1940s child TV star Don Van Vliet, from California, dreamed of stardom, became avant-garde rock star Captain Beefheart and ended up eccentrically painting strange pictures in the Mojave Desert.

It started for Van Vliet with a fantasy called *Captain Beefheart Meets The Grunt People*. He went to school in Lancaster, California, where he became buddies with ▷ Frank Zappa, moving to Cucamonga to make *Beefheart* into a film and further aid and abet Zappa. They worked on the movie scenario, formed a band called The Blackouts and planned another called The Soots.

Some aficionados maintain Van Vliet first thought of the script while others claim it was Zappa's idea. A similar Captain Beefheart had existed as a story book familiar for a century. Van Vliet effectively reinvented the character, while Zappa was soon applying it to *him*. Van Vliet had a strong heart and had "beefs" against convention.

The name was outrageous in the early 1960s. Beefheart was backed by ever-changing Magic Band members rechristened such ridiculous things as Zoot Horn Rollo, The Winged Eel Fingerling, Antennae Johnny, The Mascara Snake, Rockette Morton and Orejon: "it means Big Ear," he explained enigmatically. "They all lived happily ever after."

Beefheart inspired the naming of ▷ Dali's Car.

The Bee Gees
The name has been explained variously as coming from any or all of the following:
1. From "The Brothers Gibb" – Barry, Maurice and Robin – who were born in the U.K. but partly brought up in Australia. They made an early, experimental debut at a Manchester cinema in 1956 as The Blue Cats before leaving for Down Under in 1958. They were billed as The Bee Gees (Brothers Gibb) Comedy Trio in Brisbane in 1962, performing novelty songs.
2. From Barry's initials. This is the most popular theory; he's several years older than the others and the early band leader.
3. From speedway driver and promoter Bill Gates, who spotted the trio singing at a race track and gave them support.
4. From local Aussie deejay Bill Goode, who first championed their music.
5. From the musical notes used in their early close-harmony style in Brisbane.

The answer is they were always The Bee Gees (Brothers Gibb): it was good fortune that Gates and Goode had the same initials so there was no renaming required. It's preferable to two alternatives – Rattlesnakes and Wee Johnny Hays and the Blue Cats.

The Bee Gees tag was kept despite a solo career by Robin between 1969 and 1971. Barry recorded as The Bunburys in 1986, telling a children's story about rabbits.

See the trio's book, as told to David Leaf: *Bee Gees: The Authorized Biography*.

Bees Make Honey
Like many other names in rock, and many "honey" choices, this was chosen for sexual overtones. As in "the birds and the bees".

B.E.F.
Abbreviation for British Electric Foundation, the production organisation behind U.K. electronics band ▷ Heaven 17. The aim was to sound like a public corporation, complete with a mission statement: "The new partnership – that's opening doors all over the world." Plus a ludicrous Dunhill-style international slogan: "Sheffield-Edinburgh-London."

The yuppie 1980s was a time when stars saw themselves as business figures. Cf ▷ Public Image Ltd, ▷ Sigue Sigue Sputnik.

Beginning Of The End
This U.S. band was protesting at funk creeping into Nassau music: hence the 1974 hit *Funky Nassau*. The phrase's most famous use was by British prime minister Sir Winston Churchill who said victory in Africa was not "the end" of the war, probably not "the beginning of the end" but perhaps "the end of the beginning". Cf ▷ Blood, Sweat And Tears.

The Belle Stars
This 1980s U.K. female pop band's name and image recalled the west's most notorious female outlaw Belle Star, who was celebrated by a well-known 1941 film.

Belly
1990s band, offshoot of Throwing Muses, with a name that resembles ▷ Echobelly. Tanya Donelly said belly suggests "different things to

different people. Some people think of babies, some of beer; others think of dead fish or of sex. I think of the one black hair on my body that grows from my belly and it gets to be very long sometimes."

The Belmonts
▷ Dion And The Belmonts.

Pat Benatar
This New York singer was born with the less catchy name Pat Andrzejewski. Her first husband was Dennis Benatar. The marriage didn't last; Pat kept the name after her 1982 remarriage to guitarist-producer Neil Geraldo, by which time she was an established artist.

The Benders
This jazz band explain their name: "It's a word which means nothing in our home, Australia, and that is what we wanted." If it meant the same Down Under as it does in many other English-speaking countries they wouldn't have stood a chance.

Ben Folds Five
Not a sentence, as in Ben folding up five somethings. Mid-1990s group led by Ben Folds. A trio; they thought this sounded better, with alliterative prospects for growth.

Cliff Bennett And The Rebel Rousers
In the early 1960s, British bands were trying to sound American. By mid-decade, with the success of ▷ The Beatles, this changed. This U.K. group belongs to the earlier phase. Rabble-rousing was practised on-screen by stars such as James Dean and Marlon Brando – while Bennett liked Duane Eddy's 1958 hit *Rebel Rouser.*

Benny Profane
These U.K. rockers named after an eccentric figure in U.S. writer Thomas Pynchon's debut book from 1963, *V*, set in New York, Cairo and Malta.

Bent Fabric
A Danish pianist who anglicised his name Bent Fabricus Bjerre.

Berlin
Like ▷ Spandau Ballet and ▷ The Berlin Blondes, a group from outside Germany under the spell of the once-divided city. This Los Angeles act liked ▷ Velvet Underground founder ▷ Lou Reed's 1973 solo album *Berlin*, which also inspired the naming of ▷ The Waterboys. The city name is probably a corruption of *bärlein*, or bear cub.

Berlin Blondes
They may have been blonde but they were from Glasgow, Scotland. Not ▷ Berlin either. Cf ▷ Texas.

Irving Berlin
The pronunciation of famous U.S. songwriter Israel Baline's name led to a printer crediting an early piece to Irving Berlin.

Chuck Berry
There's confusion on his birthplace and birthdate, but not his name – Charles Berry. He inspired the name ▷ Jo Jo Gunne.

Dave Berry
Born David Grundy, Sheffield, U.K., he renamed in honour of ▷ Chuck Berry, whose songs he covered.

Bethnal
British band named from their native Bethnal Green, in London.

B-52s
The American Air Force B-52 bomber, delivered between 1955 and 1963, was retained in regular use 30 years later. The plane, with a wingspan the size of a football pitch, played a major role in both the Vietnam and Gulf Wars.

A beehive hairstyle popular in the 1950s and 1960s was so large it therefore acquired the Southern nickname B-52.

Kate Pierson and Cindy Wilson used to go to a nightclub in Athens, Georgia in the early 1970s before they formed the band. Because they couldn't afford anything else, they went to a secondhand store and bought sixties clothes. Cindy had a pink bouffant so high she looked in danger of falling over and Kate sported a blue version a foot high.

While their stage image had evolved almost by accident, the hair made the name obvious. It was apt because their early work plundered 1950s and 1960s references.

Yet it also caused some problems: the beehives were later replaced with shorter, simpler styles saving on hairspray, while the group had to play down militaristic associations.

Tribute band: ▷ The Rock Lobsters.

The B.H. Surfers

Name unilaterally given by sections of the U.S. media – especially in the Bible Belt – to ▷ The Butthole Surfers. That is, of the papers and TV stations who reported the band: many didn't mention them because of the name and hoped they'd go away.

Bhundu Boys

These Zimbabweans named from the bush fighters who freed what was Rhodesia from the iron hand of the Ian Smith white regime.

The Bible

Like ▷ The Christians, they had to fend off religious references. They wanted to be as well thought of, and sell as many, as the world's best-selling book. Cf a novel by ▷ Jonathan King, entitled *Bible Two*.

Biff Bang Pow

They name checked the song by Creation because they liked it.

Big Audio Dynamite

The abbreviation B.A.D. was chosen by ex ▷ Clash guitarist Mick Jones. This carries the U.S. connotation of meaning very good. Bad was so used by Isaac Hayes on his *Hot Buttered Soul* LP of 1969, exploited by George "Bad" Benson in 1975; and used by ▷ Michael Jackson on his 1987 album *Bad*.

Jones had to consider what it meant and Beyond Alien Destruction was one possibility. He explained he wanted an explosive sound which would "go with a bang". Another choice, in 1982, was ▷ Real Westway. The band became BAD II after a re-formation.

Big Black

U.S. musician Steve Albini stirred up controversy

with this and his subsequent band ▷ Rapeman. He's denied allegations of racism (here) and sexism (there). This name's supposedly not phallic and portrays the evils of society being represented by a large dark devil figure.

Big Bopper

Born Jape Richardson, Texas, he adopted the name J.P. Richardson, based on a common mispronunciation of his name, when he became a disc jockey on KTRM Radio, Texas. Because of his size and enthusiasm for the fifties heel-and-toe Bop dance, he adopted the nickname The Big Bopper.

Big Brother And The Holding Company

This San Francisco band got their name in 1965, before they started backing Janis Joplin and when they were managed by Chet Helms.

He took Big Brother from George Orwell's 1949 nightmarish novel of the near future *Nineteen Eighty-Four*. Big Brother was the nameless dictator of the superpower Oceanea. His portrait adorns every wall – complete with moving eyes and the logo "Big Brother Is Watching You". He's apparently based on Stalin. See also: ▷ Country Joe And The Fish.

Helms, as promoter, financier and *éminence grise*, additionally saw it as an amusing comment on his role. After he left, journalists thought it referred to extrovert guitarist James Gurley.

The group additionally chose The Holding Company to rival ▷ The Great Society's name. Joplin said it was an apposite comment on faceless capitalist institutions which were becoming Orwellian monoliths. Cf – years later – the naming of ▷ Public Image.

Gurley added in an interview: "It had, like, a double meaning because of common slang at the time. 'Holding' meant 'possessing' [drugs] – it just was safer to say. It was a long name but it worked well, real well."

Après Joplin, the band played under their full name: as The Holding Company; and as Big Brother, although the latter was their favourite.

Spin-off: ▷ Dinosaurs.

Big Country

Seen by some as applying to Stuart Adamson's Scottish home.

Surprisingly, the rest of the band were non-

Scottish, born in England and Canada. The twin guitars still sounded like bagpipes on their 1983 title track *In A Big Country*. The act was formed by session musicians Rhythm For Hire, coming together with Adamson after his time in ▷ The Skids.

He says the name was meant to imply vastness, ambition and new discovery – in whatever country, whatever field. The music was described as "panoramic" and "wide-screen".

The name's shared with the successful 1958 film *The Big Country* starring Gregory Peck. The group, on the other hand, proved a cinema box-office flop at first, and dropped from supporting ▷ Alice Cooper after a show at Birmingham's Odeon.

Big Easy

From their native New Orleans. The term for the city was further popularised in a steamy film of the same name; its origin is uncertain.

A Bigger Splash

Named in tribute to American artist and film maker Andy Warhol (1927–88). His painting *A Bigger Splash* shows a Californian swimming pool with the water disturbed after someone has dived into it.

Big Guitar Yeah

Scottish three-piece from Edinburgh; hopefuls of the early 1990s. "Why? Because we like loud guitar, heavy grooves, using and abusing technology."

Big In Japan

"Big In Japan" is one of the music businesses's greatest jokes and used to surface like this:

Record plugger to DJ: "You've *got* to play this new single, it's absolutely brilliant and it will sell loads! It's by The Turgid Dirges!"

DJ: "The Turgid Dirges! But I've never heard of this band."

Plugger: "They're still to make it here, but they are already really big in Japan/Italy/El Salvador!" And so on.

The phrase was spotted by this British group in a late 1970s *New Musical Express* issue which said: "▷ Led Zeppelin big in Japan". They said the advent of punk music was time for a fresh start, new gods, new music and new ideas.

A seminal Liverpool band whose membership rivals the similar Crucial Three for talent, Big In Japan briefly featured Holly of ▷ Frankie Goes To Hollywood fame, who asked if sex and horror had became the new gods; Budgie, later of ▷ The Slits and ▷ Siouxsie And The Banshees; Bill Drummond of ▷ The KLF; Ian Broudie of ▷ The Lightning Seeds; and Jayne Casey of ▷ Pink Military.

No relation to either German band ▷ Alphaville, who cut a single called *Big In Japan*, or ▷ Japan.

The Big "O"

▷ Roy Orbison.

Big Star

This 1970s band from Tennessee, U.S.A., were looking for a name after a hard day's night working in a recording studio. As they emerged into the evening, increasingly sure they were going to be big stars, their eyes alighted on a neon display on the other side of the street: "Big Star Foodmarket". "It must be a sign," they said.

Big Thing

This U.S. band spent years playing under this moniker. Singer-songwriter Robert Lamm said it was chosen in the hope their music would be the Next Big Thing.

It worked on other levels: first, it was Mafia-inspired slang – "doing the big thing" is to murder someone. Second, it was saucily suggestive. (This mildly lewd idea became an album title for ▷ Duran Duran years later.) Such factors may have explained why the band got bookings in no more than small mid-west clubs.

It was their mentor Jim Guercio who was the drive behind their change to (yes!) ▷ Chicago. Then they indeed became the Next Big Thing in jazz-rock.

The Big Three

1960s Merseybeaters named after the six-foot stature of the three members.

Big Yin (Band)

Billy Connolly and friends: the comedian was variously known as "the big one" and "the big girl" for his long hair.

Acker Bilk

Born Bernard Bilk, known as "acker" from now rarely heard Southern English rural slang for "friend".

The Billion Dollar Babies

▷ Alice Cooper was originally the name of the band; later it came to refer to the singer alone. When the original line-up later re-formed without him they tried to avoid any risk of trouble by choosing a new name.

They liked the cover of the 1973 Cooper album *Billion Dollar Babies* because it showed them wallowing in heaps of greenbacks. Even this name produced court threats, subsequently settled.

Biloxi Blues

A name taken from the title of a musical about a man called up for service in the dying days of Word War II. The comedy was filmed in 1988.

Bing

▷ Bing Crosby.

Bird

The nickname became bigger than the man: Charlie Parker. Within hours of his death in 1955, "Bird Lives" was daubed on the walls of the New York subway. Everyone understood.

Arranger and composer Gil Evans insisted the name came when Parker was a teenager fending for himself in Kansas City. "He would joke: 'Well, I'm going home to catch one of the yardbirds and cook it' - that's what he called chicken".

Parker was responsible for ▷ The Yardbirds' name but *not* ▷ Birdland. The nickname was also applied to jazz arranger Bert Johnson, although his fame is eclipsed by Parker's.

Birdland

U.K. Midlands band of the 1990s named after an arty track on Patti Smith's 1975 album *Horses*. It's a poem about a young man being attacked and killed by a flock of birds on his New England farm. She was inspired by Alfred Hitchcock's 1963 movie *The Birds*. The bleached-blondes of Birdland gave the game away by recording Smith's *Rock 'n' Roll Nigger*.

They were therefore *not* named after Charlie ▷ "Bird" Parker's nightclub, Birdland.

Birds

This 1960s English band showed how to get into trouble with a name: they started as The Thunderbirds – after the car – found another band had the name, renamed The Birds, then were overtaken in popularity by ▷ The Byrds and sued the Americans for loss of income. The Brits lost and had to become Bird's Birds.

Most lucky of these early Birds: Ron Wood, later of ▷ The Faces and ▷ The Rolling Stones.

The Birthday Party

This Australian band started as The Boys Next Door in 1980 and briefly used this concurrently with The Birthday Party, conscious both names sounded ordinary and unthreatening.

They were inspired by *The Birthday Party*, a doomy 1957 play by British dramatist Harold Pinter, later filmed, in which an ordinary event becomes desperate and dangerous.

Their leader Nick Cave, who favoured decadent lyrics inspired by Pinteresque visions of destruction, returned to literary references with ▷ The Bad Seeds.

Bitch

The in-yer-face name was part of the sado-masochistic image of this American heavy metal band fronted by Betsy Weiss. The unit later changed the moniker to Betsy – in an attempt to be taken seriously. Shorn of their headline-grabbing tag, they found it harder to get hits.

Bix

Jazzman Leon Bismarck Beiderbeck was called Bix; a corruption of his Germanic real name.

Björk

She was born Björk Gumundsdóttir but figured her second name would never be spelled or pronounced properly outside her native Iceland. As a member of ▷ The Sugarcubes, she became the latest in a line of one-name stars – cf ▷ Sting, ▷ Madonna etc.

Pronounce it "Be-urk" (rhymes with "work") *not* "Bee-ork" (rhymes with "York").

Bjorn Again
Tribute band, with lookalikes playing cover versions of ▷ Abba songs. Name taken from original member Bjorn Ulvaeus.

Black
Black were always white, although they were a trio which became one: Liverpool singer Colin Vearncombe, whose wonderful lifestyle included a penchant for black clothes. A wise name change from his punk band Epileptic Tits.

Black Box
These rappers insisted it was a reference to the flight monitor fitted to aeroplanes, but they said it with a sly wink – leaving open the possibility this is another lewd reference.

Blackbyrds
This loose aggregation is widely reported to have named after ▷ The Byrds. In fact their leader was Donald Byrd, who first had a hit with *Black Byrd*.

Black Caesar
One of a plethora of nicknames for ▷ James Brown, this came from his score for the 1973 ghetto gangster film of the same name. Like ▷ Little Caesar, it recalls Julius Caesar, though it's more to do with West Indian escaped slave John Caesar.

Cilla Black
She was born in Liverpool, U.K., as Priscilla Marie Veronica White, and began singing as Swinging Cilla. Deciding Cilla White didn't sound right, she hit back as Cilla Black. The change was suggested by inventive ▷ Beatles manager Brian Epstein.

The Black Crowes
Chris and Rich Robinson, from Atlanta, Georgia, started as Greasy Little Toes. A friend said this wasn't auspicious and suggested Mr Crow's Garden after the fairy tale. They were offered $50 for a concert in Chattanooga in 1984 … the cheque bounced and they renamed again … adding the extra "e" to confuse people and developing a logo of crows with long black hair cut in ▷ Keith Richards style like their own.

They're informally known as The Crowes in the same way as ▷ The Rolling Stones, whom they have emulated, are called The Stones. No relation to other musical crows, for example ▷ Rain Tree Crow.

Black Flag
Named after the U.S. insect-killer aerosol. This Californian band thought it recalled ▷ Black Sabbath. Spin-off: ▷ The Circle Jerks.

Blackfoot
Blackfoot was a U.S. band and Blackfoot Sue a British act, both named after American Indian tribes, Blackfoot and Sioux.

Black 47
A name of a 1990s U.S. band who chose to commemorate Ireland in 1847, the height of the Irish Famine. At least one million people were estimated to have died. Some of the ancestors of the band, and many others, emigrated from Ireland bitter at the English, who did little to help.

The Black Gladiator
▷ Bo Diddley.

The Blackhearts
Named by Joan Jett of ▷ The Runaways. She was a part-time graffiti artist who drew little hearts on walls across America.

Blackmore's Rainbow
▷ Rainbow.

Black Moses
Nickname given to Isaac Hayes, for his biblical dress and philosophical introductions to songs. ▷ The Real Black Moses.

Black Oak Arkansas
The Knowbody Else failed to break through despite endless tours and they moved back to Arkansas in 1971 for a home-truths rethink. They lived round vocalist ▷ Jim Dandy's home town Black Oak and still have large ranches there.

Black Sabbath
Started in 1967 by John Michael Osbourne,

AKA ▷ Ozzy Osbourne. The band went through hippy-inspired names Polka Tulk, Mythology, Whole Earth and Earth. Unfortunately, there was another U.K. act called Earth: audiences would turn up expecting soft rock – and get blown away at full volume.

They took the final appellation from one of their songs, written round bassist Geezer (Tony) Butler's interest in black magic. He was inspired by a book by author Dennis *The Devil And All His Works* Wheatley, not the 1963 film of the same name. The same interest influenced other heavy metal stars including Jimmy Page of ▷ Led Zeppelin.

Spin-off band: ▷ Dio. The act partly inspired the naming of ▷ Black Flag. Black Sab's work inspired the naming of ▷ Masters Of Reality.

Black Snake Moan

Named after a track by Blind Lemon Jefferson. Vocalist Robert Plant went on into the similar-sounding ▷ The Crawling King Snakes, also named after his fondness for U.S. blues, and became the voice of ▷ Led Zeppelin. He returned to the blues theme years later with ▷ The Honeydrippers.

Black Uhuru

The politically motivated reggae band formed in Jamaica as Uhuru, Swahili for liberty.

Black Umfolosi

Named after a nineteenth-century Zulu regiment.

Black Widow

Like ▷ Black Sabbath, another U.K. band with an interest in the occult. Not a reference to the spider.

Blancmange

Seen by some as revolting, the name was chosen by Neil Arthur and Stephen Luscombe to avoid over-seriousness of other synth bands of the 1980s. It was reinforced by jokey record sleeves and titles such as *Mange Tout*. They might have done better if they had remained The Viewfinders. Many U.S. interviewers didn't know blancmange was a jelly-like dessert.

Bleep + Booster

This British 1990s duo's name comes from a boy and his extra-terrestrial companion who starred in a 1960s BBC TV cartoon.

The choice caused problems, as ▷ Bros/ ▷ Pet Shop Boys/ ▷ East 17 svengali Tom Watkins found when he took them on. Everyone wanted to ask Stephen Singleton and David Lewin: "Which one's Bleep and which one's Booster?"

Blind Faith

One-LP wonders made up of Steve Winwood, ex ▷ Traffic; Ric Grech, ex ▷ Family; and ▷ Eric Clapton/Ginger Baker, ex supergroup ▷ Cream. *Melody Maker* revealed the band, calling them "the ultimate supergroup" before they'd even played. The name was a response to "blind faith" of fans more impressed by "Clapton Is God" solos than group performances. Clapton further hid from acclaim as ▷ Derek And The Dominos.

Independent On Sunday reporter John Windsor, quoting photographer Bob Seidemann, casts doubt on Clapton as the originator, saying the moniker came from the title of the album's cover photograph. It showed a pre-pubescent girl toying with a phallic spaceship. Seidemann was lodging with Clapton at the Pheasantry Studios, Chelsea, and spotted a likely subject on an underground train – 12-year-old Sula Goschen. He gave her a card and her parents gave their consent, though it was her 11-year-old sister Mariora who finally posed.

Blind Owl

Al Wilson of ▷ Canned Heat; from his short-sightedness and nocturnal lifestyle.

Blizzard Of Oz

▷ Ozzy Osbourne mixing his nickname with the British underground *Oz* magazine and musical *The Wizard Of Oz*.

The Blockheads

Q: Why do groups give themselves self-mocking names? Cf ▷ Simple Minds etc.

A: In this case U.K. singer/songwriter ▷ Ian

Dury told his backing group they were useless learning tunes: "Y'er'll block'eads!!" Formed from ▷ Kilburn And The High Roads.

Blodwyn Pig

Spin-off from ▷ Jethro Tull, a name also with an agricultural origin: after a hog depicted on the cover of their debut album. They later became Blodwyn, Welsh for white flower. No relation to ▷ Henry Cow or ▷ Pearls Before Swine.

Blonde On Blonde

A tribute to ▷ Bob Dylan's 1966 double album of the same name.

Blondie

Naturally brunette Debbie Harry started in folk-rock band ▷ Wind In The Willows and performed with Angel And The Snake, backed by Chris Stein, ex-Magic Tramps. The bottled-blonde look came in three-girl band The Stilettos.

"It was a good choice," she said in an interview. "It was a strong visual image and proved blondes can have more fun."

It also referred to a much-loved U.S. strip cartoon series *Lil' Abner, Blondie And Dagwood*, made into TV shows and films. The original Blondie Boopadoop is no relation to Betty Boop, inspirer of ▷ Betty Boo later. Unlike her, Harry escaped legal action – partly because "blondie" was in wide use. *Blondie* actress Penny Singleton wasn't the only blonde bombshell.

Harry later formed Tiger Bomb, appearing as Deborah Harry: a lengthening of name usually means serious intent: cf ▷ John Cougar Mellencamp.

Terrible punning album title: *Once More Into The Bleach*.

Harry's appeared in a number of films, ironically sometimes with a brunette look. So much for the sort of Marilyn Monroe *Blonde Ambition* of ▷ Madonna.

Blood, Sweat And Tears

This New York band was toiling in a dark, sweaty rehearsal room in 1968. Al Kooper cut his finger, felt nothing so certainly didn't cry but the name hit him when he saw the red puddle as the lights came up.

The phrase turns up many times in literature and was famously used by British prime minister Sir Winston Churchill in May 1940. A Churchillian phrase was also picked by ▷ Beginning Of The End.

The Bloomsbury Set

Named after intellectuals who met in the Bloomsbury district of London. The original Bloomsbury Group, including Strachey, Russell, Huxley, Forster, Sackville-West, Woolf and Keynes would be appalled that 80 years later they christened a band from Birmingham playing vulgar *popular* music.

Bloomsday

Arcane literary reference to Irish writer James Joyce's pun on Doomsday, a day in the life of Leopold Bloom in the 1922 masterpiece *Ulysses*. Joyce scholars celebrate Bloomsday every 16 June. Perhaps predictable pretentiousness from former cohorts of ▷ Lloyd "Literary Namedropper" Cole, who namechecked Joyce, Simone de Beauvoir and Norman Mailer among others in early songs.

The Blow Monkeys

Taken from a less-than-complimentary term for aboriginal didgeridoo musicians, heard by singer ▷ Dr Robert during his teenage years in Australia.

Blue Angel

New York rock quintet known for nurturing Cyndi Lauper. The name's from the 1930 film which catapulted Marlene Dietrich to stardom.

The Bluebells

Formed by Glaswegian Robert Hodgens 1979, who renamed Bobby Bluebell. The Bluebell Girls of Paris started legal action over the group name. The Scotsmen won: a court ruled Scottish bluebells were well known so a local band was entitled to the name – and there was no way the acts could be confused.

Blue Cheer

A blue cheer is a rude noise – and a strain of the hallucinatory drug LSD. This U.S. West Coast band, formed in the long-off hippy hazey Boston daze of 1967, named after the latter. Cf ▷ Jefferson Airplane.

The Blue Flames

Countless bands have used this name including outfits led by Junior Parker, Jimmy James – AKA ▷ Jimi Hendrix – and Georgie Fame. Parker's band named after their blues repertoire; Hendrix named his band after Parker's.

Blue Jays

The original vocal Blue Jays – formed in California in 1958, enjoyed hits in the 1960s and re-formed in 1989 – named after a baseball team.

In the interim a duo appeared, wearing plenty of Blue Jays on their record sleeves. Jays from their first names, Justin (Hayward) and John (Lodge); blue from their main band, ▷ The Moody Blues, then undergoing a hiatus. This passed for cleverness in some 1970s rock circles.

The Blue Nile

Not from Africa but Scotland, these musicians were looking through an atlas when they found the Blue Nile river. There's a Nile, Blue Nile and White Nile: everywhere the water's mainly mud colour.

Blue Öyster Cult

This Long Island act tried for size the radically different names of The Stalk Forrest Group, Oaxoa, The Cows and Soft White Underbelly (ugh) – nearly all suggested by leading light Sandy Pearlman.

Underbelly were praised in U.S. magazine *Crawdaddy* but Clive Davis, president of CBS records, summarily rejected their demo tape as "horrible". Maybe he disliked the name.

Pearlman, who'd moved from rock journalist to manager, was casting round for ideas when he was outside a New York seafood restaurant selling Blue Point Variety oysters. He wrote a song called *Blue Oyster Cult*. The name applied to the band "because it sounded cool" and the umlaut was added for a mysterious air.

He denied suggestions it came from the link between PEARLman and OYSTER and resubmitted the Underbelly tape to Davis under a new name. This time Davis listened, and signed the group: it was two years before they told him the name story.

B.O.C. inspired other heavy metal bands to garnish their names with cod-Germanic symbols for no reason. Those who succumbed to this umlaut/diaresis diarrhoea include: ▷ Die Ärtze, ▷ Einstürzende Neubauten, ▷ Foetus Über Alles, Helmet (early ▷ Helmet), ▷ Mötley Crüe, ▷ Motörhead, ▷ Münchener Freiheit, ▷ Queensrÿche and Rëktum (▷ Gaye Bykers On Acid spoof).

Band members include Buck Dharma, who was born Donald Roeser and renamed according to Buddhist teachings.

B.O.C. played various semi-secret gigs and one-off projects as The Stalk Forrest/ Forest Group, reviving one early name. Acts as varied as ▷ The Cure and ▷ R.E.M. have adopted similar tactics, guessing only true fans are likely to know the identity of those playing.

The Blue Ridge Rangers

Not so much a band, more a smokescreen by former ▷ Creedence Clearwater Revival star John Fogerty to avoid the limelight. He disguised his 1973 solo album as a one made by a new band with an appropriately rural name.

Similar motivations resulted in the naming of ▷ Derek And The Dominos by ▷ Eric Clapton, ▷ The Notting Hillbillies and ▷ The Traveling Wilburys.

Blue Rondo A La Turk

This short-lived 1980s U.K. band named from a swinging tune by Dave Brubeck. It sounded exotic and fitted their cosmopolitan ▷ Kid Creole image. It interested the fashion magazines but the music press and punters weren't impressed.

Blues Boy

▷ B.B. King.

Bluesbreakers

John Mayall, inspired by Alexis Korner's Blues Incorporated, formed The Blues Syndicate first. He wanted to break up old blues with jazzy and electric ideas pioneered by Cyril Davis and others.

▷ Cream, ▷ Eric Clapton, ▷ Mark-Almond.

Blues Project

Mid-1960s East Coast U.S. group – taken from the name of a jamming outfit in which they'd previously played.

The Blue Turtles

▷ Sting had a bizarre dream one night about cyan turtles digging up his garden. He thought it a significant symbol, celebrated with his 1985 LP *The Dream Of The Blue Turtles* and name of his jazz-tinged backers of the time.

Blue Whale

▷ Fleetwood Mac founder Mick Fleetwood moonlighting in the 1990s. His hobby band played blues; backed his environmental concerns for marine wildlife and recorded at his studio, already named Blue Whale.

Blur

The contenders for the Britpop crown started under the bland name ▷ Seymour, taken from one of singer Damon Albarn's characters. One of their concerts was reviewed under the mis-spelled name "Feymour" in *Music Week*.

Seymour sent a tape to Andy Ross, the former *Sounds* journalist who was head of Food Records, a nascent off-shoot of EMI. He and his partner Dave Balfe, ex ▷ Teardrop Explodes, signed them for a £3,000 advance on condition they change their name.

A proposed list of alternatives considered in a West End pizza restaurant included The Shining Path, Sub, Sensitise, Blur and Whirlpool. So there was everything from a group of Peruvian revolutionaries to a maker of "white goods" – the latter could have caused trademark problems.

Blur was chosen for its multi-meanings which could refer to the effect of alcohol, drugs or the passage of time; it could relate to vision, memory or psychedelia.

The list was drawn up by Ross and Balfe and submitted to the band for them to pick a name. This is presumably not often stated because it appears damning of the Blur's creativity – although Albarn's songwriting has dispelled doubts.

As part of the deal, drummer Dave Rowntree reportedly had to undertake never to play concerts in his pyjama bottoms. Ross/Balfe thought the same stunt had done ▷ The Boomtown Rats no good. Johnny Fingers in Bob Geldof's band used to be similarly attired, leading to distracting publicity and unwelcome lunges by female fans.

Within weeks of signing, Blur heard of a band called Blurt, whose second album was absurdly called *Kenny Rogers Greatest Hits: Take Two*. A dispute was avoided because there have been at least four Blurts, the best known of which was led by Ted Milton.

So it is another short, vague 1990s name, again with a nicely ambiguous sound. There has been a debate on whether these less-is-more contemporary choices are clever. These include: Aloof, Ash, Bawl, Bay, ▷ Beck, Blow, Bis, ▷ Bob, ▷ Bush, Cake, Case, ▷ Cast, Clock, Come, Curve, Eat, ▷ Gene, Grace, Gun, ▷ Hole, ▷ Jale, ▷ KoRn, Lamb, Live, ▷ Loop, Low, ▷ L7, Lurch, ▷ Lush, Main, Mice, Moist, Moose, ▷ Neck, Nut, ▷ Oasis, Olive, Paw, Phish, The Pod, ▷ Pulp, ▷ Reef, Rex, Ride, Salad, Salt, Smog, Space, Spin, ▷ Suede, Swell, Swirl, Tism, Tool, Top, Wedge and Whale. Expect a reaction soon with a swing back to efforts like ▷ Big Brother And The Holding Company.

See also Linda Holorny's 1995 book *Blur: An Illustrated Biography* and Martin Roach's more comprehensive *Blur: The Whole Story*, published in 1996.

Blur's fanzine is called *Blurb*.

Albarn has gone under the anagramic pseudonym Dan Abnormal, and wrote a song of the same name. He said it was given to him by his girlfriend Justine Frischmann from Elastica: "I thought it was brilliant. It represents a lot of my less savoury habits." He appears as Abnormal on Elastica's 1995 album, playing keyboards.

Blyth Power

Taken from the name of a steam engine which they liked. Not the only band to name after a contraption of this sort: cf ▷ Buffalo Springfield.

BMX Bandits

BMX bikes became valuable at the height of the 1980s cross-country craze and newspapers were full of headlines about them being stolen by "BMX bandits". A synonym of the classic title *Bicycle Thief*.

BOB

BOB – note capital letters – formed in North London, U.K. in 1986 and named after ▷ Bob Dylan. They have become reluctant to admit this, doubtless worried at getting pigeonholed like ▷ The Dylans. True, there have been enough "new Dylans" without people openly admitting the link. They later denied even owning one Dylan record between them and said the name was chosen because it was almost meaningless and so short that if it went on a poster it needed to be printed up bigger. ▷ The Who chose their name for this reason.

But as songwriter Simon Armstrong told one interviewer: "When you think about it, the whole concept of picking a name for a band is ridiculous."

Bob B. Soxx And The Blue Jeans
▷ Bob B. Soxx.

Bobby "Blue" Bland
Blues singer, born Robert Calvin Bland.

Bobby Charltons
This U.K. group name pays tribute to the legendary English soccer star and World Cup hero. Another name of a sporting hero ripped off by a band: ▷ Babe Ruth.

The Bodines
Like ▷ The Boo Radleys, another band to name affectionately after an idiot. In this case they named after Jethro in *The Beverly Hillbillies*. This was a classic U.S. sitcom about a family of hicks-from-the-sticks Ozark farmers called Clampett who strike oil on their ranch and are baffled by all the money that results. They move to California where they are hilariously out of place despite their obscene wealth.

Jethro is the family's nephew; while his proper name was Bodine the world sees him as a Clampett. He is usually described as a muscle-bound, good-looking womaniser let down by his minimal IQ.

The TV series also inspired U.K. star offshoots ▷ The Muswell Hillbillies and ▷ The Notting Hillbillies.

Body Count
▷ Ice T under another name. He first used the rubric for the notorious *Cop Killer*. The name comes from a line in *Born Dead*.

Bodysnatchers
From the horror book and film *The Invasion of The Body Snatchers*.

Another act to name after a Bela Lugosi flick: ▷ White Zombie.

Marc Bolan
Born London, U.K., 1947 as Mark Feld, he flirted with the stagey name Toby Tyler and sung in John's Children before forming ▷ T Rex. He thought Tyler a little lightweight and wanted something more serious. His choice was taken from the king of seriousness, ▷ Bob Dylan, who inspired many other artists. Bolan comes from the first and last letters of His Bobness's name ie: Bob Dylan. Bolan's record company, DECCA at one stage credited him as Bowland, reportedly as a result of a mis-hearing. There is no connection with Mack Bolan, the hero of *The Executioner* series of novels begun by Don Pendleton in 1969.

Name notes: Bolan cut a flop singles in 1970 and 1973 respectively credited to Dib Cochran's Earwigs and Marc Bolan's Big Carrot. The first was a tribute to Eric Cochran: Bolan had been a fan aged just seven. Perhaps thankfully, he didn't explain the second ... His son was called Rolan(d) Bolan – cf his friend ▷ David Bowie's Zowie Bowie. More details in books by Paul Sinclair; George Tremlett; and Chris Welch and Simon Napier-Bell. Nickname: The Electric Warrior.

The Bolshoi
U.K. 1980s band who named from the Russian state ballet company.

Bolt Thrower
Long before *Doom* captured the attention of computer kids everywhere with its chainsaw massacres, this U.K. band liked this war game character so much as to swipe his name. Before he could get them.

Bomb Everything
These U.S. hipsters started shakin' the house under the blunt name Bomb Disneyland, reasoning there was no better way of establishing anarcho-syndicalist credentials. They are reluctant to discuss this name, and had to change it after legal action loomed. Hence Mickey Mouse and Donald Duck live to fight another day.

The name caused similar problems during the Gulf War to force Iraqi troops out of Kuwait.

Bomb The Bass

Rookie British producer Tim Simenon found himself with a massive hit on his hands with his first recording, *Beat Dis*.

The name came from a term used by engineers for one recording technique he was learning in the studio.

"Bombing" means taking one sound, such as a piece of music, and undermining it by mixing something completely different on top, such as a sampled sound effect or deejay speech.

So Simenon had started with a powerful bass guitar line and overlayed a tape he had compiled of familiar samples from popular dance records. So he was "bombing the bass" and made this doubly clear by including the sampled repeated words "bomb de bass!"

The group virtually ceased operations during the 1991 Gulf War in case the name was misunderstood. Simenon had by then moved on to lucrative fields afresh in production. ▷ Bomb Everything ran into similar problems during the war; ▷ Massive Attack briefly abbreviated to Massive.

For more, see *The Directory Of Hip-Hop Terms*.

Beki Bondage

It seemed an ideal name for a punk at the time that bondage gear was the height of fashion. Actually the lead singer of ▷ Vice Squad found her name very easily: she was born Rebecca Louise Bond.

Gary "U.S." Bonds

Born Gary Anderson in Florida, U.S.A., he was renamed U.S. Bonds by his record company in 1960 as part of a promotional con. Producer Frank Guida sent out copies of the *New Orleans* single in a plain sleeve which ripped off the famous slogan "Buy U.S. Bonds". His astute hope was that announcers would think it a federal announcement and give it a play. An angry Anderson only learnt of this later but he accepted it as the record charted. Meanwhile the Bond Authority was furious, and the record company was forced to compromise with the name Gary "U.S." Bonds.

U.S. was said to mean Ulysses Samuel.

Cf ▷ John Cougar Mellencamp – another artist renamed without his consent on the release of his first record.

Boney M

This West Indian band had wanted to be called M because three of the original members had names starting with this letter. Producer Frank Farian wanted to call them Boney, after an imported TV show then highly popular in Europe. It was 1976. Farian had already recorded the single which had been a hit outside Germany and merely wanted the "band" to present it at home. In the end they compromised with Boney M. The band went on to record a string of tracks which were hits, despite the silly name.

Another Farian band: ▷ Milli Vanilli.

Bongwater

So what sort of person names a band after a hookah water pipe? Say "Hi" – or was that "high"? – to Bongwater. *Hits From The Bong* followed.

Bonham

Shameless family reference by Jason Bonham, son of ▷ the late "Bonzo" Bonham of ▷ Led Zeppelin fame.

Jason is the leader of this particular group.

Bon Jovi

From the name of the lead singer, former studio tea boy from New Jersey, U.S.A., John Francis Bongiovi Jnr, who became Jon Bon Jovi. His name is Italian, his ancestors Sicilian.

Bono

▷ U2's lead singer acquired his nickname, later stage name, from a shop-front sign BONOVOX seen in his native Dublin, opposite the Gresham Hotel in O'Connell Street.

The shop was advertising hearing aids and the teenage friends were intrigued by the name. As all the members of the youth community called "The Village" were adopting nicknames, Paul Hewson, already nicknamed The Judge, also became Bono Vox (of) O'Connell Street, Bono for short. The name also translates as "good voice" which is apt for a singer. Compare to the unrelated Simon Le Bon of ▷ Duran Duran, ▷ Ultravox.

Pronounce "Bon-oh/ Bonno" as opposed to "Bown-oh/ Boh-no".

Interviewed by *Vox* magazine in May 1997, Bono said: "Maybe it wasn't actually me who changed it [the name]." It was given to him. Asked if it was important he killed off his name of 15 years he said: "Maybe so. Looking back identity was always a problem, because I was neither Protestant nor Catholic, neither middle class nor fully working class."

For the 1995 Passengers project he became Pi Hoo Sunn.

▷ The Edge, ▷ Feedback, ▷ The Hype. Unflattering derivative: Bozo.

See also Eamon Dunphy's book *Unforgettable Fire – The Story of U2*.

Sonny Bono

Anglicisation of Salvatore Bono. He's nothing in common with ▷ Bono of ▷ U2 apart from the name spelling. It's pronounced differently: "Boh-no" not "Bonno".

▷ Cher.

Bonzo

▷ Led Zeppelin's John Bonham. Largely, a play on his name (and a better one than, say, Bozo: Bonham could have happily floored anyone suggesting as much). Also from his goofy friendliness and similarity to the daffy, docile and lovable cartoon character Bonzo. Cf ▷ Bonzo Dog Doo-Dah Band. Related: ▷ Bonham.

Bonzo Dog Doo-Dah Band

Bonzo has long been in use as a pet name. It may have come from the Australian word "bonzer", meaning good, but probably has the same root as bonnie, another popular choice for canines.

It gained currency when Captain Bruce S. Ingram, editor of the British newspaper the *Sketch*, created a lovable puppy dog called Bonzo. He was drawn by British artist George E. Studdy in the 1920s – and by the 1930s had become a major hit, appearing on everything from postcards and posters to toys and tea towels.

This takes us to the 1960s, where a group of London art students behind this initially pub-rock band wanted a whimsically silly name with a 1920s variety flavour and adopted The Bonzo Dog Dada Band.

The Bonzos also namechecked the Dada art movement of the roaring twenties. This later inspired the naming of several bands called ▷ Dada. It was wilfully anarchistic and featured "found" objects presented as art.

The name got mispronounced so much that the group gave up, bowed to popular opinion and they officially became Doo-Dah not Dada. "Doo-dah", like ▷ Showaddywaddy, was a repeated phrase used in such popular songs as *Camptown Races*. It also well fitted the hit *I'm The Urban Spaceman*, with its "doh-doh" backing. They later made it just The Bonzo Dog Band.

All with a little help from their friend, ▷ Beatle ▷ Paul McCartney, AKA ▷ Apollo C. Vermouth.

No relation therefore to Bonzo of ▷ Bonzo Goes to Washington.

Bonzo Goes To Washington

This is ▷ Talking Head Jerry Harrison in disguise.

U.S. President Ronald Reagan acquired the unflattering nickname "Bonzo", apparently relating to his mental ability – or lack of it – and in reference to his 1951 film *Bedtime For Bonzo*, in which he was upstaged by a chimpanzee called Bonzo, who seems much smarter than him. The film inspired a sequel the following year, *Bonzo Goes To College*.

This band's highlight, in 1984, was therefore based around a recording of Mr Reagan's microphone outtake "we begin bombing in five minutes", an essayed joke which became a major gaffe.

The nickname was also used by ▷ The Ramones on their 1985 single *Bonzo Goes To Bitburg*, about Reagan's visit to a cemetery containing graves of Hitler's SS.

Both recall ▷ Frankie Goes To Hollywood.

Betty Boo

Betty Boo, like ▷ The Thompson Twins, came on at first like a cartoon character and indeed her name also came from a cartoon.

It was inspired by Betty Boop, the sexy star of short animated films produced by Max Fleischer in the 1920s and 1930s. Betty was at first Betty Boopadoop – no relation to ▷ Blondie Boopadoop. She had a squeaky voice and, like the later character Jane, always seemed to be losing her clothes.

Boo's real name is Alison Clarkson, who was born in Shepherd's Bush, London, but is half Scottish and half Malaysian.

She adopted her stage persona at the tender age of 17 when she joined the all-female rap group The She-Rockers.

Boop the singer became Boo after lawyers stepped in representing her namesake cartoon character.

Booker T And The MGs

A shortened version of their full name, Booker T. Jones and the Memphis Group. All were session musicians at Stax Records Memphis studio who backed Otis Redding among others and also recorded as part of the Mar-Keys. One of the band members pointed out Jones had a convertible English MG car. However, the car only came with the band's success: Booker thought it an apt purchase. Somehow Booker T. and the Morris Garages wouldn't sound the same …

The name inspired ▷ The LAGs.

Individual band member: Donald Duck Dunn, named in reference to the Disney legend.

The Boomtown Rats

In 1975 they begun rehearsals as Mark Skid and The Y Fronts. (Cf similar idea: ▷ The Skids.) Leader ▷ Bob Geldof thought this juvenile and offensive. He wanted something which was "dark and brooding … People have to respond to everything, including the name. It must be exciting."

Subsequent rejected suggestions included: Traction (too heavy metal); Darker Days (sounded like second-rate song scrapped by ▷ The Doors); Nightlife (not easily shortened) and Nightlife Thugs. This **was** liked because it could be shortened to just The Thugs, in the same way ▷ The Rolling Stones were often The Stones.

It was the night before the band's first gig, a Halloween bash at Dublin's Bolton Street College Of Technology, where some of them were studying. Geldof had been reading folk-singer Woody Guthrie's autobiographical 1943 book *Bound For Glory* – a great aspirational

name for a band in itself although never used by them. On page 114 the character Colonel, in Guthrie's home area, makes a passing reference to a gang he greatly disapproves of : "yore pack of mangy curs! Boom town rats!" (sic). The Rats were a gang of youths recently arrived in the Oklahoma town after oilfields were found.

The phrase came into the singer's mind in the interval of that first gig and they played the rest of the concert after the promoter announced – much to everyone's amusement – the sudden name change to The Boomtown Rats. It could also be abbreviated, Stones-style, to The Rats.

The band then tried many individual names – Max Volume, Max Headroom, the Van Rentl Brothers Hertz and Avis, Cup O'Tea, Ray Di Ator among them. But only two names stuck. Johnnie Moylet became Johnny Fingers: it was obvious for a keyboardist. Bassist Pat Cusack became Pete Briquette. They thought his name was very Irish so made it more so: it was a pun on Irish fuel cakes made from peat. There's more in Geldof's always articulate 1986 biography *Is That It?* Albums include compilation *Ratrospective*.

The Boo Radleys

They took their handle from a strangely named village idiot character in *To Kill A Mockingbird*, Harper Lee's best-selling novel about justice – or, rather, the lack of it – in the U.S. Deep South earlier in the twentieth century. It was a nicely self-disparaging name which suggested a sense of humour rather than pomposity. See entry on ▷ Simple Minds and many others.

Nothing to do with ▷ Boo Yah T.R.I.B.E.

After a run of poor sales, they acquired the unflattering derivative: The Do Badlys.

Bootleg Beatles

Tribute band, with lookalikes playing cover versions of ▷ Beatles songs. Beats the bootleggers.

Boots

Nickname for Nancy Sinatra, ▷ Frank Sinatra's singing daughter, from the bossy persona assumed on her first hit, *These Boots Are Made For Walkin'*.

According to one account, one of her songs inspired the naming of ▷ Prefab Sprout.

The Boo-Yaa T.R.I.B.E.

Veterans of the internecine Los Angeles ghetto gang wars, they decided to turn their energy to creative force and rapped it up (geddit) by calling themselves variously The Boo Yaa Gang/ Tribe/ Family.

The name was instant street cred even before their LP *New Funky Nation*. Boo Yaa is street slang for the sound of a shot, especially from an uzi, or machine gun. Audiences at concerts were soon chanting "boo-yaa" at their heroes.
▷ A Tribe Called Quest.

The Boss

Nickname for concert supremo ▷ Bruce Springsteen, acquired at the time of his legendary five-hour-plus shows.

Boston

The band began in 1975 making demo tapes on a portable studio in the basement of a house in – you've guessed it – Boston, Massachusetts, U.S.A.

There's a lot of dispute about who thought up this brilliantly imaginative name. Most of the original band were born and brought up in Boston and they claimed to have considered "dozens" of alternative names. One may well imagine how good these were if the band ended up as boring old "Boston".

Eve Boswell

From Boswell's Circus, in which she began her singing career: she married the owner.

David Bowie

Born David Robert Jones, London, U.K., 1947, he cut early records as David Hayward-Jones or Davie Jones with The Buzz and The King Bees. The names were apparently a tribute to ▷ Muddy Waters, sometimes called King Bee – after his *Honey Bee* song.

Jones was also in ▷ The Mannish Boys, named after another Waters number, and The Lower Third – billed as "South-east Kent's best rhythm-and-blues group".

The Christian name change from David linked him with the old maritime saying about dead sailors going to "Davy Jones's locker".

His first manager Ken Pitt suggested a name change in 1966 after hearing a singer called Davy Jones who had just been found for new U.S.A. TV creation ▷ The Monkees. The name change was wise, because The Monkees went on to conquer the market for a few years, but in retrospect the two Joneses have absolutely nothing in common.

Jones chose the name Bowie from the Bowie hunting knife, which was in turn named after Col. Bowie, its inventor, who died in 1836. And Jim Bowie fought with Davy Crockett at the Alamo.

Hence the name. Hence the laughing gnome.
Misc. name notes:

His early bands also include the experimental Feathers and The Hype – a name also favoured by the early ▷ U2, see ▷ The Hype. He has also recorded as, simply, Bowie. His son is called Zowie Bowie, though more generally known as Jowie Bowie, or just Joe Bowie. *Wowie Zowie* was a track on ▷ Frank Zappa's 1966 ▷ Mothers debut *Freak Out*.

One 1971 single was credited to a fictitious group called Arnold Corns. This name, "the most unsexy one I could think of", was in tribute to Bowie's favourite ▷ Pink Floyd track *Arnold Layne* – appropriately about a transvestite. Publicity shots showed his favourite dress designer Freddi Buretti, in new guise as the Corns's lead singer.

Bowie's manifold *alter egos* have also included Major Tom, the subject of *Space Oddity*, The Thin White Duke – 1970s emaciated image – Aladdin Sane – 1973 album punning on "a lad insane", possibly his half-brother Terry Burns – and ▷ Ziggy Stardust in 1972. The last gets a separate entry and also, incidentally, inspired ▷ a rejuvenated Alvin Stardust. His unworldly and gender-bending ever-changing images inspired nicknames including The Dame and The Alien.

Bowie's backing bands have been equally legion and include The Spiders, from the Ziggy Stardust tale, and The Glass Spiders. They were a totally different band, formed 1987, after a track called *Glass Spider*, for The Glass Spider concert Tour.

Also ▷ Tin Machine. Bowie inspired ▷ Simple Minds' name and an early appellation of ▷ Joy Division, Warsaw. He probably inspired the naming of ▷ Slaughter And The Dogs, after *Diamond Dogs*.

Pronunciation guide: Bowie (Boe-ee) rhymes with Snowy, it's not bOw-ee to rhyme with wow-ee.

Bow Wow

Long-established Japanese group; the onomatopoeic name is English children's slang for dog or "barking dog", although it means nothing specific in Japanese. Formed mid 1970s: no relation to ▷ Bow Wow Bow.

Bow Wow Wow

1980: Initially a production by ▷ Sex Pistols manager and rock entrepreneur ▷ Malcolm McLaren. Some of the original members of ▷ Adam And The Ants brought their African tribal Burundi drum sounds to the early recordings. Mohican-haircut Burmese teenager Annabella Lwin added the screeches.

1982: Later McLaren left them.

1983: Still later the group left Annabella to start a new career as The Chiefs Of Relief.

Oh, and McLaren's Bow Wow Wow name has nothing to do with ▷ Bow Wow. He thought the name reflected the group's animal/ anarchic *Go Wild In The Country* sound with a pun on "Wow". Wow!

It's from the dog, Nipper, who is one of their record label EMI's trademarks. Nipper is the confused mutt listening to an old-style horn phonograph playing a record of his owner: the caption says "His Master's Voice". The entry on ▷ HMV label says more on the original painting.

Name notes:

1. The group briefly featured ▷ Boy George, billed as Lieutenant Lush.
2. Among names considered: ▷ Sex Gang Children. Boy George used it as a name, allegedly after a line in a Bow Wow Wow song.
3. Other bands named after dogs: ▷ Jefferson Airplane, ▷ Poi Dog Pondering and hundreds more.

The Box

Much-vaunted 1980s band, widely predicted to be massively successful but they never made it as big as the *NME* headlines predicted. They said the name was primarily a reference to television: cf ▷ Monochrome Set, ▷ Television, ▷ Terrorvision, ▷ The Tubes etc. But it worked on a number of levels, particularly sexual. "Box" being slang for female pudenda: cf ▷ Pandora's Box.

Boxcar Willie

Like so many other boys, Lecil Travis Martin wanted to be an engine driver: his father was a part-time railway hand and he became fascinated by trains at an early age. After learning guitar, he wrote a country song called *Boxcar Willie* and the name stuck. In tribute to his father, he sings *Daddy Was A Railroad Man*. AKA Boxie.

Boy George

Londoner George Alan O'Dowd had given G.O.D. as his initials for years. The pretty boy – sometimes mistaken for a girl – was given plenty of cruel nicknames even before he began to explore cross dressing.

Then came singing. He worked with ▷ Bow Wow Wow for a one-off concert on the suggestion of pop entrepreneur Malcolm McLaren, who billed him as ▷ Lieutenant Lush.

There's more in *Take It Like A Man*, George's candid autobiography co-written with Spencer Bright and published in 1995.

He says in the book: "The name Boy George went with the reggae vibe too – lots of DJs had titles like King Tubby, Prince Jammy, Jah Whoosh."

The "Boy" was partly to indicate what sex the gender-bender night clubber really was: cf ▷ (Boy) Marilyn.

"I also liked the idea of playing with sexual ambiguity. Is is a bird? Is it a plane? No, it's Boy George."

As his successful solo career developed, he was sometimes billed simply as "George".

▷ Culture Club, ▷ Jesus Loves You, ▷ Sex Gang Children.

Unflattering derivative: Boy Gorge. This was first bestowed on the Boy by his friends in his St John's Wood days – the author of this book was a close neighbour. George would go out for a walk, dodging the fans, and return to his luxury home with bags of cakes, crisps and chocolate. "Boy Gorge" was later used by unkind U.K. tabloid newspapers after he put on weight following the first flush of stardom.

The Boy Scoutz

All-girl Irish rock band whose biggest claim to fame is having been chosen in preference to ▷ U2 to play one concert in Dublin. Obviously they named after the youth movement, recalling one of the simplest dirty jokes in the book: "the boy scouts and the girl guides".

Boyzone

A pop teen sensation of the 1990s designed to appeal to all girls whose fantasy was a zone filled with boys. Actually they didn't have the immediate success of ▷ Take That or ▷ East 17, but soon made up for that; and the name came from the British comic *Boy's Own*.

Boyz II Men

Because this U.S. act were mere lads when they started. They were born in 1972–4 and formed the band in 1988. Since then they have fulfilled their aim and literally grown up in public.

Similar pun, different band: ▷ Soul II Soul.

B.Q.E.

A capella specialists of the late 1980s and 1990s, they named from Brooklyn Queens Expressway. The motorway connects the two New York boroughs; the vocal group's members are from both areas. As they drove back and forth along it for rehearsals, they realised that they had the road in common.

Brand X

Phil Collins's band-on-the-side during his ▷ Genesis peak. The name questions whether the same philosophy of branding, say, a commercial item such as a can of baked beans can be applied to a group. Advertising and marketing professionals often referred to new items as Brand X until a suitable name was found. Collins also said that the name was nicely neutral.

No relation to Group X, early ▷ Hawkwind.

Brass Monkey

U.K. readers simply need to know this folk band featured a selection of brass instruments.

Many Victorian mantelpieces in England used to feature an ornament of three brass monkeys, one covering his mouth (speak no evil), another his eyes (see no evil) and the third his ears (hear no evil). From this came the Northern English expression, said on freezing winter days: "It's cold enough to freeze the balls off a brass monkey." *Hence the name.*

Bread

Oklahoma, U.S.A., pop band, formed 1969. David Gates and his friends were trying to think of a name when they got stuck in a traffic jam caused by a bread van.

After half an hour of looking blankly at its rear doors, they realised the name was staring them in the face.

In 1969 bread meant not just the most basic food but money, which was what Gates and co. hoped to make. But their loyal fans always disliked the hippy taunt breadhead, meaning capitalists, those concerned with money above all else.

▷The Jam.

Terrible punning LP title: *Manna*.

Breeders

From gay slang for heterosexuals.

Made up of members of Throwing Muses and the ▷ Pixies.

Like ▷ Belly, this is seen by some as a feminist allusion to a woman's reproductive powers. Guitarist Kim Deal had actually come up with the name some years before, for a part-time touring group which never really got off the ground.

Brides Of Funkenstein

Funk star ▷ George Clinton came up with dozens of persona down the years but one of his favourites was Dr Funkenstein, punning on Frankenstein. The novel originally written by Mary Shelley tells of a researcher who makes a man – or monster – which then turns on him. The name of this band was inspired by the 1935 film *The Bride Of Frankenstein*, a sequel to the best-known Boris Karloff movie. Many people confuse the name Frankenstein, who is the scientist, with his monster.

The Bridewell Taxis

British slang for vans used by police, security firms and prison officers to take people to jail. The "black marias" originally passed between the seventeenth-century house of detention at

Clerkenwell, the clink, and Bridewell women's prison, named after St Bride. Clerkenwell was built as an overflow and inmates were held there pending sentence. "Bridewell" has come to refer to any jail; this band actually formed in Leeds not London.

Brilliant

Spin-off from ▷ Killing Joke, whose dreadlocked bassist Youth, born Martin Glover Youth, teamed up with ex ▷ Hitmen vocalist Ben Watkins. The name? "Simple," they told BBC Radio. "We are called brilliant because we are." Jaz of Killing Joke apparently thought otherwise.

Brilliant Corners

U.K. 1980s pop/rock band named after *Brilliant Corners*, a 1957 jazz album by pianist ▷ Thelonious Monk and tenor saxophonist Sonny Rollins.

Brinsley Schwarz

U.K. pub rock band named after guitarist Brinsley Schwarz rather than charismatic bassist-vocalist ▷ Nick Lowe because it was thought Schwarz had a name both more unusual and therefore more memorable. The act started life as Kippington Lodge.

British Electric Foundation

▷ B.E.F., ▷ Heaven 17.

British Lions

A British band who patriotically named after a U.K. rugby football team. ▷ Mott The Hoople.

Bromley Contingent

Called because they lived in this area of London, U.K.; they were more a social club of sorts centred on gay discos and punk gigs. ▷ Steve Severin has claimed this was more a press invention than anything. But the Contingent's one real gig – including him, Siouxsie and later ▷ Sex Pistol Sid Vicious – metamorphosed into ▷ Siouxsie And The Banshees.

Graduates also went on to become ▷ Adam And The Ants and ▷ Billy Idol.

Bronski Beat

U.K. pop group founded in London 1984. The original line-up included Jimi Somerville, later of the even more successful ▷ Communards. Other members were Larry Steinbachek and Steve Bronski, whose adopted surname christened this unit.

Brooce

▷ Bruce Springsteen knew that he had arrived amid the upper strata of superstars as his name became abbreviated to just "Bruce". Cf "Elvis", ▷ Elvis Presley; "Keith", Keith Richard(s) etc. This led to the nickname "Brooce" – add as many "o"s as you feel fit. Often yelled by female fans at his marathon concerts.

Elkie Brooks

She was born in Manchester, U.K., as Elaine Bookbinder. Elkie is the Yiddish name for Elaine and she abbreviated Bookbinder. In 1988 she reasserted her own name with *Bookbinder's Kid*.

She was one of the main vocalists in ▷ Vinegar Joe, alongside Robert Palmer.

Nickname: Elk.

Tina Brooks

… was a man called Harold. The sax player became Teeny Brooks because of his juvenile appearance and he became Tina after someone misheard the nickname one day.

Bros

The group started with London brothers Matt and Luke Goss, together with Craig Logan, under the name Gloss (which they felt would mean more to people than Goss). They later decided on similar-sounding Bros, pointing out their brotherly relationship. A less than brotherly relationship to Logan may have been indicated by his dismissal, albeit with a big pay-off.

Note: Bros fans were called Brosettes. (Yes: past tense. There can't be any left.)

Spin-off: ▷ Band Of Thieves.

Brown Dirt Cowboy

No relation to ▷ Cowboy Joe.

Nickname for ▷ Elton John's lyricist and brief solo star Bernie Taupin.

Because of his fascination with westerns, as displayed in many songs such as *Roy Rodgers*, much of *Tumbleweed Connection* and the album *Captain Fantastic And The Brown Dirt Cowboy.*

James Brown

He made up for the ordinary name with an extraordinary career crowned by plenty of nicknames, some self-bestowed but still accurate.

They include: ▷ Black Caesar; ▷ Butane; Mr Dynamite (Himself); The Forefather of Hip-Hop; ▷ Funky President; ▷ The Godfather of Soul; ▷ The Hardest Working Man In Showbusiness; The King Of Soul (also applied to Otis Redding); The Minister Of The New Super Heavy Funk; The Original Disco Man; ▷ The Real Black Moses; Soul Brother Number One; etc etc. He was originally Mr Star Time, after his star time spot in every show as captured on *Live At The Apollo* Volumes One and Two (1963 and 1968). (Also the title of a 1991 CD box set.)

One of his songs inspired the naming of ▷ Pigbag.

Brownmark

Minnesota star spotted by ▷ Prince. No relation to the like of Mark Sid and the Y-Fronts (early ▷ Boomtown Rats), his real name was simply Mark Brown.

Brownstone

Because solid brown stone homes were the symbol of the successful bourgeoisie in the Eastern U.S. for years. (Cf *A Portrait In Brownstone.*)

Brownsville Station

In might seen odd to name after the southern-most city in the U.S.A. when you come from Detroit. It seemed the obvious name for this quartet because of their interest in southern roots music.

In the States, you can't get much further south than this.

Cf ▷ Graham Central Station.

BT Express

Like ▷ Guns N' Roses, a combination name from previous groups they had worked in. In this case, of Madison Express and Brooklyn Brothers Trucking. Somehow King Davis House Rockers got thrown away along the way. The American disco-funk specialists came from Madison, starting in 1972 and coming together in the existing form about 1974.

BTO

▷ Bachman-Turner Overdrive.

Buckingham Nicks

Made up of Lindsey Buckingham (the bloke) and Stevie Nicks (the lady) who later joined ▷ Fleetwood Mac for its most commercially successful incarnation.

Before that, they were in Fritz (not related to ▷ Fritz The Cat).

Buckinghams

From Chicago, Illinois, they named themselves after the city's famous fountain after an agony of indecision in which they toyed with the names The Pebbles, The Centuries and many more. Their manager wanted a British name at the time of the British beat boom. (Cf ▷ Beau Brummels etc.)

The choice was a good compromise. Fans from Chicago saw it as local reference whereas most fans thought it English – like the U.K. county town and London royal residence, Buckingham Palace.

Lord Buckley

Another star with an assumed aristocratic name (cf ▷ Lord Sutch etc), the comedian claimed to have won his "title" in a card game with a blue-blooded opponent.

He inspired the naming of ▷ The Nazz.

Bucks Fizz

Bucks Fizz is a term, at one stage most commonly heard in the U.K. Home Counties, for a cocktail of champagne or sparkling wine mixed with orange juice, first created by a barman at Buck's Club, London. It was less commonly used in the U.S.A., because of the confusion with "dollar". (▷ Dollar also failed to break through in America.) The band came together from session singers in 1981 for a Eurovision Song Contest entry.

Oh, and the real name of Bobby G was Robert Guppy. Should you be interested.

Buckwheat Zydeco

Band best known for their support to ▷ Eric Clapton. They were formed by Stanley Buckwheat Dural. The buckwheat is the Creole name for the staple food French haricot beans, commemorated in a number of traditional songs. Zydeco is a type of U.S. cajun, R&B and blues music.

Budgie

Rock band from Wales of the 1970s. Cue terrible punning LP titles: *Squark, Impeckable*. Chosen as a humorous domestic budgerigar riposte to ▷ The Byrds and other avian names. No relation to drummer Budgie, of ▷ Siouxsie And The Banshees and many other bands.

Buffalo Springfield

They formed in 1966 and were to be called ▷ The Herd – but this fine punning rubric was soon appropriated by a U.K. vocal band.

In January 1967 they renamed after a sign on an old steam-traction roller seen by percussionist Dewey Martin during road repairs in Los Angeles, California. "You hear Buffalo Springfield, and think, what does it *mean*, man?"

Band members came from many sources (including ▷ the Au Go-Go Singers, ▷ The Mynah Birds and The Squires) and went in into groups as varied as ▷ Poco and ▷ Blood, Sweat And Tears.

For more see Dave Zimmer's 1984 authorised biography.

This 1960s act are no relation to an L.A. trio of the 1990s, ▷ Grant Lee Buffalo.

Buggles

Musician producer Trevor Horn (▷ Art of Noise, ▷ Frankie Goes To Hollywood, ▷ Yes etc) wanted to find a really revolting name.

In that respect, he spectacularly failed: most listeners probably thought buggles was a reference to his bug-eyed glasses. Buggles is hardly in the league of genuinely offensive names such as ▷ The Skids, Severed Head In A Bag or the various incarnations of ▷ Foetus.

B. Bumble And The Stingers

The pun came from "singers". Fitted in with their *Flight Of The Bumble Bee* theme, taken from Nikolai Rimsky-Korsakov. They called the late great composer "Rimsky With His Corsets Off". No relation to ▷ Sting.

Burning Spear

The name came from writings by Kenyan Jomo Kenyatta. A reggae band who wore their hearts on their sleeves, they established their black power credentials with the track *Marcus Garvey*. Cf ▷ Spear Of Destiny.
Cf ▷ Spearhead.

The Burrito Brothers

▷ The Flying Burrito Brothers.

Bush

Named from their native Shepherd's Bush, a west-central area of London, U.K. This band made it big in the U.S.A. while they were still virtual unknowns in their home country. In America, the band's fanatical young followers just took Bush as another short mid-1990s name (▷ Blur etc, etc) – few related it to President George Bush and even fewer were put off by knowing what Shepherd's Bush is really like! "It must be a pretty groovy place," said one. Ignorance is bliss.

Name notes:

1. No relation at all to Kate Bush.
2. This group "paid their dues" on their way to fame, originally playing tiny London clubs in the early 1990s as Future Primitive.
3. In 1997 there was a legal dispute. Obscure act Bush, from Canada, hadn't objected to the hugely popular British band using the same moniker. This changed when lawyers acting for the British act objected to anyone else using the name. The newcomers' misguided move backfired completely. The veterans had been going since the 1970s and could prove rights to the name, so won an order saying the upstarts should be called Bush X for releases in Canada. Further negotiations are possible.

Buster Brown

Australian rock band named from the 1950s *Fanny Mae* rocker.

Butane

One of many nicknames for ▷ James Brown, this one based on his Famous Flames backing band and dating from about 1957.

Butterfield 8

Taken from *Butterfield Eight*, a 1960 film starring Elizabeth Taylor, about a society call girl with a confusing love life. The band were movie soundtrack buffs and liked the flick's advertising slogan: "The most desirable women in town – and the easiest to find!"

Spin-off from ▷ Madness and ▷ The Higsons.

Butthole Surfers

Usually seen as being pretty damn rude: the band know it sounds offensive, maintain it isn't. They are politely unhelpful when asked to explain further and refer back to the song *Butthole Surfer* on their difficult-to-get first EP. A butthole surfer is apparently a follower of trendy Texas bands, if you can make sense of the lyric, although plenty of people think it a revolting reference to gay sex.

Despite the denials the name has been censored in some U.S. newspapers, who have self-righteously taken it upon themselves to rename the act ▷ The B.H. Surfers, the BHs, The Surfers etc. (The last recalls early ▷ Beach Boys.)

Guitarist Paul Leary is quoted in *The Rough Guide To Rock* as saying that even his mother has been known to use the name now – about a decade after the band started. Presumably she was fed up of answering the question of what her son did with "he's in a band" which inevitably led to the question "which one?". Multi-million royalties bring their own middle-class respect, irrespectable name or not.

The Butts Band

Because they were the butts – or the remnants – of ▷ The Doors after Jim Morrison's death and Ray Manzarek's departure for a solo career.

The Buzzards

These zany punksters took the name from their native Leighton Buzzard, U.K.

Buzzcocks

1970: Howard Trafford (as he was then) started in a comedy combo at his school in Leeds, U.K. It was called The Ernest Band after the headmaster.

1971: Peter McNeish (as he was then) was in a Leigh Grammar School group called Kogg.

1973: McNeish formed a new outfit called Jets Of Air, after a term he heard in a physics lesson.

1975: The two met at Bolton Institute Of Technology, Northern England, and set up a group playing ▷ Stooges' songs "in people's front rooms".

1976: After hearing of another band who played one Stooges' song, *No Fun*, they went to London to see them play live on 20 and 21 February. Trafford said they were impressed by the gigs and decided to "go back to Manchester and be like them … but up North". The other band was, of course, ▷ The Sex Pistols.

The duo chose their new stage names within hours of returning home to Manchester. McNeish became ▷ Pete Shelley (which would have been his mother's choice if her child had been a girl). Trafford became ▷ Howard Devoto (based on a story told in a philosophy lecture).

The initial Pistols inspiration not only influenced their music but their obviously phallic/Freudian name. It was also, neatly, a catchphrase in TV show *Rock Follies*: "What's the buzz, cocks?"

The duo had seized upon London listings magazine *Time Out* hoping to see something on the Sex Pistols. All they found was a review of *Rock Follies* headlined "It's The Buzz, Cock!" and an article by Andrew Nicholds which started with the same words.

The Buzzcocks name also tied in with their first single, entitled (apty enough, really) *Orgasm Addict*.

Ex-band members joined ▷ Flag Of Convenience and ▷ Magazine; the band later re-formed with Mike Joyce, ex ▷ The Smiths.

The group is profiled in Tony McGartland's 1995 book *Buzzcocks – The Complete History*.

The Byrds

In the late 1940s and 1950s – after Sonny Til and The Orioles' *Cryin' In The Chapel* – it was almost *de rigueur* for black vocal bands to name themselves after various birds, especially songbirds: The Bluebirds, The Flamingoes, The Quailtones.

Similar names later became popular among rock bands: for example, The Hawks, precursors of ▷ The Band, ▷ Wings, ▷ The Eagles, ▷ The Nightingales, ▷ The Housemartins and Rare Bird – to name just a few. The Byrds avoided a possible clash with the U.K.'s ▷ Yardbirds, saying they were unlikely to be confused.

Some of these other "bird" bands were paying homage to the jazzman known simply as "Bird", ▷ Charlie Parker.

James Joseph McGuinn III, the main brains behind this particular ensemble, came to the job after Brill Building songwriting: he co-wrote a song for ▷ The City Surfers.

Looking for a catchy name for his new band, he latched on to his aeronautics hobby to come up with The Jet Set – a name seen as inappropriate by manager Jim Dickson. McGuinn always liked the name, later saying their music had replaced the "rrrrroooooaaaaahhhhh" of 1940s aircraft with the "krrrriiiissssshhhh" sound of a jet.

The Jet Set decided to do a one-off record which did not prejudice their other contracts and therefore needed a temporary pseudonym. Jac Holzman of Elektra decided to exploit their long-haired Beatle image and wanted a British-sounding name. This was at the time of the British invasion of the U.S. charts – see the consequent naming of ▷ Sir Douglas Quintet and others. Holzman took the name off a nearby gin bottle depicting the Tower of London guards. None of the group felt sufficiently strongly about vegetarianism to reject The Beefeaters, but nobody took it seriously.

Meanwhile Christopher Hillman joined, fresh from leading his own band, aptly named ▷ The Hillmen.

The final name came about when the band met for a Thanksgiving Day meal at the home of joint manager Ed Tickner. Gene Clark said the turkey dinner reminded him of the Dino Valente song, *Birdsies*, which he really liked and which Dickson had helped record.

The other members were not impressed, although McGuinn said it met his plan of a name suggesting soaring flight like The Jet Set. When Ticker suggested "Birds", the others said it was British slang for girls, which could cause some sexual confusion. This led to the idea of a misspelling such as the Beatles' pun on beetles: they had been very influenced by *A Hard Day's Night*. Berds, Burds. Then McGuinn's comments on flight made them remember aviator Admiral Byrd. The clincher was that it had "the all-important Magic B" of both ▷ The Beatles and ▷ The Beach Boys, Tickner recalls.

Meanwhile the band were indeed flying, from folk to rock and ending up somewhere in between. Clearly, the name was meant to suggest uplifting music which transported the listener high above everyday cares.

Jim McGuinn, who legally became Roger in about 1968 as the result of his adoption of the Subud faith, still has the rights to the name. He also formed The Thunderbyrds, getting in an automotive pun.

There's more on McGuinn's name change under his own entry.

Another member, drummer Michael Clarke, was born Michael Dick. He renamed after broadcaster Dick Clark, adding the final "e" to distinguish himself from Gene Clark. Clarke (3 June 1944–19 December 1993) was not the only star to cut off his Dick, so to speak: ▷ Fish and ▷ Paul Revere did the same.

Former member ▷ Gram Parsons named ▷ The Flying Burrito Brothers after a Byrds project.

The Byrds also obviously influenced name choices for The Pigeons (early Vanilla Fudge), ▷ The Mynah Birds and ▷ Sweethearts Of The Rodeo and for more obscure reasons ▷ The Turtles – a spelling of Tyrtles was mooted – and ▷ Budgie, although possibly not ▷ The Blackbyrds and ▷ The Long Ryders.

Many other minor bands respelled their names similarly: The Myddle Class, The New Dymension etc.

Terrible punning LP title: *Preflyte*.

They were sued over the name by the British ▷ Birds and threatened action against a British band which wanted the name ▷ The Ded Byrds.

An exhaustive account of the naming is given in Johnny Rogan's book *Timeless Flight: The Definite Biography of The Byrds*.

Hence the name. Hence all those "bird" photo opportunities with the band stuck up trees.

Cabaret Voltaire

Recalls the literary nightclub in Zurich, 1916, which was named after French philosopher-writer Voltaire (1694–1778). It was the focus of the Dada 'art/anti-art' movement, known for defaced Mona Lisas and anarchist shows with axes provided to smash exhibits.

There have been two experimental bands of this name. One avant-garde outfit was formed in 1972 and renamed ▷ Henry Cow. The better-known Cabaret Voltaire formed in Manchester in the mid-1970s and were called "The Cabs" (as opposed to the Fabs, i.e. ▷ The Beatles). Their early shows were performance art with Dada-like looped noise.

Cactus World News

Dublin protégés of ▷ U2. Singer Eion McEvoy discarded an early lyric called *Cactus World News* but recycled the title.

J.J. Cale

Discount stories he was born John Cale and lengthened the name by adding a non-existent J. He was born Jean Jacques Cale in Oklahoma City and shortened it to produce a name reminiscent of the likes of ▷ B.B. King. (Cf ▷ ZZ Top.) He kept it after he was overtaken in the fame stakes by John Cale, the Welsh ▷ Velvet Underground star.

Camel

From the cigarette packet, featured in modified form as an album cover. No relation to Peter Frampton's Camel, or ▷ Sopwith Camel.

Cameo

Because they made intricate songs like cameos – an inlaid jewel, not a theatrical reference.

Camille

▷ Prince maintained he had a "dark side" which showed itself on *The Black Album* as Spooky Electric. The "good side" was Camille as shown on *Lovesexy*. A Minneapolis magazine had said his lyrics were as anguished as the death scene from *Camille*.

Camper Van Beethoven

Californian act named by early member Robert McDaniel. It's been suggested the moniker, like ▷ Moby Grape, was the punchline to a bad surreal joke. The existing members deny this. ("Who can drive all night, bed six women and write a symphony at the same time?")

Can

The influential German band began as Inner Space in 1968, renaming The Can by the end of the year. They noted the word was short and multi-meaning in English: as in "metal container", "headphone" and "recorded". Cf ▷ Canned Heat.

The Can Book (1989) by Pascal Bussy and Andy Hall noted: "The Turkish word *can*, pronounced 'chan', means life or soul, the Japanese word *kan* means feeling or emotion, and the Japanese word *chan* means love when used in salutation."

The definite article was dropped between the release of *The Can Soundtracks* in 1970 and 1971's double *Tago Mago*. Several of their sleeves featured Andy Warhol style cans, notably the 1972 album *Ege Bamyasi*, which inspired D. Ege Bam Yasi.

El Canario
"The Canary" – nickname for José Alberto, from his sweet singing voice.

C&C Music Factory
Named from studio wizards Robert Clivilles and David Cole.

Candle box
Taken from a phrase in a song by ▷ Midnight Oil.

Candy Flip
Retro 1960s drug reference for the 1990s, referring to a cocktail containing a sugar cube of LSD. Cf ▷ The Sugar Cubes.

Canned Heat
From the title of Tommy Johnson's song *Canned Heat Blues*, recorded many times in the 1920s and 1930s. It was about Sterno, a chemical used by some in the U.S. depression and prohibition as the cheapest method of getting "canned" (= totally smashed).

The name was also a pun on canned (= recorded, taped) heat (= emotion); a slogan in heating advertisements and a Vietnam War-era bullet-holder.

The Johnson single was in the 60,000 plus record collection of Bob Hite, who founded Canned Heat in California in 1966. He was known as The Bear because of his great size and weight, and his co-founder Al Wilson became Blind Owl for his short-sightedness.

Freddy "Boom Boom" Cannon
Freddie Karmin thought this name change would make his career go with a bang. It certainly led to album titles such as *The Explosive Freddy Cannon*. Cf ▷ Cannonball Adderley.

Capability Brown
Like ▷ Jethro Tull, a British band harking back to the rural past. Landscape gardener Brown (1715–83), a contemporary of Tull, often said: "I see great capability of improvement here." None of the group was called Brown – they found the name in a history book.

Capp-Pierce Juggernaut
A newspaper article by Leonard Feather on a U.S. jazz band just formed by Frank Capp and Nat Pierce was headed: "A Juggernaut on Basie Street". It was thought the large band would be impossible to stop once it had momentum, like a large truck. No relation to 1980s heavy metal band ▷ Juggernaut.

The Cappuccino Kid
Nickname for ▷ Paul Weller, formerly of ▷ The Jam, during his time with ▷ The Style Council. The name came from records such as *Café Bleu*. Also known as ▷ The Modfather.

The Captain And Tennille
Los Angeles keyboardist Daryl Dragon and Toni Tennille were touring with ▷ The Beach Boys. Mike Love gave Dragon the nickname "Captain Keyboard" because of his frequently worn naval officer's cap.

Captain Beefheart
▷ Beefheart.

Captain Fantastic
Nickname for ▷ Elton John. Cf ▷ The Brown Dirt Cowboy.

Captain Sensible
Sensible people should also refer to ▷ The Damned.

The band's bassist was Ray Burns and his stage name commented on his lunatic behaviour and dress – nurse's or nun's outfit or tutu – or lack of dress at all.

The name was given to him in 1976 when the band played a punk rock festival in France. The bands travelled there in coaches. Sensible tells the story in a 1995 TV documentary and Jon Savage's 1991 book *England's Dreaming*.

In both cases the words are about the same: "I had got a shirt with epaulettes. I was

C

pretending to be the pilot, and shouting: 'It's all right! Everything's under control! It's on autopilot!' People were getting upset. And someone said: 'Oh, it's Captain Fucking Sensible.' We called ourselves by wacky names, so we could keep signing on the DHSS. [Claiming for unemployment benefits and other compensation at the U.K.'s Department of Health and Social Security.] I thought it would last five minutes. I didn't know I would still be called Captain Sensible at 35."

Captain Trips

The late ▷ Jerry Garcia got this nickname during the early days of ▷ The Grateful Dead. The band's music, with its long solos and psychedelic lyrics, was described as "the soundtrack to an acid trip". Garcia, as the band's head honcho and purveyor of all things far out, naturally became Captain Trips.

Caravan

This British art rock band from Canterbury formed as The Wilde Flowers – many of this original line-up becoming ▷ Soft Machine. The name came from a song about the joys of life on the road. Some of the band members went on into ▷ Hatfield And The North and ▷ Matching Mole.

Carcass

Because these committed vegetarians sing of slaughterhouses in blood-and-guts songs full of technical terms used by butchers, vets and medics. Sample titles: *Feast On Dismembered Carnage* and *Exhume To Consume*. Spin-off from ▷ Napalm Death.

Caretaker race

Taken from science fiction series *Star Trek*, it was a "green" comment on humans as caretakers of the environment for future generations. *Star Trek* also inspired ▷ T'Pau.

Carlton And His Shoes

Donald Carlton was backed by The Shades in the 1960s: they renamed after a misprint on their debut record. Carlton wasn't the first of the group of stars called "shoegazers" – although many of his audience cast curious eyes over his footwear and were doubtless disappointed to see nothing unusual.

Carmel

Like ▷ Sade, the name of a band as well as a singer. Her real name: Carmel McCourt.

Hoagy Carmichael

From his full name Hoagland Howard Carmichael.

Carpenters

Real names, a brother and sister team; nothing to do with woodworkers. In case you were wondering.

Carrig

Gaelic for rock. A more interesting pun than ▷ Roxy Music, Rock Salmon, Rock Steady Crew, Roxette etc.

The Cars

This mid-west U.S. band started as folksters Grasshoppers, then Milkwood (from Dylan Thomas's radio play *Under Milk Wood*) and adopted more electric sound as Cap'n Swing. Their final New Wave name was suggested by David Robinson of ▷ The Modern Lovers. He said it was short, simple and suggested music that could move you. Cf many other auto names: ▷ The Cortinas, ▷ The Corvettes etc.

Similar name abbreviations applied to founders Ric Otcasek – who became Ric Ocasek – and Benjamin Orzechowski – Ben Orr.

Carter USM

These South Londoners were first in Jamie Wednesday. Carter The Unstoppable Sex Machine are Jimbob (James Morrison, gtr/vocals) and Leslie Fruitbat Carter (gtr). Asked if USM refers to him, Fruitbat now says the origin's obvious. This creates a nice legend: he's not exactly a sex symbol and authenticated details of his sexual prowess are fortunately absent.

However, Jimbob let slip in 1988 that it came from a newspaper cutting – about someone else – given to Fruitbat as a joke. They went with it because they thought Carter USM was the stupidest handle they could use (excepting ▷ Ned's Atomic Dustbin).

The Cascades

Californian band named for their 1963 debut release *Rhythm Of The Rain*.

Casey Jones and The Engineers

Early ▷ Eric Clapton band, named after the legendary railroader Casey Jones for a joke.

Johnny Cash

The country superstar was born J.R. Cash (in line with the now rare U.S. habit of giving initial-only names) and only became Johnny when he joined the army.

Cassandra Complex

Psychology has dozens of "complexes" referring to mental conditions. This band liked one named from people like the mythological figure Cassandra, who spoke of spectacular disasters waiting to happen.

Cast

The late lamented lauded ▷ La's closed their first and only album with an epic track, *Looking Glass*. As the 1990 song accelerated into feedback, we are told: "Everything must pass … The glass is smashed … The change is cast." Lee Mayer's song impressed bassist John Powers, who lifted one word. He said it was apt: "everything must pass", like ▷ George Harrison's song as a comment on the end of ▷ The Beatles. Cast were the future.

This is well known yet has sometimes been played down. Liam "Skin" Tyson, asked about it in an Internet interview, replied: "I don't know. It probably came out of a dictionary, knowing John."

Catherine Wheel

U.K. band named after the spiked wheel on which St Catherine of Alexandria was to be executed. According to legend the wheel splintered and shards killed her tormentors. It is symbolised in firework displays (and coats of arms of two Oxbridge colleges). The 1990s act thought the choice "spellbinding" and potent.

The Cat In The Hat

Nickname for ▷ Jamiroquoi, after his omnipresent big woolly Rastafarian-style hat. It recalled Dr Seuss's learning-to-read *Cat In The Hat* book series.

The Cats And The Fiddle

"Cats" from jazz slang; "fiddle" from Chuck Barksdale's stand-up bass; the whole from the nursery rhyme. People kept names simple in the 1940s.

Cavedogs

Obscure U.S. band named from an insult for ugly women.

CCS

British 1970s outfit formed by Alexis Korner, who said it stood for "Collective Consciousness Society". Korner also helped name ▷ Free.

The Celibate Rifles

This Australian rock band aimed to be different from ▷ The Sex Pistols so named the opposite.

Central Line

Named after the Central Line, their local line, on the London Underground system. Cf, in America, ▷ D-Train. Another band to name after a London Tube line: ▷ Bakerloo.

A Certain Ratio

▷ ACR.

Chad And Jeremy

British 1960s acoustic duo whose full names are Chad Stuart and Jeremy Clyde.

Champaign

Not a pun on champagne. They came from Champaign, Illinois.

Champs

This instrumental band was stuck for a name when Los Angeles record boss Gene Autry heard them in the late 1950s. In an intended compliment, he named them after his pet Champion, "The World's Wonder Horse", who became a cowboy film star.

Gene "Duke of Earl" Chandler

U.S singer, born Eugene Dixon, Chicago, 1937. He borrowed the surname in tribute to his favourite actor, Jeff Chandler. The actor had been named after Chandler Boulevard, Los Angeles. One of many musical "aristocrats".

Channel Light Vessel

The three Brits in the band took the name from

the very-British BBC Radio 4's shipping forecast. Channel Light Vessel Automatic is an unmanned ship used by the Meteorological Office to monitor weather conditions. The group later dropped the final word: it reappeared as the title of their first album.

The forecast has been celebrated by Barry Hines in *A Kestrel For A Knave*, ▷ Blur's *This Is A Low* and ▷ Thousand Yard Stare's *Junketing*.

Chantays

Californian 1960s band, strangely named by Bob Spickard from the French verb *chanter* (to sing) although they had no singer and found fame with instrumentals. Also known as The Ill Winds. Cf ▷ The Chantels, ▷ The Chanters.

Chantels

Members of this all-girl group attended St Anthony Of Padua school in the Bronx, where they supported the school's basketball team. According to Jay Warner's 1992 *Billboard Book Of American Singing Groups*, in 1957 the team faced St Francis de Chantelle college. "One of the girls [to this day no one remembers which] suggested calling themselves the Chantelles. It soon became the Chantels." Cf ▷ The Chantays etc.

The Chanters

Chosen from a dictionary by soon-to-be-manager Bernie Johnson, the mother of one of the band, in 1957. They were later Bud Johnson and The Chanters, although Bud Jnr never sang lead.

The Charging Tyrannosaurus of despair

It was supposed to be a serious comment on the state of mankind. In reality, it's hilariously stupid: imagine being introduced at a concert as this: how do you live up to it?

It was later changed to Detroit Edison White Light Company because, just as amusingly, the drummer refused to be associated with despair. The name – nothing to do with Tyrannosaurus Rex – deserves an award as perhaps the most silly hippy name ever. Mind you, it has some strong competition: here are some examples: Cybernetic Serendipity; The Flowerpot Men; Mobile Freakout; The Moving Sidewalks;

Melvin Q. Watchpocket; Ballpoint Bananas; Chocolate Watch Band; Celestial Hysteria; Colossal Pomegranate; Evergreen Tangerine; Everpresent Fullness; Frumious Bandersnatch; Hmmm; It's A Beautiful Day; Marshmallow Pillow; The Only Alternative And His Other Possibilities; Purple Earthquake; and ▷ Strawberry Alarm Clock.

Charlatans

Another of those nicely self-disparaging names (cf ▷ Simple Minds et al), this choice has been used by bands from the U.K. (from 1989) and U.S.A. (from 1961). The better-known British outfit felt its definition suited them perfectly: "pretenders to some exeptional knowledge or skill". They were learning music at the time. The ghost of the other group came back to haunt them during a U.S. tour: the Brits had to rename Charlatans U.K.

Another band to use the dictionary: ▷ The Commodores.

Ray Charles

Ray Charles Robinson from Albany, Georgia, U.S.A., lost his sight in childhood, and was billed as R.C. Robinson on his debut aged 17. He wanted to use his full name, however, and nearly did. But the following year American boxer Walker Smith became Sugar Ray Robinson. The singer-keyboardist settled on his first two names to avoid confusion with the champion pugilist.

Fighter Sugar Ray Charles Leonard named after the music star, who is also known as The Genius.

Charlie's Angels

A 1990s band who are great fans of the similarly named U.S. detective drama which ran from 1977 to 1982.

Chas And Dave

Christian names of British "rockney" duo Charles Hodges and David Peacock. No relation to ▷ Sam And Dave.

Cheap Trick

This Illinois band had antecedents with names as diverse as ▷ The Grim Reaper, The Boyz, Fuse and Sick Man Of Europe (the last was a nineteenth-century phrase for the ailing Turkish Empire). They renamed after one critic commented little things please little minds, whereas cheap tricks attract big audiences.

Chubby Checker
1958: Ernest Evans, an aspiring Philadelphia singer, bore a more than passing similarity to the young ▷ Fats Domino. His record management wanted to exploit this. The wife of TV host Dick Clark suggested: fat to chubby, dominoes to checkers. The same logic inspired ▷ The Fat Boys, who later teamed with Checker for a 1988 remake of *The Twist*. ▷ The Dreamlovers.

Cheech and Chong
Richard "Cheech" Martin and Thomas Chong, respectively of Mexican and Chinese extraction.

Chelsea
In U.S. popular consciousness, Chelsea means The Chelsea Hotel, ▷ Joni Mitchell's *Chelsea Morning* written there, and perhaps Chelsea Clinton – named after the song.

These British punksters named after their base, the original Chelsea, in west-central London, famous for its well-heeled areas, football team and fashionable King's Road, where they formed. ▷ Billy Idol.

Chemical Brothers
One of the reasons behind this book is that one can go through hundreds of articles on a group without names being explained. The only full explanation for the name of this British dance-rave duo – who are not blood brothers – came as late as June 1997, well into their career. Ed Simons and Tom Rowlands had originally formed a disco company.

Simons, interviewed in *Esquire* magazine, finally said: "We thought of London Dust Explosion but then decided it had to have 'brothers' in it."

Rowlands added, more obscurely: "Someone asked us to because it was someone else's name. So we did."

It transpires they became The Dust Brothers after the Dust production team in the U.S. Things changed as the disc jockeys moved into

recording: the American Dusts saw the choice as a rip-off, not a tribute, and a legal dust-up was threatened.

The Britons renamed, at the time enigmatically explaining "dust is a chemical", and sparking controversy as reporters speculated it was a drug reference. Simons now explains: "We liked Chemical Brothers as it's all about chemical beats, and because chemistry bonds things."

Cher
Half Cherokee, half Armenian, Cherilyn Sarkesian La Pier was born in El Centro, California. She cut the 1964 novelty *I Love You Ringo* as Bonnie Jo Mason, a name chosen for its "all American, girl-next-door" sound. Still, she worked as Cherilyn before meeting and marrying Salvatore Phillip Bono, known as ▷ (Sonny) Bono.

Their act's name was briefly Caesar and Cleo, then Sonny and Cher – the simple abbreviation punning on French for "dear" and neatly referring to her American Indian origins. Her 1973 album was called *Half Breed*. (Rita Coolidge is also half Cherokee; also cf ▷ Redbone).

Sprog notes: Child, with Sonny Bono: Chastity Bono. Pronunciation guide: Share not Sheer or Chur. Nicknames: The Great American Navel, ▷ The Queen Of Flash.

Neneh Cherry
… was born Neneh Mariann Karlsson. She's the stepdaughter of late jazz trumpeter Don Cherry.

Cherokees
While ▷ Cher is Cherokee and dozens of U.S. bands tried to sound British after the success of ▷ The Beatles, this group went the other way. They hailed from Worcestershire, England, and thought the name would be exotic on concert bills.

Chic
Immodestly, they thought they were well described by the French word which variously means "fashionable, sophisticated and skilful". So much in a small word.

Chicago

Chicago businessman Jim Guercio, a self-confessed autocrat, was delighted to find a promising jazz-rock band in his city. They had started as ▷ Big Thing, renaming The Missing Links. The group had formed at the local university – all but one came from the Windy City – and Guercio had a new appellation in mind. He liked the corporate anonymity of Chicago Transit Authority: CTA was on billboards everywhere.

Their first album was released in 1969, eponymously titled *Chicago Transit Authority* – and there the trouble began.

There have been dozens of similar cases, many of which miss the point that it's not easy to confuse (for example) a long-haired rock act selling records with short-haired corporation selling bus tickets. (See ▷ T Rex, ▷ Yazoo etc for similar disputes: the U.K. generally has taken a more liberal view than the U.S.A.)

The real CTA claimed breach of copyright and infringement of a long-established trade-name. The group could drag the CTA into disrepute, the authorities said, and the city wanted no link with them, formal or informal.

Guercio argued that it was the title of the record, not the band name – but to no avail – and he cut the name to Chicago. This was again presented to the band as unilateral decision. By now they were getting fed up with Guercio's heavy-handedness. After his inevitable departure, the band released more than 20 albums and came to be seen as good upstanding citizens honoured by the city for their contribution to tourism and its musical life. Like ▷ Lynyrd Skynyrd, it all came right in the end for the group and their initial inspiration. Trivia note: Chicago is a contraction of the Algonqian meaning "the place of the garlic cabbage".

Chicken Shack

From the song *Chicken Shack*, recorded by Alex Korner's All-Stars among others. Like Korner, they championed obscure U.S. blues songs; Christine Perfect went on into ▷ Fleetwood Mac, then doing much the same. More Korner: ▷ CCS, ▷ Free.

Chicory Tip

This British 1970s novelty band named after a

vegetable – explaining it was a pun on "chic" and "chick". Later album title: *Salad Days*.

Chiffons

All-female group who named from the women's dress material. One of many bands to name after fabrics: ▷ Suede etc.

Chi-Lites

Four steps to heaven:
1. In 1960 they formed as the Chanteurs (cf ▷ The Chantays etc). Then renamed The Hi-Lites, after a local club.
2. Another band claimed the name.
3. Leader Marshall Thompson suggested The Chi-Lites, which kept the "highlight", needed only marginal changes to posters and was different enough to stop legal action. The C showed they came from Chicago.
4. They were often Marshall And The Chi-Lites, in the style of many groups with a "highlighted" front man.

Chilli Willi And The Red Hot Peppers

Not to be confused with ▷ The Red Hot Chili Peppers, this 1970s U.K. pub rock band were named by a friend after a drinking session. They couldn't think of anything better before their first gig.

China Crisis

This U.K. duo took their name from a 1982 newspaper headline – it was always thought, and for deep underlying reasons. Gary Daly talked darkly in interviews about international relations. But the game was up when Eddie Lundon candidly admitted it was his revenge after years of racist jibes at his Chinese-featured appearance: he has narrower eyes than most westerners.

Chinchilla Green

Canadian-Germanic band based in Berlin whose name was an environmental statement combining "the animal used for decadent fur coats and a positive, life-affirming colour, especially in Germany".

Chinnichap

Songwriters (Nicky) Chinn and (Mike) Chapman.

Chocolate Watch Band

This U.S. psychedelic group formed in 1965 with a moniker which punned on "band". Chocolate gave a Dali-esque name like ▷ The Soft Watches or ▷ The Strawberry Alarm Clock.

Chris and Cosey

Chris Carter and Cosey Fanni Tutti (geddit) of ▷ Throbbing Gristle. ▷ CTI.

The Christians

The Christians were a family of 11 in Liverpool, U.K.; this vocal band contains three brothers, Garry, Russell and Roger. The name's won them some religious fans yet alienated audiences in non-Christian or secular societies. They had rejected other monikers including The Gems and Natural High (a hippy expression for anyone who reached ecstasy without drugs).

The Chrysalids

Named after John Wyndham's 1955 novel. Same literary source: ▷ The Midwich Cuckoos, ▷ The Triffids.

La Cicciolina

The Italian star of pop, porn and politics was born Ilona Staller. Her name means "the dumpling", a lovey-dovey affection.

Ciccone Youth

Guitarist-singer Thurston Moore formed ▷ Sonic Youth in New York in 1981. As they became successful, he watched with fascination the greater commercial triumph of ▷ Madonna. By the mid-1980s, she was generating broadsheet profiles and magazine covers galore. Moore added to the acres of newsprint with a piece on Madonna in his samizdat fanzine. Sonic Youth released a track in their 1986 *E.v.o.l.* album entitled *Madonna, Sean And Me* or *The Crucifixion of Sean Penn*.

Ciccone Youth took "youth" from the parent band and "Ciccone" from ▷ Madonna's original, discarded surname. They parodied Madonna's hit *Into The Groove*, retitled *Into the Groovey*.

Meanwhile the Madonna studies industry has grown apace with several students doing doctorates on her work. As Moore commented: "She's *good*. I was saying it's all got a bit out of hand."

Cinderella

U.S. band named after the soft porn movie *Sinderella*, in which Cinders is successively and successfully led into sin by her ugly sisters (who turn out to be transvestites), Buttons (who's into bondage), fairy godmother (with magical powers to remove her clothes) and the handsome prince (the only tiny thing he has is a glass slipper: the rest's king size).

Circle Jerks

Circle Jerk is defined by Dr Robert Chapman's *New Dictionary of American Slang*: "1. (Especially teenagers) a sex party of mutual masturbation. 2. Any futile meeting etc." The parties were in shared "frat houses" – usually as an initiation rite and entailing an unconventional use of milk bottles. Outside the U.S., the name was meaningless. Naïve inquirers were referred to the dictionary.

Band members made up many origin stories such as references to "square berks". In some parts of America the name ran into as many protests as ▷ The Butthole Surfers. The CJs, as they were known, were a spin-off from the controversial ▷ Black Flag. The criticism didn't stop them entitling their 1980 debut *Group Sex*.

Cirth Ungol

Author J.R.R. Tolkien inspired ▷ Marillion as well as this British 1980s band, who admired his Lord Of The Rings (1954–5) and named from one of the towers in the trilogy.

The City Surfers

Named to match their ▷ Beach Boys spoof, *Beach Ball*. The song was co-written by Jim McGuinn (as he then was), soon to be main man of ▷ The Byrds.

The CJs

▷ The Circle Jerks.

Clannad

Folk band consisting of the sons and daughter of an Irish band leader, all named Brennan

(Bhraonain in its original Gaelic form) or Duggan. They first sang only in Irish. The name comes from Gaelic *clan a Dobhair*, or family from Dore, or Gweedore, County Donegal. They've links with ▷ U2. Solo artist who left the band: ▷ Enya.

Eric Clapton

He was born Eric Patrick Clapp, a name which had to go ... the interest is in his pseudonyms and band names.

His early groups included The Roosters (after the blues number *Red Rooster*), Blues Incorporated, ▷ Casey Jones And The Engineers, ▷ The Yardbirds (more roosters), ▷ Bluesbreakers and The Glands. Later bands – with the guitar hero often trying to shun the limelight – included Clapton And Powerhouse, ▷ Cream, ▷ Blind Faith, and ▷ Derek And The Dominos. Nicknames: ▷ God, ▷ Slowhand.

The Clash

Why the Clash? Various explanations come in newspaper articles, John Tobler's 1981 book *The Clash*, Jon Savage's 1991 biography *England's Dreaming* and on the liner notes to *The Clash On Broadway* 1991 CD set.

London SS were breaking up in 1976; part went into ▷ The Damned and the rest – Paul Simonon, Mick Jones and Viv Albertine – were undecided. While going to claim unemployment benefit they met ▷ Joe Strummer, whose outfit ▷ The 101'ers were established on the pub-rock circuit. Management hopeful Bernard Rhodes wanted London SS to rename because of their swastika logo offended his European refugee mother.

Strummer said they drove to the squat where the others lived "and put together the group there and then". He told Savage: "For about a week we were the Psychotic Negatives, then we were The Weak Heartdrops, after a Big Youth lyric, then Paul thought of the name The Clash." (Big Youth also inspired ▷ Sonic Youth.) Bassist Simonon, on the box set, recalls the discarded possibilities lasted for "minutes" and included The Mirrors.

Marcus Gray's 1995 book *Last Gang In Town: The Story And Myth Of The Clash* adds they discarded The Phones – a "modern" name recalling ▷ Television; and The Outsiders –

possibly from the Albert Camus or Colin Wilson books, or recalling another antecedent of the band, The Delinquents. The Psychotic (or Psycho) Negatives was from a track called *Psychotic Reaction* and the Weak Heart Drops from a song called *Lightning Flash*.

Many encyclopedias say Mick Jones chose the name; Simonon confirms Strummer. Simonon found it while looking though the London *Evening Standard*. Several headlines featured the word "clash", a word sub-editors favour as much as "hit", "rap", "slam" and "blast".

Strummer liked the word because it was short. As they became a leading punk group, they realised the name meant Clash not just as in a mild shock-horror-probe argument or headline. They were fed up with the bloated state of music and U.K. politics and wanted a name with impact. It meant complete confrontation, class conflict, radical rebellion, revolution, short sharp shocks and the smashing of the state. Only original guitarist Keith Levine didn't like the choice. "He wasn't crazy about it – but there you go."

Hence the name. Hence the trashed hotel rooms.

Their political stance was further explored in the 1980 factional film *Rude Boy*, countless songs and by the individual band member Tory Crimes.

Name trivia notes:

1. The liner notes to *The Story of The Clash Volume 1* were written by one Albert Transom, almost certainly Joe Strummer "playing silly buggers".
2. They inspired Four Horsemen.
3. Billing name: The Only Band That Matters.
4. Spin-offs: ▷ Real Westway and ▷ Big Audio Dynamite.

Classics IV

There were five people in this Florida band. They were originally billed "Dennis Yost and The Classics IV", thought this too long, and considered a change to Classics V would be confusing.

The Clean

This New Zealand band named after a review said their live sound was "not very clean". ▷ The Great Unwashed.

Jimmy Cliff

Born James Chambers in Jamaica. Later recorded an album titled *Cliff Hanger*.

Climax Blues Band

From their love of Chicago Blues; indeed they even considered Chicago Blues Band as a name. One group member said in a 1975 interview: "I wish we'd stayed with the Chicago Blues thing, even if it produced problems with ▷ Chicago. People think our name's kinda rude … climax … it's not what we meant."

Climie Fisher

Simon Climie and Rob Fisher, who'd also worked with the basis of ▷ Tears For Fears.

Patsy Cline

This country star from Virginia, U.S.A., was born Virginia Patterson Hensley. She was known as Patsy from her second name then married Gerald Cline. Nickname: ▷ Country's Leading Cowgirl. Cf ▷ The Queen Of Country. ▷ The Reclines.

Clint Eastwood And The General Saint

Named in honour of the real Eastwood, who had a hit in his own right, 1970's *I Talk To The Trees*. This rap star wasn't the only one inspired by the spaghetti western hero: ▷ High Plains Drifters.

George Clinton

Leader of ▷ The Brides Of Funkenstein, ▷ Funkadelic and ▷ Parliament(s). Fanciful nicknames: Dr Funkenstein, Interstellar Cosmic Funkfather, The Minister of All Funkadelia, Starchild and Uncle Jam.

Clitoris That Thought It Was A Puppy

▷ Meat Loaf collaborator Jim Steinman chose the name from a word association game as "plain silly, not plain offensive".

Clonk

From the character in their single *Captain Clonk*.

Clouds

A tribute to ▷ Joni Mitchell's second album *Clouds* recorded in 1969. The title's a reference to the track *Both Sides, Now*.

Cloven Hoof

This British band named from their ▷ Black Sabbath sound and satanic themes.

The Coasters

This group started as The Surf Boys. This and their final name may have inspired the naming of fellow Californians ▷ The Beach Boys five years later.

Kurt Cobain

▷ Nirvana, ▷ Hole, ▷ Courtney Love. Pronunciation guide: Co-bane, not C'bane.

Cochise

More American Indian influence. Cf ▷ Blackfoot, ▷ Crazy Horse etc. This band, playing all-American music, named from one of the major figures in Apache history. Cochise (*c.* 1812–76) led the Chiricahuas.

Joe Cocker

He hails from Sheffield, U.K., but is no relation to ▷ Pulp's Jarvis Cocker. His bands include ▷ Mad Dogs – a name considered by ▷ Led Zeppelin – and ▷ The Grease Band. Nickname: ▷ Cowboy Joe. His version of a Leon Russell song inspired ▷ Delta Lady.

Cockney Rebel

▷ Steve Harley. ▷ The Sex Pistols on tour once named themselves Acne Rebel in reference to this band.

Cockney Rejects

Londoners, beaten by ▷ Steve Harley for the name Cockney Rebel, chose the nearest they could get.

The Cocktail Cowboys

Formed by Dave Pegg (▷ Jethro Tull and ▷ Fairport Convention) and named after his autobiographical solo *The Cocktail Cowboy Goes It Alone*.

Joey Coco

▷ Prince writing for ▷ Sheena Easton and others, named after the provocatively sweet *Sugar Walls*.

The Cocteau Twins

Nearly every music reference work incorrectly

states the group named from French writer and film-maker Jean Cocteau (1891–1963), author of *Les Enfants Terribles*. The band's vocalist is Elizabeth Fraser; the twins of the book are called Elizabeth and Paul. The book inspired ▷ The Rich Kids. The Cocteaus didn't counteract this story for years but put out a statement after being bemused and besieged by bookish autograph hunters.

The name actually came from a line in a song by fellow Scottish musos ▷ Johnny And The Self-Abusers, the punk band which evolved into ▷ Simple Minds. They also worked on a single by ▷ The Lillies.

Lloyd Cole and The Commotions
The singer/songwriters's name is Lloyd Cole. He chose his band's name to match 1950s groups, although only early tracks had a real rock 'n' roll sound. ▷ Bloomsday, ▷ The Bob Dylan Band.

Nat King Cole
Nathaniel Adams Coles got his name from *Old King Cole* – another of music's "aristocracy", along with scores of "dukes", "counts", "lords" and "earls". His daughter is also a "Nat": Natalie Cole. Nickname: Mr Velvet Voice.

Phil Collins
Nickname: ▷ Thumper. ▷ Genesis, ▷ Brand X.

Colorblind James Experience
Mix-'n'-match for "blind" blues players and ▷ The Jimi Hendrix Experience. Among those being namechecked: Blind John Davis; "Blind" Rev. Gary Davis; Sleepy John Estes; Blind Lemon Jefferson; "Blind" Willie McTell; "Blind" Willie Johnson and Blind Joe Reynolds.

Colosseum
This British band's namesake Roman stadium capacity gave something to aim for in concert numbers. They beat it. Later Colosseum II. ▷ Greenslade.

Robbie Coltrane
The Scottish comedian and rock figure was born Robin MacMillan but renamed after his favourite jazzman John Coltrane.

The Comets
Bill Haley's backing band were called The Four Aces of Western Swing, then The Saddlemen, to fit their cowboy image and music. As Haley made plans for rock 'n' roll, scientific discoveries were made about his near-namesake (Edmund) Halley's Comet. The group's chase for stardom would have been doomed under their old name, he admitted.

Commander Cody and the Lost Planet Airmen
Sci-fi inspiration, recalling ▷ Captain Beefheart. Cody was George Frayne IV, who named after a 1940s-vintage film, *Adventures of Commando Cody, Sky Marshal*; the band named after another movie, *The Lost Planet Airmen*.

The Commitments
Band in Booker-winning Roddy Doyle's first novel, *The Commitments*, published in 1988 and filmed by Alan Parker in 1991. The Commitments became a fully fledged real group, playing covers. Glen Hansard went on into ▷ The Frames, while many of the act re-formed in 1997 as The Committed.

In the novel they form as And And! (And) – while manager Jimmy Rabbitte says their name should reflect sex, politics and working-class commitment.

The Comodores
When two fledgling groups – The (Mighty) Mystics and the Jays – combined in Tuskegee, Alabama, in 1967, a change of name was needed to keep the peace.

Singer Lionel Richie takes up the story in an interview: "We had all kinds of wonderful ideas – 'The Fantastic Soulful Six', 'The Mighty Wonders'. In fact, we almost broke up just trying to come up with a new name.

"We finally turned to the dictionary and [trumpet player] William King just stuck his finger on a page and we came up with 'commodore', and old naval term describing someone who ranks between captain and admiral. We were lucky because that word was real close to the word 'commode', and we might have ended up as 'The Commodes', wearing suits made out of toilet paper!" There have also been makes/models of boats, cars and aeroplanes named Commodore.

The Communards

▷ Bronski Beat boy Jimmy Somerville wanted to sing about social and sexual politics. Hence the name of another band he worked with, Body Politic. This time, he saluted radical inhabitants of the Paris Commune in the 1870s. Other possible choices were The Committee and ▷ Consenting Adults, to signal support for gay rights.

Perry Como

U.S. singer who anglicised his name Pierino Como.

Company Of Wolves

British writer Angela Carter (1940–92) included this novella in her 1979 collection *The Bloody Chamber*. Based on the fairy tale *Little Red Riding Hood*, it became a horror movie five years later. Heavy metal bands love names like this and it was promptly snapped up …

Comus

This 1970s prog-rock band in the ▷ Caravan/ ▷ Quintessence mould named after a 1630s masque by English poet John Milton. His writing also inspired ▷ Eyeless In Gaza.

Concrete Blonde

Invented by ▷ R.E.M.'s Michael Stipe, who is well known for obscure references, oblique lyrics and obtuse titles – and being politely unhelpful when asked why.

Stipe gave it to DreamSix because he wasn't convinced by their old name: "Sounds like *Number Nine Dream*. [▷ John Lennon song.] Concrete Blonde is much better." The band, bemused, thought he was right, accepted the superstar's suggestion and perhaps wisely didn't press an explanation. Maybe there **are** some things such as names which should have a veil drawn over them and remain shrouded in mystery.

Coney Hatch

Canadian band named after a corruption of a once infamous North London asylum.

Consenting Adults

U.K. 1970s band, named from a phrase in British law legalising homosexual relations in private between "consenting adults" of over 21.

▷ Bronski Beat's 1984 first album was independently named after the same laws, *The Age of Consent*.

Sam Cooke

He began as a gospel star, but when he tried to enter the pop market he was credited as Dale Cook, in a bid not to alienate his core audience. His distinctive voice gave the game away and he reverted, saying honesty was best. His later adding of an extra E to his surname inspired ▷ Dionne Warwick(e).

His song *The Chain Gang* in part led to the naming of ▷ The Kane Gang; while his version of *The Great Pretender* inspired ▷ The Pretenders. Nickname: ▷ Mr Soul.

Alice Cooper

The band went through names each as The Earwigs, The Spiders and Nazz. The last, suggested by drummer Neal Smith, was changed because there was another act called ▷ The Nazz, led by ▷ Todd Rundgren.

The Alice Cooper name related first to the group, but after 1975 to the singer, as he came to dominate and then legally renamed. For he is of course a *man*, born Vincent Damon Furnier in Detroit, U.S.A.

Alice said they started dressing up in lipstick, powder and paint in desperation: "We wanted to draw attention to ourselves because we weren't getting anywhere fast." This simple explanation emerged in recent television interviews where Alice admitted the moniker just tied in with their *Alice in Wonderland* act. He came up with it "on the spur of the moment" and could have as easily said "Carrie Carter," "Suzie Smalls" or "Billy-Jo Melons".

The act featured axes, snakes and electric chairs with Alice dressed as a ghoul with "blood" dripping off his face: he saw "little innocent Alice" as the victim of his attacks. These shock tactics, combined with feedback guitars and screams, caused entire audiences to walk out of concerts: some probably took the name at face value and expected to see a quiet ▷ Joni Mitchell style act. The appellation has the same ring of innocence as axe killer suspect ▷ Lizzy Borden, though it's subtler than ▷ Molly Hatchet. The confusion impressed ▷ Frank Zappa, who signed them to his label.

Alice has made a lot of publicity out of his name – as well as the bizarre fact he's the son of a preacher. (Another minister's son: ▷ Lemmy.) Additionally, he's generated headlines with bizarre explanations, all of which he has now confessed to be untrue.

False explanation 1: Alice suggested the intention was prove "people are both male and female". He later admitted he hated ▷ New York Dolls drag.

False explanation 2: It is frequently reported the name was produced at an ouija session. Alice originally claimed the board revealed he was the incarnation of a seventeenth-century witch called Alice Cooper. This story certainly generated more notice for the band and is so apt it deserves to be true.

Spin-off: ▷ The Billion Dollar Babies.

Copperhead

Their "money" logo was confusing. This was actually another snake name. Chosen in tribute to fellow rockers ▷ Whitesnake.

Cop Shoot Cop

These New York rockers say it was taken from a newspaper headline. It was only marginally less controversial than Shoot The Cops, their first choice.

Cornershop

This Asian band's name comments on the demise of local shops in Britain as out-of-town supermarkets take over.

Cortinas

Younger or non-U.K. readers may need to be told this British punk act named after the best-selling Ford family car, a sister of the Consul and the Capri. Poorer relations of ▷ The Jags.

Corvettes

Another car name. This time from the U.S.A., after the speedy and sexy Corvette Stingray, itself named after a warship and fish.

Cosmo

No relation to the magazine *Cosmopolitan*. Rather ▷ Creedance Clearwater Revival's Doug Clifford, who thought everything "cosmic". Hence the album *Cosmo's Factory*.

Elvis Costello

Born Declan Patrick MacManus in London, U.K., he was the son of Joe Loss singer/bandleader Ross MacManus (usually written McManus).

The name's seen by some as a cheeky attempt to combine ▷ Elvis Presley and 1950s American funnymen Abbott And Costello by virtue of his own early geeky appearance – not that of the typical rock star.

In fact Costello was his mother's maiden name and he played early gigs with pub combo Flip City as D.P. Costello. The surname Costello had been used by his father who charted in some countries in 1970 with a version of ▷ The Beatles' song *The Long And Winding Road*.

The "Elvis" was suggested by Jake Riviera, who became Declan's manager and signed him to the independent Stiff Records, on condition he changed his first name. Costello said the idea initially struck him as insane. The equally un-Elvis-like ▷ Reg Presley of ▷ The Troggs had thought similarly when he was urged by his manager to adopt a similar name. Costello's first success coincided with Presley's death, which led to the shock value nearly backfiring, with critics attacking "bad taste". As he became the critics' darling, he was seen as a worthy successor to The King. His 1986 album was entitled *The King Of America*. On this work he featured his own name, McManus, which also cropped up on film soundtracks.

He used the pseudonym The Imposter for the 1983–4 spoof 'Is It Or Isn't It Him' political protest songs *Pills And Soap* and *Peace In Our Time*. Costello fans would know this pseudonym was appropriated from the title of the track he wrote and recorded in 1980.

Costello also hid his identity, electing to be credited as Eamonn Singer, for the artwork of the 1986 LP *Blood And Chocolate*. He had produced a painting, entitled *Napoleon Dynamite*, and also used that pseudonym. He opted for greater anonymity on the Out Of Our Idiot compilation by "various bands", going for names such as The Emotional Toothpaste.

▷ The Attractions. ▷ The Tragically Hip.

The Cotton Club

Several acts have considered this name, most famously ▷ The Crickets. It was inspired by a famous Harlem nightclub, immortalised in a 1984 film.

The Couch Potatoes
This English band named as a protest at compulsive television watchers. "Watch your life away" was their slogan.

Johnny Cougar
▷ John Mellencamp.

The Counterfeit Stones
Group mimicking the ▷ Rolling Stones, and acknowledging their magpie status. Mick Jagger-style front man: Nick Dagger.

Counting Crows
Post-grunge Californian rockers. The band's singer-songwriter Adam Duritz said the name was inspired by the film *Signs of Life*, starring his ex-girlfriend Mary Louise Parker. In one sequence two men stand contemplating their lives as a murder of crows – as they are collectively called – fly by. The idea also inspired the 1993 song *A Murder Of One*.

The Country Hams
▷ Paul McCartney.

Country Joe And The Fish
▷ Country Joe McDonald.

Country's Leading Cowgirl
Billing name for the late, great ▷ Patsy Cline. Cf ▷ The Queen Of Country.

Jayne County
… deserves an entry because she was born a he and christened Wayne. The singer chose the new name because it was "as close as you can get" to her masculine alter ego. She elaborates in the 1996 biography *Man Enough To Be A Woman*.

Courage of Lassie
This Canadian outfit figured the risible title of a 1946 film about a collie dog would make a memorable moniker.

Cowboy Joe
Nickname for ▷ Joe Cocker, from his interest in western films. No relation to ▷ The Brown Dirt Cowboy.

The Cowboy Junkies
This Canadian quartet said this eye-catching and misleading moniker doesn't mean anything: "We were just thinking of a name which would make folks think, what the hell …" Still, it sums up their trademark stoned-sounding country songs. During an experimental stage they were *Germinal*, after the Emile Zola book.

The Cowsills
All Cowsills: six brothers, mum and sister, with dad as manager.

Crabby Appleton
Los Angeles band led by Michael Fennelly, named after the U.S. TV cartoon character.

The Cramps
U.S. band reviving rockabilly with shockabilly tactics … even to the name. In the U.K. it refers to muscle spasms in either sex after working out; in the U.S. it is a female term for menstrual pains and in parts of Europe it means a male erection.

Awards for individual names to Erick Purkhiser, who goes under the *nom de kitsch* Lux Interior, "Poison" Ivy Rorschach (*née* Kirsty Wallace) and Slim Chance.

Cranberries
Embarrassingly, this band from Limerick, Ireland, originally liked comic songs and was known as The Cranberry Saw Us, a pun on Cranberry Sauce. The comedy, and the name, was cut when singer Delores O'Riordan joined.

Crash Test Dummies
They wanted an "unusual collective" name, and rejected the bad-taste medical offerings The Chemotherapists – after cancer therapy – and The Skin Grafts.

Crass
Anarchistic band whose name was a reaction against crass pop pap and party politics. Individual band members: Steve Ignorant, Joy De Vivre. Album name: *Stations Of The Crass*.

Crawling King Snakes
Robert Plant, later of ▷ Led Zeppelin, named this act after traditional/ John Lee Hooker song *Crawling King Snake*, covered by ▷ The Doors.

He also played with ▷ Blind Snake Moan: more snake inspiration. ▷ Percy, ▷ The Honeydrippers.

Crazy Horse

Prior to working with ▷ Neil Young, they were The Rockets. He convinced them "rock it" was old fashioned; they suggested War Babies.

Crazy Horse was the commander of the Sioux and Cheyenne at 1876's Little Big Horn battle. Young has long been interested in native U.S. culture. The name had also been lifted by a Parisian nightclub – though this isn't why Young chose it. He felt their music was like a bucking bronco. After the renaming, they recorded the 1969 track *Requiem For The Rockets*.

Cream

This name worked on three levels. First, it had sexual overtones. (Cf ▷ 10CC, ▷ The Lovin' Spoonful.) Second, it allowed "milky" titles such as *Fresh Cream* and *Cream On Top*. Third, the trio's players had established reputations, supposedly the widely acknowledged finest performers on their respective instruments.

They were bassist Jack Bruce (ex ▷ Manfred Mann, John Mayall's ▷ Bluesbreakers), drummer Peter "Ginger" Baker and guitarist ▷ Eric "God" Clapton (The Yardbirds, ▷ Bluesbreakers etc). Cream pre-dated Clapton's ▷ Blind Faith – another supergroup – by several years.

▷ George Harrison played with them pseudonymously.

Creaming Jesus

The author apologises in advance if this name upsets. This book attempts to be more comprehensive than censorious. If it offends, this is exactly what this 1990s British band intended. "If you're offended, question your preconceptions not us." It also guaranteed them minimal publicity, which they called a sad reflection on tolerance of free expression.

Creation

Alan McGee thought Creation a great choice for a band so he launched a record label of this name. No relation to 1960s act Creation. Label stars: ▷ Oasis.

Creedence Clearwater Revival

This Californian band began as Tommy Fogerty and The Blue Velvets, then traded as The Visions. Their manager rechristened them The Golliwogs in a strange attempt to make them sound British. The band hated both it and their uniforms but promotional posters had been printed. Fortunately their 1965 debut single didn't chart: in a racially naïve yet divided America they didn't realise the storm that could have followed. Among many U.S. bands who used supposedly British names: ▷ Sir Douglas Quintet and ▷ The Byrds (at one stage called The Beefeaters).

A string of flops followed, with a hiatus and change of record company management, to Fantasy. The group considered a new name and the three words evolved:

1. Creedence, from acquaintance Credence Newball. They thought his name had a ring of truth but amended it so as not to offend him.
2. Clearwater was from an advert about the benefits of pure drinking water used in Olympia beer. They liked its refreshing sound with environmental overtones.
3. Revival. Myths have mushroomed round this, partly becaiuse John Fogerty was for years evasive. Plenty of reference books say Fantasy boss Saul Zaentz urged a revival of American roots music in a final attempted assault on the charts. In fact Fogerty told the writer Zaentz urged neither a change of moniker nor music. "Revival" showed their hope for better times at home after a disastrous few months, being forced into an image and appellation they "despised". "And, sure enough, both the name and the new records seemed to strike gold."

It was Christmas Eve 1967 when they agreed on Creedence Clearwater Revival (C.C.R. for short), saying the finished name sounded good as a whole.

Spin-off: ▷ The Blue Ridge Rangers. The band inspired the names ▷ Green River and Willie And The Poorboys ▷ Cosmo.

Kid Creole And The Coconuts

U.S. producer Darnell Browder was of Haitian origin, hence Creole. The "Kid" echoed the ▷ Elvis Presley film *King Creole*. His collaborator,

Ray "Sugar Coated" Hernandez, chose a similarly fanciful tag: Coati Mundi. Their first effort was Dr Buzzard's Original Savannah Band before recruiting The Coconuts for a totally tropical name. Cf ▷ Blue Rondo A La Turk.

Crew-Cuts
Canadian singers whose clean-cut name fitted their early image. This didn't last long: their first album was *The Crew-Cuts Go Longhair*. Cf ▷ The Ivy League.

The Crickets
Members of the band known for backing ▷ Buddy Holly chose the name in the late 1950s after consulting reference books. Niki Sullivan said they found a page about insects. An earlier group was The Spiders – and remarkably, they considered Beetles. "Jerry said, 'Aw, that's just a bug you'd want to step on,' so we immediately dropped that." They chose Crickets as a joke "because they make a happy sound … they make music with their legs".

They weren't bothered that it could also refer to the English sport. It was this double meaning that not many years later helped inspire ▷ The Beatles, all Holly fans.

The name was needed partly because Holly's could not be used for their first recording: DECCA had an option on him, although it showed no sign of picking it up.

The band also considered ▷ The Cotton Club – until during a 1957 tour, when they were given a hotel room infested with crickets. Also that summer, while they were recording *I'm Gonna Love You Too*, a cricket got in to the echo chamber. On the last version, its chirping came only on the fade-out and at the right tempo. They kept its sound and the name.

It's wrong to say – as several books have done – that the hotel and studio incidents inspired the moniker, which had been around for some time. But both were seen as good omens.

For definitive accounts, see *Remembering Buddy* by John Goldrosen and John Beecher, 1987, revised and updated 1996, and Philip Norman's *Buddy – The Biography*.

Later members included ▷ Ric Grech.

Trivia note: "The Crickets" was used by a group of balladeers who named four years before Holly's cohorts and were led by Grover Barlow. He later renamed as Dean Barlow, using his mother's maiden name.

Tory Crimes
The original drummer with ▷ The Clash was born Terry Chimes but renamed in a street credibility bid. His calculated cynicism still didn't make him sufficiently politically correct and he soon left the band.

The Cro-Mags
Cro-Magnon means "the grotto of Magnio". It's in the Dordogne and known for the 1860s discovery of the remains of a human-like creature, with an important part in evolution. Cf ▷ Piltdown Men.

Bing Crosby
Harry Lillis Crosby became "Bingo" in high school in Spokane in reference to big-eared Bingo in *The Bingville Bugle* comic strip. Bing insisted it was because he liked the character, rather than because of any supposed physical similarity, as is sometimes suggested. ▷ The Old Groaner.

Christopher Cross
U.S. singer-songwriter who was born with the less stagey name Christopher Geppert. No relation to Chris Cross of ▷ Ultravox.

Crowded House
Formed by ▷ Split Enz founder Neil Finn, after his move from New Zealand to Los Angeles. The name's a reference to the hectic life at his small house in Hollywood while putting together the band and planning their first album in 1985–6. They pondered the moniker ▷ The Mullanes but decided it was old fashioned and also played gigs in California as The Largest Living Things. Spin-off: ▷ ALT.

Crown Heights Affair
New York grouping from Crown Heights; recalling Steve McQueen's film *The Thomas Crown Affair*.

Crucifucks

A Michigan band who wanted "the most offensive name ever". Outcome: commercial crucifixion. Cf ▷ Creaming Jesus.

Crusaders

This Texas band began as The Jazz Crusaders and aimed to proselytise jazz. After their first crossover hit the name was shortened but the intention stayed.

Cruzados

Latin-influenced 1980s U.S. band who deserved to be much better known; like ▷ The Crusaders, their name recalled the religious crusades. In addition, cruzados refers to the cross and a Portugese coin.

Cry Of Love

From ▷ Jimi Hendrix's album of this name. Hendrix's influence emerges via Audley Freed's guitar. A 1990s rock band.

The Crystals

Shortly after forming, the New York all-girl group met musician Leroy Bates, who suggested the name after his daughter Crystal. Bates co-wrote some of their material including – aptly – *There's No Other Like My Baby*.

CTI

Abbreviation for Creative Technology Institute, ▷ Chris and Cosey of ▷ Throbbing Gristle.

The Cuban Heels

Crawling from the wreckage of seminal punksters ▷ Johnny And The Self-Abusers: two bands. The lucky ones became millionaires with ▷ Simple Minds. The unlucky ones had no money, just smart footwear – *hence the name*. The band lasted from 1978 to 1982.

The Cult

This British band started as The Southern Death Cult – taken from a book in Bradford Library, an anthropological study of American Indians from Mississippi.

It was in keeping with singer Ian Astbury's interests and taste in clothes (while he briefly adopted the stage name of Ian Lindsay). It could also be seen as a Northern attack on Southern England (cf ▷ The Beautiful South).

They regrouped, moved from punk to heavier metal and abbreviated to Death Cult, though this didn't last: "We didn't think we'd sell many records called that." The Cult's music, coincidentally, recalls ▷ Blue Öyster Cult. Spin-off: ▷ Four Horsemen. More American Indian influence: ▷ Cochise, ▷ Crazy Horse, ▷ Eagles etc.

Culture Club

The central figures in the band were discovered in 1979–80 by the U.K. media exploring the London dance crazes, New Waves and New Romantic fashions.

This resulted in verbose articles about nightspots Heaven, Hell and Blitz in the "Club Culture" capital. ▷ Boy George – tired of In Praise of Lemmings and ▷ Sex Gang Children – switched round this headline to get his new group's name, although it was only selected after "debates" with Jon Moss, whose musical CV includes work with ▷ The Damned and ▷ The Stranglers.

"We all agreed Sex Gang Children was the wrong name. We toyed with new names, Caravan Club, Can't Wait Club. Jon said: 'Look at us: and Irish transvestite, a Jew, a black man, an Anglo-Saxon.' That's how I came up with the name Culture Club. Nightclubbing, roots and culture," George remembers in his autobiography. Caravan Club would well have produced legal problems, so it's as well it wasn't pursued. Cf ▷ Marilyn, ▷ Visage etc.

The Cure

Founded 1976 by Robert Smith after school in Crawley, Sussex, U.K. He had earlier played in a band called Obelisk.

The story is set out in *The Cure: Faith* by Dave Bowler and Bryan Dray (1995). The group named Easy Cure, after a song by first drummer Lol Tulhurst, who thought love a cure for all ills. Smith thought this bland: he wanted the group to be a more definite article.

Spin-offs include The Cry (Simon Gallup), ▷ The Glove (Smith and ▷ Steve Severin) and The Cult Heroes (early joke single entitled *I'm A Cult Hero*). Playing small venues, they have adopted ▷ R.E.M.-style "coded" names, such as ▷ Five Imaginary Boys, to avoid drawing big crowds. Tribute act: ▷ The Lovecats.

Curiosity Killed The Cat
Singer Ben Volpeliere-Pierrot was nicknamed "The Cat" because of his coolness, he claimed. This suggested the idiom about a feline's constant curiosity. The teen band abbreviated to Curiosity as they tried to keep momentum but their nine lives of chart success ran out as people lost curiosity ...

Curly Leads And Switches
Louisiana star Max de Frost renamed Curly Leads to fit in with his song *Plug Me In* and catchphrases such as "turn me on".

Curved Air
British art-rock band formed 1970, named in praise of ▷ Terry Riley's 1969 album *A Rainbow In Curved Air*. Terrible punning LP title: *Air Conditioning*. Graduates joined ▷ The Police, ▷ Sky.

Cybernetic Serendipity
Far out 1960s band with far-out cosmic (or is that comic?) name. They explained: "Cybernetics means brain communication; serendipity is the gift of finding valuable things by luck."

Cymarron
Not Welsh; a U.S. band named after a television cowboy show.

Cypress Hill
Although hailing from Cuba in part, they lived in Los Angeles, California, and named after part of the Southgate suburb.

Cyrkle
This Pennsylvania singing group started as The Rondells. A rondel or rondeau is a musical or poetical form suggestive of a recurrence.

They signed with the same management company as ▷ The Beatles. ▷ John Lennon asked: "What's a Rondell?" They said: "Well ... like a circle." He came up with the misspelling.

C

Dada

Not baby talk for "father". Dada was French for "hobby-horse", a word chosen at random to name an art movement in the early twentieth century. It inspired three bands: Dada, dada and ▷ Bonzo Dog Doo-Dah Band.

Daddy Longlegs

From Jean Webster's novel *Daddy Longlegs*, a sugary love story made into a musical and film. The epistolary novel's hero isn't a crane fly but a tall sugar-daddy.

Daddy Stovepipe

Wandering U.S. guitarist Johnny Watson was named after his trademark top hat. He was married to the equally wonderfully named Mississippi Sarah.

DAF

DAF stands for Deutsche Amerikanische Freundschaft (German-American friendship). The band, producing ▷ Yello-style pop, hailed from Germany. No relation to the DAF car which inspired another band, ▷ New FADS.

Daisy Chainsaw

The band combined the fragile Daisy looks of Katie Jane Garside with chainsaw guitars.

Dalek I

It was somebody which a cold saying "Darling, I love you" which gave this U.K. group their name, referring to the sinister aliens from the BBC cult science fiction series *Doctor Who*.

Band members went on into ▷ Orchestral Manoeuvres In The Dark and ▷ The Teardrop Explodes. Cf ▷ The Mekons, ▷ The Timelords.

Dali's Car

Mick Karn (born Tony Michaelides, ex ▷ Japan) and Pete Murphy (ex ▷ Bauhaus) named their collective outing after a track on ▷ Captain Beefheart's 1969 double album *Trout Mask Replica*. This in turn came from surrealist Salvador Dali. Cf ▷ The Soft Watches.

Damascus

In fact from Banbury, U.K. They thought the name "exotic and mysterious". ▷ To Damascus.

Damian Thorne

From the name of a character in *The Omen* film.

The Damned

Might have been called ▷ The Sex Pistols according to some reports, both names favoured by impresario Malcolm McLaren. This isn't quite correct: McLaren had considered The Damned as a moniker for The Pistols, who had been named for a while before the new band came along. McLaren planned on calling the new boys Masters of the Backside – with Chrissie Hynde, later of ▷ The Pretenders, among them.

Ray Burns was brought in and became ▷

Captain Sensible, replacing Tony James, later bassist with ▷ Sigue Sigue Sputnik and ▷ Sisters of Mercy. He said McLaren and Johnny Rotten of The Pistols heard them play with Chrissie and weren't impressed; she left; the hapless band carried on regardless thinking nothing was going right. In Jon Savage's 1991 book *England's Dreaming* he adds: "The name 'The Damned' was Brian James's idea. We were damned really: everything that could go wrong did."

James was thinking of Luchino Visconti's 1969 picture *The Damned* starring Dirk Bogarde and Vanian-style gore make-up. Marcus Gray writes in his 1995 book, *The Last Gang In Town*: "True to the band's origin in the ▷ London SS, they stuck with the 'Nazi decadence' theme."

The Damned was appropriate because of the Dracula stage outfit of singer David Vanian – who was born David Letts and was briefly David Zero. He was a cemetery worker; his Hammer House of Horror garb recalled ▷ Alice Cooper. It was coincidence that *The Damned* was the title of other films including a Hammerscope horror film of 1963.

Vanian had a foil in drummer Christopher Miller, who proudly proclaimed he'd suffered from scabies and was rechristened Rat Scabies by James.

After a 1978 break-up, they fragmented into Kings, The Edge and Tanz Der Youth before re-forming as Les Punks, a French term for punkoid musos, and briefly as The Doomed while legal rights to the name were sorted out. Related band: ▷ Lords Of The New Church.

Damned Yankees

When Ted Nugent formed this so-called supergroup – actually the next most famous member was from ▷ Styx – in 1989 he was asked to describe them. Coining the title of a 1950s musical, he joked they sounded like "Damn Yankees". ▷ The Amboy Dukes.

Dana

This Belfast-born Eurovision-winning singer was born Rosemary Brown and was nicknamed Dana as a child: it's a Gaelic word meaning mischievous.

The Dancing Did

A 1980s band from Evesham, Worcestershire, with a rural agenda and a name that confused many people who asked: "The dancing did **what?**" The answer is that a "did" is country slang for a peasant.

Jim Dandy

The ▷ Black Oak Arkansas singer was born Jim Mangrum and renamed after LaVerne Baker's 1956 hit.

Danny And The Juniors

Philadelphia schoolboy Danny Rapp formed the band in 1955 with friends about to do their junior college year.

Danny Wilson

Scottish band named after the 1952 film *Meet Danny Wilson*, starring ▷ Frank Sinatra. They probably chose the wrong movie. They said in an early release their moniker came from a flick in which Sinatra gets embroiled in a plot to assassinate the President. This exactly fits the storyline of 1954's *Suddenly*.

Danzig

U.S. rockers who named from leader Glenn Danzig; not a reference to the Polish town now known as Gdansk, birthplace of Solidarity.

Dare

Named after leader Darren Wharton, ex ▷ Thin Lizzy, with a few letters wisely shaved off at the suggestion of ▷ Lemmy from ▷ Motörhead.

Bobby Darin

Walden Robert Cassotto, from The Bronx, took his new tag after hours leafing through the New York phone directory.

Dark Star

This British art rock outfit named from a science fiction film rather than the ▷ Grateful Dead's identically titled epic song.

The Darling Buds

A Shakespearean quote from sonnet 18, *The Darling Buds* was used by H.E. Bates as a novel title, which is where this Welsh band found it.

They named one album *Pop Said*, also a quote from the same Bates book. Cf ▷ This Mortal Coil.

Darts

They named after an instrumental rock 'n' roll track, while saxophonist Horatio Hornblower namechecked the C.S. Forester seafarer.

Dave Dee, Dozy, Beaky, Mick and Tich

This U.K. novelty group, formed by David Harman, was called Dave Dee And The Bostons … until they confessed on BBC television this was "rubbish". They resorted to their joke nicknames.

Skeeter Davis

She was born in Kentucky as Mary Penick. "Skeeter" was the name for a mosquito: as a child she was always flitting around. Her singing partner Betty Jack Davis was killed in a 1953 car crash and Skeeter renamed in her memory.

Dawn

Producer Hank Medress, a former singer with The Tokens, named the new band after Dawn Siegal, daughter of his former colleague Jay Siegal.

Lady Day

▷ Billie Holiday became known as "Lady" on the 1930s Harlem club circuit because of her near-regal bearing. It was used as the credit for 1943's *Trav'lin Light*.

Dazz Band

The Cleveland-based band set out to create "danceable jazz"; the name is a contraction of a phrase by leader Bobby Harris.

The dB's

… a name explained by the title of their 1981 debut, *Stands For Decibels*. This American group's concerts were deafening.

Deacon Blue

Vocalist Ricky Ross confirms it was from the ▷ Steely Dan track *Deacon Blues*, on the 1977 album *Aja*. He loved its music and aspirational lyric about seeking stardom.

The Dead Boys

One U.S. book says these Cleveland punks' name inspired an early song *Dead Boys*. Actually, the song came first. It's also called *Down In Flames* and includes the line "dead boy, running scared".

They included the delightfully designated "Master Bator", Stiv Bators, later with ▷ Lords Of The New Church. During his life the S on the end of Bators came and went. The Dead Boys also featured Jimmy Zero, Cheetah Chrome, Jeff Magnum and Johnny Blitz.

Dead Fingers Talk

One of many rock homages to U.S. writer William S. Burroughs (1914–97). This 1970s band named after the title of a book compiling some of his best work, including *The Soft Machine* and *The Naked Lunch*.

Also owing a naming debt to the same cult writer: ▷ The Heavy Metal Kids; ▷ The Mugwumps; ▷ Naked Lunch; ▷ The Nova Mob; ▷ Sex Gang Children; ▷ The Soft Boys; ▷ Soft Machine; ▷ Steely Dan and ▷ Thin White Rope. So far nobody seeking a name has latched on to other Burroughs titles such as *Queer, The Ticket That Exploded* or *Junkie*. Get in there soon! University theses have been written on his influence on pop and film.

Dead Kennedys

The name refers to members of the jinxed American political family, especially President John F. Kennedy (assassinated 1963) and Senator Robert Kennedy (1968).

It has been seen as brave, suicidal, amusing, revolting, or a pathetic play for attention and cashing in on the misery of others. Leaders Jello Biafra and East Bay Ray know they were beaten to the most repulsive designations by ▷ Foetus.

The Deadly Fumes

This British band chose a silly collective name because it made them laugh. "Deadly" is an expression meaning "very good" – see Roddy Doyle's ▷ *The Commitments*.

Deadly Hume

Australian band named after the notorious accident blackspot, The Hume Highway, running into their native Sydney.

Dead Milkmen

Thought up as a joke akin to ▷ The Dead Boys. Unrelated to ▷ Death By Milkfloat.

Dead On Arrival

From *High Time* magazine's review of a ▷ Sex Pistols film.

Dead Or Alive

This Liverpool act came together from ▷ The Mystery Girls and Nightmares In Wax. Is he-a-she frontman Pete Burns took the name from a wild west "wanted – reward" poster seen in a club.

Deaf School

It might seem a handicap to be deaf as a composer but it never stopped Beethoven. These musicians weren't deaf, maybe tone deaf. They started in 1974 at Liverpool Art College, part of which was once a deaf school.

Elton Dean

Saxophonist who played with ▷ Long John Baldry, ▷ Soft Machine and Bluesology. Now famous, with Baldry, for inspiring ▷ Elton John.

Death

Seminal exponents of thrash rock named from leader Chuck Schuldiner's phrase "death metal". He said: "The name perfectly describes the music, and it's not a joke."

Some more death rock names: Abattoir, Autopsy, Blessed Death, ▷ Carcass, Christian Death, Coroner, Corpsegrinder, Cryptic Slaughter, Death Angel, ▷ Death By Milkfloat, Deathrow, Died Pretty, ▷ DOA, Doom, Entombed, Evildead, Exquisite Corpse, Gravediggaz, ▷ The Grim Reaper, Killdozer, Killer Dwarves, ▷ Killing Joke, Kill For Thrills, ▷ Lawnmower Deth, Massacre, ▷ Megadeth, ▷ Napalm Death, Obituary, Overkill, Poison, Poison Idea, ▷ Sepultura, Sexton, Six Feet Under, Slayer, The Stormtroopers Of Death, Suicidal Tendencies, ▷ Suicide, Xecutioner.

Death By Milkfloat

They topped ▷ Lawnmower Deth by saying the most embarrassing way to die was to be run over by a slow-moving electric milk wagon.

Death Cult

▷ The Cult.

Death In Vegas

This band's name is misleading for two reasons:
1. They come from the U.K., not Las Vegas.
2. It refers to Elvis Presley – who died at Graceland, Whitehaven, Memphis. Dead Elvis was their original moniker. Programmer Steve Hellier and disc jockey Richard Fearless reconsidered after anger from fans of The King. Dead Elvis became the title of their 1997 debut album.

Fearless told *The Face*: "A lot of people think Elvis died in Vegas. He didn't, but that's where he did his sell-out gigs to fat, middle-aged American women and that was the death of him creatively."

DeBarge

Like ▷ The Cowsills, The Jacksons and The Osmonds (to name but three), they were all members of the same family – in this case a family of ten.

Chris De Burgh

He was born Christopher Davidson in Argentina: the stage name salutes his Irish ancestral home.

Decameron

They loved the title of Giovanni Boccaccio's work written 600 years before in Italy and thought it nicely meaningless.

DECCA

The U.K. record company took its name from a portable gramophone, which played a signature tune on notes D-E-C-C-A.

The Ded Byrds

This British guitar band kept coy about their name which used the ▷ Led Zeppelin misspelling to recall ▷ The Byrds. This didn't stop threats from representatives of the latter act and the project crashed to earth.

Kiki Dee

Bradford singer born Pauline Matthews. The stage name was one of a number suggested by songwriter Mitch Murray in the mid-1960s to fit his own compositions. She was later an ▷ Elton John protégée.

Deep Forest
A straight description of this French group's inspiration: tribal music fused with jungle sounds.

Deep Purple
The story began in the U.K. in 1968 when drummer Chris Curtis of ▷ The Searchers contacted keyboardist Jon Lord of ▷ The Flowerpot Men. Curtis wanted to start a band called Roundabout – because the stage was to feature a circular platform which the musicians would jump on and off. This idea having been ditched, deservedly, and Ritchie Blackmore (ex ▷ Lord Sutch's Savages) recruited, they shared a house where a piece of paper was pinned up for anonymous name suggestions.

One entry said "Deep Purple". This sounded strange and it emerged it had the same colour references as ▷ Black Sabbath and ▷ Pink Floyd. It was emphatically not – as some reference books have suggested – chosen as a contrast with the name ▷ Vanilla Fudge. The heavy name got better as the group's rock got heavier.

Initially, nobody admitted to making the suggestion or would explain what it meant. Then they discovered: *Deep Purple* was a light song by ▷ Bing Crosby, of all people. It was made into a hit in 1962 by Nina Tempo and April Stevens. Few fans guessed their favourite band was named after a slightly embarrassing slow trad song which they wouldn't be seen dead keeping in their record collection.

The Hoagy Carmichael version of the tune was a particular favourite of Blackmore's granny and finally he admitted he was to blame for a moniker now seen as worthy of purple-period ▷ Prince.

Spin-offs include ▷ Gillan, ▷ Rainbow (more colour) and ▷ Whitesnake. The Purps inspired the naming of Swiss rockers ▷ Stormbringer and 1990s act ▷ Machine Head.

Def Leppard
The Sheffield, U.K., heavy metal band started as Atomic Mass (1977). The name change came from a suggestion of Joe Elliott when he joined.

He reasoned:
1. Many HM fans accept deafness as an occupational hazard (for example, later, Motörhead's *Deaf Forever* etc).
and …
2. Plenty of other bands had named themselves after big cats (e.g., ▷ Shabby Tiger, ▷ The Tygers of Pan Tang) but rarely leopards.

The others in the band soon chose to write the name phonetically to make it more interesting. Re-spell "Deaf" and you may as well mess up "Leopard" too.

All of this resulted in three happy co-incidences.

First, the spelling made them more acceptable for the American market, which became their primary target.

Second, it was not their specific intention to pay homage to ▷ Led Zeppelin but the spelling of "Def" directly recalled the bigger band. While it was never very likely that U.S. fans would call them "deef leo-pard", the new spelling appeared a tribute to "leeeed zeppelin". (Led Zeppelin was spelled thus to make the pronunciation clear.) The band rapidly spotted the similarity and said they would prefer to attract Zep fans than punks to their early gigs.

The third coincidence is that the name also – as it happened – fitted in with U.S. street slang: "Def" is short for "definitive", meaning "very good", as in the record company Def Jam.

They are informally called by fans Def Lep, like Led Zep.

Defunkt
They meant funk music was alive and well, not defunct.

Del Amitri
This Glasgow act named at an embryonic stage: their name is "in the womb" in Greek.

Delaney And Bonnie
Delaney Bramlett and Bonnie Lynn; they married five days after meeting in 1967 and divorced in 1972.

De La Soul
This act combined hip-hop with soul to produce a hybrid, DAISY Age standing for Da

Inner Sound Y'All. Hence Daisy Soul, hence De La Soul.

Delfonics
Producer Stan Watson adapted it from the ▷ Del-Vikings, with whom he'd worked.

Del Fuegos
Del Fuego is the furthest south on the South American mainland continent. This American outfit found the name in an atlas and thought it sounded "like a hot car or a cool band".

Delicate Vomit
These mid-1990s hopefuls wanted to be called Vom, until they discovered another act of the same name. They told *NME* it was an interesting contrast between violence and sensitivity.

Del-Lords
Taken from the "over-the-top" name of a TV executive they met; it sounded like a U.S. street gang, many of whom start with a "Del".

The Del-Rons
In honour of similarly named groups, particularly ▷ the Del-Vikings (sometimes spelled Dell-Vikings) and The Del-Satins.

Delta Lady
▷ Joe Cocker inspired this lot, who named after his hit *Delta Lady* on the 1970 cover-versions album *Joe Cocker!*

The Del-Vikings
The Vikings was the name of a basketball and social club which founder Clarence Quick supported in Brooklyn. The "del" was fashionable at the time although redundant because it means "the". Cf The Dells – roughly "The Thes"; in turn ▷ The The; and ▷ Delfonics, ▷ The Del-Rons.

Terry Dene
U.S. 1950s rock star, born Terence Williams. He renamed in honour of actor James Dean (1931–55), who died in a car crash the year before.

John Denver
Born Henry John Deutschendorf Junior in Roswell, U.S.A., he chose to use his second name coupled with his favourite city.

Department S
Early 1980s U.K. band named from a highly popular ATV 1969–70 spoof-thriller series which starred Peter Wyngarde. The lead singer gets an award for an individual band member's name: Vaughn Toulouse.

Depeche Mode
Life changed for this young band from Basildon, Essex, when a copy of a French trade and general interest fashion magazine – *Depeche Mode* – found its way to nearby Southend, where vocalist David Gahan was studying. They borrowed the title, which means "Fashion Dispatch" or "Fashion Express". It is sometimes translated as "hurry up fashion", "fast fashion" and even "by telegraph". Some of these interpretations are a *péché* (sin).

Fans are called Modeheads. Vince Clarke got out to form ▷ Yazoo, ▷ The Assembly and ▷ Erasure.

Deram
Named after a brand of cartridge.

Derek And The Dominos
An attempt by guitar hero ▷ Eric Clapton to disguise himself. As such it was a failure, but resulted in the magnificent *Layla* (and other assorted love songs).

Clapton was soured by experiences in ▷ Cream and ▷ Blind Faith – after all the hysteria and slogans saying "Eric Clapton is ▷ God". He joined three ex-members of ▷ Delaney And Bonnie's band and they were slated to debut as Eric Clapton And Friends at a June 1970 charity concert in London, but the star wanted anonymity. Clapton's friend Tony Ashton often called God "Del" and suggested the 1950s-sounding Del And The Dominos. The more formal Derek was accepted. It was simultaneously seen by some as a tribute to ▷ Fats Domino.

Clapton had intended the name only to last the night – then used The Dominos as the name for a U.S. tour. He wanted to play small clubs – still, the promoter took every opportunity of dropping his name, forcing larger venues.

Similar hiding-talent-under-a-bushel names: ▷ The Blue Ridge Rangers, ▷ The Traveling Wilburys, ▷ Notting Hillbillies.

Derringer

Soon-to-be U.S. star Rick Zehringer changed his name before his massive hit with ▷ The McCoys, *Hang On Sloopy*. The band was signed to the Bang label, which had the picture of a small pistol on its label. He later led a band called Derringer.

Des'ree

Full name Des'ree Weeks.

Destroy All Monsters

A truly silly name, lifted from a 1968 science-fiction film. The U.S. band, ex-members of ▷ The Stooges and ▷ MC5, saw the Godzilla movie and thought it truly awful. It's meant to be terrifying; it's actually hilarious. The group said: "The title made us laugh every time we say it."

Detroit Spinners

▷ Spinners (U.S.A.).

The Detroit Wheels

▷ Mitch Ryder's backers, originally The Rivieras. The new name reflected their origins in the U.S. auto-making capital and helped win them a large local following.

Devadip

Name used by ▷ Carlos Santana during his time following Buddhist teachings. Cf ▷ Roger/ Jim McGuinn of ▷ The Byrds.

Devo

Devo is de-evolution, the opposite of evolution. The group was formed as The De-Evolution Band in 1974 as the by-product of a U.S. Kent State University documentary video project.

It was a prizewinner at the Ann Arbor Film Festival and in 1977 they made another film, *In The Beginning Was The End*, to further advance their view the world is going backwards biologically. Fast information processing will far overtake human mental power and as we need to use our brains less and communicate seldom we will regress back to monkeys or mere robots.

Maybe it was something to do with the fact they came from the Mid-Western industrial city of Akron, Ohio, but they extended the concept to a stage show designed to show the de-humanising aspects of high-tech life. They pretended to be automatons and played increasingly metronomic/monotonous/moronic music.

Ultimately a pretentious way of building up to covers of the ▷Rolling Stones' *Satisfaction*. Fans called: Devo-tees. The band's antecedents include Jackrabbit, an outfit which featured Chrissie Hynde, later of ▷ The Pretenders.

Howard Devoto

Howard Trafford renamed in February 1976 after seeing ▷ The Sex Pistols. He and ▷ Pete Shelley were consequently inspired to re-invent themselves. Devoto was the name of a man who was mentioned in a moral story recounted by Trafford's philosophy lecturer. "Devoto" sounded pretentious, mysterious and a like "devoted". ▷ The Buzzcocks, ▷ Magazine.

Dexy's Midnight Runners

Widely reported to be a reference to the amphetamine dexedrine, usually taken in pills known as Dexys. These drugs were issued to troops in wars, taken by bored housewives (the "Mother's little helpers" which were the subject of a ▷ Rolling Stones song) and still swallowed by young soul rebels attending all-night Northern soul parties at the time the group started as The Killjoys; their early sound resembled sixties soul.

As Peter Laurie's textbook *Drugs* says, the pills can increase short-term vitality for short spells – but they're potentially dangerous. Perhaps for this reason, Dexy's followed a strict no-drugs code, banned alcohol from early gigs and leader Kevin Rowland has always been vague about the name.

In an apparent attempt to play down the drugs reference the band was even pictured in an alarmingly literal interpretation of their appellation, out jogging in darkened streets.

The Dharma Bums

There are a few cult writers whose influence on pop culture has been arguably greater than their sway on literature itself. William Burroughs is one such. Another was Jack Kerouac. *The Dharma Bums* (1965) was seen as nowhere near as important as *On The Road* (1957) but ultimately named a rock band. ▷ Elmerhassell, ▷ The Subterraneans.

Diamond Head

British heavy metal band who named from a locomotive on the Canadian-Pacific railroad. It is also: an LP stylus; an album by Phil Manzanera of ▷ Roxy Music; a 1965 hit for The Ventures; a Hawaiian volcano.

Neil Diamond

Neil Diamond insists he was born Neil Diamond, has never toned down his heritage and is proud of his past. Therefore, many magazines and encyclopedias are incorrect in giving his real name as Noah Kaminsky.

Still, it is true that many stars have moved away from Jewish-origin names (▷ Bob Dylan etc). And Kaminsky/Kominsky as a name was thrown away by ▷ Danny Kaye and Melvyn Kaminsky, who became Mel Brooks.

Charles Dickens

Briefly successful U.K. pop star who took the name of the famous Victorian author.

Dickens the writer also inspired the naming of ▷ Uriah Heep.

Bo Diddley

He was born in Mississippi as Otha Ellis Bates, then put out for adoption and became Elias McDaniel.

His rebirth as rock 'n' roll legend Bo Diddley came in 1955. Harmonica player "Billy Boy" Arnold gives the story in George R. White's 1995 biography *Living Legend.*

Arnold recalled how one time, walking along the street, bassist Roosevelt Jackson said: "'Hey Elias, there go Bo Diddley', speaking of a comical-looking, bow-legged, little short guy. To me it was the funniest word I'd ever heard: I just cracked up!"

Arnold suggested this to Chess Records co-founder Leonard Chess, who wasn't sure, thinking it was a discriminating word for black people. He was soon convinced otherwise, and Elias was renamed – like it or not.

Elias had been known as Bo before – while training as a boxer. This also came from Southern patois and means roughly "a bad boy".

Bo Diddley as a comic character had been around a while: Chess found another southern singer had been called the same 20 years before while other Diddley acts existed in Chicago (1935) and even Shanghai (1929).

Diddley said of the name: "I would **love** to know where the sucker same from. The other day, I read there was an instrument in the South, in the old days, called a diddley bow ..." So his name was an inversion of this – but only coincidentally.

The New Grove Dictionary Of Musical Instruments defines it as "a single-string chordophone of the Southern U.S.A." usually made up of a long wire attached to a frame house. "The wire is played with a nail and the house acts as a resonator."

Bo inspired the naming of ▷ The Roadrunners and ▷ The Pretty Things. Nicknames: Black Gladiator, Big Bad Bo.

Die Kreuzen

A Milwaukee, U.S.A., band, they thought the German word, seen in a book, sounded like "cruising" and reportedly assumed it meant "the crosses". Kreuzen is actually a verb meaning to cross.

Digable Planets

Named after the philosophical stance that every individual is a separate planet.

Dillinger

Another Jamaican reggae star named after a U.S. mobster. Lester Bullocks remembered John Dillinger.

Dils

This San Diego band started as Dilrod, a science-fiction-influenced name.

Dingoes

They wanted a word to reflect a native of Australia, their home. Strange they rejected The Koalas, The Kangaroos and The Wombats ...

Dinosaur Jr

They named Dinosaur after a children's show –

long before the 1990s *Jurassic Park* obsession. They denied it had anything to do with wanting to be big in a ▷ T. Rex way. The "Junior" was added after complaints by ▷ The Dinosaurs, including Barry "The Fish" Melton (▷The Fish).

The Dinosaurs

An ironic name chosen when these ageing West Coast rock stars came together for an ad hoc supergroup. At least one newspaper said they were a bunch of dinosaurs. The band played art-rock with long passages like it was dying out, recalling their work with the likes of ▷ Big Brother And The Holding Company, ▷ The Grateful Dead, ▷ Country Joe And The Fish, ▷ Jefferson Airplane, ▷ Hot Tuna and ▷ Quicksilver Messenger Service.

This band forced the renaming of ▷ Dinosaur Jr.

Dio

Named after leader, ex ▷ Black Sabbath, ▷ Rainbow singer Ronnie James Dio.

Dion And The Belmonts

New York-born Dion DiMucci said the name was chosen as an affectionate childhood memory of the Belmont area of the city.

Dippermouth

Louis Armstrong was known of ▷ Satchmo because of the size of his mouth. The big-breath trumpeter could put a water dipper into his cheeks, hence another nickname.

Dire Straits

Reflects the near-insolvent state of 27-year-old Mark Knopfler in 1977, then a part-time teacher and small-time musician playing with pub rockers such as Brewer's Droop. Knopfler, sharing a flat in Deptford, South London with two others, had just scraped together a hard-earned £120 to pay for a demo tape.

They toyed with the name Café Racers. The Straits name was a joke suggested by a friend. It was at first too close for comfort but later ironic in the extreme (cf ▷ Willy And The Poorboys). ▷ The Duolian String Pickers, ▷ The Notting Hillbillies.

Disposable Heroes Of Hiphoprisy

Rappers with strong views on the hypocrisy of American politics; band member Michael Franti said their music was "news you could use" before being disposed, like papers. Spin-off: ▷ Spearhead.

The Divine Comedy

Italian poet of about 1320 inspires rockers of the 1990s. Dante Alighieri (1265–1321), author of the symbolistic *Divina Commedia*, might be turning in his grave. Singer Neil Hannon disclosed that the name had more to it than met the eye. He was an atheist; his father, a Church of Ireland bishop. The same poem inspired the very different ▷ Styx.

The Divine Miss M.

▷ Bette Midler.

The Dixie Cups

Little Miss And The Muffets wisely decided to rename and get in a reference to their origin. Dixie(land) cups were cocktails sold in New Orleans.

DJM

U.K. record label with a name standing for Dick James Music. Its signings ranged from ▷ Satan's Rats to ▷ Elton John – whose name James helped inspire.

D.L.R.

Disciples Of Lyrical Rebellion; U.S. band. ▷ Arrested Development.

D-Mob

These Britons' name had the briefly *de rigueur* soul "D" (cf ▷ D-Train etc). Countless bands have named after mobs (▷ The Amboy Dukes, ▷ Sigue Sigue Sputnik), while this added a "wicked demobilisation pun".

DNA

Why do so many supergroups combine boring music with boring names (cf ▷ Asia, ▷ GTR)?

This name means ▷ (Rick) Derringer 'n' Appice (drummer Carmine Appice), i.e. D and A, DNA, geddit?

The same name has been used by two other

bands. It is quite widely known that DNA is a chemical found in cells coded with genetic information. It stands for dioxyribonucleic acid: not a lot of people know that.

DOA
Canadian punk: dead on arrival.

DOB
Japanese band's date of birth.

Doctor Feelgood
This U.K. band, formed 1971, recalled 1960s music such as the early ▷ Rolling Stones.

It was therefore natural they should be named after the 1961 song and album *Doctor Feel-Good*, written and recorded by seminal blues figure ▷ Piano Red. His band was renamed Dr Feelgood And The Interns for some years after recording the album.

The title also gained currency thanks to versions by ▷ Johnny Kidd and Aretha Franklin; the band was named after neither of these.

Dr Funkenstein
▷ George Clinton, ▷ Brides of Funkenstein.

Doctor Hook (And The Medicine Show)
U.S. singer Ray Sawyer had a patch over one eye, like the character in *Peter Pan*, after an accident. (Another eyepatch = piratical name ▷ Johnny Kidd.) The "quack" additions tied in with the band's act, inspired by shows selling dodgy potions to gullible cowboys.

Doctor John
New Orleans session player Malcolm John "Mac" Rebennack helped run the AFO label which included Prince Lala, who adopted black magic trappings akin to ▷ Screamin' Jay Hawkins. "Mac" was interested in voodoo too: the 1960s saw the birth of Dr John Creux The Night Tripper. The name was a tribute to Professor Longhair and ▷ The Beatles' *Day Tripper*.

Dr Phibes And The House Of Wax Equations
This band named in tribute to two films: the British-made 1971 *The Abominable Dr Phibes* and *The House of Wax Equations*, an obscure television horror flick.

Doctor Robert
Bruce Robert said he was called "The Good Doctor" at King's Lynn School, Norfolk, "because I was a sympathetic listener ... I got lumbered with everyone else's problems". ▷ Blow Monkeys.

Coxsone Dodd
An "aristocrat" in the Jamaican reggae world, Clement Dodd became styled "Sir"; the Coxsone came from the then popular cricketer. He named ▷ Horace Andy and ▷ The (Wailing) Wailers.

Dodgy
When they were called Three Cheers For Tokyo, these 1990s British musicians were told that being in a band was a dodgy career option. The word, meaning anything shady, unreliable or legally uncertain, was backed by series of "Dodgy press releases", one of which was reported to contain cannabis seeds.

Snoop Doggy Dogg
He says this is a first name and nickname, not a surname. ▷ Snoop.

Dojo
U.K. label named after founders Dougie Dudgeon and John Beecher.

Thomas Dolby
Newspapers point out that he was born – in Egypt – as Thomas Morgan Dolby Robertson. The third name proved apt, given his reputation as an eccentric electronics wizard. It was already a household name via the Dolby System of noise reduction developed by a different Dolby.

Dolby Laboratories reportedly tried unsuccessfully to sue him for trademark infringement in 1987. The dome-headed keyboard boffin pointed out it was his real name too – and won.

Dollar
This British pop band duo wanted a word already in the widest circulation. Dollars are

D

used in many countries but the name was a liability in the U.S., and seen as an English eccentricity. Another name misunderstood on the other side of the pond: ▷ The Fall.

Dolly Mixtures

This all-female group's pun may not be understood outside their home country. U.S. readers note: this U.K. trio named from a brand of candy.

Fats Domino

New Orleans singer, born Antoine Domino, he was in Billy Diamond's Band when their leader gave him the Fats nickname because of his 220lbs frame. His moniker inspired that of ▷ Chubby Checker and partly inspired ▷ Derek And The Dominos.

Lonnie Donegan

Glaswegian singer Tony Donegan got his new name from New Orleans blues player Lonnie Johnson. He was on the same bill at a big London concert as the U.S. guitarist and was mistakenly introduced as "Lonnie Donegan". The gig went well and young Donegan decided not to confuse the new fans. Nickname: ▷ The King Of Skiffle.

Ral Donner

Chicago singer who was born Ralph Donner.

Donovan

Born in Glasgow, Scotland, Donovan Phillips Leitch always used his prenomen only on stage (although his name was used in full to provide the title of a 1970 album). He inspired ▷ Open Road and ▷ This Machine Kills.

The Doobie Brothers

These Californians' name was suggested as a joke by an acquaintance. They weren't brothers and didn't know what "Doobie" meant, innocently thinking it had something to do with "dooby-doo music". Caught on the hop a few hours later, they gave it as their name rather than "Pud", their previous choice, which was unlikely to lead to success.

They soon found a "doobie" was 1960s slang for a cannabis cigarette. It had already found its way into literature via Armistead Maupin and Richard Merkin. After the truth dawned, the Doobies often said it was a family name to avoid radio bans.

Compare to the similarly innocent sounding ▷ Jefferson Airplane; there the band say the device for smoking marijuana came after they started.

The Doors

U.C.L.A. students James Douglas Morrisson and Dennis Jakob were discussing Dionysus (as one does) and remembered a line from William Blake, the eighteenth-century English poet and artist: "If the doors of perception were cleansed, man could see things as they truly are, infinite" (*The Marriage Of Heaven And Hell*, 1790).

The quote had been borrowed by British writer Aldous Huxley in 1954 for *The Doors Of Perception*, an essay on experiments with mescaline and LSD. Jim was soon conducting his own "experiments". (Cf Huxley influences ▷ Eyeless In Gaza, ▷ The Feelies.)

Jim and Dennis said they wanted to form a band called The Doors: Open and Closed. Sans Dennis, the act formed from LA bands Rick and the Ravens and the Psychedelic Rangers.

The new members thought the name far out, and by now Jim had added doubtless sincere but pretentious philosophy. "Our music opens the door for a new era of enlightenment ... There's the known. And there's the unknown. What separates the two is the door, and that's what I want to be ..."

It related to titles such as *Break On Through (To The Other Side)* and *The Doors Are Open*.

Name notes: There's more under ▷ Jim Morrison about his surname spelling. ▷ The Lizard King, ▷ Mr Mojo Riser/ Risin'. Spin-off: ▷ The Butts Band. The Doors inspired ▷ Horse Latitudes and ▷ The Australian Doors. Best reference: Jerry Hopkins and Danny Sugarman's 1980 book *No One Here Gets Out Alive*.

Lee Dorsey

U.S. singer, born Irving Lee Dorsey, had a short-lived career in the boxing ring under the charming name Kid Chocolate.

Nickname: Mr T.N.T.

Bijou Drains

Wonderful incognito choice of ▷ The Who's Pete Townshend, producing ▷ Thunderclap Newman.

Judge Dread

This appears under "D" not "J" because the Judge wasn't a band but solo Alex Hughes, christened after a ska song by ▷ Prince Buster (who also named ▷ Madness). That's "Dread" as in "dreadlocks"; no relation to comic book character Judge Dredd.

Mikey Dread

Michael Campbell named after his Rastafarian dreadlocks, "the longest in Jamaica".

Dread Zeppelin

Another Californian spoof on ▷ Led Zeppelin. Extent of joke: "Dread", as in dreadlocks; "Zeppelin", as the Led Zep catalogue sampled and translated into reggae form. The Zeps had already tried reggae thanks to the offbeat *D'Yer Mak'er*.

Humour likely to wear thin, fast, as ▷ Fred Zeppelin. Singing star: Tortelvis (real name Greg Tortill, inspired by tortilla-loving ▷ Elvis Presley in overweight Vegas mode). Guitarist: Jah Paul Jo (after Zep's John Paul Jones). Title of first album: *Un-led-ed* – a similar pun was used by Robert Plant and Jimmy Page when they worked together on an *Unplugged* style acoustic reunion.

D:Ream

"Because dreams are vital for life." The colon stems from the "D" fashion of ▷ D–Mob *et al*.

Dream Academy

British group named after 1964's The Dream Syndicate, an avant-garde New York project by LaMonte Young, joined by Welsh classical prodigy John Cale, later of ▷ The Velvet Underground. Cf ▷ The Dream Syndicate.

The Dreamlovers

▷ Chubby Checker's band formed in 1960 but couldn't become The Checkmates: the name was snapped up by Emile Ford in 1958. They named after a number one hit of the previous year, ▷ Bobby Darin's *Dream Lover*.

Dream Syndicate

The Dream House was an American ensemble which became The Dream Syndicate. It inspired ▷ Dream Academy and Dream Syndicate, a 1980s West Coast rock outfit.

Drella

Nickname for artist Andy Warhol, nominal producer of ▷ The Velvet Underground's debut album. His character was said to be a combination of Dracula and Cinderella; it was recycled in his posthumous lauding by ▷ Lou Reed and John Cale on 1990s *Songs For Drella*.

DRI

This Texas band named after a newspaper article which accused all young people who listen to rock music of being "dirty rotten imbeciles".

The Drifters

Formed round Clyde McPhatter, ex The Dominos. (No relation to ▷ Derek And The Dominos, ▷ Fats Domino.) Because the founders had moved through many bands – and the group went through dozens of changes. They moved from McPhatter's blues (1953–57) to Ben E. King's pop (1958–79) and had 12 different lead singers. The name was also used by the early ▷ Shadows. No relation to ▷ High Plain Drifters.

The Drones

Named in a tongue-in-cheek way, after the rudimentary noise they made. More influenced by ▷ The Banshees than ▷ The Buzzcocks.

The Droogs

Los Angeles 1970s garage band making reference to Anthony Burgess's book *A Clockwork Orange*, like ▷ Heaven 17, ▷ Korova Milkbar, ▷ The Mixers *et al*. The book's hero Alex is surrounded by a gang of "droogs". The word translates quite well as "dudes": the characters are hardly friends and will happily kick each other's faces in.

The Drowning Pool

They thought this 1975 murder mystery movie title was "really deep".

Drugstore

Brazilian singer Isobel Monteiro said: "We were going through some film titles and thought *Drugstore Cowboy* great. It goes beyond druggy connotations. It's this imaginary place where you can buy … pleasure or pain. It's open to interpretation."

D-Train

Tom Waits saw a *Downtown Train* full of Brooklyn girls; ▷ Bob Dylan had *Visions of Johanna* with escapades on the D-trains. The route was becoming rock history as these New Yorkers named after their local railway line.

The DTs

Oxford band named "because we can recognise symptoms of alcohol withdrawal". Their slogan: "Shake with the DTs". More medical bad taste: ▷ The Epileptics, ▷ St Vitus Dance.

Dubliners

Because they came from Dublin, Ireland; not primarily a reference to James Joyce's book.

Stephen "Tin Tin" Duffy

Duffy's hair was black not red, but he did have a quiff similar to the hero of *The Adventures of Tin-Tin* by Hergé, Georges Rémi. In a farcical dispute, Hergé moved to protect its "intellectual property" and "attendant earnings potential"; but how anyone could confuse the cartoon character with The Man Who Left ▷ Duran Duran Just Before They Made It Big is beyond comprehension. ▷ The Thompson Twins escaped heavy-handed legal threats from Hergé.

Unflattering derivative : Stephen "Duff Duff" Tinny, ▷ The Lilac Time.

Sly Dunbar

Noel Dunbar renamed in honour of Sly Stone of ▷ Sly And The Family Stone. ▷ Sly And Robbie.

The Duolian String Pickers

Named after a twangy instrument made by National Guitars. Included later members of ▷ Notting Hillbillies and ▷ Dire Straits; a National is pictured on 1985's *Brothers In Arms*.

Champion Jack Dupree

The Louisiana musician started as a boxer and retired an undefeated champion, *hence the name*.

Duran Duran

Vocalist Simon Le Bon (his birth name: "Simon The Good") said the Duran Duran tag was chosen because it meant nothing to most people so didn't tie them to an image.

It was taken by bassist John Taylor from the 1968 Roger Vadim cult classic film *Barbarella*, starring Jane Fonda, where Milo O'Shea plays a pervy, mad scientist called Durand Durand. Female spacefarer Barbarella was created five years before by Frenchman Jean-Claude Forest. Significantly, the young band played many gigs (1978 on) at the Barbarella Club in Birmingham, U.K.

All kept their original names with the exception of Nick Bates, who adopted the more exotic Rhodes, from the Aegean island. Later in their career (1988) they tried dropping one Duran from their name, then (*c.* 1989) were billed as duranduran. Spin-offs: ▷ Arcadia, ▷ The Power Station. Former member: ▷ Stephen "Tin Tin" Duffy. More double names: ▷ Talk Talk. Fans called: Durannies. They dubbed John Taylor "Mr Beautiful". Cf ▷ Japan's ▷ David Sylvian, "The World's Most Beautiful Man".

Durutti Column

Don't be misled by the columns on their record covers: this **isn't** an architectural term. The Durutti Column was an extreme left-wing faction described in Hugh Thomas's book *The Spanish Civil War*. The name was also used by a ruthless group of European anarchists, Situationiste Internationale, and it was from here the Mancunian group took their appellation. Three of them went on into ▷ Simply Red.

Ian Dury

After ▷ Kilburn And The High Roads, this singer has favoured ironic names. ▷ The Blockheads was followed by The Music Students. Dury's Lord Upminster nickname, used as a 1981 album title, comes from his Essex home.

The Bob Dylan Band

This was the self-effacing name for a New York group formed by ▷ Lloyd Cole. He explained they covered Dylan's *She Belongs To Me* – and he had learned to play the harmonica. The real ▷ Bob Dylan didn't take legal action.

Bob Dylan

The spokesman for a generation has said much, and eloquently. Yet he's uttered little on his name. And when he has, Dylan's given contradictory accounts of what it means (if anything) and where it comes from (if anywhere). This might show contempt for the journalist or journalism, indifference, boredom and/or a desire to weave new myths. Maybe, like his music, the name defies explanation; it just is. The following isn't an attempt to spoil the magic but an honest attempt to investigate.

Perhaps the strongest clue is an outburst from the great man after the publication of a "definitive" biography. In summary, he dismissed the "Dylan Thomas" theory and experts have now returned to the "favourite uncle" or "plucked from the air" explanations.

He was born Robert Allen Zimmerman, in Duluth, Minnesota, U.S.A. Could a man called Zimmerman have become world famous, you may wonder. Possibly yes, given the greatness of his songs. In the event, he didn't take the chance to find out. He was following ▷ Ethel Merman, a major star of the 1930s, who was born Ethel Agnes Zimmermann. A new name gave him the opportunity to create whatever background he desired, free from the identifier of being a middle-class Jewish kid. This made sense if he was to emulate ▷ Woody Guthrie and sing about paupers. The renaming also recalls ▷ Ramblin' Jack Elliott, who met Guthrie in the 1940s and recorded an album of his songs in 1960. Dylan concluded his poem *Advice For Geraldine On Her Miscellaneous Birthday* with the thought that one should never give one's real name.

Explanation one: he named after Dylan Thomas.

The usual and generally accepted theory, from the early 1960s on, reported by many papers and books, is that he adopted the surname in 1960 in honour of Welsh poet Dylan Thomas (1914–53). This relies on the poetry of Dylan's lyrics; he'd read Thomas while young. In addition, when working with Steve Goodman, Dylan chose to be known as Robert Milkwood Thomas in tribute to Thomas's play for voices *Under Milk Wood*.

Much of this is set out in Robert Shelton's 1986 biography *No Direction Home: The Life And Music Of Bob Dylan. Oh No! Not Another Bob Dylan Book*, 1991, by Patrick Humphries and John Bauldie, explicitly says: "Dylan Thomas had been dead for six years by the time Zimmerman hijacked his name." Dylan Thomas has influenced many rockers: Paul Simon, ▷ King Crimson and ▷ Frankie Goes To Hollywood have lifted quotes.

For years Dylan had little to say about Thomas. It had been assumed this was to disguise his indebtedness. After publication of the biography Dylan went out of his way to speak to Shelton to say: "I didn't take the name from Dylan Thomas." In a 1965 interview Dylan said: "I've read Thomas's stuff. It's not the same as mine." He also emphasised the difference between a lyric and a poem. In another interview he claimed doing more for the name Dylan than Thomas ever did. Paul Ferris's 1977 biography *Dylan Thomas* says: "Dylan was an obscure figure from the *Mabinogion*, the Welsh medieval prose romances. As a noun the word means 'sea' or 'ocean'." The young Zimmerman was not especially enamoured by the sea.

Explanation two: a television tie-in.

A less conventional alternative is that "Dylan" came from sheriff Matt Dillon in Dodge City, played by James Arness in U.S. TV western *Gunsmoke* (1955–75), later known as *Gun Law*. The theory came from unkind critics, suggesting the uncouth Zimmerman wasn't sophisticated enough to refer to Thomas. He'd certainly watched the programme, as thousands of American teenagers had done. Plus Dylan used the cowboy name Elston Gunn when working with ▷ Bobby Vee. Still, Dylan's own hints on this later, never explicit, look attempts to confuse people in the face of other rumours.

Explanation three: A favourite singer.

In the absence of confirmed theories, writer Ian Woodward has speculated it could be from an otherwise little-known 1950s folk singer called Dylan Todd. There's no proof, though Dylan was certainly seeking an authentic-sounding "down-and-out drifter's" appellation.

Explanation four: a favourite relative.

Evidence for the family theory comes in a direct quote from the winter 1965 interview – with the *Chicago Daily News* – already mentioned. Dylan said: "I took the name Dylan because I have an uncle named Dillion." He deliberately changed the spelling because it "looked better". It's surprising this explanation was not offered before, while it it possible Dylan wished to protect his family or found the truth too prosaic. The story gained little currency at the time because it was in a local paper, and scant credence because of the misleading *Gunsmoke*-style stories.

Explanation five: random choice.

The singer once said he just "plucked it out of the air" when applying for a gig at the Ten O'Clock Club in Minneapolis. "Dylan" has a sound not too far away from the syllabic end to "Zimmerman". So, failing the "uncle" version, this is the most conceivable.

Hence the name. Hence the mixed up confusion.

Dylan's other names:

His Bobness, to use his *Q* nickname, has played as Tedham Porterhouse (with Ramblin' Jack Elliott), ▷ Blind Boy Grunt, Roosevelt Cook (backing Tom Rush), Elmer Johnson, Big Joe's Buddy, Egg O'Schmullson and Keef Laundry. He took the part of Alias in the 1973 film *Pat Garrett And Billy The Kid* and played as part of the ad hoc superstar band ▷ The Traveling Wilburys as Lucky (1988) and Boo (1990). Nicknames: to many people, he is simply Bob or Dylan. He is also known as The Zim (from his surname), The Great White Wonder (title of legendary bootleg recording) and (less kindly as he gets older) Bob Zimmerframe.

Dylan's backing bands have often been nameless, apart from: ▷ The Band and The Hawks, The Billy 4, and The Rolling Thunder Revue, named after 1976 The Rolling Thunder Revue tour. ▷ Area Code 615 formed after backing him. His work inspired ▷ Dylan's Trashcan, ▷ fIREHOSE, ▷ Blonde On Blonde, ▷ John Wesley Harding, ▷ Mystery Trend, ▷ Starry Eyed And Laughing and ▷ The Weathermen. Contrary to many reports ▷ Judas Priest did **not** name from him. Some articles have said a Dylan track inspired ▷ Yazoo.

Not related: ▷ The Bob Dylan Band, ▷ BOB and ▷ The Dylans. Related: Jacob Dylan, his son, also a musician. Dylan's followers, who spend fortunes following his concerts round the world, style themselves as Bobcats.

There are so many Dylan books that to list all source material for this entry would take a long time. Apart from *The Telegraph*, the Dylan magazine, there's also Clinton Heylin's *Bob Dylan: Behind The Shades*, dating from 1991, and Daniel Kramer's *Bob Dylan: A Portrait Of The Artists's Early Years*, from 1992.

The Dylans

Vocalist Colin Gregory says: "It had to be The Dylans didn't it?" He suggests the Sheffield combo's name is a tribute to, first, the rabbit Dylan in the children's TV series *The Magic Roundabout*, and second, to ▷ Bob Dylan. Closer examination shows the second is the true explanation: the band admitted loving "Our Bob's Music".

Dylan's Trashcan

Short-lived 1980s band from Oxford University, U.K., named after the fascination with fans for ▷ Bob Dylan. One man, A.J. Weberman, has made something of a career of going through the superstar's garbage in a search for discarded lyrics or "clues" to the mysterious maestro's lifestyle.

Cf: ▷ Ned's Atomic Dustbin, ▷ the Trashcan Sinatras etc.

Napoleon Dynamite
▷ Elvis Costello.

Vince Eager
One of a wide range of 1950s stars named by entrepreneur ▷ Larry Parnes – often after cursory meetings on an initial indication of their personality. Roy Taylor's enthusiasm was the quality that first struck Parnes here.
Cf ▷ Tommy Steele etc.

Eagles
The band's precursors included Soul Survivors, North Serrano Blues Band, Teen King And The Emergencies and The Poor. Bassist Randy Meisner said of the latter: "We lost all our money and our house … We got to thinking what would be a good name for a band." (Cf ▷ Dire Straits, ▷ Willy And The Poorboys.)

The best account of the naming comes in Marc Shapiro's 1995 book *The Story Of The Eagles: The Long Run*.

Some versions say guitarist singer Glenn Frey came up with the name. Shapiro, however, credits fellow guitarist Bernie Leadon.

They wanted a simple, non-dating all-American word. The eagle is the symbol of the U.S., its currency and other countries. It had American Indian and astrological tie-ins. "In the Hopi mythology, the eagle is considered a sacred animal," Leadon said. "It symbolised the highest spirituality. I hoped the music would soar that high. Frey wanted a name that could have been a Detroit street gang and everybody wanted a name that was tough … Hey we're the fuckin' Eagles man!"

The "king of birds" came after dozens of other avian names: cf ▷ The Byrds. Joe Walsh arrived via ▷ James Gang.

Earth, Wind And Fire
Singer and co-founder Maurice White, on a world tour with Jimmy Reed, became fascinated with the three elements in astrology, mythology and Egyptology.

Easterhouse
This band from Manchester, U.K., named in solidarity with the residents of a rough and rundown area of Glasgow, Scotland.

East Of Eden
A Biblical story of Cain and Abel; a literary phrase from the time of Milton; a book title for John Steinbeck and a film in the 1950s; a band name in the 1970s. Steinbeck also inspired: ▷ The Grapes Of Wrath, ▷ The Tortilla Flats. The band denied the name was after ▷ Iron Butterfly's 1968 release *In-A-Gadda-Da-Vida*.

Sheena Easton
Sheena Shirley Orr, from Glasgow, Scotland, had a short marriage to singer Sandy Easton before hitting *The Big Time* on BBC television. Prince links: ▷ Joey Coco, ▷ Alexander Nevermind.

East 17
British 1990s teen sensations who named after the postal district of their London homes, E17.

Higham Hill and Walthamstow were never considered ... Cf ▷ Area Code 615.

Clint Eastwood And The General Saint
▷ Clint.

Easybeats
Many American bands pretended to be British after the British invasion led by ▷ The Beatles. (Cf ▷ Beau Brummels, ▷ Sir Douglas Quintet etc.) This Australian band tried the same trick, with some success, after adding a Liverpool-born member.
▷ The Merseybeats.

Echo And The Bunnymen
Crazy name, crazy group.

There's controversy and curiosity about the moniker, sparked by the band's evasiveness. According to some, a friend called Paul Ellenbach kept suggesting strange soubriquets, such as Glisserol And The Fan Extractors and Echo And The Bunnymen – which was chosen for no particular reason.

The outfit was formed quickly as a support for ▷ The Teardrop Explodes. There wasn't much time to find a billing for what was planned as a short-lived unit. Guitarist Will Sergeant was on record as saying he always thought the alias too off-the-wall, cutting airplay in America. Vocalist Ian McCulloch commented the appellation would counteract pretentiousness.

The 1978-vintage group had a drum kit which they christened Echo – perhaps to prevent a leader developing. They may have been thinking of their home city paper, *The Liverpool Echo*. Pete de Freitas later took over drum duties, until his death. "Mac" denied *he* was Echo, a claim proved when the full designation was kept after his departure for a solo career at one point.

The "Bunnymen" tag also provides false trails. Suggestions seem doubtful about "bunny girls" or talkative people who "rabbit" a lot. Another theory refers to *White Rabbit* by ▷ Jefferson Airplane. More plausible is the explanation of the *New Musical Express*'s Dave Quantick who declared: "The Bunnymen bit is the result of too much dope."

McCulloch's first band, in 1977, was The Crucial Three with fellow Liverpudlians Pete Wylie (▷ Wah!) and Julian Cope (▷ The Teardrop Explodes). McCulloch and Cope also worked in A Shallow Madness – a most revealing handle.
Hence the name. Hence the far-out lyrics.

Echobelly
Sonya Aurora Madan was interviewed for Amy Raphael's 1995 book *Never Mind The Bollocks: Women Rewrite Rock*.

She said of the name: "The name Echobelly existed before the band. I wanted a word that was quite female and organic and voluptuous, and Echobelly had it. It also had the meaning of being hungry for something, which I thought was quite potent. I wanted something almost birth-like. We [Madan and Glen Johansson] just sat together and wrote all these names down and it stuck out. I like the idea of a word that doesn't actually mean anything by itself but which expresses succinctly that we're doing."

The U.K.-based band formed in 1992 and broke through with their debut EP *Bellyache* and album *Everybody's Got One* (it's an acronym).
Cf ▷ Belly.

Eclection
That's eclection, not election. As in eclectic, "borrowing freely from various sources". Which is what this folk group did, with all its members from widely differing U.K., U.S. and Australian backgrounds.

Related bands: ▷ Fotheringay, ▷ Fairport Convention.

The Edge
Guitarist successively with (commercially unsuccessful) ▷ Feedback and ▷ The Hype; then with (wildly successful) ▷ U2, he was born David Evans in London, of Welsh parents. The name came during his teenage years in Dublin, and was suggested by ▷ Bono, then an active member of "The Village" youth community.

Among reasons given for this name:
1. Dave, with his Welsh background and different outlook on life was on the edge of "The Village" community.
2. He was also quiet, watching and listening on

the fringe rather than joining in conversations.

3. His mind was sharp.
4. His head was angular.
5. He was like The Edge, the hero of Western novels by George Gilman.

Unflattering derivative: The Hedge.

Obviously, no relation to Edge, a band formed by members of ▷ The Damned after a short-lived band split in 1978, and including Jon Moss, who went on into ▷ Culture Club.

For more see Eamon Dunphy's 1988 biography *Unforgettable Fire – The Story of U2*

Edsels

Band from Ohio who reportedly named after a Ford car. Cf: ▷ The Cortinas, ▷ Thin Lizzy.

Edward Bear

The original name for Milne's Winnie the Pooh character. More Milne: ▷ Pooh Sticks.

Efua

Efua means "Girl born on a Friday" in Ghanaian, although neither of her parents are from that country. They just liked the name. Her father is a Cuban-born Jamaican and her mother an Englishwoman of Russian Jewish extraction. 1990s pretender to the singing crown shared by the likes of the also singularly named ▷ Sade and ▷ Enya.

Ege Bam Yasi

From *Ege Bamyasi*, the 1972 album by German act ▷ Can. The London-based 1980s dance-technopop outfit, with Pimlico Jones on guitar, released a record called *Circumstance*.

The name of the album originally came from a can of okra vegetables found in a Turkish restaurant.

Eggs Over Easy

Not a meaningless term, as one U.K. rock encyclopedia states, but from an American phrase meaning turned-over fried eggs.

The Egyptians

The name was not apt because they were British, but it reflected their interest in mythology.

Related band: ▷ The Soft Boys.

18 Wheeler

Singer Sean Jackson told *Q* magazine this 1990s Scottish combo named after "a gay black truckers' porn mag in the 1970s which featured enormously endowed men and their vehicles. We found it in a catalogue of exotic literature, although we've never seen a copy."

8th Day

God spent a busy week making the world then took it easy for a day. This band took as their slogan: "Today is the first day of the rest of your life."

Eighth Wonder

How to succeed in pop lesson one: say there are the seven wonders of the world, and then there's you. Patsy Kensit was not scared to say this. She later married Jim Kerr of ▷ Simple Minds and then Liam Gallagher of ▷ Oasis.

808 State

It sounds like a zip or phone number (▷ Area Code 615). Mancunian Martin Price took it from an early Roland beat box in preference to The Hit Squad.

801

▷ Roxy Music's Phil Manzanera took it from the lyric of ex-colleague ▷ Brian Eno's *True Wheel* on 1974's *Taking Tiger Mountain*. Related acts: ▷ Curved Air, ▷ Matching Mole.

Einstürzende Neubauten

These Berliners used drills, girders and power tools for a grating beat which was "like the sound of new buildings being demolished". The name translates as "collapsing new buildings". Their first album, from 1982, was *Kollaps*.

Eire Apparent

Most people think it cringeworthy. Still, this Irish band – who also considered Eire Today – thought the patriotically punning name "hilarious".

Eldritch

The black-clad Gothic prince of ▷ Sisters Of Mercy fame surprisingly wasn't born wearing shades in a bat-infested Berlin belfry but was plain Andrew Taylor in Leeds, U.K. Eldritch means "poetic, weird, uncanny, unearthly".

The Electric Light Orchestra (ELO)

This U.K. band was initially the brainchild of Birmingham musical ▷ Wizzard Roy Wood, who wanted to move on from ▷ The Move.

The aim was to develop Wood's interest in the orchestral rock explored by ▷ The Beatles with *I Am The Walrus* and *A Day In The Life*. He wanted to carry on where they left off, combine "jazz and classically influenced" tunes with classical themes, electric instruments with cellos, violins and instruments usually found in a classical orchestra. *Hence the name.*

The pun is continued via album titles such as *Light Years Ahead* and covers depicting light bulbs. The abbreviated name continues the classical orchestra trend for abbreviating names to initials, as in LPO, CBSO, etc. "Light" was the term used by the BBC for all pop and non-classical music played on the radio "light service" channel prior to its being split into Radio 1, originally for pop, and Radio 2, for popular tunes. (Radio 3, for classical, was similarly called "the music service", as if the rest wasn't music, and speech-based Radio 4 was ▷ The Home Service.)

Main band leader Jeff Lynne (ex ▷ Idle Race), after drawing the ELO story to an effective end, freelanced, did sessions and produced before jointly helping to form the 1987 supergroup ▷ The Traveling Wilburys under the name Otis Wilbury (later becoming Clayton).

ELO continued without him, led by drummer Bev Bevan, under the name Electric Light Orchestra Part II.

Electric Prunes

The Seattle surrealists explained: "electric" came from their instruments: and it wasn't derogatory to be called a prune in the 1960s.

The Electric Warrior

Nickname for ▷ Marc Bolan, from the 1971 ▷ T Rex album of the same name.

Electronic

This band briefly brought together musicians from ▷ The Pet Shop Boys, ▷ The Smiths and ▷ New Order into "A ▷ Blind Faith for the 1990s". They said the name "explains our aims" – to marry computerised keyboards, beatbox and guitar into a new whole.

Bernard "Barney" Sumner said he got the idea when someone spiked his drink in a loud New York nightclub and all of a sudden "this electronic music made sense".

After a one-off single and an eponymous album the core duo, Sumner and Johnny Marr, reunited for a second album in 1996.

Elephant's Memory

These New Yorkers wanted to be like an elephant's memory: very big and lasting for ever. Despite work with ▷ John Lennon they didn't live up to this promise.

Elevation

Like ▷ Marquee Moon and ▷ Friction, named after a track on ▷ Television's debut LP.

Elixir

"We mean the elixir for superhuman ability." Cf ▷ Ambrosia.

Duke Ellington

Another music "aristocrat" along with other "kings", "lords" etc, he was born in Washington as plain Edward Ellington. He acquired the nickname as a child because of his "upper-class" bearing and dress. His father was a White House butler. Most musical "aristocrats" got their names only later as they rose to the top of their profession. Arguably, Ellington was at the top from the start.

Ramblin' Jack Elliott

… was born Elliott Charles Adnopoz. He knew you couldn't sing ▷ Woody Guthrie songs such as *Dust Pneumonia Blues* convincingly if it emerged you're the son of a famous physician. The romantic ramblin' referred to his life on tour, although he could afford good hotels and cars.

Elmerhassell

A minor character from a major beat generation novel of sex, freedom and jazz, *On The Road*. Narrator Sal Paradise says Elmer Hassel is a "slinking criminal" with "a hip sneer". Jack

Kerouac is said to have named him after one Herbert Hunke. Cf ▷ The Dharma Bums.

ELO

Not an English North country greeting ('ello), but an abbreviation (E.L.O.) for ▷ the Electric Light Orchestra.

ELP

Keith Emerson, Greg Lake and Carl Palmer felt they were so famous they didn't need a proper name for their supergroup. Later E and L linked with strategically named drummer Cozy Powell.

Related: ▷ Asia, ▷ King Crimson.

Elvis The Pelvis

▷ Elvis Presley, ▷ The Pelvis.

Emanon

No, not Eamonn, Emanon. ▷ Manfred Mann offshoot, a jazz outfit. Why the name? It's simply "no name" backwards.

Cf ▷ Emmenon.

Emerson, Lake And Palmer

▷ ELP.

EMF

Singer James Atkins was vague about the initials, telling journalists surely they knew what it meant. This led to reports it stood for Electro Motive Force.

The real answer, with apologies (but not many – anyone with any sense would know some names are rude) ... the band's concerts included a chant which usually started off as "Epsom Mad Funkers" and degenerated into "Ecstasy Mother Fuckers".

Emmenon

▷ Madonna being offensive with her first band. Emmenology means menstruation. They later became Emmy, a name with less emotional baggage but too close to the name of the U.S. TV awards.

The Emoticons

Emoticons are used by computer geeks sending e-mail messages. They are pictures made up of punctuation marks, viewed by turning the image on its side. Thus :-) is a smile, :-(is unhappy, ;-) its winking equivalent, 0:-) is a saintly figure and so on. This British band thought it an interestingly up-to-date marriage of emotion and technology.

Empress Of The Blues

▷ The Queen Of The Blues is a title claimed by a number of stars. As the field became crowded, supporters of the most-fancied candidate, Bessie Smith, upgraded her title to fend off lesser pretenders.

England's Glory

Peter Perrett in his days before forming ▷ The Only Ones. The name was a patriotic reference to the long-established make of matches sold in the U.K.

The English Beat

▷ The Beat (U.K.)

The Enid

The Enid; later just Enid. The obscurity of the in-joke nickname, never fully explained, says it all. This much-praised, long-lasting yet commercially unsuccessful band rarely strived for accessibility.

Eno

British keyboard genius who was born Brian Peter George St John (le) Baptiste de la Salle Eno. The abbreviation mirrors similar moves by double-barrelled members of ▷ Queen and ▷ The Rolling Stones. He was a mainspring behind ▷ The Warm Jets and ▷ Roxy Music. No relation to ENO (English National Opera). ▷ Portsmouth Sinfonia. He inspired ▷ 801 and worked with ▷ David Bowie, ▷ Talking Heads (▷ King's Lead Hat) and ▷ U2, where he used an anagram to become Ben O'Rian for the Passengers project.

John Entwistle

▷ Ox, ▷ Rigor Mortis, ▷ The Who.

En Vogue

This U.S. soul act named after French fashion, "the coolest in the world". Cf ▷ Depeche Mode.

Enya

She was born Eithne Ni Bhraonain, renamed the non-Gaelic Brennan as the rest of the family did for showbiz work (▷ Clannad) and became Enya as the closest Anglicisation. Like ▷ Sting, ▷ Madonna and others, she's now a single-name artist.

Epileptics

Band with usual punk desire to shock. Instead of going down the "flirt with Nazism" route, this lot tried mocking others. The British Epilepsy Association objected and they became Epi-X then ▷ Flux Of Pink Indians.

EPMD

Formed by Erick Semon and Parrish Smith. Optimistically stands for Erick And Parrish Making Dollars.

Erasure

Vince Clarke is said to have chosen this name because "erasure is more important than recording in the studio".
▷ Depeche Mode.

Esperanto

Named after the international language created by a Warsaw linguist in 1887, it roughly translates as "hope".

Esquerita

He telescoped his real name Eskew Reeder. The now all-but-forgotten 1950s rock 'n' roll star deserves better than his epitaph as the man who tried to out-do ▷ Little Richard.

Gloria Estefan

Gloria Fajardo married Emilio Estefan, a fellow member of ▷ Miami Sound Machine.

Sleepy John Estes

U.S. bluesman who suffered from a medical condition which sapped his energy and eyesight.

The "E" Street Band

Backing band for ▷ Bruce Springsteen. E Street was the road where original keyboardist David Sancious's mother lived in Belmar, New Jersey. Springsteen's second album was 1974's *The Wild, The Innocent And The E. Street Shuffle.*

Etchingham Steam Band

Spin-off from ▷ Fairport Convention, named after an old traction engine.

Ethiopians

The name is less misleading than it may seem. Strictly speaking, this group should have been The Jamaicans. They all had strong Rastafarian beliefs, so they had no compunction in naming themselves after the people of their adopted homeland.
Cf ▷ Abyssinians.

Eurythmics

Eurhythmics was a regime of rhythmical bodily movements developed in the early twentieth century by Professor Jacques-Dalcroze in France. The system of gymnastic dancing exercises with a musical accompaniment was used to teach rhythm and time. The spelling soon changed, says *The Oxford English Dictionary*.

Annie Lennox and David Stewart thought the name interesting – although the duo's seditious electronic grooves and sexy lyrics were more suitable for nightclub dancing than classroom. They were previously members of ▷ The Amazing Blondel and ▷ The Tourists; both went solo later. Stewart used the credit David A. Stewart to avoid confusion with another Dave Stewart (ex ▷ Hatfield And The North).

Vince Everett

Rock 'n' roll singer Martin Benefield purloined the name of ▷ Elvis Presley character in the 1959 film *Jailhouse Rock*.

Everything But The Girl

A certain Yankee-style second-hand furniture and *bric-à-brac* shop in Hull, U.K., bore a sign saying: "For your bedroom needs we sell everything but the girl." Despite the chauvinistic reference, the shop was a favourite of students Tracey Thorn and Ben Watt, who were at the city's university studying English.

One version of the story claims the shop was having a closing-down sale at the time (wrong).

Another says that everything was for sale but the staff (true, while the "girl" was actually a dummy in the window holding the sign).

The name was obviously potentially misleading for a male-female duo; yet it was also apt, reflecting the soon inseparable Thorn and Watt's not-for-sale feminist concerns. Both had also recorded separately under their actual names. Related bands: ▷ The Marine Girls, ▷ Grab Grab The Haddock. Best reference: Cherry Red's 1996 re-released *Pillows And Prayers*, at last on CD.

Excalibur

Named from the sword-and-stone legend of King Arthur (not the model of U.S. car).

Exciter

Canadian three-piece band named after the classic ▷ Judas Priest song *Exciter*, best heard on the 1979 live album *Unleashed In The East*.

The Ex-Pensive Winos

Unofficial name for the backing group for ▷ Rolling Stone ▷ Keith Richards's *Talk Is Cheap* tour, promoting the eponymous LP. Named in lousy 1970s Marquee jam style, but in the words of Keef: "It's all clever stuff!"

You see, it was chosen after he found three of them guzzling a big bottle of ultra-expensive Lafitte Rothschild behind the drum kit during rehearsals. Rebel Yell tippler Richards told them he was spending all his money on winos. They told him it takes one to know one: "We're winos man – but at least we're *expensive* winos!" (He approved; the rest is history.)

Music journalists have sometimes spelled this name as X-Pensive Winos. Like Richards or Richard, it doesn't seem to matter very much.

Exploding White Mice

Mice have provided the inspiration for some very silly musical names: Eek-A-Mouse (who was born Ripton Joseph Hylton), Deep Freeze Mice and this lot to name three. This group liked ▷ The Ramones, played Ramones style

music and named after the mice who go pop in the 'Mones film *Rock 'N' Roll High School*.

Extreme

These hard rock musos stalled as they were overtaken by grunge – music even extreme than they were playing. Yet their creed was supposedly in their name: Extreme wanted to "take music to its limits".

Extreme Noise Terror

A thrash combo of the 1980s on, their appellation describes their feedback din which was more noisy than musical. It was taken from a newspaper headline, "extreme noise danger", warning that listening to rock at loud volume on headphones could cause deafness and tinnitus.

Exultation Of Larks

A better bird collective than ▷ A Flock of Seagulls. There were also a Murder Of Crows (not to mention a Counting Crows and Black Crows).

Gets a Beech Award for an impressive name. Possibly after ▷ King Crimson's album *Larks' Tongues In Aspic*.

EYC

Stood for Express Yourself Clearly. Possibly a reference to ▷ Madonna's hit *Express Yourself*.

Eyeless In Gaza

English poet John Milton's verse play *Samson Agonistes*, dating from 1671, enlarges on the Biblical story of Samson after he is made captive, blinded, and put in the prison at Gaza. Milton was blind himself as he dictated the work to his family.

These words, in Samson's opening speech, were also used as the title of British writer Aldous Huxley's 1936 novel about pacifism, *Eyeless In Gaza*. Huxley, of course, also provided the inspiration for ▷ The Doors and name of ▷ The Feelies is said to show his influence.

1980s band on U.K. independent Cherry Red label.

Fab Four

▷ The Beatles, ▷ Prefab Four.

Fabian

Fabiano Forte Bonaparte, from Philadelphia, U.S., anglicised his name like his friend ▷ Frankie Avalon, and became one of the first big "single name" stars.

The Fabulous Poodles

Taken from a magazine headline on the winners of a dog show fur-cutting contest "because it was ridiculous". "Poodle" is in some slang dictionaries as meaning "a ladies' man", though this was a secondary consideration.

Fabulous Thunderbirds

Taken from the car, although the name was used as a reference to the Gerry Anderson puppet show series *Thunderbirds*, with its 1960s catchphrase "F.A.B" for fabulous.

The Faces

A "face" was a luminary in the British beat subculture world of the swinging sixties. ▷ The Small Faces were minor celebrities of the genre, named partly from their physical stature. After a shake-up they felt confident to rename, so growing in stature in the fame game. The first time they played with Rod Stewart in 1969, they used the abortive name Quiet Melon (thankfully, swiftly rejected). Spin-off: ▷ Slim Chance.

Factory

The Manchester record label was home to ▷ Joy Division and ▷ New Order but missed ▷ The Smiths, ▷ The Stone Roses and ▷ Oasis. It collapsed in the 1980s and risen again as Factory Too. Some reports said it was christened after Andy Warhol's New York arts collective. In fact promoter Alan Wise suggested it as a club name to entrepreneur Anthony H. Wilson after seeing a sign which said: "Factory clearance." See *The Factory Story* by Mick Middles.

Sammy Fain

Anglicisation of Samuel Feinberg.

Fairer Sax

"Obvious but dubious" pun by this all-female saxophonist band.

Fairground Attraction

The band, name and travelling fair visual image were built around Mark Nevin's acoustic songs. Cf ▷ The Attractions.

Fairport Convention

1967 : The tale starts at a home in Fortis Green, Muswell Hill, North London. This large detached house had a general medical practice on the ground floor and the rest was let out to lodgers. It was owned by a widow of one of the doctors, who allowed her son Simon's band to rehearse in the attic. And the point of this story? The woman was called Mrs Nicol, her son was guitarist Simon Nicol, the house was called Fairport, and hence Simon's band became Fairport Convention.

1968–71 : As they became an acclaimed folk-rock act, Tyger Hutchings transmuted into a more traditional Ashley Hutchings. They hid their real names backing Al Stewart on 1969's *Love Chronicles*, Richard Thompson for example becoming Marvin Prestwick.

1976 : The band name was briefly formally abbreviated to Fairport after years of being informally called such.

Spin-off and related bands include : ▷ The Albion Band, ▷ The Cocktail Cowboys, ▷ Etchingham Steam Band, ▷ Fotheringay, ▷ The GPs, ▷ Matthews Southern Comfort, ▷ The Pheasant Pluckers, ▷ Plainsong, ▷ Steeleye Span and ▷ Whippersnapper. The band probably inspired ▷ The Men They Couldn't Hang.

For more see Patrick Humphries's *Meet On The Ledge*, now updated.

Fair Weather
From Andy Fairweather-Low, attempting to find fairweather friends after his teenybopper days with ▷ Amen Corner.

Adam Faith
Born Terence Nelhams, London, his first appearance was with the skiffle group The Working Men. He ploughed through books of boys' and girls' prenomens for stage names. He played a role in the renaming of ▷ Sandie Shaw and helped ▷ Leo Sayer to find his moniker.

Faith No More
These San Francisco residents' name sounds profound – while explanations are rarely so. At one stage they claimed it was a greyhound on which they placed a large winning bet – while this is now accepted to be a tall story, on a par with their many practical jokes. Instead, bassist Bill Gould recalls: "At first we were called Sharp Young Men but that was just too hokey, we wanted something cryptic. So it came to be called Faith No Man." Mike Morris was the singer, known as "The Man" because he was older; he was later sacked amid "musical differences".

An old friend of Gould, Will Carpmill,

suggested a revision as revenge on Morris, seeing "The Man" was no more. They subsequently had Chuck Mosely and Mike Patton as ever-more-outrageous figureheads. Another aspiring vocalist (who failed the audition) was ▷ Courtney Love. (▷ Hole, ▷ Nirvana.) There's more in the detailed *Faith No More: The Real Story*, by Steffan Chirazi (1994).

The Fall
Mancunian Mark E. Smith took it from the novel by Frenchman Albert Camus (1913–60), the last published in the author's lifetime and arguably his best. The 1956 book reflects the Bible story of the first sin and man's expulsion from the Garden of Eden. The appellation caused confusion in the U.S.A., where it was thought to refer to the autumn. Spin-off: ▷ The Adult Net. See also ▷ The Smiths. Smith is sometimes referred to as Mark-ah E-ah Smith-ah because of his singing pronunciation which emphasises the end of each line-ah.

Georgie Fame
This was one of the names manufactured by U.K. entrepreneur ▷ Larry Parnes, who gave his stars similar monikers. In this case he was confident keyboardist Clive Powell would be famous. He had joined The Blue Flames, who at first backed ▷ Billy Fury before supporting Fame himself.

Family
They formed in 1962 as The Farinas and renamed Family at the suggestion of producer Kim Fowley. Their communal life was reflected in Jenny Fabian's *Groupie* book and their own album *Music In A Doll's House*.

Related bands: ▷ Blind Faith, ▷ Traffic, ▷ Streetwalkers. Not related: ▷ Prince's The Family.

The Family Cat
An "ordinary," "everyday" name along the lines of ▷ The Smiths or ▷ The Birthday Party. Chosen as the opposite to rivals Wild Dogs.

The Family von Trapp
Scottish band *c.* 1980 founded by Muriel Gray

and named after the subjects of *The Sound Of Music*, Baron Georg von Trapp and his happy family.

Famous Potatoes

Novelty act who named because their "rootsy, underground" audience-pleasing sound was called soil music. LPs include *Dig (It)* and *The Sound of the Ground*, the latter a rip-off of ▷ Human League's *Sound of the Crowd*.

Fanny

Their record company ditched the appellation Wild Honey in favour of this, spelling out the *double entendre* by promoting them as "the first female rock band". This was 1969, when phallicism and sexism were less widely understood. The name was reportedly suggested by no less than ▷ Beatle ▷ George Harrison, probably to his eternal shame. Cf ▷ The Slits.

Fantastic Four

Comic inspiration for this band, one down from Enid Blyton's *The Famous Five*.

The Farm

From Walton Farm in the band's native Liverpool. It's known for its links with Robert Tressel (pen name of Robert Noonan), who wrote *The Ragged Trousered Philanthropists*, published posthumously in 1914. This book is one of the British socialist gospels, an account of the self-help of a group of building workers. It was read by guitarist Keith Mullen at 15, while vocalist Peter Hooton said they wanted to express "The Soul of Socialism".

Embarrassingly for the band, it emerged that the book – always on sale at Labour Party conference book stalls – was also a favourite of Conservative Prime Minister John Major. Their record label is called Produce.

The Farmers Boys

British early 1980s group, at one stage always the band-most-likely-to, but the band-who-never-were, named in jest after their rural Norfolk background. Cf ▷ The Pet Shop Boys (late 1980s, city background, band-who-always were).

Perry Farrell

Was born in Queen's, New York as Perry Bernstein. He renamed Farrell, after his brother's first name, to make a pun on "peripheral". The name behind ▷ Jane's Addiction, Lollapalooza and ▷ Porno For Pyros.

Faster Pussycat

Heavy metal group of the 1980s – yet another feline name (▷ Def Leppard, ▷ Tygers Of Pan Tang etc). Yet another band named after a movie too. In this case, *Faster Pussycat! Kill! Kill!*, now seen as one of the great cult films. The 1966 flick helped erotic film director Russ Meyer to break into the big time thanks to its fetishist and sci-fi overtones and part of its kitsch appeal is that it has aged terribly. More Meyer inspiration: ▷ Mudhoney etc.

Fastway

Taken from leaders "Fast" Eddie Clarke (ex ▷ Motörhead) and Pete Way (ex ▷ UFO, soon to join ▷ Ozzy Osbourne). Almost as bad a pun as Way's ▷ Waysted.

The Fat Boys

From their size and backing of similarly large ▷ Chubby Checker on a remake of *The Twist*.

Father Of The Blues

William Handy composed famous songs such as *Memphis Blues* and bestowed the title on himself.

Fatima Mansions

Irish rockers referring to a badly named Dublin housing estate, where their run down homes had deteriorated from the mansions they once were.

The Fat Lady Sings

These four Irish folksters are quite thin males. They chose the name precisely because it was misleading in a ▷ Les Negresses Vertes way. At least one journalist thought it was a tribute to some obscure 1960s chanteuse. It was from the phrase "it isn't over until the fat lady sings": at the end of baseball games a lady used to sing the National Anthem. It has come to refer to any show, contest or sporting event which "isn't over until it's over".

Fat Mattress

Noel Redding founded the band as a break from his day job as bassist of ▷ The Jimi Hendrix Experience. He told underground papers of the late 1960s that the new project was to provide music which people would recline on, like a soft bed, to ease their cares away.

Fat Tony

Hi to Fat Tony, who became one of London's best club DJs and … fairly thin person. Explanation: Anthony Marnoch was 17 stone and people called him Fat Tony behind his back. At 21 he had glandular fever and lost it all but thought Fat Tony "a good name" and kept it.

Faust

A medieval legend tells of a man who gained skills by handing his soul to Satan. In the sixteenth century it was attached to conjuror Johann Faust (1488–1541). Hence literature by Marlowe, Goethe and Mann. Also music by Spohr, Wagner, Schumann, Liszt, Gounod … and *Faust* by Faust – not a masterpiece of German prog-rock but with an identical heritage.

Feedback

The first name for the famous ▷ U2, formed after drummer Larry Mullen Junior placed a notice appealing for fellow musicians on a notice board in his Dublin school. Bassist Adam Clayton was competent but the band named from the screeching noise that came from his portable amplifier. ▷ The Hype.

The Feelies

Mid-1980s American band who took the name from a children's blindfold "guess the object" contest. They said the name didn't come directly from Aldous Huxley's 1932 masterpiece *Brave New World*, although they knew the book. He suggested that as movies were replaced by talkies, so modern film might be replaced by feelies, in which audiences could experience sensations felt by the actors.

Felt

This British 1980s act's ▷ Velvet Underground reference was the past participle of to feel or experience. An excellent pun, on a par with ▷ The Herd.

The Fendermen

U.S. 1960s duo behind *Mule Skinner Blues* who both played Fender guitars.

Shane Fenton And The Fentones

Londoner Bernard Jewry became Shane Fenton in the 1960s, seeking a U.S.-sounding name; unfortunately the And The Fentones name sounded about ten years out of date. Come the 1970s and retro-chic was getting acceptable; he made it as ▷ Alvin Stardust.

Byron Ferrari

Or ▷ Bryan Ferry. This derivative was sneeringly coined by *NME* as Bry, as he is sometimes known, continued with his cocktail-bar-lounge-lizard-tux look while punk revolted into a new style.

Bryan Ferry

Solo and ▷ Roxy Music star, ▷ Byron Ferrari icon.

FFW

These Germans specialising in weird satire were "Freaky Fuckin' Weirdos". The record company insisted on its emasculation to the incomprehensible FFW.

Fiat Lux

Nothing to do with luxury Italian cars. These Britons used Latin "let there be light" from *Genesis*'s opening.

Fields Of The Nephilim

The name came from *The Nephilim*, on this U.K. band's first album, 1987's *Dawn Razor*. It fitted their spaghetti western image and Clint Eastwood-cowboy-meets ▷ Andrew Eldritch-garb. AKA The Nephs, pronounced "nefs". After a split they became The Nefilim and The Rubicon.

The Fifth Dimension

Before this Los Angeles five-piece went *Up, Up And Away*, they were The Versatiles, then the Hi-Fis – names declared "dated" by record boss Johnny Rivers. Vocalist Ron Townson said they could salute their five interests: pop, jazz, classical, gospel and folk.

Band from Vancouver, Canada, whose name attacked U.S. colonialism. "Fifty-four forty or fight" was the presidential campaign slogan of James K. Polk, who promised to go to war unless Canada accepted his territorial demands.

Fine Young Cannibals

Founded by graduates of ▷ The (English) Beat, with gifted young vocalist Roland Gift from The Akrylix. Guitarist Andy Cox said he tossed aside a well-thumbed thesaurus and found the title in a book called *Jazz In The Movies*. The 1960 MGM film *All The Fine Young Cannibals* is about how two naïfs find New York a culture shock.

Cox said the selection was greeted with unanimous approval: "It was so weird that nobody would sue us over it." In fact, a garage band called The Cannibals took action, though the case was soon dismissed. A single later appeared by a group called Five Young Cannibals, and went nowhere.

Misguided critics who thought it was something to do with violence also made a meal of the 1988 album title *The Raw And The Cooked*, actually a reference to French anthropologist Claude Lévi-Strauss. The band soon became FYC, avoiding controversy.

▷ Guinness, ▷ 2 Men, A Drum Machine And A Trumpet. For more see Brian Edge's 1991 book *The Sweet And The Sour*.

The Fire Engines

The aftermath of punk saw this anarchistic Scottish band name in tribute to nihilists of a different time: ▷ The 13th Floor Elevators, who had a song about fire engines.

fIREHOSE

▷ Bob Dylan used D.A. Pennebaker's 1967 film *Don't Look Back* to make one of the first pop videos. As *Subterranean Homesick Blues* plays, he casually discards cards of the key words including "fIREHOSE".

This U.S. band was formed by two of ▷ The Minutemen in the 1980s. They wanted to get a clip of the film with Dylan "advertising" their band 20 years before formation. The odd capitalisation was carried across to many of the band's song titles and their own names. The same Dylan track inspired ▷ The Weathermen. No relation to Firehouse.

The Firm

A Jimmy Page post ▷ Led Zeppelin band, formed with Paul Rodgers. The name has sexual overtones and means a business. In addition, Page tells Stephen Davis in the 1985 book *Hammer Of The Gods*: "The term 'The Firm' in England is when all the boys go out together at night, without the wives or girlfriends." No relation to the outfit behind novelty singles such as *Arthur Daley*.

First Cow Over The Moon

Based on a child confusing "first man on the moon" and the cow "jumping over the moon" nursery rhyme.

The First Lady of Jazz

Usually said to be Ella Fitzgerald, America's First Lady of Song; however, another hotly contested title.

Fish

Singer with ▷ Marillion, later solo. "Fish" is sometimes used as an insult for women but this Scottish forestry student wasn't bothered. He tells the story on *The Funny Farm Interview*, recorded in July 1995 for his information club The Company: "I was at school with the moniker 'Derek William Dick' ... I used to get really upset with 'Dirty Dick', 'Dicky Bird' and stuff like that."

He was working at Fochabers, Grampian, where his landlady, a Mrs Fraser, objected to the number of baths he was taking. In protest "I would go in with my cans of beer and my radio and my books and sat there for two and a half hours in the bath. One night a friend hung about waiting for me to come out and he said: 'Are you some sort of fish or something?' and I said: 'That's it'. I just could not imagine being introduced on stage as Derek Dick ... it just doesn't work."

He later founded the Dick Brothers record label.

Name notes:

1. Absolutely no relation to ▷ County Joe McDonald And The Fish, ▷ The Fish. Also no relation to Fish, drummer in Los Angeles

band Fishbone, or the bands Phish and Citizen Fish.

2. Another famous "Dick" in rock is Paul Revere Dick. He also discarded his surname. ▷ Paul Revere And The Raiders. Then there's Mike Dick, who became better known to the world as ▷ Byrds drummer Michael Clarke.

The Fish

Barry Melton's name came from a Chairman Mao quote about revolutionaries being like fish in water. ▷ Country Joe McDonald, ▷ The Dinosaurs. No relation to ▷ Fish.

Five Guys Called Moe

Five Guys Called Moe is a track by 1940s jazzman Louis Jordan and a musical which starred fives guys all named Moe: Big Moe, Four-Eyed Moe, Little Moe, No Moe and Eat Moe. It has also been purloined by a four-piece band, three guys and a girl and none called Moe, in 1980s ▷ Fat Lady Sings misleading style.

Five Imaginary Boys

▷ The Cure have played "secret" gigs at small venues which would be overwhelmed if they advertised under their usual name. The hope was that only dedicated fans will spot the reference to their song *Three Imaginary Boys*.

Five Star

These siblings of the Pearson family from Romford, Essex, were aspiring "five stars" – the international term to signify the best hotels, restaurants and service.

Five Thirty

London 1990s band determined to avoid the rat race and the daily grind of faceless 9 to 5 employment. They said, "5.30 p.m. is the time everybody goes home and gets ready to go out."

The Fixx

This British band began as The Banana Boats (trouble – racist allegations), became The Portraits (trouble – another band of similar name) and then The Fix (trouble – seen as a drug reference). It was intended as a slightly obscure "fixing it" ▷ Cure name. They hadn't made the obvious link with "fixing" an addict's craving by taking more. An "X" was added to make it less X-rated.

Roberta Flack

Her real name, but she self-produced her LP *Feel Like Makin' Love* – and others – under the name Rubina Flake "to avoid the flack".

Flag Of Convenience

▷ Buzzcocks spin-off who used a naval term, saying any name is "like a flag of convenience to allow you protection".

The Flamin Groovies

This U.S. band combined fashionable words in (another) bid to recreate swinging sixties London and sound British. Inspired ▷ The Teenage Heads.

Flatt And Scruggs

Using their real names, this U.S. act styled themselves: "Lester Flatt and Earl Scruggs, purveyors of bluegrass to the gentry".

Flea

Member of ▷ The Red Hot Chili Peppers "who scratched a lot".

Fleetwood Mac

When ▷ Eric Clapton quit John Mayall's ▷ Bluesbreakers, he was replaced with a shy lad from London's East End, Peter Greenbaum (born Greenbaum). Like Clapton, he was unhappy at the adulation. Mayall gave Green some studio time in 1967, to cheer him up and as a birthday present.

Green cut an instrumental called *Fleetwood Mac*, named from his two recording colleagues: fellow Bluesbreakers Mick Fleetwood, the drummer – they had earlier played together in Peter B's Looners – and bassist John McVie. Desperately wanting to hide his identity behind others, Green also nominated the tune's title as the group name. He was annoyed when it was credited, at the record company's insistence, to Peter Green's Fleetwood Mac. While he got his way on this in the end, he quit in May 1970.

Fleetwood and Mac have stayed more or less constantly throughout dozens of other personnel and style changes. The appellation almost went, amid legal action over its ownership in 1974 when their manager put together a "fake" band to play concert bookings. Spin-off: ▷ Blue Whale. No relation to ▷ The Fleetwoods.

The Fleetwoods

The Saturns, from Olympia, Washington, added Gary Troxel as lead singer in 1958 to become Two Girls And A Guy – a disingenuous yet unusual name which long predated ▷ 2 Men, A Drum Machine And A Trumpet. Liberty Records promoter Bob Reisdorff phoned singer Barbara Ellis to offer the trio a contract, while urging they come up with a catchier tag. At this point he glanced down at his phone and said: "Like Fleetwood." This was the local dialling code. Their debut single was at number one within three weeks. No relation to ▷ Fleetwood Mac.

Flesh For Lulu

In the 1960s, ▷ Lulu was a pop star at 15. Twenty years on and her star had faded. Still, she remained a recognisable figure thanks to her television and modelling work. This band reportedly saw her eating in a restaurant. No great Lulu fans, they named only as a meat-eating protest and claimed *Flesh For Lulu* was the title of a cult film made many years before.

A Flock Of Seagulls

Britons who named from Richard Bach's best-selling novel *Jonathan Livingston Seagull*. This thin volume was later made into an LP and a 1973 film. The group said: "We read the book. Saw the seagulls in the sky. Listened to the album an' that was it!" "Nobody liked the name so we thought we'd keep it." "What about ▷ Scritti Politti's name? It's worse than ours."

Despite this defence they acquired unflattering derivatives in the music press: A Flock Of Sheep, A Pack Of Gerbils, A Bunch Of Wallies and A Flock Of Haircuts – singer Mike Score was renowned for his increasingly preposterous coiffure.

Flowered Up

The 1990s band say the name "popped up" naturally after a party. To be flowered up is to be inebriated on drugs, carrot juice or anything you can get hold of. Dancer Barry Mooncult over-illustrated the point by wearing a four-foot yellow sunflower round his head.

Flowerpot Men

▷ The Ivy League hailed from the British Midlands, despite the U.S.-style moniker. By 1967 crew cuts were out and dropping out was in. So, with absurd hippy apparel and repertoire they renamed ... after a BBC television children's serial. Rationale: Flower power was everywhere, everybody seemed to be smoking pot. Jon Lord went on into ▷ Deep Purple. Cf ▷ The Woodentops.

Flowers Of Romance

Named on the suggestion of John Ritchie, AKA ▷ Sid Vicious. Viv Albertine told Jon Savage: "John thought up the name. It was perfect. You're the flowers and what's romance? Lies. These children are the flowers of romance."

Vicious went on into ▷ The Sex Pistols, which included ▷ Johnny Rotten. John Lydon, still later, named a ▷ Public Image Ltd album after the Flowers Of Romance. Vicious died in 1979; the 1981 LP, with a wreath cover, was in one respect a tribute to him.

Fluff

Nickname for disc jockey Alan Freeman, who didn't fluff his lines but favoured ancient pullovers.

Flux Of Pink Indians

These U.K. punksters reasoned it made some sense: they were not Indians, nor Red (American) Indians but pink. Previously ▷ The Epileptics.

Flying Burrito Brothers

They were not called Burrito, not brothers, and couldn't perform Mr Kite style aerobatic tricks. The name was first used for a short-lived 1960s informal bunch of musicians, including Jess Davis, in Los Angeles – then borrowed by ▷ Gram Parsons for jam sessions before his time in ▷ The Byrds. Davis said it sounded like a flying circus act or a mob of southern desperadoes: a burrito is a U.S.-Mexican dish, giving a clue to their origin.

The Byrds had released their 1968 folk-rock LP *The Notorious Byrd Brothers* (none of them were brothers either) when he joined with the intention of making a country-rock answer. They considered his idea of calling the album

The Flying Burrito Brothers because of its coincidental reference to the last. "Burrito" sounded like Byrds; "Flying" fitted their avian connection. (Some fans wrongly protested the idea was a dig at former Byrd Gene Clark, who left the band because of a reported fear of flying.)

Months later Parsons quit; the record became late 1968's country-influenced *Sweetheart Of The Rodeo* and he was free to use the name for his next project. For more see *Timeless Flight* by Johnny Rogan. Cf ▷ Sweethearts Of The Rodeo.

Flying Pickets

Flying pickets were British trade unionists who went to help strikers outside factory gates, persuading or forcing others not to go into work. The 1980 U.K. Government clamped down on picketing, saying large numbers of activists were travelling considerable distances to interfere in disputes not involving their direct employers.

The move infuriated this *a capella* act with a political conscience. "We wanted to encapsulate the struggle for a better standard of living, a fairer society," explained band member Brian Hibberd. Individual member name: the lager-and-politics-inspired Red Stripe.

FM

They considered the vaguely risqué VHF (Very High Frequency) but settled on Frequency Modulation, which they wanted to broadcast their AOR, adult-orientated rock. Which is enough abbreviations for one entry.

FMB

They were the subject of a 1993 U.K. Channel 4 documentary, *The Next Big Thing*. Which guaranteed they weren't. Perhaps because they were coy about the name, which means "fuck my boots".

Foetus

Bywords for a family of bands chosen by Anglo-Australian, adopted New Yorker, Jim Thirlwell, AKA Jim Foetus, Clint Ruin, Stinkfist, Flesh Volcano, Steroid Maximus … this man likes identity changes and says: "Shock 'em before you rock 'em." Revolting names include Foetus Inc., Scraping Foetus Off The Wheel, You've Got Foetus On Your Breath, Foetus Under Glass, Foetus In Your Bed, Foetus Interruptus, Foetus Corruptus, Foetus All-Nude Revue, Foetus Art Terrorism, Phillip Toss And His Foetus Vibrations, Foetus Über (Alles) and Foetus Over Frisco. Spin-off: ▷ Immaculate Consumptive.

Foghat

This 1970s British bluesy band recalled the cartoon character Luther Foghat.

Follow 4 Now

Named after a song by ▷ Public Enemy, *Bring The Noise,* on the 1988 album *It Takes A Nation Of Millions To Hold Us Back*. It advises following people power.

Wayne Fontana

He was born Glyn Ellis in Manchester, U.K. His name was chosen in honour of ▷ Elvis Presley's 1950's drummer D.J. Fontana. The stage name came long before he signed a recording contract with the coincidentally named Fontana Records. ▷ The Mindbenders.

Foo Fighters

From U.S. military slang for fighter pilots who can be called out to investigate sightings of "foos" or UFOs, unidentified flying objects. Dave Grohl's band after ▷ Nirvana; their opening song was called *This Is A Call*; with early sleeves picturing the Roswell Incident, in which U.S. doctors are examining alien-like forms, now said to be crash test dummies. No relation to ▷ UFO.

Foreigner

Named because they formed in 1976 with two Brits and three Americans. The personnel later changed slightly, making the band 75 per cent foreign for their main, U.S., market. Singer Lou Gramm was born Louis Grammatico.

Forrest

An American soul act, named after leader Forrest Thomas.

The 49ers

Singer Dawn Mitchell walked in to the studio, having earlier met producer Gianfranco

Bortolotti in a disco. She was the 49th person to be auditioned by this Italian house outfit ... knocked them out with her performance ... and they had found a vocalist and name.

Fotheringay

British folk-rock band formed by Sandy Denny after her first ▷ Fairport Convention stint. Named after her folk composition which opens their 1969 LP *What We Did On Our Holidays*. Fotheringay, Northamptonshire, was the place of the imprisonment of Mary, Queen of Scots. The name can hardly be beaten for its British folk pedigree.

Foundations

British 1960s popsters – discovered by a record dealer while playing in a London basement below his office. *Hence the name.*

Four Horsemen

This spin-off from ▷ The Cult took their name from a track by ▷ The Clash on 1980's *London Calling*.

400 Blows

This band named after a 1959 film by François Truffaut, *Les Quatre Cents Coups*, about an unhappy 12-year-old boy on the run.

The Fourmost

Manager Brian Epstein amended this quartet's name from The Four Mosts in 1963 and exploited their connection with another Merseybeat group, who proved to be a foremost fabber four. ▷ The Beatles.

Fourplay

This quartet thought it better than The Sensational Alex Harvey Band (Without Alex Harvey). If the foreplay was bad, the rest was worse.

The Four Seasons

They had nearly ten years of moderate but mundane success as Variatones and The Village Voices (a reference to the New York city Greenwich Village newspaper).

Given the group's popularity it is natural that a number of other clubs have claimed they inspired the final name. The best known is the top restaurant a few doors from their New York record company offices. One theory is that the music executives wanted to get free meals in exchange for "advertising". Lead singer Frank Castelluccio became Frankie Valli. ▷ The Sandpipers, ▷ Wonder Who.

The 4 Skins

A Oi!/hardcore quartet with a skinhead following, their name was seen as anti-Semitic; the band's politics built on the Nazi stance affected by many punks. Cf ▷ Redskins for the other side of the skinhead coin.

The Four Tops

Many 1950s band names were hardly adventurous: that came later. This quartet from Detroit, Michigan, thus started as The Four Aims (1953) and only revised this because of possible confusion with the Ames Brothers. Lead singer Levi Stubbles, often the target of shaving jokes, became Stubbs.

Fox

From singer Noosha Fox.

John Foxx

▷ Ultravox.

Frabjoy And Runcible

U.K. band, a forerunner of ▷ 10CC. The name comes from two nonsense words, the first (frabjous) invented by Lewis *Alice In Wonderland* Carroll and the second (runcible spoon) Edward *Pobble* Lear.

Fra Lippo Lippi

Another "we've read a book" obscure reference. Indie band named from the 1855 work by English poet Robert Browning.

The Frames

Spin-off from ▷ The Commitments by Glen Hansard, who said the name was "multi-meaning ... not just films".

Connie Francis

Born Concetta Rosa Maria Franconero, she made the change aged 10 based on a suggestion by TV chat show host Arthur Godfrey. He said before her appearance on his *Talent Scouts* programme that her name was long to remember and difficult to pronounce.

The Frank And Walters

None of this threesome was called Frank or Walters. They were from Cork, Ireland, and named after two vagrants who were well-known local characters.

Frankie Goes To Hollywood

The usual explanation is given on the B side of 1983's *Relax*, called *One September Monday*. "There was a band I was in, I was just jamming. We needed a name quickly because we had to get a gig … and there was a piece of *The New Yorker* magazine stuck to the wall in the rehearsal room, and it said 'Frankie Goes To Hollywood' and showed a picture of ▷ Frank Sinatra getting mobbed by teenyboppers."

Young William Johnson, who gave this account, earlier changed his name to Holly (▷ Holly Johnson), played with ▷ Big In Japan and formed a band punningly called Hollycaust. What he doesn't say is that the headline contained the magic word "Holly" – just as he was re-forming the group with Paul Rutherford, ex ▷ Opium Eaters.

Some pop trivia books say the story was about Frankie Laine. It wasn't. Neither was Holly right about the source: it was *Variety* which wrote about Sinatra moving from Las Vegas. (See Nick Cohn's book *Rock Dreams*.)

Hence the name. Hence the "Frankie Says" tee-shirt slogans.

The act became informally known as "The Frankies" (▷ The Hollies had already been done after all) and the remnants toyed with the name of The Lads after the departure of the two main front men. (Cf another Liverpool band, ▷ The La's.) They inspired ▷ Bonzo Goes To Washington and ▷ Paddy Goes To Holyhead.

The Frantic Elevators

Forerunners of ▷ Simply Red. They liked a track by ▷ Television, *Elevation*, on the 1977 album *Marquee Moon*. (Cf ▷ Elevation.) This was finally ruled too hippy and they switched to The Elevators. Mick Hucknall considered adding an adjective such as Rancid (this was punk after all). Then he saw an advert in *New Musical Express* which said: "Are you frantic yet?" There's more in *Simply Mick* by McGibbon and McGibbon, 1993.

Frazier Chorus

This 1980s U.K. group started off as Plop! the idea being an antidote to ▷ Wham! They evolved into Frazier Chorus, the name of a baseball club.

Freddie And The Dreamers

Leader Freddie Garrity chose the name for the Mancunian group, originally the Kingfishers, because it fitted with a summer residency at Dreamland, Margate, U.K.

Fred Zeppelin

Short-lived California band formed by Moon Unit, daughter of ▷ Frank Zappa, parodying ▷ Led Zeppelin's name.

Free

Named by U.K. musician and radio personality Alexis Korner after his then-defunct group Free At Last which featured Ginger Baker, who sprang to fame with ▷ Cream. Free called their 1972 LP *Free At Last* – it was too good to waste in the end.

Island Records unsuccessfully implored the band to become ▷ Heavy Metal Kids. For a short while later they went under the immortal name of Kossoff, Kirke, Tetsu and Rabbit (!) Korner also named ▷ CCS. Spin-off: ▷ Back Street Crawler. Related band: ▷ Bad Company.

Friction

Named from the third track on ▷ Television's *Marquee Moon* album. Chosen by Peter Laughner, ex ▷ Pere Ubu, because of his enduring love for the record.

Frijid Pink

One hit wonders from Detroit whose frigid name was supposed to mean "cold excellence".

Fritz The Cat

U.S. band named after the lewd feline character created by cartoonist Robert Crumb for U.S. underground "comix". Fritz was the star of the risqué 1971 Steve Krantz film *Fritz The Cat*.

No relation to 1970s Bay area group Fritz which featured Lindsey Buckingham and Stevie Nicks, later of ▷ Fleetwood Mac.

Lefty Frizzell

U.S. singer, at his peak in the 1950s; the Lefty comes from his early boxing career, where he had a lethal left hook.

Frogman

Clarence Henry got the name from his "self produced" frog imitations on *Ain't Got No Home*.

Fruitbat

Member of ▷ Carter USM.

The Frustrations

U.S. punk band formed by Bill Berry and Ian Copeland – the name expressed their feeling about young life in Macon, Georgia. Berry found fame later as part of ▷ R.E.M.

FSA

Short for Flying Saucer Attack.

Fuck Off

Sorry. Yes, a band called themselves this. They were Spanish, and played heavy metal, which explains it. Their 1989 album *Another Sacrifice* was big in Europe – the name was too much for it to chart in any English-speaking country. A cleverer attempt is the 1990s act King L.

Fugazi

Like ▷ Snafu, a name taken from U.S. military slang, and meaning "a fucked up situation".

The Fugees

An abbreviation of refugees; the prime movers were originally from Haiti. They later used *Refugee Camp* as a title.

The Fugs

U.S. 1960s poets Ed Sanders, Tuli Kupferberg and Ken Weaver shotgun-married works by William Blake to rough-hewn guitar and named from Norman Mailer. In making his World War II experience in the Pacific into *The Naked And The Dead*, he faced a problem in accurately recording U.S. servicemen's language. It needed to be liberally sprinkled with "fucks" – but this was 1948, less tolerant than now, so he rendered it as "fug".

Fun Boy Three

This trio wanted to have fun after ▷ The Specials – and produced a misnomer. Their songs were often doomy: for examples *The Lunatics Have Taken Over The Asylum* and *The More That I See The Less I Believe*.

Funkadelic

U.S. star ▷ George Clinton relaunched ▷ The Parliaments in 1969. The new moniker combined his own funk music with psychedelia, then at its height. Associated bands: ▷ The Brides Of Dr Funkenstein and Bootsy's Rubber Band. One of their songs inspired the name ▷ Urge Overkill.

Funky President

Nickname for ▷ James Brown after his well-publicised 1971 lunching with Republican President Richard Nixon. It's not every day a mere American leader is granted the privilege of meeting such an all-powerful and distinguished personage, The Minister Of The New Heavy Super Funk.

Fun Lovin' Criminals

A New York trio who wear their interests and influences prominently on their well-tailored mafia-style silk suit sleeves. Legal Pulp Friction with Quintin Tarantino followed as they sampled his films. Singer and guitarist Huey stole the name from an acquaintance who ran a graffiti crew in Queens. "It represents the duality that goes with living in New York," he told *Q*. "It's hard to always be on the right side of the law."

Billy Fury

Another of the names created by U.K. pop entrepreneur ▷ Larry Parnes, the man affectionately known as "Mr Parnes, Shillings And Pence". He chose this one because young Ronald Wycherley, from Liverpool, had obvious vitality and daring. He had been sacked from jobs for fighting and got a contract by gate-crashing Parnes's dressing room before a gig, then jumping on stage to sing.

FU-Schnickens

Brooklyn rappers who explain their FU means "for unity". Schnicken is a word they invented themselves to mean "coalition". "Together it means we are together, work together."

Fuzzbox

Birmingham rockers of the 1980s. The fuzzbox, which blurs chords together, was used on their guitars, apparently to disguise their lack of ability. Leader Maggie Dunne adapted the old "I've got a horn and I'm going to play it/got a dress and I'm going wear it" joke, saying: We've Got A Fuzzbox And We're Gonna Use It. This excellent but long name was later abbreviated to simply Fuzzbox. Additionally, it's often said to have Freudian overtones, Fuzzbox being both an all-girl band and a slang term for female pudenda.

Fuzztones

▷ Jesus And Mary Chain, ▷ My Bloody Valentine, ▷ the Pixies, Sugar ... the 1980s and 1990s saw many bands using feedback and fuzzbox on poppy sounds. This U.S. band named after their sound.

FYC

▷ Fine Young Cannibals.

F

The Gallaghers

The key members of ▷ Oasis are Liam and Noel Gallagher. This tribute band named after them. More Oasis covers: ▷ No Way Sis.

Gallon Drunk

Named after student gallon-drunk induction rituals, where freshmen have to consume eight pints of alcohol. Why the boozy name? Because, like ▷ Lush, this lot like their liquor.

Ganelin Trio

Named after their leader Vyacheslav Ganelin.

Gang Of Four

Before the group adopted it, Gang of Four was a political term. It described:
1. A group of figures engaged in a power struggle in China who were punished for airing "unacceptable" views;
2. Four British middle of the road politicians who founded the Social Democratic Party. This band was British. Their brand of militant Marxism, however, made it quite clear that they were inspired by the Asian plotters. Later events left them successively as a Gang Of Three, Two and One.

The Gap Band

Oklahoma band who named from their three home areas: Green Wood, Archer and Pine.

Jerry Garcia

He was born Jerome Garcia. He was commemorated by Ben & Jerry's (no relation) ice-cream with a "new flavor" called Cherry Garcia. It remains to be seen if he will be remembered as an ice-cream, as ▷ Captain Trips or simply the founder of ▷ Grateful Dead. He also played with ▷ Jefferson Starship.

Art Garfunkel

▷ Simon And Garfunkel.

Gaye Bykers On Acid

The name summed up their campy image and music, which blended acid rock with motorbike movies. It proved to be a real albatross though, with members being constantly asked: "Are you gay?", "Are you bikers?" and "Are you on acid?"

They tried countering by saying Gaye Bykers was a female fictional character. The appellation was said to have been taken from a drawing by Ray Lowry. Apparently, he also came up with the monikers Fashionably Celibate, Hitler On Acid, Six Grown Children and the superb Burn The Churches Rape The Nuns at the same time – none of which has been taken up by anyone to the knowledge of the author.

Singer Ian Hoxley played up the ▷ Alice Cooper-like sexual confusion by becoming Mary Mary. They played up the joke, with alter egos including Lesbian Dopeheads On Mopeds (supposedly a butch band from down under); and Rëktum (masquerading as German heavy metal freaks).

Marvin Gaye

Marvin Pentz Gay reportedly added the E to

deflect homosexual jibes. There are reasons to doubt this however: he was so named before "gay" was commonly used in this way.

Crystal Gayle

She was born Brenda Gail Webb, sister of ▷ Loretta Lynn, who tells of the renaming in her autobiography *Coal Miner's Daughter*. Brenda followed her into showbusiness and signed with the same record label, which already had a Brenda on its books, ▷ Brenda Lee. They were discussing this as they drove past a Krystal hamburger sign. Loretta said: "Crystals are bright and shiny, like you."

The G Band

▷ Gary Glitter.

GBH

GBH is British legal jargon for Grievous Bodily Harm, an offence more serious than Actual Bodily Harm. This aggressive band was part of the *Oi!* movement.

Geile Tiere

German band whose name means "wild animals".

Bob Geldof

His early journalism appeared as Rob Geldof; his full name was Robert Frederick Zenon Geldof. The third name led to comments his father christened him after an inert gas. "Sir" Bob denied his first child was saddled with the ridiculous name Fifi Trixibelle as revenge. It came from his favourite Auntie Fifi and then-wife Paula Yates's desire to be a Southern Belle. Fifi was allowed to name their next Peaches, followed by Pixie.

Nicknames: ▷ Saint Bob; ▷ Sir Bob; Modest Bob – ironic: he's got many qualities but shyness or modesty certainly aren't among them. Yates further indulged her taste for way-out appellations by calling her daughter by ▷ INXS's Michael Hutchence: Heavenly Hiraani Tiger Lily.

Gene

This British group of the 1990s pay joint tribute to 1950s star ▷ Gene Vincent and 1960s sensation Gene Pitney. The idea came from drummer Matt James.

Gene Loves Jezebel

Not boy loves girl actually, but twins Mike and Jay Aston from Wales, with accomplices. Jay's *alter ego* Jezebel came from a character in a film he worked on, based on ▷ Gene Vincent. The love-hate relationship soured and Mike/Gene left (presumably leaving Jezebel loves, er, Jezebel?) Spin-off: ▷ All About Eve.

General Kane

U.S. band gratefully named by Mitch McDowell in tribute to an officer who helped him during his military training.

General Public

U.K. 1980s band founded by graduates of ▷ The (English) Beat and ▷ The Specials with an alias protesting at faceless authority. Cf ▷ Big Brother And The Holding Company, ▷ Public Image.

Generation X

Taken from the title of the 1964 book survey by Jane Deverson and Chris Hamblett. Its original cover said: "What's the rebellious anger of Britain's untamed youth? here – in their own words – is how they really feel about Drugs, Drink, God, Sex, Class, Colour and Kicks."

The pulp-factual volume was in a bookcase owned by ▷ Billy Idol's mother and selected by Tony James, later of ▷ Sigue Sigue Sputnik. The 1970s band ran into management problems and tried a ▷ T Rex type shortening of its name to Gen X.

Genesis

Record executive ▷ Jonathan King chose the name of the first chapter of *The Bible*, often used to mean a beginning, because the group members were starting out. Many were at school (Britain's exclusive Charterhouse, King's *alma mater*), having played in The Garden Wall and The Anon.

A receptionist asked for the band's name prior to an initial meeting with King, misheard and introduced them as "The Janitors". That understanding resulted in them nearly being thrown out. So much for the old boy network. They were soon working on their debut, a concept piece called *From Genesis To Revelation*.

The alias produced another problem as it

emerged that there was another Genesis in the U.S.A. The Britons had to be known as Genesis at home and Revelation abroad. Fortunately for them, the American group was unsuccessful and they ended their schizophrenic two-name-compromise policy with relief.

Spin-offs include ▷ Bankstatement, ▷ Brand X and ▷ Mike And The Mechanics. ▷ King has named many other bands including ▷ 10CC, ▷ Thumper.

Johnny Gentle

Another name cooked up by U.K. businessman ▷ Larry Parnes. Ingredients: take one unknown willing to do anything for fame. Method: saddle him with any old handle emphasising the sort of music you have decided he will perform. (Gentle = in this case, slushy ballads.) Stir well, and you have an early 1960s star. (This guy was even supported on one tour by ▷ The Beatles; their subsequent success swept away names like this, hopefully for good.)

Gentlemen Without Weapons

Their experimental music was created by sampling natural sounds and without conventional instruments ("weapons": guitars are often called "axes").

Bobbie Gentry

Roberta Streeter, of Chicasaw, Mississippi, took her last name from the 1952 film *Ruby Gentry*, starring Charlton Heston. Chicasaw officials later considered renaming the town Gentry.

Geordie

This U.K. band were all Geordies – inhabitants of the Tyneside region – and proud of it. Singer Brian Johnson later joined ▷ AC/DC.

George

▷ Boy George, ▷ Culture Club, ▷ Marilyn.

Georgia Satellites

Came from Georgia – U.S.A., not Russia. A reference to the aerospace industry.

Gerry And The Pacemakers

In 1959, the Pacemakers – as in the leaders who set the pace in a race – sounded like a good name for a band. How could Liverpudlian Gerry Marsden foresee the word's common use as an electronic heart stimulator? He had considered calling them The Mars Bars, after the child's favourite. This punned on Marsden and was a naïve attempt to win cash from the confectionery industry.

G-Force

G as in Gary (Moore) attempting a "clever" reference to the figure representing total gravity experienced by astronauts etc.

Giant Sand

From creatures in the *Dune* books (1963–4 and sequels), which were made into a 1984 science fiction film starring ▷ Sting.

Gigolo Aunts

Named after the track *Gigolo Aunt* on former ▷ Pink Floyd man Syd Barrett's second solo album *Barrett* (1970).

Gillan

From leader, ex ▷ Deep Purple singer Ian Gillan.

Dizzy Gillespie

John Gillespie got his nickname from trumpeter colleague Fats Palmer based on his onstage clowning, playing inspired solos while dancing round in circles.

Otis "Elevator" Gilmore

Cincinnati's Danny Adler fabricated the name after record companies refused to listen to him because he had a "white name" and therefore wasn't an authentic bluesman. He took Otis from a make of lift car; he was working as an elevator attendant in a Ohio warehouse.

The Gin Blossoms

Named from a picture of W.C. Fields's gin-reddened nose, which he had likened to "a giant strawberry". Founder member Doug Hopkins reportedly suffered drink problems of his own later.

Girls At Our Best!

The misleading tag – they weren't an all female group – was a line lifted from their first song, *Warm Girls*.

Girlschool

An all-girl heavy metal band, started when two members were still in full-time education. They teamed up with ▷ Motörhead as ▷ Headgirl.

Giuffria

From keyboard player Gregg Giuffria.

Kenny G

U.S. saxophonist who abbreviated his name Kenneth Gorelick, not the best of monikers for anyone other than a horror film star.

Glass Tiger

Heavy rock band, named in surreal style from a paperweight. More tigers: ▷ Shabby Tiger, ▷ Tygers of Pan Tang.

The Glimmer Twins

Mick Jagger and Keith Richards of ▷ The Rolling Stones. From 1970s glam rock: big stars don't need to shine, they just twinkle.

Gary Glitter

He's had lots of names in a sparkling career, but, like ▷ Alvin Stardust, it took him a long time to find one that worked best. In 1971, Paul Gadd had been in showbiz for 12 years without much success. He had taken his stepfather's surname to became Paul Russell And His Rebels; then Raven And The Boston Sound; Paul Raven; Paul Monday; Boston International and finally Rubber Bucket (really; it was a single about a hippy squat).

He was advised by his record company to "bring more sparkle" into his act and took this literally. He and manager/co-writer Mike Leander (born Michael Farr) dreamed up a range of flashy sequin jump-suits and contemplated names said to include Davey Dazzle, Gary Glitter, Horace Hydrogen, Stanley Sparkle, Terry Tinsel and Vicki Vomit (▷ Queen singer Freddie Mercury had a similar *alter ego*, Larry Lurex).

They chose well and glam bam, thank you ma'am, the glitter rock bandwagon was born. Gary's back-up musicians, The Glitter Band, later became The G Band, while his hunky frame squeezed into silver shirts became a parody as he grew older. His similarity to an over-stuffed turkey tanned from the oven and covered in cooking foil led to the nickname The Bacofoil Bulk.

The Globs

No relation to ▷ BOB, The Blobs, ▷ The Nabob Of Sob or ▷ The Nobs! Stands for Global Village Tracking Company.

The Glove

This 1983 British band, made up of ▷ Cure and ▷ Siouxsie And The Banshees members, recalled 1960s ▷ Beatles psychedelia with an LP *Blue Sunshine* named after a type of LSD. They named after a character from The Fab Four's 1968 cartoon film *Yellow Submarine* – saying it sounded like hippy hero band ▷ Love and had a surreal feel, meaning "an iron fist in a velvet glove".

The Gloved One

The loved ▷ Michael Jackson, wearing his famous single, white-sequinned glove.

The Go-Betweens

Because the musicians act as go-betweens between the music and the audience. This Australian band get the idea from L.P. Hartley's 1953 story *The Go-Between*, later filmed.

God

▷ Eric Clapton nickname based on the "miracles" of his virtuoso playing. Fans of the 1960s scrawled "Eric Clapton is God" on walls in London.

The Godfather Of …

Nicknames for some of music's elder statesmen. The Godfather of Grunge: ▷ Neil Young. The Godfather of Punk: ▷ Malcolm McLaren, ▷ Lou Reed. The Godfather of R&B: ▷ Johnny Otis. The Godfather of Soul: ▷ James Brown. Cf ▷ The Modfather: ▷ Paul Weller.

The Godfathers

▷ The (New) Sid Presley Experience found celluloid inspiration in 1985, taking the title of Francis Ford Coppola's 1972–4 films. They liked it for its religious and Mafioso associations.

G

Godley Creme

Lol Creme (born Lawrence Creme) and Kevin Godley. ▷ 10CC.

Gogmagog

▷ Jonathan King thought the name memorable. It refers to a Biblical character Gog, from Magog; a legendary British giant; and masked figures above stages.

Go Gos

Like the ▷ Au Go-Go Singers, this female act named after go-go dancing. At least it bettered their first choice: The Misfits.

Golden Dawn

From Aleister Crowley's book *The Sect Of The Golden Dawn*. Crowley also inspired ▷ The MacGregors and ▷ 23 Skidoo.

Golden Earring

This Dutch band formed in 1961 and played soft numbers such as ballads from 1947 film *Golden Earrings*. Their music changed greatly and by the 1970s they were making driving rock such as *Radar Love*, a million miles from their name inspiration.

Goldie

From his home made gold tooth-caps; he has also worked under the name Metalheads.

Golliwogs

From the ridiculous image forced on this band, who fortunately escaped this – and racist allegations – by becoming ▷ Creedence Clearwater Revival.

Gordon And The Gekkos

Band formed by financier whizzkids in the City of London, named after the finance wheel-dealer Gordon "greed is good" Gekko, played by Michael Douglas in 1987 film *Wall Street*.

Gordon The Moron

▷ Jilted John's eponymous single led to a riposte by Gordon The Moron, the character who wins the heart of the fickle Julie.

Go 2

Shakespearean inspiration. "Go to!" was a frequent interjection and shortening of "go to hell".

Go West

Instant band formula: rip-off of the standard advice to those exploring the new America. Take cowboy boots, add fringed jackets, don't forget the stetsons. You'll inadvertently namecheck films by Buster Keaton, Glenn Ford and many others. Trouble is, it's been done. Cf ▷ Westworld.

The GPs

Grazed Pontiffs, not Grand Prix or General Practitioners. ▷ Fairport Convention spin-off christened by Richard Thompson in reference to shots fired at Pope John Paul II.

Grab Grab The Haddock

Spin-off from ▷ The Marine Girls, the impulsively chosen silly name tied in with their nautical lyrical obsession. Related: ▷ Everything But The Girl.

Bill Graham

The concert promoter was a refugee called Wolfgang Grajonka who found his name after a quick flick through the Bronx phone book.

Graham Central Station

The name, recalling New York's Grand Central Station, was the idea of the band's founder, former ▷ Sly and The Family Stone musician Larry Graham, who especially wanted to name-check himself.

Grand Funk Railroad

They were Grand Truck Railroad – a well-known Canadian route – then Grand Funk Railroad and abbreviated in 1970 to Grand Funk.

Grandmaster Flash

Grandmasters, from the chess term, were MCs at disco or scratch events and Joseph Saddler was named from his flashy show with rapper Melle Mel (later Grandmaster Mel).

Grant Lee Buffalo

A Los Angeles trio led by Grant Lee Phillips.

The near-extinct Buffalo was chosen "as a symbol, of what's gone wrong with this century," reported *Vox* in 1993.

Grapefruit

Tony Rivers And The Castaways were renamed by ▷ John Lennon on signing to Apple in 1968. *Grapefruit* was a book of poems by Yoko Ono.

The Grapes Of Wrath

Vancouver trio named after Nobel prizewinner John Steinbeck's 1939 meisterwerk about the depression. Steinbeck had taken the phrase from Julia Ward Howe's *The Battle Hymn Of the American Republic*. Cf ▷ East of Eden.

The Grateful Dead

What a long, strange trip it's been for this band who started in 1963 as The Hart Valley Drifters. They tried names such as The Sleepy Hollow Hog Stompers and the Thunder Mountain Tub-Thumpers, then became Mother McCree's Uptown Jug Champs, playing country, before metamorphosing into the rock-based Warlocks. The hair got longer, as did the beards, the 1960s, the "acid tests" and the songs. The songs especially. Perhaps understandably, the details of the renaming have become sketchy, through the haze of Haight-Ashbury, hash and time …

"Grateful Dead" is variously said to have come about when they learnt of other bands called The Warlocks. These included precursors to the ▷ Velvet Underground and ▷ ZZ Top. Another version asserts ▷ Jerry Garcia was at a party when he suddenly decided psychedelic music warranted a deeper name.

There is agreement that he found "Grateful Dead" in a book. Still, he either discovered it rapidly and randomly, while playing Valentinian Chance – fortune telling by blindfold selection of passages; or, after deliberation. Some accounts say the other Warlocks accepted the name with varying degrees of enthusiasm; other versions say it was backed instantly.

The party is variously said to have been in bassist Phil Lesh's Palo Alto condo; at the band's manager's house in downtown Los Angeles.

Some say Jerry was on DMT; others that he was on pot; others that he was on both and everything else he could get his hands on.

And the moniker itself is variously said to have come from:

1. An American alphabetical encyclopedia, Funk and Wagnall's *New Practical Standard Dictionary*;
2. A phrase in *The Tibetan Book Of The Dead*;
3. An Egyptian prayer book;
4. *The Oxford English Dictionary*;
5. *The Oxford Companion To Classical Music* or even
6. A volume of Egyptian prayers.

For what it's worth, the best history of the band – as given by their publicist – gives the answers as all 1.

The Grateful Dead legend in western and eastern folklore tells of people who come back from the dead to help those still alive who helped them. The "quick and grateful dead" story, in various forms, often involves the burying of corpses, who help the diggers to win fame, fortune or true love.

Hence the name. Hence the love-ins, sit-ins, and cannabis smoke-ins.

Name notes:

1. The band is often called The Dead, and followers are known as Dead Heads/Deadheads; ▷ New Riders Of The Purple Sage are a spin-off.
2. Drummer William Kreutzmann was at first known as Bill Somers to match a fake identity card he carried to avoid trouble with the U.S. Draft and Labor Law.
3. Garcia was known as ▷ Captain Trips. His death led to the band dissolving; the name remains for a diversified recording and marketing organisation.
4. Another band member was Ron McKernan, renamed Pigpen after the *Peanuts* cartoon character.
5. Spin-off: ▷ Dinosaurs. Related: ▷ Jefferson Starship.
6. For further information see Paul Grushkin's 1983 work, *The Official Book Of The Deadheads* and the countless web sites on the Dead.

The Grease Band

Originally The Heir Apparent, also from the length of their hair. Resulting LP title: *Amazing Grease*. ▷ Joe Cocker.

The Great American Navel

Wake up America: enough of literary novels! For something literally novel, here's ▷ Cher, whose outfits have often gone for the bellybutton-on-show approach. ▷ Queen Of Flash.

Great Society

Grace Slick's band made sardonic reference to promises in U.S. President Lyndon B. Johnson's "Great Society" speech of 1964, swept away by the cost of the Vietnam War. ▷ Jefferson Airplane.

The Great Unwashed

▷ The Clean broke up after under two years recording and later regrouped. The New Clean name was jokingly dropped in favour of The Great Unwashed, a nickname for many young people by middle-aged types, in response to the many cleanliness puns which constantly cropped up in New Zealander music press when the band was reviewed. Their first LP was called, incidentally, *Clean Out Of Our Minds*.

Ric Grech

The ▷ Blind Faith, ▷ Traffic and ▷ Family star's name is Ric, but he's been billed as Rick and Rik. Grech, who died in 1990, said he didn't care as long as his bank accepted the cheques.

The Greedy Bastards

A great punk name and protest at capitalists everywhere; ▷ U2 once played support to this lot.

Al Green

U.S. singer and pastor, born Al Greene.

Green Day

From their song *Green Day*, which is about innocence and pot smoking.

Peter Green

Splinter Group leader, ▷ Fleetwood Mac star, AKA Peter Greenbaum.

Green River

Seattle band named from the north-west region of the U.S.A., and 1969 ▷ Creedence Clearwater Revival song. ▷ Pearl Jam.

Greenslade

Led by Dave Greenslade, ex ▷ Colosseum. Related: ▷ If. Unrelated: ▷ Slade.

Grifters

Memphis 1990s act knowingly named after 1990 Martin Scorsese film about three confidence tricksters who make money by lying, cheating and stealing.

Grim Reaper

A reference to the skeletal figure who cuts down the dead with his scythe like harvesting sheaves of corn. A moniker which is an antecedent to many "Death Rock" bands such as ▷ Carcass.

The main interest in this name is its acquired irony – Grim Reaper played with Otis Redding on the night of his death. They later found fame as ▷ Cheap Trick.

The Groaner

▷ The Old Groaner, ▷ Bing Crosby.

The Groundhogs

This British R&B band made an early LP with ▷ John Lee Hooker and named after one of his suitably earthy songs (a groundhog's an American marmot).

Group Therapy

A psychological name. This 1960s U.S. band referred to co-operative treatment, getting in a pun on groups. Compare with (but note this act is no relation to) U.K. band Therapy or 1990s Belfast band ▷ Therapy?

Blind Boy Grunt

▷ Bob Dylan pseudonym, used several times. According to the notes of the CD box set *The Bootleg Series Volumes 1–3* he used it for a 1963 Broadside disc because he was contracted to Columbia. He had run out of words to sing and was asked to improvise to test the recording level. He was grunting into the microphone when someone asked for his name.

GTO

Stands for "Girls Together Outrageously". ▷ Frank Zappa.

GTR

Co-founder Steve Hackett said the name showed they planned "to take the guitar into the '90s and re-establish it as the foremost rock instrument".

Guadacanal Diary

Post-punk Atlanta band who liked the title of a 1943 action flick about a group of U.S. Marines.

Guess Who

The Canadian band was floundering after four changes in less than two years: The Silvertones, The Expressions, Allan And The Velvetones, then Chad Allan And The Reflections. Meanwhile British bands doing American songs were everywhere. When The Reflections decided to do the opposite and record the ▷ Johnny Kidd hit *Shakin' All Over* their record company had the idea of marketing it as "Guess Who?" with a press release suggesting it was made by a well-known U.K. group, moonlighting. The name ▷ The Who was whispered ... the Britons didn't take legal action and the record was a hit.

Unrelated: ▷ ? And The Mysterians. Related: ▷ Bachman-Turner Overdrive: The Guess Who evolved into them.

Guild

Taken from medieval trade guild fairs.

Guinness

Nickname for Roland Gift during his time with The Ackrylix, sporting bleached-blond hair. ▷ Fine Young Cannibals.

Guitar Bass & Drums

Prize for unimaginative name to this short-lived supergroup plan by Ry Cooder, ▷ Nick Lowe and Jim Keltner.

Guns 'N' Moses

This British-based Jewish 1990s heavy metal act deny being a tribute band. Singer Ax'l Rosenberg (cf ▷ W. Axl Rose) even tried to sue superstars ▷ Guns N' Roses over the name in 1992.

Guns N' Roses

Part of the band, featuring ▷ W. Axl Rose, had started playing as A.X.L., recalls guitarist Chris Webber. "After A.X.L. we changed the name to Rose, and then we became Hollywood Rose, because we'd seen a band called Rose from New York in a magazine and we wanted to make the distinction," he said.

"In fact, we'd pin different names on the band all the time, because it didn't really matter what we were called."

Axl left to play with LA Guns (formed by Tracii Guns) and finally the two bands merged, combining Americans with English-born ▷ Slash.

The composite name was chosen in preference to unlikely legends such as Heads of Amazon and AIDS (which, according to legend, was suggested when one of the band saw a headline saying AIDS would be "the next big thing").

Guns N' Roses implied both a heavy metal, explosive sound and recalled protesters putting flowers in the barrels of the guns carried by troops and police. Similar flower-power actions were carried out by anti-Vietnam crowds in America and pro-democracy activists in China.

There's more in Mark Putterford's 1993 book *Over The Top: The True Story of Guns N' Roses*.

Cf ▷ Guns 'N' Moses.

Guru

Gang Starr's rapper was born Keith Elam. Guru is an acronym for the Gifted Unlimited Rhymes Universal he churned out.

Woody Guthrie

Born in 1912, named Woodrow Wilson Guthrie in honour of 28th U.S. President Woodrow Wilson (Democrat 1913–21). ▷ Bob Dylan.

The Guv'nor

Nickname for ▷ Frank Sinatra.

Guys And Dolls

They recalled the film and musical of the same name.

GWAR

Art students pushing ▷ Alice Cooper tastelessness to extremes. GWAR means: "God, what a racket!"

H

Named after Steve Hogarth, who wanted some distance from his role as ▷ Marillion frontman.

Haircut 100

Clean–cut 1980s U.K. popsters, their name suited their image. It was chosen in preference to the ridiculous Captain Pennyworth And The Blatant Beavers.

Hair, Nose and Teeth

Inspired by the name Head, Hands and Feet. Alias the hairy Rod Stewart, the nosey ▷ Elton John and toothy ▷ Freddie Mercury of ▷ Queen. The latter said: "The band never really got going because we could not decide on the name order." Maybe one lead vocalist and one ego's enough.

Hairy Monster

U.K. radio personality Dave Lee Travis. His hirsute appearance and beard led to the slogan: "The hairy monster from 200 miles up the M1."

Bill Haley

Born William John Clifton Haley Jnr. Bill Haley And His (or The) Comets took the name from Halley's Comet. ▷ The Comets.

Half Man Half Biscuit

These Scouse scallies chose this to recall *The Elephant Man* film and Victorian freak shows.

Hall And Oates

Daryl Hall was born Daryl Hohl and his first record with John Oates was credited to Whole Oates because of a misunderstanding at the printers.

Johnny Halliday

Frenchman Jean-Philippe Smet got his stage name from touring with U.S. dancer Lee Halliday.

Hallows Eve

Death-rockers with lyrics firmly in the ▷ Napalm Deth school, they name checked All Hallows Eve or Halloween when the dead are remembered.

Halo James

From a cartoon strip. No relation to ▷ James.

MC Hammer

Californian Stanley Kirk Burrell was a teenage baseball fan and idolised the local Oakland Athletic team, going to see every game. Soon he became their team mascot and someone remarked on his resemblance to famous player Hank Aaron. Hammerin' Hank was known for his hard shots – and Stan became Little Hammer. While all rappers are MCs (originally Master of Ceremonies), he was known as McHammer and later became simply Hammer.

Herbie Hancock

▷ Mwandishi.

Hannah And Her Sisters

Potentially misleading. This combo adored Woody Allen's 1986 flick of the same name. The bittersweet comedy of sibling relationships won three Oscars.

Hanoi Rocks

… were not from Vietnam, but the U.K. and Finland. The attraction of an exotic name, like ▷ Damascus, ▷ Berlin; from their early glam rock composition *Hanoi Rocks, Bangkok Shocks, Saigon Shakes*. They were styled on ▷ The New York Dolls, whose Johnny Thunders recorded *China Rocks* which makes the drugs reference clearer. Guitarist called Nasty Suicide.

Happy End

From a Broadway musical rather than a 1984 Joe Jackson song on the album *Body And Soul*.

Happy Mondays

Thought to be a not very good joke, or an ironic comment, depending on how you look at things, on fellow Mancunians ▷ New Order's 1983 magnum opus *Blue Monday*. This was interpreted by some as a song about Ian Curtis, singer with New Order's predecessor ▷ Joy Division, who killed himself on Sunday, 18 May 1980 as they were just about to start a U.S. tour. The others found out on the Monday. New Order recently said this version of lyrical inspiration is flawed: the doomy lyrics nevertheless refer to hearts running cold and death.

Mark "Cow" Day sought an antidote to all the doom and gloom which was being disseminated by local band ▷ The Smiths. Bez (real name, Mark Berry) is on record, so to speak, as saying they kept the name because they thought it was "rubbish".

There is one theory that fellow Manchester band ▷ Oasis named after a Mondays track – though there are some reasons to doubt this.

Pearl Harbor

Pearl Gates adopted the Harbor surname after the main U.S. naval base in Hawaii. Her band name, The Explosions, recalls the events of Sunday, 7 December 1941. Japanese carrier-borne aircraft attacked, sinking or disabling 19 ships – including five battleships – destroying 120 aircraft and killing 2,400 people. It led to the U.S. declaring war on Japan the next day.

E.Y. "Yip" Harburg

Songwriter Edgar Harburg was affectionately called "yip" as a child because of his similarity to a squirrel (slang "yipsel" = squirrel).

The Hardest Working Man In Showbusiness

The nickname king ▷ James Brown: this one based on his hectic 400-shows-a-year (nights plus matinees) concert schedule in the late 1950s and early 1960s.

John Wesley Harding

British folk-singer whose name is from ▷ Bob Dylan's album of the same name. Dylan was paying tribute to the Texas outlaw, actually called John Wesley Hardin, who was shot dead in August 1895. Cf ▷ Tim Hardin, ▷ Judas Priest.

Tim Hardin

Discount suggestions that he chose it as a tribute to one Charles Hardin Holley (better known as ▷ Buddy Holly). Hardin **is** his real name: he's a direct descendant of outlaw John Wesley Hardin. Cf ▷ John Wesley Harding.

Steve Harley And Cockney Rebel

Londoner Steve Nice chose his surname from the upmarket street at the heart of the British capital's medical area, and the band name from natives of the city. ▷ Cockney Rejects.

Harlow

The appearance of vocalist Teresa Straley – platinum Jean Harlow. An American heavy metal band: therefore no reference to Harlow in Essex, U.K. Cf ▷ Newtown Neurotics.

Harpers Bizarre

Californian vocal harmony combo, initially The Tikis. The new name came from magazine *Harper's Bazaar*. Cf the closely related ▷ Beau Brummels, an attempt to sound English at the height of the British invasion of the American charts.

George Harrison

During the time fellow Silver ▷ Beatles/Beetles were called Johnny Silver and Paul Ramon, he was Carl Harrison – in honour of one of his heroes, rockabilly guitarist Carl Perkins.

Harrison's extra-curricular Beatle work includes scores of other people's LPs, playing mainly guitar but even percussion and Jew's Harp. He has adopted a multitude of *alter egos*, including the anagram-like Son of Harry (with Dave Mason); Hari Georgeson (with Splinter and Ravi Shankar); and George Harrysong (with ▷ Harry Nilsson).

More imaginatively, playing with ▷ Cream and Jack Bruce, he became L'Angelo Misterioso. This translates as "The Mysterious Angel": Harrison was dubbed "the mystery Beatle" in one article. Media reports also led to his name The Dark Horse – lending this to the title of a 1974 LP and record label. He also set up Harrisongs for his compositions. He joined ▷ The Traveling Wilburys in 1988, co-producing their first album under the name Nelson and then renaming Spike Wilbury.

Peppermint Harris

Texas blues record label boss Bob Shed was enthusing to an important customer about his new signing: "This boy's gonna be big!" Shad was put in an awkward spot when asked the name of his new signing, which he had temporarily forgotten. He was chewing on a mint at the time and without hesitation firmly said the first thing that came into his mind. Singer Nelson Harrison was thus renamed without consent yet did not complain: he was pleased to have a record deal and the minty moniker was more memorable than his own.

Harvest

Record label widely reported to have been named after ▷ Barclay James Harvest.

P.J. Harvey

Polly Jean Harvey shortened her name to P.J. Harvey when playing with her backing band for similar reasons to ▷ k.d. lang, although she has never disguised her sexuality which contributed to her image once described as "bitch woman from hell".

Hatfield And The North

This is a destination on U.K. roadsigns, familiar to those heading north from London. The signs produced press criticism that they gave excessive prominence to the town of Hatfield; were confusing to those who were unsure if their destination was "north". A spin-off from ▷ Caravan, last seen missing somewhere on the North Circular having missed the signposted route to Major Fame.

Screamin' Jay Hawkins

Jalacy Hawkins, born in Cleveland, Ohio, found his name through his fondness for wild grunts and groans, as on the 1956 hit *I Put A Spell On You*. Cf ▷ Screaming Lord Sutch.

The Hawks

Backing groups of Ronnie Hawkins, the avian origin obvious and maintained through many personnel changes. One incarnation flew to success as ▷ The Band.

Hawkwind

Space rock band, formed from ▷ Mobile Freakout, The Famous Cure and Group X. Hawkwind was lauded by a generation of stoned hippies who thought the appellation deep: something to do with the slipstream from a flying predator perhaps. The connection was enhanced by a hawk logo. Indeed the name was originally Hawkwind Zoo, from a "heavy" story by cult writer Michael Moorcock (cf ▷ Tygers Of Pan Tang). He later appeared with them in concert and narrated the 1975 album *Warrior On The Edge Of Time*.

Still, the complete truth is so prosaic it's hilarious. One ex-member of the group, ▷ Lemmy, told the author the Moorcock title was only picked as a juvenile in-joke at singer Nik Turner, who had aquiline features and a flatulence problem.

For legal reasons the band became known as The Hawklords in 1978–9. ▷ Liquid Len. Lemmy later formed ▷ Motörhead, named after a Hawkwind song. ▷ Strontium 90.

Isaac Hayes

▷ Black Moses. Inspired the band ▷ Shaft.

Headgirl

▷ Motörhead and ▷ Girlschool, perpetrating the *Saint Valentine's Day Massacre* EP. The name had added significance for those with dirty minds (▷ Lemmy).

Max Headroom

Computer-generated talking head who introduced videos and made "music", Max was formed after a crash in which he collided with a sign bearing his name.

The Heads

Fans' name for ▷ Talking Heads (1975–91). In the 1990s, the group was re-formed by the ▷ Tom Tom Club faction. They were minus David Byrne and the abbreviated tag reportedly annoyed him.

H.E.A.L.

This was a loose group including Billy Bragg; members of ▷ Run DMC and ▷ R.E.M.; and rappers ▷ LL Cool J and KRS-One. The latter said it stood for "human education against lies".

Hear 'N' Aid

Charity project of the 1980s. "It's no worse than ▷ Band Aid and we made a lot of money."

Heart

This Californian hard rock band tried Whiteheart and Heartbeat – the latter used by many others – before saying: "less is more".

Heartbreakers

There's a few bands called this. One was an offshoot of ▷ The New York Dolls, featuring ▷ Richard Hell of ▷ The Voidoids. Another combo played with ▷ Tom Petty. Name inspirational sources include an ▷ Elvis Presley hit of 1956 and a Clint Eastwood film of 1986.

Heaven 17

The Sheffield band was originally part of ▷ B.E.F. (▷ Human League.) Heaven 17 comes from the novel *A Clockwork Orange*, the 1962 view of the future by Anthony Burgess, later filmed. Burgess may well have been adapting "seventh heaven".

The anti-hero lists some acts: The Heaven Seventeen, Luke Stern, Goggly Gogol, Johnny Burnaway, Stash Kroh, The Mixers, Lay Quiet Awhile With Ed and Id Molotov. The book inspired ▷ The Mixers, ▷ The Droogs and ▷ Korova Milkbar.

Heaven West Eleven

This 1990s duo have a home studio in London's west-central district: Notting Hill and Shepherd's Bush. (Cf ▷ Bush.) Cf ▷ East 17.

Heavy D And The Boys

Jamaican-born Dwight Myers wanted to be known as McCloud after the U.S. TV cop. Instead he was putting on weight and the kids on the block preferred Heavy D(wight). The diets failed and he decided they knew best.

Heavy Metal Kids

British rockers named after a William S. Burroughs quote about "heavy metal thunder" in his 1959 work *The Naked Lunch*. The phrase soon applied to a style of pounding rock, although ironically The Heavy Metal Kids were not typical of the HM genre. For more Burroughs: ▷ Dead Fingers Talk etc. ▷ Free were almost named Heavy Metal Kids too.

Richard Hell

Richard Myers said the name fitted his new hell-raising personality and spiky hairstyle. Punk showed it was possible, indeed desirable, to "reinvent yourself". The image was based on French nineteenth-century poet Jean Rimbaud; Hell's stage sparring partner at the time was inspired by Rimbaud's foil Paul Verlaine. ▷ Tom Verlaine, ▷ Television, ▷ The Heartbreakers, ▷ The Voidoids.

Helmet

Ex ▷ Band of Susans star Page Hamilton, like a surprisingly large number of other heavy rockers, was interested in Germany and so acquired the Germanic nickname Helmut after Chancellor Helmut Kohl. He narrowly avoided Adolf and Wolfgang.

He called the band Helmet, adding a possible sexual connotation and got in a headgear reference by calling the first album (1990) *Strap It On*.

Jimi Hendrix

Official records list his birth name as Johnny Allen Hendrix, but his father insisted his son should have been James Marshall Hendrix and altered the name four years later. As Jimmy James he played with ▷ The Isley Brothers before forming Rainflowers, later Jimmy James And The Blue Flames – named after the Junior Parker's ▷ Blue Flames.

He reverted to Hendrix and changed the spelling to Jimi on crossing the Atlantic. The Experience appellation was suggested by ex ▷ Animal-turned-manager Chas Chandler from the slogan "The band you have to experience".

Later bands were impulsively named The Band Of Gypsys and Electric Sky Church. He inspired in whole or part the naming of ▷ Cry Of Love, ▷ Colorblind James Experience, ▷ The Jean-Paul Sartre Experience, ▷ The Sid Presley Experience, ▷ Kiss The Sky, ▷ Kinky Machine, ▷ The Red House Painters, ▷ Third Stone and ▷ Voodoo Chile. His roadies included ▷ Lemmy. Spin-off from the Experience: ▷ Fat Mattress.

Hennessys

No reference to cognac: Welsh 1960s band led by Frank Hennessy.

Henry Cow

Nobody in the band was called Henry Cow.

It was a reference to U.S. pianist and composer Henry Cowell (1897–1965), who moved from conventional music to experimentation after the style of John Cage. This U.K. band also showed an interest in experimentation.

Notes for name nuts:
1. This band, formed at the U.K.'s Cambridge University in 1968, were briefly called ▷ Cabaret Voltaire, a name later made famous by another act.
2. In no way related to the similar-sounding animal ▷ Blodwyn Pig.
3. Related band: ▷ Comus.

The Herd

Late 1960s U.K. bopper band who made a fine pun on the collective for a group of animals – nicely disparaging – and the past tense of hearing – their records were, after all, Heard.

One of the best punning names, along with ▷ Felt, ▷ The Jam, ▷ XTC, ▷U2, The Swankers (▷Sex Pistols), ▷ Riff Raff, Voxpoppers, N-Trance, The Hit Squad (▷ 808 State), ▷ The Spin Doctors, Heartbeat, ▷ INXS, The Pop Tarts (▷ Pop Will Eat Itself), Altern8, King L and ▷ Linx. Spin-off: ▷ Humble Pie.

Herman's Hermits

The U.K. band noticed the similarity between leader Peter Noone and Sherman in U.S. television's *The Rocky And Bullwinkle Show*. They got the name wrong, but thought it "hilariously American". The Hermits gave alliterative effect.

Later releases were by "Peter Noone and Herman's Hermits" (which one was Herman then?). Their initial choice – Heartbeats – was much better, though it may have got them noticed less quickly.

Hetch Hetchy

Athens, Georgia, band who worked with Michael Stipe of ▷ R.E.M. The name comes from a valley in Yosemite National Park.

The High

"We're all tall, man, what's the problem?" The problem was they were of average height, making this a thinly disguised drug reference.

High Plain Drifters

Birmingham 1980s band inspired by Clint Eastwood's 1972 film *High Plains Drifter*. Not related: ▷ The Drifters, ▷ The Grifters.

The High Priest of Bop/ Be-bop

Appropriately religious-sounding nickname for the devotionally named ▷ Thelonious Monk, ▷ The Mad Monk.

The Highwaymen (country)

This country band, featuring ▷ Johnny Cash, ▷ Kris Kristofferson, Waylon Jennings and Willie Nelson, named from a J. Webb composition.

The Highwaymen (folk)

Predating the country act of the same name, they named after the famous poem by Alfred Noyes.

Higsons
Named after their leader Charlie Higson.

The Hillmen
From Chris Hillman, later of ▷ The Byrds.

The Hi-Los
Pronounced "high-lows" not "hillows". U.S. combo with two extremely tall members and two of less than average height. With suitably contrasting voices to match.

Hindu Love Gods
Warren Zevon and ▷ R.E.M. almost stumbling through cover versions and named after an earlier, abortive R.E.M. offshoot. The name, like R.E.M., was supposed to be deep and meaningless.

His Latest Flame
After the number one ▷ Elvis Presley 1961 song. Earlier they were called Sophisticated Boom Boom (also title of ▷ Dead Or Alive's 1984 album).

His Name Is Alive
Reference to the spirit of emancipation living on after the assassination of U.S. President Abraham Lincoln.

Hitlerz Underpantz
Jejune punk shock tactics, predecessor of ▷ Orchestral Manoeuvres In The Dark.

Hitmen
There were two 1980s Hitmen – from Australia and London. The latter said it takes in "business [troubleshooters], firearms [sharp shooters] and pop [makers of hits]". Related bands: ▷ Brilliant, ▷ Depeche Mode. Cf The Hit Squad (▷ 808 State).

HMV
Stands for His Master's Voice. Name of record label and chain of record stores. Taken from a Francis Barraud painting bought by EMI chairman William Owen, showing Barraud's bull terrier cross, Nipper, looking quizzically at a gramophone. The make of phonograph depicted was changed at Owen's request. Helped inspire ▷ Bow Wow Wow's naming.

The Hoboken Canary
▷ Frank Sinatra's nickname The Hoboken Canary stems from his voice and origin. His earliest group was The Hoboken Four, named after the singers' home in New Jersey.

Hole
Another short 1990s name (cf ▷ Blur), chosen by ▷ Courtney Love "to confuse people". Papers called it an "in the face" phallic name recalling ▷ The Slits. Love dismissed the dirty minds, saying she took it from Euripides, where Medea talks of a hole piercing through her soul. "It's about the abyss that's inside," she told Amy Raphael in the 1995 book *Never Mind The Bollocks: Women Rewrite Rock*. ▷ Riot Grrrl.

Billie Holiday
The U.S. jazz singer was born Eleanora Fagan – the second name was her mother's; she later learned her real father was musician Clarence Holiday. Billie was from her long-time favourite movie star, Billie Dove. ▷ Lady Day.

Jools Holland
The piano player took the middle-class edge off his real first name Julian. ▷ Squeeze.

Michael Holliday
The British singer was born Michael Miller and finally used his mother's maiden name.

The Hollies
Manchester, U.K., band formed 1961 as The Fourtones, later The Guytones and The Deltas, whose final name was chosen simply as a tribute to ▷ Buddy Holly, who died in 1959. It seemed obvious, there already having been a band called The Iveys (no relation to the band of 1968 which evolved into ▷ Badfinger). Still, there was no excuse for an album to be entitled *Holliedaze*.

The Hollow Men
Indie band named after T.S. Eliot. *The Hollow Men* was a long poem of the mid-1920s.

Buddy Holly
Charles Hardin Holley was known as Buddy from an early age in his home town of Lubbock, Texas. The "e" in Holley was accidentally

dropped when his first record contract was drawn up, a change he decided to keep for professional use (but his grave says "In loving memory of Buddy Holley").

His first real band, Buddy and The Three Tunes, was a self-consciously disparaging name (despite the fact that they could play considerably more than three songs, as anyone listening to their 1956 recordings, released as the 1961 LP *That'll Be The Day*, will know). ▷ The Crickets. He influenced ▷ The Beatles, ▷ The Hollies and ▷ The Iveys.

The Home Service

Spin-off from ▷ The Albion Band; Albion meant "England" or "home". They wanted a suitably nostalgic name and considered the cricket term The First Eleven as well as Villagers. The Home Service was the old name for the BBC's domestic radio station, specialising in news, talks and plays as opposed to the Music, Light and World Services.

The Honeycombs

British 1960s group. Drummer Ann Lantree was called "honey" and she and another member had day jobs as hairdressers.

Honeycrack

In the face of claims their name is a sexy or druggy reference, they reply it's the nominal marriage of "something very sweet with something hard". Go figure.

The Honeydrippers

Honeydripper was a 1945 hit for Joe Liggins And His Honeydrippers; he later set up the Honeydripper label. It was also apt for a northern English R&B band who specialised in performing similar music by the likes of Albert King and ▷ Gene Vincent. They became famous after teaming up with former ▷ Led Zeppelin singer Robert Plant.

The Hoochie-Coochie Men

This band was formed by ▷ Long John Baldry in the mid-1960s, recalling a ▷ Muddy Waters song which says a hoochie-coochie man, or practitioner of voodoo, has sexual powers to seduce women. More voodoo: ▷ Hoodoo Gurus, Hoodoo Rhythm Devils, The Mojo

Men, ▷ The Mojos, ▷ Wall Of Voodoo, ▷ Voodoo Chile.

Hoodlum Priest

This act celebrated celluloid heroes and recalled the 1961 movie of the same name.

The Hoodoo Gurus

This Australian 1980s group is no relation to the San Francisco 1970s outfit Hoodoo Rhythm Devils. Both named after black magic but have little else in common. They were originally Le Hoodoo Gurus, hoping the French sound was classy, until they got announced as "Three Loose Zulus".

John Lee Hooker

This Mississippi bluesman has sometimes used a string of pseudonyms, sometimes for contractual reasons, including the similar Johnny Lee and John Lee Booker. He inspired ▷ The Crawling King Snakes and ▷ The Groundhogs.

The Hooters

Reportedly from a musical term for a harmonica, and not drugs slang for marijuana cigarettes.

Hootie And The Blowfish

They had a hit with their first album, the magnificently titled *Cracked Rear View*, in 1994. The moniker refers not to the band but two of their friends, Ervin "Hootie" Harris and Donald "Blowfish" Feaster. The nicknames were in-jokes among the University of South Carolina choir which also included band leader Darius Rucker.

Lightnin' Hopkins

Sam Hopkins got his name for his fast guitar picking while playing with piano-bar star Thunder Smith: they were called Thunder and Lightnin'.

Hornets Attack Victor Mature

An anarchistic choice. Victor Mature, as one of Hollywood's leading men of the 1940s, was a cinema icon whose handsome features were not designed to be wrecked by hornet stings. It was taken from a Los Angeles newspaper story about the actor who was out playing golf when he had to run for safety when he stirred up a swarm. The band were no great fans of Mature, whom they said had "larger breasts than most women".

This Georgia band went on to become ▷ R.E.M. They returned to the name once after becoming famous for a 1985 gig; they guessed only true fans would recognise it.

Horse Latitudes
North London 1990s band named after the classic track on the October 1967 album *Strange Days* by ▷ The Doors, based around Jim Morrison's high school poem about becalmed sailing ships jettisoning cargo in the doldrums.

Hot Chocolate
The London band were signed to ▷ The Beatles-owned Apple label in 1969, where they had an internal "suggestions please" contest for a moniker. A secretary suggested it in reference to their hot music and racial origin.

The Hothouse Flowers
Taken from a Wynton Marsalis title. A talent nurtured by ▷ U2. Spin-off: ▷ ALT.

Hot Metal
Heavy metal band who named after a 1986–88 U.K. television sitcom starring Robert Hardy as an unscrupulous media baron. "Hot metal" refers to the old-fashioned method of printing newspapers.

Hot Tuna
Do not read this entry if you are eating your dinner or feel slightly unwell.

This is one of those appalling names, like ▷ Peanut Butter Conspiracy and ▷ Vanilla Fudge. This band, an off-shoot of ▷ Jefferson Airplane, wanted to be Hot Shit because they had "shit hot tunes". After resistance from RCA, they agreed to a slight change. Spin-offs: ▷ Dinosaurs, ▷ SVT.

The Housemartins
Supposedly named after the bird and song. However, the birds are (unlike, say, ▷ Nightingales) not particularly noted for their tunes. Related band: ▷ The Beautiful South.

House Of Love
This band ripped off Anaïs Nin's 1954 novel *Spy In The House of Love*. They denied any connection with ▷ Was Not Was single of this name, noting they formed in 1986, before its release. Their 1988 album features the book prominently in its cover photo.

Whitney Houston
Born in Newark, New Jersey, Whitney was named after a character in her mother's favourite soap opera.

The Howling Success
Nickname for the lachrymose ▷ Johnnie Ray.

Howlin' Wolf
Mississippi-born muso Chester Arthur Burnett knew it was normal for a wolf to howl at the moon, and this he did each night to close his evening Memphis KMW Radio slot – adapting Jimmie Rodgers to a tortured blues cry which became *Moanin' At Midnight*. He was also known as Bull Cow and Cow Foot because of his height and size. His name was parodied by U.K. 1980s singer Howlin' Wilf.

H.P. Lovecraft
This entry is under "H" not "L" because it refers to a band, not an individual star. Still, it came from one person: the original H.P. Lovecraft was a haunted New England writer. Little of his work appeared in his lifetime, but this U.S. act helped in its reappearance. A number of their songs quote directly from Lovecraft's stories.

HSAS
From founders Hagar, Schon, Aaronson and Schrieve. Spin-off from the equally boring ▷ Journey.

H2O
Glasgow band who decided the chemical symbol for water was smarter than their original choice, the misspelling Skroo. "We're all 80 per cent water, so we must feel some affinity to it," they explained.

Huang Chung
The name suggests a non-British band, and

their music was heavy with Chinese influences. Bassist Nick Feldman admitted it was chosen because of its onomatopoeic representation of a guitar chord. Later respelled Wang Chung.

Hue And Cry

This duo named after "an angry chase, an outcry or a clamorous disapproval," to quote one definition. They just thought it unusual. Neither was called Hugh/Huw – neither was especially lachrymose. Like ▷ Gene Loves Jezebel/▷ Bleep + Booster (which one's which?) and ▷ Pink Floyd (which one's Pink?) they found the non-member name a problem in interviews.

Hues Corporation

A nice faceless corporate name, like ▷ Big Brother And The Holding Company, ▷ The Firm and ▷ Public Image Ltd. This American band named after a conglomerate owned and run by the billionaire Howard Hughes. Los Angeles producer Wally Holmes wanted to call them The Children Of Howard Hues but was informed this was legally dangerous.

Huggy Bear

British 1990s band in the ▷ Riot Grrrl movement. They named after successful U.S. television show *Starsky And Hutch*. Huggy wrongly fancies himself as the super-cool street contact of the plainclothes detectives who spent 1975–79 leaping in and out of fast cars. ▷ David Soul; ▷ Lovebug Starski.

Hullabaloos

Because they came from Hull, U.K.; still, their music was far from a hullabaloo as defined as "uproar or din".

Human League

The League's antecedents all date from Sheffield, U.K., in the mid-1970s, including the punkish Musical Vomit – not an auspicious beginning. By 1977, Martin Ware and Ian Craig-Marsh were The Dead Daughters, a moniker from the science fiction computer game *Star Force*. They renamed The Future – a good choice, noting their futuristic electronic divergence. Phil Oakey saw them in mid-1977 and declared them "ahead of their time". Later

he joined as the appellation changed to The Men And The Human League. This last was one of two rival empires battling to rule earth in 2180 in the sci-fi game. The tag was trademarked as early as 1980, a typically far-sighted move.

Ware and Craig-Marsh, the band's founders, later left to form ▷ B.E.F. and ▷ Heaven 17. Oakey and company kept the rights to the Human League appellation, despite the reputed £20,000 payment that this would involve to Heaven 17. He explained that it was worth the money and just right: it sounded cool, with "human" adding just a touch of emotion.

Related band: ▷ The Rezillos. For more, see Peter Nash's 1982 book *The Human League: Perfect Pop*.

Human Sexual Response

From a standard psychological textbook of the same name.

Humble Pie

Press speculation was generated by the group's impressive antecedents which included ▷ The Herd, ▷ The Small Faces and ▷ Spooky Tooth. Steve Marriott responded with this name to show they weren't suffering from over-inflated egos. The expression "to eat humble pie" means to act humbly or to eat one's words. Spin-off: ▷ Rough Diamond.

Engelbert Humperdinck

Born Arnold George Dorsey, he was singing from before 1956 but only found fame with the ridiculous name performing ballads in 1965. It was suggested by his former flatmate Gordon Mills, who was then managing ▷ Tom Jones. As with Jones's name, Mills looked to the past for inspiration but this time went for the most complex option in the hope it would be memorable. He borrowed it from a nineteenth-century German opera composer, the man behind *Hansel And Gretel*. "Enge" later became known as "Mr Romance". Mills later helped ▷ Gilbert O'Sullivan.

Hunters And Collectors

This Melbourne band made a self-consciously sexist joke about men naturally being "hunters" and women "collectors of berries and fruit".

Hüsker DU

This critically lauded American mid-1980s band took their name from a Scandinavian children's board game. It means "do you remember?" and is meant to encourage memory skills. They weren't so much hailing the past as selecting a tag which they hoped would mean nothing to most people.

The Hype

These Dubliners began as ▷ Feedback, making fun of themselves, then renamed to make fun of the music business. They soon realised this could alienate record companies and could be taken as meaning they were only a hyped act without talent. They changed again and proved this false by becoming mega-group ▷ U2. No relation to The Hype who backed ▷ David Bowie or Hazel O'Connor's Megahype.

H

Ibex

A precursor of ▷ Queen, the moniker was suggested by drummer Mike Smith, who thought it sounded cool and Dadaist. He was unaware it was the name of a wild goat. ▷ Freddie Mercury renamed the band Wreckage.

Icehouse

Australian act Flowers ran into two problems. First was the commercial death of their debut album,1980's *Icehouse*. Second, they discovered there was a Scottish act called The Flowers. Their icy response was to remix and relaunch the record, renaming after its title cut. An icehouse in this context is slang down under for an asylum, a "cooler" for cooling off lunatics. Similar "Mad Aussie" name: ▷ Mental As Anything.

Ice T

A champion of black rights, he named from political author Iceberg Slim. It fitted U.S. underworld terminology: "ice" = "very cool". His real name is less cool, Tracy Marrow: his first name was abbreviated to pun on iced tea. This happened before the drug ice started to appear widely. Ice, smokeable methamphetamine, has proved to be addictive and dangerous. Ice T responded by speaking out against drugs. A self-confessed former criminal, he was known as O.G.; this became an album title and means "Original Gangster".

Cf ▷ Vanilla Ice, ▷ Body Count.

Vanilla Ice

A millionaire rap king at 23, Ice was born Robert Van Winkle and recalls his Miami youth: "Ice came from the kids I hung out with. Every one was black, and I had the vanilla skin, so that's what they called me … " He was less pleased by later reports saying he was "a flavour of the month" who had "melted away". ▷ Ice T (similar *alter ego*, another embarrassing real name).

The Icicle Works

This British act took it from a 1959 short story called *The Day The Icicle Works Closed* by U.S. writer Frederik Pohl. They thought it far-out, interesting and surreal.

The Id

Forerunner of ▷ Orchestral Manoeuvres In The Dark, so named from the psychology student interests of one of their number.

Ides Of March

Illinois band formed on 15 March; the anniversary of the claimed date on which Roman emperor Julius Caesar was assassinated. He had been warned to "beware the Ides of March".

Idle Race

Jeff Lynne's humble start came in a Brummie band who named after an early song. He went on into ▷ The Electric Light Orchestra, ▷ The Traveling Wilburys and produced ▷ George Harrison and ▷ The Beatles. Not so idle.

Billy Idol

Born William Michael Albert Broad, he joined the ▷ Bromley Contingent, ▷ Chelsea and ▷ Generation X. One report of the time suggested he wanted a name to reflect his cult hero status and nearly resolved on Billy Starboy. Unflattering derivatives: Billy Idle, Bone Idol (because of his leisurely recording schedule). Son: Willem Wolf Broad.

If

Formed in the late 1960s, following the influential Lindsay Anderson 1968 film *If*, about rebellion at a boys' public school. Related band: ▷ Greenslade.

Iggy

AKA Iggy Stooge, ▷ Iggy Pop.

Ikettes

Because they backed the husband-and-wife team of Ike and ▷ Tina Turner.

Illinois Speed Press

From Chicago, they named from a local newspaper and general printing company whose slogan was Speedy Service With A Smile. Have a nice day!

Immaculate Consumptive

▷ Madonna was not the only star to take off the religious term immaculate conception, referring to Jesus being miraculously conceived in the Virgin Mary. (Her 1990 greatest hits CD was called *The Immaculate Collection*.)

This international band contained the talents of ▷ Mark-Almond, Nick Cave, ▷ Foetus man Jim Thirlwell and Lydia Lunch. They took the name in reference to the fashionable appearance of all of the band and their thinness – all looked liked consumptives, even Lydia Lunch, who looked like she'd had none.

The Immaculate Fools

One of the many to chose a self-mocking name (cf ▷ Simple Minds), this 1980s U.K. outfit accepted they "may not be Einstein" but "wear it well". No relation to ▷ Immaculate Consumptive.

The Impediments

Because these musicians from Minneapolis, Minnesota, started with a greater reputation for their hard drinking than playing ability. They later straightened up as ▷ The Replacements.

Imposter

▷ Elvis Costello incognito for the political tracks *Pills And Soap* and *Peace In Our Time*. Not quite anonymous: the Imposter appeared on *Top Of The Tops* looking and sounding exactly like Costello. And his fans would have recognised it as the title of a Costello track from three years before.

Incognito

U.K. producer Jean-Paul Maunick, always a backroom boy, thus chose to keep out of the spotlight when forming his own band.

Incredible String Band

U.K. folk trio boasting their proficiency over a vast array of instruments, including mandolins, harps, dulcimers, violins and guitars.

In Crowd

They were Four Plus One – a handle too similar to ▷ Unit 4 + 2 and they changed in 1965. They confirmed in an interview the new identity came from Dobie Gray's *The In Crowd* single of the same year.

The Ink Spots

The 1930s name, one of the oldest in this book, came from the days when groups kept things simple: it referred to their individual "spot" in concert as well as their colour. They were King, Jack and Jester until complaints from The King's Jesters. The new tag was thought up "in minutes" by manager Moe Gale.

Innocents

Californian trio who named after the car club they had joined.

Inspiral Carpets

Pronounced "In-spiral", as in inspirational, mind expanding, shimmering 1960s songs, spinning records, swirling shirts, even spirals in carpets – possibly as seen after acid tabs. All this was just fantasy to the schoolboys who launched the band in Oldham, U.K., in 1980. They launched as The Furs, a tribute to early heroes

▷ The Psychedelic Furs. Later commonly called by fans The Inspirals. One of their roadies, Noel Gallagher, said his time with them helped provide the name ▷ Oasis.

The Intelligent Hoodlum
The real name of this New York teenager was a secret; his alias came about because he was a reformed criminal. "I was much too intelligent for crime." Music paid better and had the advantage that he could do naughty things without getting sent to prison.

Lux Interior
Member of ▷ The Cramps.

INXS
The pun works if you spell it out. Say "In Excess", not "Inks". They began as The Farriss Brothers (1977), after the three members of the Australian Farriss family. But they had a rethink after criticism this was "dated", "boring" and "like a circus act". The new name was suggested by ▷ Midnight Oil manager Garry Morris. Bassist Garry Gary Beers was christened in a family tradition for double Christian names.

IQ
These intellectual U.K. musos of the 1980s said it was intended as a comment, not a boast. It reportedly came from a 1960s headline about Oxford-educated *Privilege* singer Paul Jones: "Can a pop star have too high an I.Q.?" Cf ▷ The Zombies.

Iron Butterfly
U.S. group leader Doug Ingle said the name needed to reflect the band's desire to move easily from heavy music to lighter sounds. He found it after reflecting on the popularity of insect aliases such as ▷ The Beatles and ▷ The Crickets. Ingle was equally influenced by the Aztec god Izpapaloti, meaning "stone butterfly", according to one account. This surreal translation was very 1960s and akin to countless psychedelic offerings such as ▷ The Soft Watches.

The Californian band's success proved influential. Jimmy Page said it had some bearing on the naming of ▷ Led Zeppelin, another "light and heavy metal music" description.

The handle had been applied to a very different musical star before. Singer Jeanette MacDonald, who did a mean *Madama Butterfly*, was often billed as Iron Butterfly. She died in the mid-1960s, just before Ingle's group sprouted from its chrysalis. There's no evidence that they were paying tribute to her. Even more coincidentally the nickname was given to Imelda Marcos, widow of President Ferdinand Marcos of the Philippines.

Ironhorse
Railroad inspiration for this ▷ Bachman-Turner Overdrive offshoot, in keeping with a mechanical and transportation theme.

Ironing Board Sam
South Carolina musician Sammy Moore acquired his name when he makeshift-mounted his keyboard on an ironing board for a show. He hated his nickname at first but later realised its commercial value and even gave away ironing boards to concert-goers.

Iron Maiden
An Iron Maiden was a medieval torture instrument. The gory details as follows.

Historians say there were at least two iron maidens, the early and less sophisticated Middle Ages version simply consisted of a human-shaped cage of a rope. This ducked unfortunates in water and left them there until they drowned or confessed. The later medieval version was more fiendish, putting the victim in wooden or metal "maidens" – coffin-shaped sections, one with sharp inward-facing spikes, which was gradually closed.

Fun for all the family and an apt tag for a band with the decibels to inflict their own musical torture on the willing and unwilling.

The choice was based on a song of the same title which they played at their first gig in 1976 after dropping their old name Smiler or Smile – a moniker, incidentally, also used by the early ▷ Queen. Bassist Steve Harris had also considered the moniker Gypsy's Kiss.

It had absolutely nothing to do with the 1962 film *The Iron Maiden*, about a man and his traction engine, by the way. It had similar contradictory qualities to ▷ Iron Butterfly and ▷ Led Zeppelin though.

Fact for factoid freaks: The author is informed * that singer Bruce Dickinson, who came to the Maiden via ▷ Samson, was once part of a gender-bender act provocatively called Rear Entry. Do these people have *taste*?? Silly question, really.

* This information was provided by a university acquaintance of Bruce's but is hard to verify. Most encyclopedias start with Dickinson springing to life fully-formed as the moustachioed frontman of Samson first. Yes, perhaps unbelievably, Bruce Dickinson went to *university*. The sometime *Lord Iffy Boatrace* novelist and tattooed millionaire also attended a relatively exclusive public school.

Yusif Islam
▷ Cat Stevens after his religious conversion.

Isley Brothers
They **were** all brothers: Rudolph, Ronald, O'Kelly, Vernon and later recruits Ernie and Marvin. Then they cheated and added Chris Jasper – their cousin.

Isotope
One of several atoms of the same element identical in chemical properties while differing in mass number. The term was chosen by the group because it was "basic … just like people".

I Start Counting
This name's stupidity is only partly alleviated by knowing it's the title of a film, a 1969 British effort about a suspected mass murderer. It starred the young Jenny Agutter, whose movies of the period also influenced ▷ The Railway Children. Still, there are similar first-person silver-screen titles they could have picked which are even more off-the-wall: *I Didn't Do It, I Killed Rasputin* or *I Dream Too Much*.

It Crawled From The South
▷ R.E.M. being creative in a one-off concert billing, which recalls horror movies such as *It Crawled From The Deep* and *It Came From Outer Space*. Of course, R.E.M. came from the American south: they put Athens, Georgia, on the map.

It's A Beautiful Day
Inspired by the weather conditions in San Francisco on the July 1967 day they formed. The optimism had dimmed by 1978 – or perhaps the weather wasn't so good – for they briefly re-formed as It Was A Beautiful Day.

It's Immaterial
Liverpool band who said finding a name was "just a mere detail". Related bands: ▷ The Christians, ▷ Wah!

The Iveys
Early ▷ Badfinger. They signed to the infant ▷ Apple label under this name, a tribute to ▷ Buddy Holly. As in *The Holly And The Ivy* Christmas carol, of course. The renaming came because this sort of moniker was looking dated by the late 1960s. This hadn't stopped ▷ The Hollies, or indeed ▷ The Beatles, who of course founded Apple, from naming after Holly.

The Ivy League
Entirely in the North American tradition of clean-cut college names (▷ The Crew Cuts, Four Preps, The Lettermen), they hailed from Birmingham, U.K., but imitated the close-harmony sound. An interesting counterpart to many U.S. groups of the time who pretended to be British. The prestigious Ivy League consists of U.S. universities: Brown, Columbia, Cornell, Dartmouth, Harvard, Pennsylvania, Princeton and Yale. The band later became ▷ The Flowerpot Men.

I

The Jackson Five

Well, there were five of them called Jackson. It took a long time to find a name … One was called (improbably) "Jermaine La Jaune Jackson" (*jaune* = yellow). After Michael left, Randy (really) arrived so the moniker stayed. They became The Jackson Family, then The Jacksons, after a label change because Tamla Motown owned the byword Jackson Five. Cf ▷ New Edition.

Jackson Heights

Founder Lee Jackson was English and didn't know much about the Jackson Heights area of New York but thought it an apposite reference to his surname. His given Christian name was Keith; he switched during his time with The Nice so as not to clash with later ▷ ELP star Keith Emerson. The group later worked without him under the name Heights.

Michael Jackson

Born Michael Joseph Jackson. Michael Jackson, a stage name taken from a clever combination of his family surname and the first name his parents gave him at birth … If all stars were named in this way, this book would be much shorter. Still that's not to mention his nicknames and unflattering derivatives: Jacko, ▷ Wacko Jacko, ▷ The Gloved One. Tribute act: Mikki Jay. ▷ Jackson Five.

His son is Prince Michael Junior. The choice was seen by some as a slight on ▷ Prince – who had refused a duet on the song *Bad* years before. Others said it allowed Michael to invest a future Prince of Pop to rival his own title ▷ The King of Pop. However, in a 1997 interview, Michael said: "My grandfather and great-grandfather were both named Prince, so we have carried on the tradition and now have a third Prince in the family."

Jack The Lad

This ▷ Lindisfarne spin-off named from the Northern English phrase "because we're all likely lads, Jack the Lad".

Jagged Edge

They liked the title of a film so named after it, while saying the movie itself wasn't much good. "We're not endorsing that."

Jags

U.K. band named after Jaguar luxury cars. They thought it could also refer to big cats or even Mick Jagger of ▷ The Rolling Stones. They co-existed with a similarly named U.K. act, Jaguar.

Jale

All-female four-piece from Halifax, Nova Scotia, Canada, named ▷ Abba-style after their initials: Jenny (Pierce), Alyson (MacLeod), Laura (Stein) and Eve (Hartling).

The Jam

This U.K. band, arguably one of the most important of the late 1970s and early 1980s, named from breakfast conversation among Paul Weller's family. Paul's mother, Ann, recalls: "We were at breakfast one day, and Nicky (Paul's sister) said: 'We've had the bread and the marmalade, so let's have the jam." ▷ The Marmalade, ▷ Bread. U.S. readers may need to be told "jam" is the English word for breakfast jelly.

The trio used to meet for "jam session" rehearsals at their school in Woking, Surrey. "Jam" was short enough to print up big on posters like those of their idols, ▷ The Who.

More neo-mods: ▷ The Lambrettas, ▷ The Merton Parkas. Spin-off: ▷ The Style Council. The Jam inspired ▷ The Stone Roses. Paul Weller's nicknames: ▷ The Cappuccino Kid, The Guv'nor, ▷ The Modfather, The New Eric Clapton and The Uncle of Britpop.

Weller was born in Woking in May 1958. His mother was unwell when the registrar visited her and amid confusion her son was named John William Weller, his father's name. After she recovered the parents unofficially renamed the child as Paul – it's still John William on his passport.

Drummer Buckler was named Paul Richard Buckler – but known as Rick from an early age. On some early Polydor photos he was wrongly identified as "Rick Buckley".

For more see Paolo Hewitt's *The Jam: A Beat Concerto*, published in 1983 and revised in 1996. Or the less-insightful *The Jam: Our Story*, by Bruce Foxton and Rick Butler with Alex Ogg, 1994.

JAM Chain
▷ The Jesus And Mary Chain.

James
They could never have made it under their first identity, the punk Venereal And The Diseases. The next name was also a disaster. Guitarist Paul Gilbertson, a lost founder-member, had a girlfriend who worked for the Model Team International agency. He decided to lift the moniker and even had tee-shirts made with this slogan but was threatened with legal action.

At this point they decided to keep it simple and use the prenomen of one of their members. The first choice was singer Tim, but he didn't want to be too prominent. Still, the line-up had two Jameses. Bassist Jimmie Glennie explains James was "simple, unassuming and doesn't give any clues". Like fellow Mancunians ▷ The Smiths, it was a tag devoid of associations which prevented them from being labelled.

The James Gang
From the outlaws led by Jesse James. Related: ▷ The Eagles. Not related: ▷ James.

Rick James
Born James Johnson, briefly Rick Matthews. Some of his early changes were reportedly bids to avoid arrest as a deserter from the U.S. Navy. But they caught him in the end. ▷ The Mynah Birds, ▷ The Mary Jane Girls, ▷ The Main Line, ▷ Punk Funk Chorus.

Jamie Wednesday
This British band – formed on a Wednesday and named after ▷ Jim Morrison of ▷ The Doors – inspired the name ▷ Pop Will Eat Itself. Related act: ▷ Carter USM.

Jamiroquoi
U.K. star Jason Kay named after an American Indian tribe. Nickname: ▷ The Cat In The Hat.

The JAMS
One of the names used by the ▷ KLF. Stands for Justified Ancients of Mu Mu and taken from the Shea and Wilson *Illuminatus* trilogy of novels.

Jan And Dean
Jan Berry and Dean Torrence. They also used the name for solo projects.

Jane's Addiction
This 1990s act claimed Jane was a junkie Hollywood hooker through which they met in Los Angeles in the 1980s, although this may be a piece of self-mythologising to rival ▷ Alice Cooper's ouija board naming. ▷ Porno For Pyros.

Jaojoby
Dance act named from singer Jaojoby Eusebe.

Japan
This British synthesiser combo wanted a

moniker which showed they weren't another punk guitar act. They hailed from the not-so-lovely Lewisham and thought Japan more exotic, although none had been there when the soubriquet was selected. They said: "It's just a word. A country. It could be anywhere."

However, it summed up their songs, which showed traditional Eastern influences. Not surprisingly, they became big in Japan before they made it back home in Britain. Not related: ▷ Big In Japan. Related: ▷ Dali's Car, ▷ Rain Tree Crow, ▷ David Sylvian.

Frankie Half-Pint Jason
From his diminutive frame.

Jay And The Americans
The 1950s and early 1960s saw groups striving to project a decent short-haired image in the face of McCarthyism and backlash from middle America against "black music", rock 'n' roll and unAmerican values. Hence names like this, although the band's bland image may now be questioned, since members included the subversives who later formed ▷ Steely Dan.

The Jean-Paul Sartre Experience
Pure pop band with no pretensions tongue-in-cheekily named after the French writer (1905–80). Partly inspired by ▷ The Jimi Hendrix Experience. The prospect of little Sartre providing an outrageous Hendrix-type show takes some imagination.

Jefferson Airplane
This is not a drug reference but taken in 1965 from a dog's name. The pooch's full title included "Blind" – a reference to scores of blind blues players such as Blind Blake, Blind John Davis, Blind Willie McTell, Blind Willie Johnson, Blind Joe Reynolds, and especially Blind Lemon Jefferson, whose work was revered by the band's blues guitarist Jorma Kaukonen. Some biographies say the canine's tag also contained a Thomas, a reference to the American president (1743–1826), who tried to bring an end to slavery. The Airplane came from the Jefferson aeronautics company.

By the 1970s, a Jefferson Airplane was widely accepted in San Francisco slang. It was defined in *Chapman's Dictionary* as any tweezer-like device for holding a joint too small to be gripped by the fingers without burning. It was named from the group's psychedelic sounds; however, magazine articles got the truth the wrong way round. Over the next few years, this error was widely reported in rock encyclopedias.

By the 1980s, the group was trying to correct the flood of incorrect reports, although the Airplane's place in drug culture was such that their denials fell on deaf ears initially. The story was better than reality.

Cf ▷ The Roches, who were not named after the cigarette, and ▷ The Doobie Brothers, who claimed not to have known of the drug link when naming.

Hence the name. Hence all the surrealistic pillows. Name notes:
1. Related bands: ▷ Dinosaurs, ▷ Great Society, ▷ Hot Tuna, ▷ Jefferson Starship, ▷ SVT.
2. Sprog notes: Grace Slick called her daughter China, her son God.
3. Included violinist Papa John Creach – his nickname coming from his comparatively advanced age. He was in his 50s when the Airplane took off.
4. They inspired ▷ (Jefferson) Airhead and may have helped inspire ▷ Echo And The Bunnymen.
5. Another misunderstood name with a possible animal link: ▷ Pink Floyd.
6. There's more in *The Jefferson Airplane And The San Francisco Sound* by Ralph J. Gleason (1969) and *Waiting For The Sun: The Story Of The Los Angeles Music Scene*, 1996, by Barney Hoskins.

Jefferson Airhead
▷ Airhead.

Jefferson Starship
Part two of the ▷ Jefferson Airplane saga starts in 1970, when a collaboration with ▷ Jerry Garcia and Graham Nash, ex ▷ The Hollies, was christened Jefferson Starship. This higher-flying name, at the height of NASA's Apollo success, originated from co-founder Paul Kantner's science-fiction vision of the future – refer to album *Blows Against The Empire*. He denied paying tribute to *Starship*, the ▷ MC5 track of the year before. The appellation was

retained, shortened at one point to Starship; and in 1989 Jefferson Airplane was re-formed.

The Jerky Boys
Prank callers Kamal (Ahmed) and Johnny B (Brennan) ring up New York sales, delivery or repair lines with ridiculous requests and record the results, often calling their victims "jerks" or "jerky". *Hence several hit albums, hence the name.*

The Jesus And Mary Chain
Amid the dark menace of Scottish brothers William and Jim Reid, it's incredible to note they first considered the tag Death Of Joey, inspired by the demise of their pet budgerigar. Jesus And Mary Chain was an evolution of Daisy Chain and intended as meaningless.

There are many myths about the name. The duo initially said it was inspired by a cornflakes packet, which had an offer to send away for a Jesus And Mary linked bracelet. Major cereal manufacturers quickly pointed out they would be unlikely to have a religious item as a free gift. The Chain then switched to another tall story: that it was a solid gold $200 necklace advertised in a magazine. Then they said it came from dialogue in a ▷ Bing Crosby film. That it was a chain letter. That it was a order of Catholic nuns. That it was a religious shrine in Greece or Mexico. That it was an obscure satanic cult … All false.

William Reid finally spoke in a U.S. radio interview, after being challenged by a Crosby movie expert who could find no mention of the words. William said: "These stories are wrong. … We knew the word Jesus was sacred to Christians but after all Jesus is the commonest name in some places. Nobody minds the 'Mary'." (Cf ▷ Jesus Jones.) The brothers were banned from top U.S.A. TV shows on account of the shock-value name, which they refused to shorten to J.A.M. Chain as prudish producers suggested.

Jesus Jones
The band's founders were on holiday, sitting in a Spanish bar and being served by a waiter called Jesus. The Britons commented his religious prenomen was not used for babies back home, where it could be seen as blasphemous. They pictured a few names: Jesus Smith, Smith and Jones, Jesus Jones … started laughing and stopped there.

Jesus Loves You
▷ Boy George attempting a 1991 comeback. The choice was related to his conversion to the ways of Krishna.

Jethro Tull
Jethro Tull was a leading eighteenth-century British farmer, known for his creation of a labour-saving seed drill. The name was suggested by an employee at Chrysalis Records, who had seen Tull's classic book *New Horse Hoeing Husbandry*. Vocalist-leader Ian Anderson thought it described his folk-rock better than his previous choice, Bag O' Blues. A 1968 single, *Aeroplane*, mistakenly credited Jethro Toe but it flopped, saving them from an unfortunate name. Bands related to Tull: ▷ Blodwyn Pig, ▷ The Cocktail Cowboys.

The Jet Set
▷ The Byrds.

JFA
Meant Jodie Foster's Army.

Jilted John
U.K. actor Graham Fellowes created this character to fit in with his 1978 comedy single about how weedy John is chucked by his girlfriend Julie. ▷ Gordon The Moron.

Jimbob
James Morrison (no relation to ▷ Jim Morrison of ▷ The Doors). Member of ▷ Carter USM.

Jimmy The Hoover
Not content with naming ▷ The Sex Pistols and ▷ Bow Wow Wow, street wise businessman ▷ Malcolm McLaren said of this 1980s act: "I hoped they'd clean up."

Jive Bunny
Mastermind Andy Pickles saw potential in the nickname of a friend, making it into a band and range of cuddly souvenirs.

J.J.
From co-founder Jan Johnston.

Billy Joel
When fame beckoned Bronx boy William Joel he rejected calls for a stagey moniker. "Ain't nothing wrong with a downtown name."

Elton John

Briton Reginald Kenneth Dwight was born in Pinner and at 14 joined local pub R&B band Bluesology. Over six years, the act turned professional and released their first single, *Come Back Baby*, written by Dwight. They backed ▷ The Ink Spots on a British tour and Doris Troy but the piano man quit, preferring songwriting with Bernie Taupin. Urged to find a showbizzy tag by publisher Dick James (▷ DJM), Dwight cast his mind back to Bluesology – and two latecomers to the line-up. They were sax player ▷ Elton Dean (later with ▷ Soft Machine) and front-man ▷ Long John Baldry. He had created Elton John before the end of 1967.

He changed to Elton Hercules John by deed poll in May 1972. *Hercules* was one of his songs, on the contemporaneous *Honky Chateau* album. But he used his original name as the title for the 1988 LP *Reg Strikes Back*. An early budget-priced remake of others' hits was later released on CD as *Reg Dwight's Piano Plays Pop*.

▷ Captain Fantastic, ▷ The Brown Dirt Cowboy, ▷ Hair, Nose and Teeth. Spoof act: Elton Jack. A duet with ▷ Kiki Dee was credited to Ann Orson and Carte Blanche in the U.S.A.

Johnny And The Self-Abusers

The ▷ Simple Minds story starts with this 1977 Glasgow band. The self-depreciating name established their punk credentials before they'd played anything. They underlined their anarchistic stance by breaking up on the day their first single was released. They inspired ▷ The Cocteau Twins. Spin-off: ▷ The Cuban Heels.

Johnny Hates Jazz

A pop band making an in-joke reference to a friend's musical preferences.

Johnny The Fox

Nickname for Phil Lynott after 1976 ▷ Thin Lizzy track *Johnny The Fox Meets Jimmy The Weed*.

Holly Johnson

William Johnson apparently became Holly on the dance-floor when approached by a handsome hunk and asked for his name. On the spur of the moment, the camp William murmured: "Holly", after the song which was playing: ▷ Lou Reed's 1973 track *Walk On The Wild Side*. ▷ Frankie

Goes To Hollywood, ▷ Big In Japan. The star's own account comes in *A Bone In My Flute*.

Jo Jo Gunne

Early 1970s break away band from ▷ Spirit, named after a ▷ Chuck Berry song which rhymed with their hit, *Run Run Run*.

Al Jolson

Anglicisation of Asa Yoelson.

Tom Jones

Thomas Woodward was born in Treforest, Glamorgan, in 1940 and spent eight years singing for beer and small cash, first as Tiger Tom, then Tommy Scott And The Senators (a bid to sound exotic in Merthyr Tydfil clubs). He was discovered by pop entrepreneur Gordon Mills, who was visiting Pontypridd. Mills got inspiration from a film he'd seen, the 1963 release *Tom Jones* starring Albert Finney. He thought it would link the singer to a successful movie, associate him with the raffishly romantic hero, provide an easy name to remember and a visual image.

Mills also helped ▷ Engelbert Humperdinck and ▷ Gilbert O'Sullivan. Nicknames: The Voice, Jones The Voice, ▷ The Prince Of Wails.

Josef K

These Scottish neo-pop revivalists took their inspiration from *The Trial*, a posthumous masterpiece by German-speaking writer Franz Kafka (1883–1924) which highlights Josef K, an ordinary man accused of an unspecified crime.

Joshua

From leader Joshua Pehahia.

The Joshua Trio

Spoof band performing ▷ U2 material, named after the 1987 *Joshua Tree* album by their superstar inspirers.

Journey

This San Francisco combo were originally The Golden Gates, after the famous bridge. They held a contest for the new name and rejected all 3,000 entries after thinking of Journey themselves, despite allegations it was boring. Still, they've travelled a long way since ... Related: ▷ HSAS, ▷ Santana.

Joy Division

This celebrated British band started at the height of punk, the summer of 1977. Their Manchester singer Ian Curtis sought guidance from Richard Boon, manager of ▷ The Buzzcocks. Curtis's widow Deborah, in her amazingly matter-of-fact 1995 memoir *Touching From A Distance*, says Ian was "deeply irritated" when Boon offered The Stiff Kittens as a standard punk name. Contrary to some reports, the suggestion didn't come from Buzzcocks frontman ▷ Pete Shelley; nor was it seriously used.

Instead they paid homage to ▷ David Bowie by becoming ▷ Warsaw, then heard of a similarly named combo and reconsidered.

It was vital for many bands of the time to have a supposedly shocking tag to rival ▷ The Sex Pistols. So the final handle came in 1978, from a 1958 paperback novel about Nazi concentration camps called *The House Of The Dolls*, written by one 'Ka-Tzetnik 135633'. The Joy Division was the area of the prison which housed "comfort women" chosen for their attractiveness and youth to be serial sex slaves. These poor women usually contracted sexual diseases quickly and were sadistically killed.

Deborah recalled: "It was gruesome and tasteless and I hoped that the majority of people would not know what it meant. I wondered if the members of the band were intending to glorify the degradation of women. Telling myself that they had chosen it merely to gain attention, I gradually became accustomed to the provocative moniker …"

Their defenders said it didn't necessarily mean Joy Division were an extreme right-wing band – there was an essential humanity underlying their material. The Nazi theme was echoed by other punks; still, no others went as far as putting Hitler Youth pictures on their debut record's cover. It was only later they went out of their way to repudiate controversial fascist, anti-democratic views.

The ▷ New Order designation was said to have similar Germanic influences – the group said it was Cambodian.

The act never sounded joyful, with songs about depression and desolation, with isolated singer Ian Curtis perpetually on the verge of the suicide he later committed.

Hence the name. Hence the love which tore him apart.

The Joy Of Cooking

Californian vocalists Toni Brown and Terry Garthwaite wrote strongly feminist lyrics and named from a non-politically correct book which claimed a woman's role is to please her man above all.

JTQ

Stands for James Taylor Quartet.

Judas Jump

▷ Amen Corner.

Judas Priest

The British band formed in the mid-1960s and used the exclamation "Judas Priest!" sometimes euphemistically in place of "Jesus Christ!" Vocalist Ian Hill managed to hold on to the name as they evolved into the combo which was to become famous.

Many articles have said – wrongly – the name came from ▷ Bob Dylan's song *The Ballad of Frankie Lee And Judas Priest* on his 1968 album *John Wesley Harding*. These articles are incorrect for three reasons. First, the name predates the song. Second, Priest denied it. Third, the Brummies, who progressed from rock to heavy metal, never sounded in the slightest like Dylan anyway. They influenced the name ▷ Exciter.

Juggernaut

Texas 1980s band reflecting the heaviness of their metal music. Unrelated: ▷ Capp-Pierce Juggernaut.

Juicy Lucy

Taken from one of their songs and illustrated with a 1960s sexist album cover showing a nubile, naked model called Lucy lying amid succulent squashed fruit. Set the juice loose!

The June Brides

The British month most likely to be chosen for weddings has had many echoes in literature; this band took it from the film of the same name.

The Justified Ancients Of Mu Mu

Taken from the Shea and Wilson cult mythological/fiction *Illuminatus* trilogy. AKA ▷ The JAMS. ▷ The Timelords, ▷ The KLF.

J

Kaleidoscope
Because this outfit described their psychedelic-influenced music in a manifesto as "a collision of styles" within a wide scope.

Kalima
From the Greek word kalloni, or beauty.

Eden Kane
Richard Sarstedt used his admiration for the Orson Welles 1941 film *Citizen Kane*. ▷ The Kane Gang, ▷ Rosebud.

Kane Gang
Combination of *Citizen Kane*, and ▷ Sam Cooke's song *The Chain Gang*. They said: "We took the greatest film and the best song and put them together." Citizen Chain was not on the list.

Kansas
These classmates in Topeka, Kansas, thought a local name ensured them a regional following at least.

The Katydids
These Londoners named after the American grasshopper, self-consciously following the great tradition of acts naming after insects – especially ▷ The Crickets.

Danny Kaye
Anglicisation/simplification of David Daniel Kominsky. Cf ▷ Neil Diamond.

The Kaye Sisters
Not actually sisters; from founder Carmen Kaye.

KC And The Sunshine Band
Their lead singer was Harry Wayne Casey, hence KC from his surname. "Sunshine" came from Sunshine Junkanoo, a style of music imported into the U.S.A. from the Bahamas.

Keef
▷ Keith Richard(s) of ▷ The Rolling Stones.

Keel
From singer Ron Keel.

Keith
In a rock context most people will associate this with Keith "Keef" Richard(s) of The Rolling Stones. This name was used as a simplification by U.S. saxophonist James Keefer.

Kenickie
This U.K. female-led band are named after a cool Travolta-like character played by Jeff Conway in *Grease*, their favourite teen film. Among *Grease* bit-part names still to be done as band names: Cha Cha, Rizzo, Frenchie, Putzie and Teen Angel.

Klark Kent
Inspired by Clark Kent, Superman in disguise as a mild reporter, created in the 1930s. An *alter ego* of Stewart Copeland, on the

Kryponite label. Related: ▷ Curved Air, ▷ The Police.

Kerrang!

U.K. magazine named from "the sound of a powerchord struck on a heavily amplified electric guitar". Cf ▷ Huang Chung.

KGB

Almost the last of the boring-name, boring-music supergroup dinosaurs in 1976, soon to be submerged by punk, featured Ray Kennedy, ▷ Ric Grech and Mike Bloomfield, echoing the abbreviation for the U.S.S.R.'s feared spy police.

Kid Creole And The Coconuts

▷ Creole.

Johnny Kidd And The Pirates

Singer Fred Heath led a struggling band, improbably called The Five Nutters – until a broken guitar string left him with a defective eye. His eye-patch gave rise to his piratical image and swashbuckling Captain Kidd moniker which led to chart success. Cf ▷ Doctor Hook, ▷ The Pirates.

Greg Kihn

His real name was the inspiration for some of the worst name-punning album titles of all time: *Next Of Kihn, Rockihnroll, Kihntinued, Kihnspiracy, Kihntageous, Citizen Kihn, Kihnsolidation* and *Unkihntrollable*.

Kilburn And The High Roads

▷ Ian Dury's first London backing band in the 1970s. He knew the north residential area of the city for its station, Kilburn High Road. ▷ The Blockheads.

The Killer

Jerry Lee Lewis got this nickname in school – he says, from his "ladykilling" looks.

Killing Joke

Songwriter Jaz Coleman recalled a comic book story, pitting Batman against The Joker, entitled *Killing Joke*. This British band's songs included *Bloodsport*, examining how killing can be seen as a sick joke. Related act: ▷ Brilliant.

King

Band named from leader (Paul) King.

The King

▷ Elvis Presley. Name earned by virtue of his role as the king of rock and given by everyone else. Cf ▷ The King Of Pop.

B.B. King

Mississippi boy Riley B. King says of his given names: "The 'B' didn't stand for anything, but the 'Riley' was a combination." His father Albert Lee King had a lost brother called Riley – and worked for a plantation owner called Jim O'Reily, who was present at the birth. The 'O' was dropped because the child "didn't look Irish". There's more in the 1996 book *Blues All Around Me: The Autobiography*.

Riley acquired the tag "The Blues Boy from Beale Street" during his residency on a Memphis, Tennessee, local radio music show run by Sonny Boy Williamson (Rice Miller). The billing, suggested by DJ Don Kearn, was soon shortened to B.B. Meanwhile, King is sometimes credited as providing the inspiration for ▷ ZZ Top's name.

Ben E. King

Ben Nelson's pseudonym came from his work fronting semi-pro band The Crowns.

Carole King

She was born Carole Klein and while a struggling songwriter settled on the more euphonious King, which she thought would have more appeal. She was already becoming established under this name when she married her first husband Gerry Goffin.

King Cole

Old King Cole of the children's rhyme as applied to Cole Porter, the American king of popular songwriting, with dozens of hits to his credit including *I Get A Kick Out Of You* and *I've Got You Under My Skin*. Cf ▷ Nat King Cole.

King Crimson

A 1969 British concert began with the following words: "Ladies and gentlemen, Giles, Giles and Fripp – who for reasons best known to themselves have changed their name to King Crimson – will have a freakout without the aid of pot, LSD or any other drugs." (Somehow, bands don't get introduced like that any more.)

Pete Giles, Mike Giles and Robert Fripp's first appellation made them sound "like a firm of solicitors," according to *Disc* magazine. The other "reasons best known to themselves" came from their new composition *In The Court Of The Crimson King*, featuring a devil-red character called King Crimson. The moniker produced some problems in the U.S.A. because some people turned up expecting a soul act like King Curtis.

Other Fripp bands include ▷ The League Of Gentlemen and Sunday All Over The World (this last with his wife, ▷ Toyah). Bassist Greg Lake went on into ▷ ELP. Inspired ▷ Exultation Of Larks.

Kingdom Come
They lifted it from *The Lord's Prayer*, rejecting Power And Glory, which had been used by Graham Greene as a novel title.

Jonathan King
The U.K. pop figure was born Kenneth King – not bad as a showbiz name. Still, he thought it "not very charismatic". Before the release of his first record in 1965: "The boss, the producer and I decided to think of two names each and draw one out of a hat. We all came up with Jonathan, so we forgot the hat."

He has used a string of one-off pseudonyms including Athlete's Foot (an Olympics theme tune), The Smurps (a take-off of The Smurfs cartoon characters) and Sakkarin (a revival of *Sugar, Sugar*, originally by ▷ The Archies). King was responsible for naming ▷ Genesis, ▷ Gogmagog, ▷ The Piglets, ▷ Shag, ▷ 10CC and others.

King Missile
This U.S. group named after a phallic character in a Japanese cartoon – half man, half missile. Original name: King Missile Dog Fly Religion. Silly individual name: Dogbowl. Cf ▷ Rapeman.

Nosmo King
U.K. comedian and singer who was looking for a new name on his way to an important audition. His eyes alighted on a prominent sign on the bus: NO SMOKING ... and with a simple rearrangement the answer was obvious.

The King Of Pop
▷ Michael Jackson. Name usually said to have been bestowed by his record company. Cf ▷ The King.

The King Of Ragtime
American pianist Scott Joplin (1868–1917) is now remembered for 1902 rag *The Entertainer*, although it's not the most entertaining of his ragtime classics.

The King Of Reggae
▷ Bob Marley.

The King Of Skiffle
Skiffle music, often with unusual instruments such as washboards, scored its biggest hit with ▷ Lonnie Donegan's *Rock Island Line*. In a comparatively small field, he was the uncontested king.

The King Of Soul
Term applied by fans to ▷ James Brown (who has more than enough other nicknames including ▷ The Godfather of Soul). Also refers to Otis Redding, partly based on his 1967 album with Carla Thomas, *The King And Queen*, although the epithet was used before its recording.

King Of Swing
▷ Dire Straits claimed to be the sultans of swing years later, yet the true kings of jazz swing were band leaders Benny Goodman and Ted Heath.

The King Of The 12-String Guitar
▷ Leadbelly to his friends.

The Kings From Queens
From the New York origins of ▷ Run DMC.

Kingsmen
American teenager Lynn Easton was a fan of The Kings Men and acquired the name when they went their separate ways.

The Kinks

There are divergent accounts from brothers Ray and Dave Davies. The two, who have had a strained but close relationship, agree on essentials while there are differences on some specifics.

It's agreed they started as the Ray Davies Quartet, then renamed The Ramrods after a Duane Eddy instrumental hit. Other names included The Ravens, after a 1963 Boris Karloff horror movie and meant as a pun on "rave(r)"; and the Bo(ll) Weevils, after a track variously attributed to Eddie Cochran and ▷ Bo Diddley.

Ray recalls: "We were having a drink in a pub with ▷ Larry Page [manager] – and somebody commented on the fake-leather capes Dave and Pete [Quaife, bassist] were wearing. Someone else said we were wearing kinky boots, similar to those worn by Honor Blackman in *The Avengers*." This was 1963; the TV series ran from 1961 to 1969. "Larry concluded … we might as well call ourselves The Kinks." Dave maintains the suggestion came from Arthur Howes, the band's first serious booking agent.

Ray includes a detailed account of Page excitedly spelling out the appellation's virtues. He certainly exploited the choice's curiosity value, with early photos showing the group looking uncomfortable in pink hunting jackets, buckles, jodhpurs and whips. Even the drum featured a logo with high-heeled boots. The brothers thought the tag wouldn't last but didn't question Page's management experience. They agreed The Kinks was short enough to look good on posters (cf ▷ The Who). Dedicated followers of fashion that they were, they knew the epithet was in keeping with swinging sixties London, where "kinky" was in common currency as a fashion-to-sex buzzword. The saucy adjective, probably from the Dutch word *kink*, meant eccentric, perverted, out of the ordinary in a sophisticated or attractive way, or, even, homosexual. It gained wider circulation in U.K. newspapers reporting the call-girl scandal surrounding minister John Profumo.

Ray's account is in *X-Ray: The Unauthorized Autobiography*, 1994. His sibling Dave's version is *Kink: An Autobiography*, published in 1996. There are useful insights in two books published in the mid-1980s. They are *The Kinks: The Sound And The Fury* by Johnny Rogan and *The Kinks: The Official Biography* by Jon Savage.

Hence the name. Hence The Kink Kronikles.

Related: ▷ Muswell Hillbillies. Unrelated: ▷ Kinky Machine. Influenced: ▷ The Knack.

Kinky Machine

Inspired by ▷ Jimi Hendrix's track *Third Stone From The Sun* on the 1967 album *Are You Experienced?* Almost obscured by feedback, a voice declares his spaceship is watching the earth: "May I land my kinky machine?" Kinky was a very 1960s word, sometimes meant as a compliment (cf ▷ The Kinks). By the 1990s, it's usually taken as meaning "perverted", while it has a dated retro-chic. The same album inspired ▷ The Red House Painters and ▷ Third Stone.

The Kinsey Report

Named after their lead singer, "Big Daddy" Kinsey, who shared his surname with psychologist Dr Alfred Kinsey (1894–1956), whose original *Kinsey Report* was a survey of American sexuality.

Rahsaan Roland Kirk

Most people rename for pragmatic reasons. Ronald Kirk said he did because a spirit told him. Unfortunately the spirit wasn't available for comment to the author on the reasons. Inspired: ▷ Rip Rig + Panic.

Kiss

This group went for the most intimate activity they could get away with. Additionally the tag was said to have been influenced by ▷ The New York Dolls, authors of *Looking For A Kiss*. It also fitted original drummer Peter Criss (born Peter Crisscoula). KISS is usually reproduced as a capitalised logo (with Nazi-style SS) and this has prompted speculation that it is an acronym such as: "Keep It Simple, Stupid." They deny it stands for anything.

Bassist Chaim Klein was called Gene from an early age – so became Gene Simmons in reference to actress Jean Simmons.

Kissing The Pink

This 1980s U.K. band said they liked the sexy

sound of this phrase, used sometimes in snooker commentaries.

Kiss The Sky

From ▷ Jimi Hendrix's 1967 *Purple Haze,* where he tells us he's actin' funny, but doesn't know why. (Love? Drugs?) He then adds: "'Scuze me while I kiss the sky." The quote was also used as a book title by writer David Henderson.

Kitchens Of Distinction

Like ▷ And All Because The Lady Loves and ▷ Tools You Can Trust, an advertising slogan, this for luxury kitchen conversions by a U.K. company. Singer Patrick Fitzgerald said: "It was the only name we could think of which wasn't offensive." However, the 1990s band have played "secret" gigs at small venues as the Toilets Of Destruction.

Kiwis

Native avian reference to this band's New Zealand origins.

Klaatu

This Canadian band were science fiction fans and named in 1975 from the 1951 Edmund North-Robert Wise film *The Day The Earth Stood Still,* which tells of a flying saucer landing. One of its occupants, a robot called Gort, is controlled by phrases involving the key word "klaatu".

▷ Ringo Starr's known admiration for the film – he had just featured a still on a 1974 album cover – fuelled rumours Klaatu were ▷ The Beatles back together and in disguise. The record company played on this with a teasing campaign similar to that for ▷ The Guess Who.

The KLF

Or The Kopywright Liberation Front. Leading light Bill Drummond, ex ▷ Big In Japan, had a number of copyright problems after sampling other artists' records in order to create something new. Related: ▷ The Justified Ancients Of Mu Mu and ▷ The Timelords. Unrelated: ▷ EMF.

The Knack

The 1970s Los Angeles band loved ▷ The Beatles and ▷ The Kinks and chose a name similar to the latter. "Knack" was self-complimentary and offered the slogan "Get The Knack" – soon used as a record title. In addition, it was an oblique tribute to The Fab Four: the 1965 film *The Knack* was directed by Dick Lester, fresh from his success with the Liverpudlians in *A Hard Day's Night* – the cover of which was mimicked by The Knack's debut album.

Gladys Knight And The Pips

▷ The Pips.

Kokomo

The name, used by a U.K. bluesy band and an American jazz-tinged rock outfit, came from a southern U.S. town.

Kool And The Gang

Founder Bob Bell was always "cool". They renamed from Kool And The Flames to end confusion with ▷ James Brown's Famous Flames.

KoRn

Extreme offensiveness alert. An inoffensive-sounding name which *Q* magazine in 1997 said was "taken from a homosexual practice too 'alternative' to detail". A fuller explanation appears on the KoRn On The Kob web site. Leader Jonathan Davies overheard two gays talking at a party. Let's just say, the sweetcorn in question was discovered during intimate contact. Davies said everyone told this story started retching in disgust. The name was not from police slang for "kiddy porn", he states.

Korova

U.K. independent record label, home to ▷ Echo And The Bunnymen and others; same inspiration for name as ▷ Korova Milkbar.

Korova Milkbar

Another name from Anthony Burgess's 1962 novel *A Clockwork Orange,* later made into a major motion picture. The thuggish anti-heroes hung out in a café of this name, indulging in all the things kids did in 1950s milkbars (taking amphetamines, taking liberties, playing music on the jukebox, playing the fool, trying to smoke and look cool) with updated ultraviolence to boot (i.e., "flip horrorshow boots for kicking"). Cf ▷ The Droogs, ▷ Heaven 17, ▷ The Mixers. Its visual image and content influenced ▷ Sigue Sigue Sputnik.

Kraftwerk

The German electronic band rehearsed in an old factory, recorded in a refinery and produced music that reflected their industrial environment. They continued the theme by nuncupating themselves (in translation) "Power Station". *Kraft* isn't the same as English word craft: it means strength, power or force.

Spin-off: ▷ Neu! Unrelated: ▷ The Power Station. Inspired: ▷ Orchestral Manoeuvres In The Dark precursor band ▷ VCL XI.

Billy J. Kramer And The Dakotas

He was born William Ashton; the Coasters (as they once were) came from Manchester, U.K., not the American states. Kramer added a J. to his name to further Americanise it in a move suggested by ▷ John Lennon. This was at a time when many American bands were trying to sound British.

Kris Kristofferson

The Rhodes Scholar directory includes everyone from William Jefferson Clinton (Arkansas and University College Oxford, 1968) to Kristoffer Kristofferson (California and Merton College Oxford, 1958). He briefly performed as Kris/Chris Carson for impresario ▷ Larry Parnes in an era when long foreign-sounding names such as his were considered unacceptable for singing stars. Yet within a few years and the advent of acts like ▷ Simon and Garfunkel, such monikers became acceptable and he successfully reverted.

KRS-One

Means "knowledge rules supreme over nearly everyone".

Kula Shaker

The writings of 1960s intellectual and sexual guru Aleister Crowley had convinced 1990s band leader Crispian Mills that K was a special letter. It had been shared by political leaders – the Kennedys – and spiritual leaders such as Krishna, he said. Hence his band was first called The Kays. However, the name did not inspire many people and was the same as a U.K. mail order catalogue.

The son of actress Hayley Mills and grandson of Sir John Mills says on the band's Web site that the name came in a "real spiritual awakening". He had met Krishna devotee Kula Sekara, who was named after a well-known religious figure. "The original was a ninth-century mystic and emperor. A regal figure. We felt we needed a bit of regal patronage and that if we took his name he would look after us. Three months later and we had a record deal." Their first album, in 1996, was called *K*.

Crowley influenced ▷ Golden Dawn, *inter alios*.

The Kursaal Flyers

Canvey Island's finest, they formed in the Essex, U.K., seaside resort in 1974. They took their name from the most daring of the big dipper rides in Southend's local permanent funfair.

Kween

Spoof band performing material by ▷ Queen.

L.A.
They were from Britain, not California; the abbreviation means "Love Affair" not "Los Angeles". This was their second choice: West Coast band ▷ Love beat them for their preferred moniker.

Sleepy LaBeef
Thomas LaBeff changed his surname to avoid confusion and because he was from a farming family. His somnolent appearance was caused by a droopy eyelid.

Patti LaBelle
Born Patricia Holt, she became Patti LaBelle in the 1960s to front a vocal group already called The Blue Belles. The act later became LaBelle as she eclipsed the superbly named Cindy Birdsong.

Lady Day
Saxophone star Lester Young was a long-time friend of ▷ Billie Holiday, and he coined the nickname for the great singer. He called everybody, male or female, "lady", and frequently abbreviated surnames.

Ladysmith Black Mambazo
This South African group named from their home township and after defunct but fondly remembered act Mambazo, which means an axe.

The LAGs
Arthur Lee band prior to ▷ Love. Abbreviation for "Los Angeles Group", it was inspired by Memphis-born Lee's contemporaries ▷ Booker T And The MGs ("Memphis Group").

L.A. Guns
▷ Guns N' Roses.

Laibach
This group was making a separatist political statement in 1980. Laibach is an old German name for Ljubljana, the capital of Slovenia, which had been absorbed into Austria, then Yugoslavia in 1929. Slovenia declared independence in 1991.

Laika
British band of the 1990s named in memory of the unfortunate dog shot into space on a one-way mission by the Soviet Union. Laika's role as the first cosmonaut paved the way for Yuri Gagarin, the first man in space.

Lambchop
Nashville country twangers who enjoyed their first success in 1995. Singer Kurt Wagner told *NME* that the strange name was chosen because "I like the way a beautiful woman's lips make the words sound, like with a smile at the end".

Lambrettas
These musical revivalists came from Brighton, Sussex, U.K., the scene of notorious clashes 15 years before between rockers, on motorbikes,

and mods, who preferred Lambretta scooters. Cf ▷ The Merton Parkas, named after another essential item for any self-respecting mod to own.

Chancery Lane

Andrew Loog Oldham wrote his name into pop history via his work with ▷ The Rolling Stones. He made early attempts at solo showbiz success as Chancery Lane, named after the legal area of London, where he was then working.

k.d. lang

Canadian Kathryn Dawn Lang is of the feminine persuasion but chose to disguise this in her name. The lower-case, like poet ee cummings, appears an affectation, but is part of the same process. She told *Q* magazine in 1992: "I did it because Kathy's really mundane, k.d.'s generic and unlike Cherry Bomb, it's a name not a sexuality." The image became asexual, with short hair and cowboy suits, as she publicly declared her lesbianism. ▷ The Reclines.

Mario Lanza

Popular opera star Alfredo Cocozza paid tribute to *Mama Mia*. His mother's maiden name was Maria Lanza.

The La's

John Power recalls in an April 1997 *Q* magazine article: "[Guitarist] Mike Badger had this name The La's and we were like: 'What, The *La's*? As in all right, la? And he was like: 'No [sings] La, la la.'"

To explain: that's "la la" as in music such as *There She Goes*; *not* L.A. as in Los Angeles; this lot come from Merseyside, U.K. "The la's" is scouse slang for "lads"; they called everyone else "la" so it would have seemed reasonable to call themselves that as well. Related: ▷ Cast.

Lasers

Early ▷ Gary Numan, still in his punk phase. He admitted the name was derivative and an attempt to sound profound on two levels, like ▷ The Mixers etc.

Last Exit

A number of bands have taken their cue from

Last Exit To Brooklyn, the 1960s Hubert Selby Jnr novel about 1950s America which was filmed in 1989.

Lawndale

U.S. band named after their Southern Californian town base.

Lawnmower Deth

Like ▷ Death By Milkfloat, this is a ▷ Killing Joke pure and simple. The idea came from a newspaper story about a man injured in a lawnmower accident. Individual band member names: Concorde Face Ripper, Qualcast Mutilator, Mr Flymo, Mighty Mo Destructimo. It is perhaps surprising that they got a record deal; even more so that the companies involved didn't respond with writs claiming damages.

Leadbelly

Louisiana-born singer Huddie Leadbetter learned the blues during the years he spent in prison for various violent crimes. At the same time his fellow convicts christened him Leadbelly. He said this was a juvenile joke on his surname, while others said it was because of a buckshot wound. Nickname: The King Of The 12-String Guitar.

The League Of Gentlemen

A very British stiff-upper-lip name for this collection of chaps led by Robert Fripp of ▷ King Crimson, who thought it nicely upper-crust polite. It was taken from a film written by Bryan Forbes in 1960 in which an English officer teaches some toffs how to rob a bank successfully – "a rather wizzard wheeze".

Leapy Lee

Those old or unfortunate enough to remember that insidiously annoying witty ditty *Little Arrows*, a 1968 U.K. chart-topper, may want to know that he started as Lenny Graham, AKA Lee Morgan. The Leapy came from his habit of leaping from job to job as a lad.

Led Zeppelin

1. **Yardbirds.** The first chapter starts with ▷ Yardbirds manager Simon Napier Bell investigating solo discs. For his planned effort,

guitarist Jimmy Page collaborated with fellow Yardbird Jeff Beck and sessionman John Paul Jones. Keith Moon, of ▷ The Who, was wanted as the drummer but nothing came of it – apart from Page's appreciation of Jones's ability.

2. Very Heavy Lead. When ▷ The Yardbirds were on tour in New York in April 1968, their road manager Richard Cole met Moon and ▷ The Who's bassist, John Entwistle – ▷ Ox – at the Salvation disco. The latter two were bitching about how they hated Pete Townshend and Roger Daltrey and wanted to form a band with Page and Steve Winwood of ▷ Traffic. The story is taken up by author Steve Davis in his 1985 book *Hammer Of The Gods: Led Zeppelin Unauthorised.*

"Entwistle said, according to Cole: 'Yeah, we'll call it Led Zeppelin. Because it will fucking go over like a lead balloon.' Moon roared out his maniacal bray and Richard Cole told Jimmy [Page] about the idea the minute he got back to the hotel."

Still, many sources – some quoting Cole – attribute the remark to Moon. Cole, asked about it now, says he's sticking to the Entwistle version – while adding the alternative is not implausible because Moon used a similar phrase frequently to describe disastrous concerts.

They thought the act, a ▷ Cream-like supergroup, would be heavy with talent, egos, personality clashes and differing styles. It would also have a super-heavy sound, which people might not appreciate, with Page's flashy solos, Moon's manic drumming, Winwood's powerful singing and Entwistle's solid bass. It could have flown, crashed or been too heavy to ever get off the ground. In the event, the episode again produced nothing – but the name idea.

3. New Yardbirds. The Yardbirds meanwhile broke up, although new manager Peter Grant retained legal rights to the appellation. Page recruited new members to meet contractual obligations, as The New Yardbirds. The handle was a concert draw but their Scandinavian tour of late 1968 made it clear they weren't the Yardbirds and a new tag was needed.

4. Led Zep. At first they came up with ▷ Mad Dogs – the alias later used by ▷ Joe Cocker – then Whoopee Cushion. If they'd

chosen this ludicrous *alter ego*, they might never have been taken seriously.

Then Page remembered the Moon-Entwistle incident. He said: "Eventually it came down to the fact the the name was not really as important as whether the music was going to be accepted. I was quite keen about Le(a)d Zeppelin . .... it seemed to fit the bill. I had something to do with the expression about a bad joke going over like a lead balloon. And there's a little of the ▷ Iron Butterfly light-and-heavy connotation."

When the group got back to London the "Lead" was misspelled, firstly, because it would not be mistakenly pronounced as "Lee-eed Zeppelin", meaning "front Zeppelin" and, secondly, because "nobody can spell in America – colour becomes color, tonight is tonite – so they won't notice anyway." Page called in at the *Melody Maker* London offices in London when an early article called the combo "Lead Zeppelin" – suggesting Britons can't spell either. (Cf, later, ▷ Def Leppard.) It wasn't long before they were called "Led Zep".

Hence the name. Hence the long guitar solos.

5. Four Symbols. The line-up was as the mid-1968 New Yardbirds: Page, Jones, Robert Plant and ▷ John "Bonzo" Bonham. Each individual has his own moniker story and by the time of their fourth LP they became known by various runic symbols, thereby pre-dating the one adopted by ▷ (The Artist Formally Known As) Prince.

Page: chose a symbol rendered as "Zoso". The glyph is similar to the alchemical symbol for amber. Unflattering derivative: Led Wallet. Their first rehearsal ended with the already rich Page asking penniless Brummies Plant and Bonzo to chip in for food and beer.

Bonzo: symbol – three interlocking circles. He was dismissive of runes but his logo, from a book of runes, represents man, woman and child. Plant cynically remarked that it looked like three drums or the Ballantine drinks company sign.

Plant: symbol – a feather in a circle, designed by Plant himself from the ancient Mu civilisation. ▷ "Percy" had also sung with Hobstweedle, ▷ Black Snake Moan and ▷ The Crawling King Snakes.

Jones: real name – John Baldwin. Symbol –

three ovals cutting through a circle, representing confidence and competence. There's more on the runes in Dave Lewis's 1991 book *Led Zeppelin: A Celebration*.

6. Other Names. They briefly changed their designation to Nobs in protest at Count Von Zeppelin who in 1970 objected to the surname's use. Fears of court action proved groundless. Unflattering derivative: Dead Zeppelin – referring either to Bonzo's death or their flagging dinosaur appeal in the aftermath of punk. Spoof acts: ▷ Dread Zeppelin, ▷ Fred Zeppelin, The Zep Boys. Related: ▷ Bonham.

7. Aftermath. Later spin-offs: ▷ The Firm, ▷ The Honeydrippers and ▷ The MacGregors. Page and Plant had vowed not to re-form Zep but made ▷ Unleded.

8. Afterword. The act took off quickly and flew high to success, proving the handle ironic. Page is on record as saying: "We could have called ourselves the Vegetables or the Potatoes … What does a Led Zeppelin mean? It doesn't mean a thing."

Which says it all. Maybe this whole entry doesn't mean a thing.

Brenda Lee
Was born Brenda Lee Tarpley; dropped the last name as not stagey enough. Her prenomen led to the renaming of ▷ Crystal Gayle.

Dee C. Lee
A phonetic pronunciation of D. Sealey: she was born Diane Sealey. Former ▷ Wham! and ▷ Style Council singer, later solo.

Thomas Leer
Glaswegian Thomas Wishart chose this as an aggressively archetypal punk name. In the event he was beaten at the *Whiplash Smile* game by ▷ Billy Idol, who had the punkoid pouting pose down to perfection.

Left Banke
This British band said: "We took it from Rive Gauche written on a bottle of perfume from Paris."

Leftfield
This British duo saw it "an exploration of unusual areas" as much as a political statement. First album called *Leftism*.

Le Griffe
U.K. rockers whose name is from French. *La griffe* (note gender – the group got it wrong) means the claw.

Legs Diamond
Michael Diamond led this band, whose name recalls 1920s criminal Legs Diamond.

Lemmy
He was born Ian Kilmister; "Lemmy" came from his frequent remark "lemme a fiver"! The former ▷ Hendrix roadie found fame with ▷ Hawkwind and ▷ Motorhead/Motörhead. He suggested the name of ▷ Dare. His father was a vicar (incredibly). Other sons/daughters of preacher men: ▷ Alice Cooper, Terence Trent D'Arby, ▷ Tori Amos.

The Lemonheads
Massachusetts students Evan Dando (vocals) and Jesse Peretz (bassist) got the idea from a schoolfriend called Ivan. According to Everett True's 1994 biography *The Lemonheads* it came from a well-known U.S. Mid-western sweet whose packs ironically bear the motto "Just Say No To Drugs". Dando agreed it fitted "because Lemonheads are sweet on the outside and sour on the inside". The connection apparently boosted sales of the candy.

However, this "official" sweet explanation does not tell the whole sour story. One of the reasons the sweet name was ironic was because it has a drug link. Chapman's *Dictionary of American Slang* points out that "lemon" is narcotics-speak for a Quaalude: "Lemmon" is the name of a pharmaceutical business that once made it. Therefore, a lemonhead is someone who used the product.

A U.S. newspaper reported in 1995 that the Lemonhead name was a reference to ▷ John Lennon, who used a similar pun himself. This link was denied by Dando. Unflattering derivative: he was tagged Yvonne Dando after his concert appearance in a dress and pigtailed hair.

John Lennon
John Winston Lennon was born in 1940, his

L

middle name a patriotic reference to U.K. wartime prime minister Winston Churchill. The former ▷ Beatle Lennon shot dead 40 years later was officially called John Ono Lennon in tribute to second wife Yoko Ono. The legal change was made on 22 April 1969 in a ceremony at ▷ Apple headquarters in London.

While the others in ▷ the Fab Four used pseudonyms readily, he proclaimed dislike of such "pretence". He even called ▷ Bob Dylan by his birth name Zimmerman: as in the song *God*.

John excluded from this joke *alter egos* like ▷ "Dr Winston O'Boogie", "The Walrus" (references in *I Am The Walrus, Glass Onion*), "The Dreamweaver" (*Working Class Hero*) and "JohnanYoko" (signature to sundry letters).

The early group considered Johnny (Lennon) and The Moondogs, then Long John And The Silver Beetles. The latter was supposedly a reference to his height – but he pointed out he wasn't exceptionally tall. He also rejected being called Johnny Silver on their first tour, to fit the name Silver Beetles.

The Plastic Ono Band was a logical updating of "brass band". The name applied to whatever line-up the Lennons chose at the time. He also worked with ▷ Elephant's Memory.

Lennon's wordplay, evident in *In His Own Write* and *A Spaniard In The Works*, showed in his renaming of ▷ Cyrkle and ▷ Grapefruit. See also ▷ Billy J. Kramer, ▷ Poco, ▷ The Wonder Stuff.

Les Quatre Etoiles

French for "the four stars". The quartet's members were all top musicians in Zaire.

Let's Active

American Mitch Easter took the tortured grammar from a Japanese clothing company. For years the country has been making goods with English catch phrases which are considered "trendy". "Let's active" is a bad translation of the Japanese for "Let's go".

Lettermen

A clean-cut U.S. name to assure the public they were respectable guys of the sort you'd expect to find at Yale. Lettermen are the U.S.

equivalent of Oxbridge Blues: student sporting stars. Cf ▷ The Ivy League.

Level 42

Members of this 1980s British jazz-funk band started playing in humble holiday camps, so this wasn't a reference to high life in 42nd floor penthouses, says fast-thumbed bassist and sometime science fiction fan Mark King. He explains that Douglas Adams's best-selling sequence *The Hitch Hiker's Guide To The Galaxy* gives 42 as the mysteriously succinct reply to the question "What is the meaning of life, the universe and everything?" The group broke up in the mid-1990s, and the joke started to go sour in 1996, when astronomers said they found 42 deeply significant in explaining groups of stars.

Levellers

This politically aware group have a philosophy similar to that of The Levellers, a Puritanical party of the English Civil Wars (1642 on), who advocated "levelling" people to same wealth and status. Several members of the 1980s act chose Leveller as a surname. Not related to Slade The Leveller, vocalist with ▷ New Model Army, which had a similar historical impetus for their name.

Leviathan

Because they wanted to be big. And, therefore, a name chosen in a similar way to ▷ T Rex. The name for the unidentified, possibly whale-like fictional creature in the Book of Job, Isaiah and The Psalms has come to mean anything large, such as a government.

Gary Lewis

Playboys frontman Gary Levitch renamed from his father, U.S. comedian Jerry Lewis. (Unrelated: ▷ Jerry Lee Lewis).

Jerry Lee Lewis

▷ The Killer.

Leyton Buzzards

They named after Leighton Buzzard (note spelling), a town in Bedfordshire, England. The band came from Woodford and Leyton (note spelling) in Essex on the other side of London.

Leyton/Leighton are often confused, leading to post going astray.

LFO
Technically minded British duo whose name means Low Frequency Oscillation.

LHOOQ
Paris band whose lettered name pronounced in French means *elle a chaud au cul* – or "she has a hot behind". This was inspired by Marcel Duchamp who in 1919 wrote the letters under a defaced reproduction of Leonard da Vinci's Mona Lisa. Cf ▷ NTM.

Lies Damned Lies
From British Conservative prime minister Benjamin Disraeli (1804–81), who commented there are three kinds of lies: "lies, damned lies and statistics".

Lieutenant Lush
▷ Malcolm McLaren chose the name to fit a song called *The Mile High Club* about officers indulging in sexual antics on airliners. It was written for ▷ Boy George during his short ▷ Bow Wow Wow residency. Unrelated: ▷ Lush.

The Lightning Seeds
From Ian Broudie's admiration for *Raspberry Beret*, a song by ▷ Prince on the 1985 album *Around The World In A Day*. The actual line used is: "The thunder drowns out what the lightning sees." He misheard it as "lightning seeds". Related: ▷ Big In Japan.

The Lilac Time
"Lilac time" is a literary phrase similar to "purple passage" used by U.S. poet Walt Whitman (1819–92) and others. It turns up in the 1969 song *River Man* by British singer Nick Drake (1948–74). It was from here that it was taken by leader ▷ Stephen Duffy.

Liliput
This punk band formed in Zurich in 1978 as Kleenex. This produced a predictable lawsuit threat from Kimberly Clark, makers of the paper tissues. In 1980 they renamed after Lilliput (note spelling) in the 1726 book *Gulliver's Travels* by Jonathan Swift, "because we want to be giants".

Lillies
▷ The Cocteau Twins, ▷ Lush and Moose working with U.K. footballers Spurs; from the team's nickname The Lillywhite Lads.

Limahl
The singer with British 1980s heart-throb act Kajagoogoo was born Chris Hamill and made an anagram of his surname.

Lindisfarne
Founded in Newcastle, U.K., in 1967 and named from a nearby island which houses a monastery dating from AD 635. Spin-off: ▷ Jack The Lad.

Linx
David Grant chose this for its double meaning: a big cat and links as in "connections". His bassist, simply called Sketch, was born Sketch Martin and joked: "My real name is Preliminary Drawing ... but most people found that a bit of a mouthful!"

Liquid Len
Plain John Smeeton became Liquid Len, the light show king, during his finest hour, with ▷ Hawkwind. The moniker's not from his drinking ability; it came from *The Lensmen* science fiction series of novels. His early displays used real liquids over the bulbs.

Little Caesar And The Romans
Roman Emperor Julius Caesar has inspired several small-time imitators down the years. One such was 1920s gangster Al Capone, source of the name ▷ Dennis Alcapone, inspiration behind this band and the 1931 film *Little Caesar*. There was also a British singer called Julius Geezer.

Little Eva
Eva Boyd was a teenage babysitter for Gerry Goffin and ▷ Carole King before she turned to singing their songs. Her age and diminutive stature suggested their nickname for her, taken from Little Eva in Harriet Beecher Stowe's 1852 novel *Uncle Tom's Cabin*.

Little Feat
The band was formed in 1970 by Lowell

L

George and Roy Estrada from ▷ The Mothers of Invention, on Frank Zappa's advice. One account of the naming goes like this. "Lowell had unusually little, fat feet and Jimmy Carl Black of The Mothers happened to make mention of them to Lowell with an expletive. Lowell deleted the expletive and the name was born with Feat instead of Feet just like ▷ The Beatles, neat huh?" George saw the spelling change as a good luck charm.

This is from guitarist Paul Barrere, who joined a couple of years later and is a mainstay of the band called Little Feat which is still in existence. George, who always denied being too big for his boots, died in 1979; one album was punningly entitled *Feats Don't Fail Me Now*.

Little Richard
Born Ricardo Wayne Penniman in Macon, Georgia, U.S.A., he was adopted by Ann and Johnny Enotris Johnson, becoming known as Richard. And he was "Little" when he started singing at 14. Nickname: The Georgia Peach. ▷ Cliff Richard and ▷ Scritti Politti may both owe him a naming debt.

Little River Band
They saw Little River on a road sign in Victoria, South Australia, and thought it sounded like a pleasant place – although they only got to visit it after becoming famous.

Little Village
▷ Nick Lowe, John Hiatt, Ry Cooder and Jim Keltner. Supergroup formed 1992; named after a Sonny Boy Williamson tune which was the subject of a famous dispute with manager Leonard Chess.

Living Colour
Taken from a phrase beloved of photographic processors, film manufacturers and Walt Disney movies. This American band called their first album *Vivid*. They explained: "There were too many monochrome names and people wearing black … we wanted to put some colour back into music, make it real."

The Lizard King
▷ Jim Morrison of ▷ The Doors, based on his own self-mythology. The *alter ego* grew out of his epic *Celebration Of The Lizard* fantasy composition. He said the title was chosen because lizards and snakes are identified with "unconscious forces of evil". The poem finally appeared on the 1970 Doors album *Absolutely Live* and its 1991 CD re-release *The Doors Live*.

Lizzy Borden
A namecheck for another believed criminal, in this case a nineteenth-century U.S. killing suspect. The band thought she had a deceptively demure name. Borden, a 32-year-old spinster, was tried for axing to death her father and step-mother. While there was strong circumstantial evidence, police could not produce proof and she was found not guilty.

L.L. Cool J.
The New York rapper was born James Todd Smith. "Ladies Love Cool James" was a piece of graffiti written by Queens subway scrawlers. Related: ▷ H.E.A.L.

Lobo
The Florida singer-songwriter was born Kent Lavoie but chose a pseudonym, so he could start again if he flopped. His choice, like ▷ Los Lobos, came from the Spanish word for a wolf.

London SS
There's a Ph.D. to be written on the unfortunate links between punks and Nazis. Siouxsie of ▷ The Banshees wore swastikas; ▷ Sid Vicious said *Belsen Is A Gas*; ▷ Joy Division flirted with Fascist imagery; and so on. This tastelessness was for the most part based on no knowledge of politics but a desire to be noticed. Hence this band from London namechecking the German SS or Schutz Staffeln storm-troopers. Spin-offs: ▷ The Clash and ▷ The Damned.

London Suede
▷ Suede.

The Longpigs
These British rockers named from the slang for foreign sailors on shore leave. They ran into problems on tour because the word "pig" is offensive to some religious groups.

The Long Ryders

This 1980s California band named from *The Long Riders* western, released a few months before they formed. The name is sometimes reported to have been respelled in a tribute to ▷ The Byrds. However, one of the group said it was merely "to be different from the movie".

Looking Glass

Buttoned-up Victorian don Charles Dodgson would have been shocked to learn that he inspired three rock bands. For ▷ Frabjoy And Runcible and ▷ The Mock Turtles were not the only musical outfits to name after Dodgson's work as Lewis Carroll. This group named after 1871's *Though The Looking-Glass And What Alice Found There*.

Loop

Named after *Loop*, the ultra-rare first ▷ Velvet Underground single, released in December 1966 as a seven-minute one-sided seven-inch flexidisc given away with New York's *Aspen* magazine.

Loop Guru

No relation to ▷ Loop. The techno-dance experts became the self-styled "gurus of loops" because of their use of samples. The name stuck.

Lord Kitchener

Jamaican Aldwyn Roberts took the name of one of Britain's greatest war figures who is known for his recruitment poster: "Your country needs YOU." Reggae artists have appropriated names of real people both famous and infamous: ▷ Sir Coxsone Dodd, ▷ Dennis Alcapone etc.

Lord Rockingham

Scottish band leader, born as humble Harry Robinson and punningly named after a real historical character.

Lords Of The New Church

Manager Miles Copeland suggested this U.K. act should be called Lords Of Discipline. The band finally came up with the gloriously pretentious alternative because it "sounded special". Related: ▷ The Damned, ▷ The Dead Boys and ▷ Sham 69.

Los Lobos

Spanish Chicanos in California, they identified with their Tex-Mex audience by calling themselves The Wolves.

The Lotus Eaters

From a legend recounted by Homer which has had many echoes throughout western literature.

Love

Group mainstay and mainspring Arthur Lee insisted Love means not just romance but "universal love and cosmic peace". But he was speaking in the 1967 summer of love, so maybe we can understand, if not forgive him. Related: ▷ The LAGs. Inspired: ▷ Alone Again Or.

Love And Money

A film title inspired their 1987 single which said that all they wanted was *Love And Money*. Sounds quite reasonable.

Love And Rockets

From the title of a contemporary American cartoon strip. The band, former members of ▷ Bauhaus, loved the flagship of the Fantagraphics empire, which mixed lust with crime and Latino culture: emphatically, these weren't comics for children.

Lovecats

Tribute band playing material by ▷ The Cure and referring to the title of one of the Robert Smith band's most commercial singles, dating from 1983.

Courtney Love

Confused? You will be after the bewildering set of names that follow.

She was born Love Michelle Harrison in San Francisco, on 9 July 1965, to Hank Harrison and Linda Carroll. Two years later they split up. The predictably troubled scion became Courtney Michelle Harrison ("love" no longer seemed appropriate after the break), then Carroll (mother's divorce), followed by Rodriguez (mother's second marriage; she later became Ari Rodriguez, after an obscure ▷ John Denver song), then Manley (mother's third marriage).

The star-to-be tried the "decent, normal"

L

prenomen Michelle as she tried to fit in to school in Oregon, but she soon rebelled and decided that, of the appellations foisted upon her, Courtney and Love were the ones she liked most. The result resembles the implausible-sounding handles given to wives of rock musicians in Jackie Collins novels.

Courtney formed Sugar Babylon, later Sugar Baby Doll, with future ▷ L7 members and was kicked out of both ▷ Faith No More and the fledgling ▷ Babes In Toyland before founding ▷ Hole (at the suggestion of ▷ Sonic Youth's Kim Gordon) and playing a leading part in the ▷ Riot Grrrl movement. She is also the widow of ▷ Nirvana's ▷ Kurt Cobain. There's more in Nick Wises's biography *Courtney Love* (1995). It's safe to say Mrs Cobain has the most schizophrenic collection of *alter egos* in this book.

Loverboy
They named from the opposite of a magazine cover girl and didn't know the word means "toy boy" in some countries.

The Lovin' Spoonful
John Sebastian started with ▷ The Mugwumps and graduated to this group, whose name refers to the *double entendre* in Mississippi John Hurt's old piece, *Coffee Blues*. The lyric, also called *Coffee Song*, was a crowd-pleaser and featured the words: "I love my baby by the lovin' spoonful". The ambiguous subject matter was also explored by ▷ 10CC and ▷ Cream.

Nick Lowe
▷ Basher, ▷ Brinsley Schwarz, ▷ Guitar Bass & Drums, ▷ Little Village. Name-related LP titles: *All Time Lowes*, *Bowi* (after ▷ David Bowie's album *Low*).

The Low Numbers
A tribute to the ▷ The Who, who were briefly The High Numbers. This 1970s outfit specialised in covering obscure numbers by Pete Townshend and others.

L7
This loud Los Angeles female band, part of the ▷ Riot Grrrl movement, named after a postwar slang term meaning "square", a conventional or normal person. It comes from the square visual pattern made by joining the capital L and the number 7.

The group contemptuously made the symbol with their hands in reply to questions from all those "L7" reporters who didn't know the origin of the term. The reporters usually looked blank in return. In fact, most who asked **were** pretty hip. L7 was used a lot in Elvis's day but by the 1990s the term had all but died out. One of the short names of the 1990s. Cf ▷ U2.

L.T.D.
They were not Limited by scope – or name. The abbreviation meant "Love Togetherness And Devotion", spelled out as the title of their 1974 debut album.

The Lucy Show
Some dreadfully unhip critics have suggested that this British 1980s quartet were referring to Lucy, a 1960s word for LSD. More hip crits know it is a reference to another 1960s phenomenon, Lucille Ball's highly successful television series *The Lucy Show*.

Lulu
Single-name stars have become common (▷ Madonna, ▷ Prince etc) but Lulu and ▷ Fabian were among the pioneers. The little Glaswegian started with a big name – Marie McDonald McLaughlin Lawrie – which needed pruning. Manager Marion Massey chose Lulu to match a new combo, to be called The Luvvers. She inspired ▷ Flesh For Lulu.

Larry Lurex
This aspiring glam-rocker named after the shiny lurex thread used liberally in stage clothes of the time. Lurex's parodying attempt to jump on the ▷ Gary Glitter bandwagon failed: his 1973 single, a revival of *I Can Hear Music*, was a flop. He deserves a footnote in rock name history, for he became famous as ▷ Freddie Mercury of ▷ Queen.

Lush
NME answered its own question "why Lush?" by jesting: "Because they're always drunk." Sure, "lush" can refer to luxuriant vegetation

but a "lush" means anyone who lives for pleasure, especially drink. Spin-off: ▷ Lillies.

Jeff Lynne

▷ Electric Light Orchestra, ▷ Traveling Wilburys.

Loretta Lynn

She was born Loretta Webb, an elder sister of Brenda Webb, whom she renamed ▷ Crystal Gayle. Loretta was in tribute to movie star Loretta Young; the Lynn came when she married. Nickname (shared with others): The Queen Of Country Music.

Lynyrd Skynyrd

... a band, of course, therefore appearing under L not S.

All of the group but one came from Jacksonville, Florida, where most attended the same high school. They started as Mr Backyard, after the classic song *Back Door Man*, and were successively The Wild Cats, Sons Of Satan, One Per Cent, The Nobel 5 and The Pretty Ones. The personnel was constant, while they flirted with different names.

Then they unanimously decided to change to Lynyrd Skynyrd. This was how the school's officious gym coach, Leonard Skinner, pronounced his name. The handle both got revenge and immortalised the legendary hater of long-haired students. He is variously described as "the most unpopular teacher" and "the school's most notorious redneck".

Within years of leaving school, the by now very-long-haired band were worth millions: far more than their short-haired contemporaries who had obeyed Skinner's commands. Skinner publicly forgave them for taking his name in vain and said he even liked some of their music. They had completed his education, rather than vice versa, and he had realised rock music and long hair weren't so bad after all. He moved into real estate and the combo featured one of his agency boards on the back of one of their later albums.

Hence the name. Hence the Alabama anthems.

Related groups: ▷ Rossington Collins Band, ▷ .38 Special.

The band was torn apart in 1977, with a plane crash that claimed the life of singer Ronnie Van Zant. His widow objected to further use of the name. They re-emerged in 1991 as Lynyrd Skynyrd 1991.

L

M

Not from the McDonald's sign, as sometimes suggested. This group named after the M symbol for the Metro subway system in Paris.

Mabsant

From the Welsh saint of festivals.

Macca

▷ Paul McCartney.

Paul McCartney

The ▷ Beatles bassist, ▷ Fab Four mop top, lovable long-haired Liverpudlian lad, known as Macca to many friends, was born James Paul McCartney.

He had two flirtations with the pseudonym Paul Ramon – chosen "because it sounded really glamorous … Valentino-ish". He first toyed with it in 1960, when the then Silver Beetles adopted stage names during their tour supporting ▷ Johnny Gentle. It was revived when he dropped in on a London recording session for The Steve Miller band in February 1969. (Hence ▷ The Ramones.)

"It was exciting changing your name. I made it all seem real and professional," Paul says in Hunter Davies's book *The Beatles: The Authorised Biography* (1968 and updates).

Some of his 1960s material was credited to writers A. Smith or Bernard Webb, said to be anonymous French students, because Macca feared people would say his songs were only hits because of his name. (His brother recorded as

▷ Mike McGear in a bid to avoid comparisons.)

Paul has used other one-off stage names, including: Apollo C. Vermouth (producing ▷ The Bonzo Dog Doo-Dah Band), The Country Hams and ▷ Percy "Thrills" Thrillington.

He became Sir Paul after his 1997 knighthood – joining pop knights such as ▷ Sir Cliff Richard and Sir George Martin. ▷ The Smoking Mojo Filters.

The Macc Lads

Because they hail from Macclesfield, Cheshire. Cf ▷ The La's.

The McCoys

Rick and Randy Zehringer first used the name as teenagers, after they'd learned to play simple tunes from *The McCoys* album by The Ventures. The moniker was long forgotten as they turned professional as Rick And The Raiders. The advent of ▷ Paul Revere And The Raiders created a problem as they moved for a record deal. The company's talent scout saw by chance an old family photograph of the schoolboy band with McCoys on the drum and successfully urged its revival, along with slogans such as "The Real McCoys". Related: ▷ Derringer. Unrelated: ▷ Dillinger.

Country Joe McDonald And The Fish

Country: from their acoustic-folk sound. Joe: the Californian singer was named Joseph Stalin McDonald, after the Soviet dictator, by his politically motivated parents. The Fish: Joe's left-wing songs included anti-war protests and he liked the Chinese Communist idea that activists should move through the people like fish.

The Fish was used initially by journalists to either refer to Joe's backing band or main member Barry Melton. Melton made it clear it wasn't plural but singular and related solely to him. It also came to relate to the famous "Fish Cheer". This was supposedly rendered as "Gimme an F ... Gimme an I ... Gimme an S ... Gimme an H". But more often than not it was rendered as another four-letter word ... ▷ Spin-off: ▷ The Dinosaurs.

Mike McGear
Peter Michael McCartney, brother of the more famous Paul, wanted to make it on his own, not as a ▷ Beatle sibling. His appellation came from 1960s phrase "fab gear" (the four Beatles were always "fab").

The MacGregors
AKA Roy Harper and ex ▷ Led Zeppelin's Jimmy Page. They named after an alias of Aleister Crowley, who inspired ▷ Golden Dawn and ▷ 23 Skidoo.

McGuinness Flint
Songwriter Tom McGuinness and drummer Hughie Flint.

Roger McGuinn
... was born James Joseph McGuinn III and was known as Jim as ▷ The Byrds flew to stardom. In 1965 he joined the Subud faith, which maintains that everyone has a spiritual identity, "the verbal sound of the soul", hidden behind the earthly one. He sent off to his guru in Indonesia and found his son James, born in 1967, was really Patrick while he was Roger. By 1968 he had officially assumed the name.

Machine Head
Rock band of the 1990s making a clear reference to ▷ Deep Purple's 1972 album of the same name which contained heavy metal anthem *Smoke On The Water*. Cf ▷ Stormbringer.

Malcolm McLaren
Stars named by the U.K. entrepreneur and sometime star in his own right include: ▷ Bow Wow Wow, ▷ Jimmy The Hoover, ▷ Sex Gang Children, and ▷ The Sex Pistols. Sometimes called ▷ The Godfather Of Punk, a title also applied to ▷ Lou Reed.

Madder Rose
New York act whose name had been seen as a riposte to the antics of ▷ W. Axl Rose of ▷ Guns N' Roses. Guitarist Billy Cote denied this, saying it's simply a curious-sounding reversal of the reddish pigment name. How can a rose be mad? Cf ▷ Rose Royce, ▷ Rose Tattoo, ▷ Stone Roses etc.

Mad Dogs
There have been several groups of this name, inspired from the song *Mad Dogs And Englishmen (Go Out In The Midday Sun)*. The most famous rabid canines were led by ▷ Joe Cocker and it was also considered by the combo which became ▷ Led Zeppelin.

Mad Max
A fond namecheck for the Australian films about biker gangs. *Mad Max* in 1979 was followed by several more.

The Mad Monk
▷ Thelonious Monk nickname which affectionately mocks his surname and refers to Rasputin, who was known similarly.

Madness
The nutty boys from Kentish Town, London, had a three-year apprenticeship as The North London Invaders. They then considered Morris and The Minors, in tribute to the much-loved Morris Minor – then left this angle to the unrelated ▷ Morris Minor And The Majors.

The main reason for the change was because they loved the old ska song *Madness* by ▷ Prince Buster – they recorded *The Prince* in his honour ... it was their first hit in 1979. The name also matched their "Nutty Sound", with silly lyrics and bizarre videos.

After their 1988 attempted re-formation, they became The Madness. This was because they were always called Le Madness in France; they even thought of becoming Le Madness.

Notes:

1. Lead singer Suggs reverted to being Graham McPhearson for a "serious" acting career; bassist Mark Bedford was billed simply as Bedders.
2. Spin-offs ▷ The Nutty Boys, ▷ Butterfield 8.
3. It's one of the quirks of the alphabet that, bizarrely, their records are always just in front of Madonna's …

Madonna

Born in 1958 in Rochester, Michigan, U.S.A., Madonna Louise Veronica Ciccone was named after her mother. Like an increasing number of stars, she has always preferred the single name, but initially ran into misunderstandings. For one early photo session she had to fill in a form asking for Christian and surname and consequently was booked as "Madonna Madonna".

Madonna, like Jesus, is used freely in some Latin American lands but is seen as sacrilegious in some Christian countries. (Cf ▷ Jesus Jones, ▷ The Jesus And Mary Chain.) She said: "I didn't have a hard time growing up as Madonna because I went to a Catholic school."

Dictionary definitions hint at the controversy: "Madonna – a lady, especially a brothel madam; a designation of the virgin birth – from Italian *ma donna*, or 'my lady'." This connection of raunchy and religious icons, confusing prostitution and piety, made for plenty of publicity. And it has tied in with titles such as *Like A Virgin*, *Like A Prayer* and *The Immaculate Collection*. (▷ Prince has played a similar game, with titles such as *God Is Love* apparently referring more to lust than divine benevolence.)

Madonna used her name, along with talent, luck, savvy, sex and a street wise use of the media, to become the most successful-ever female solo rock artist – inspiring a whole media industry and, incidentally, the naming of ▷ Ciccone Youth and (maybe) ▷ Take That.

Name notes:

1. Anagrams: Madonna Louise Ciccone = "Occasional Nude Income"; Madonna, The Material Girl = "Ream Dim Man-Eating Harlot". See Tunstall-Pedoe and Holmes's 1995 *Anagram Genius*.
2. Madonna's marriage to actor Sean Penn saw headlines about "Mrs Madonna" and "Lady Madonna", recalling the hit by ▷ The Beatles. Penn, long eclipsed by her fame, became "Mr Madonna".
3. Nicknames: ▷ The Material Girl, ▷ The Queen Of The Pops. First band: ▷ Emmenon.
4. Madonna was with child on 14 October 1996. Her daughter was named Lourdes Maria Ciccone Leon.

Fannie Mae (And Freddie Mac)

Short-lived U.K. big-bang-era comedy duo. Fannie Mae is the colloquial name in the U.S. for the Federal National Mortgage Association (FNMA). Her sidekick, Freddie Mac, named from jargon for the Federal Home Loan Mortgage Corporation (FHLMC).

Johnny Maestro

Simplification/anglicisation of John Mastrangelo.

Magazine

▷ Howard Devoto's band after ▷ The Buzzcocks. He liked its double meaning: an attempt at mature pop covering issues like a periodical; and a case full of bullets. ▷ Flag Of Convenience.

Magna Carta

Folk group named in reference to the Big Charter signed by England's King John in 1215.

Taj Mahal

Massachusetts graduate Henry St Claire Fredericks, a multi-instrumentalist, took the name of one of the wonders of the world as mysterious and memorable. Related: ▷ Rising Sons.

Mahavishu Orchestra

From leader John McLaughlin, who renamed Mahavishu after converting to the Sri Chinmoy faith. Cf ▷ Carlos Santana.

The Main Ingredient

After one band member read the words on a bottle of Coca-Cola (the principal ingredients of which are said to be secret).

The Main Line

Another *roman-à-clef* from ▷ Rick James. He liked "innocent" names which hinted at naughtiness to those in the know. In this case, he said the name was to do with trains.

However, it didn't escape notice that mainlining is drugs-speak for injections.

The Maisonettes
The British 1980s popsters named after their leader Lol Mason. "We know it's silly ... Lots of bands used to end in -ette." Their music recalled the 1960s, when many maisonettes – a cross between an apartment and a house – were built in Britain..

The Mamas And The Papas
Taken from San Francisco Hell's Angel-speak for men and women; at one point there were two couples in the band. Ellen Naomi Cohen, AKA Cass Elliot, thus became Mama Cass Elliot and often just Mama Cass – partly because of her size. At one point she weighed 285 pounds. There's more in the memoirs of ▷ John "Wolfking Of L.A." Phillips and other members of the band. Related: ▷ The Mugwumps, ▷ Spanky And Our Gang, ▷ Wilson Phillips.

Mammoth
Not after the extinct elephant-like creature but because of the combined size of the group – all were over 20 stone in weight.

Man
Like, man, because everyone called everybody else "man" in those days (1968) even if they were, like, a chick, man. They came from Swansea, where "boy" had previously long been a form of friendly address, even for elderly men.

Manassas
Promo pictures for Stephen Stills's new band were shot in this Virginia town. A location sign was prominently featured in the best picture, so they used it as a name.

A Man Called Adam
This act's musical influences were 1960s soundtracks as well as jazz; so unsurprisingly they culled their identity from a 1966 film starring Sammy Davis Junior as a trumpeter.

Mandingo Griot Society
The Mandingo tribe of Africa pass on their legends through minstrel-bards called griots. This act came together as a collective of the cream of the griots.

M&O Band
From leaders Muff Murfin and Colin Owen.

The Man From Del Monte
U.K. 1990s band who named after advertising for Del Monte foods. The romanticised ads featured a distinguished-looking gentleman who would fly to plantations, expertly examine the succulent fruits and declare them worthy of buying. The delighted natives would shout: "De man from Del Monte, he say: 'Yes'!"

Manhattan Transfer
This American band's act was based on 1920s style swing and recalled one of the best books of that time, John Dos Passos's *The Manhattan Transfer*. The 1925 novel took its title from the New Jersey Station where passengers had to change to travel into central New York.

Manic Street Preachers
They certainly can be manic, making post-punk rock music; they certainly do preach, with plenty of political didactic messages.

Richy Edwards was quoted saying the group was walking along the street and listening to a "hallelujah come-to-Jesus man" berating the passers-by. They overheard someone remarking: "Oh look, there's a manic street preacher". A different account has guitarist James Dean Bradfield busking when the remark was made – about him. This is probably the more reliable version. Unfortunately Richy isn't around any more to cross-check events. The troubled man mysteriously vanished in February 1995 and is now presumed dead.

Unflattering derivative: Janet Street Porters.

Barry Manilow
The world's famous nose was born Barry Pinkus in Brooklyn, New York. At 13 he became Manilow, his mother's maiden name, after his father left the family. Manilow he has been ever since, apart from cutting one early single as Pinkus. It flopped – and he took this as an omen.

The Man In Black
Nicknames applied separately to ▷ Johnny

Cash and ▷ Roy Orbison. Cf ▷ The Men In Black.

The Mannish Boys

Early ▷ David Bowie band recalling the 1955 ▷ Muddy Waters single *Mannish Boy*. Bowie was a boyish man at the time.

Manfred Mann

Manfred Mann was born Michael Lubowitz, and the Mann name – supposedly from a German legend – related primarily to him but also to whatever band he was working with at the time. He founded ▷ Emanon while one of his cohorts was Jack Bruce of ▷ Cream. Terrible punning album title: *Mannerisms*.

Mano Negra

▷ Clash-style politico posing by these Paris neo-punks, who named after an Andalucian anarchist group they admired.

Manowar

Why the name? "It's the old English word for a battleship with lots of cannons and firepower. We don't mess about, you know."

Mansun

This 1990s British combo began as Grey Lantern, after a song by leading light (pun intended) Paul Draper. The choice was ridiculed by a recording studio employee and the band evolved into A Man Called Sun, a ▷ Verve B-side. Their publisher thought this too similar to ▷ A Man Called Adam, so it was crunched to Mansun. The spelling should have diverted claims they were honouring murderous psychopath Charles Manson, whose music had been covered by ▷ Guns N' Roses among others. The Manson estate threatened to sue them anyway for abuse of the name.

Draper told *The Times* of London in March 1977: "Our name was always Mansun ... but early on, we had some T-shirts printed up with the Manson spelling. We had no money to reprint them, so had had to stick with it. Apparently Charliewear is a big business." (Cf ▷ Poco, ▷ Red Krayola and ▷ Redd Kross who escaped legal threats by respellings.)

Grey Lantern, Draper's *alter ego*, is a superhero character who emerged on their debut, almost a concept album entitled *Attack Of The Grey Lantern*. No relation either to Michael Menson (of Double Trouble) or ▷ Marilyn Manson.

Mantronix

From leader Curtis Khalee. He said he took the name as a combination of "human and machine, man, mantra and electronics". Unrelated: ▷ Electronic.

Maple Oak

From Canada; a reference to the country's national tree.

Mara

From leader Mara Kiek.

The Marcels

American harmony band named after a popular layered hairstyle worn by lead singer Cornelius Harp.

Marillion

This U.K. art-rock band formed in the late 1970s with middlebrow influences such as ▷ Genesis and the literature recalled in their original name, Silmarillion. This was the title of a J.R.R. Tolkien telephone-directory-sized tome, published posthumously in 1977. It means "of the Silmarils", or jewels made of silima. The band abbreviated it slightly for greater originality after being joined by ▷ Fish. Later spin-off: ▷ H.

Tolkien's *The Hobbit* (1937) and *The Lord Of The Rings* (from 1954) inspired ▷ Steve Peregrine Took in the 1960s and ▷ Cirith Ungol in 1980.

Marilyn

Born Peter Robinson, U.K., he became friendly with ▷ Boy George in London and developed the nickname Boy Marilyn for his transvestism and his attempts to recreate the appearance of US film star Marilyn Monroe (Norma Jean Baker, 1926–62). ▷ Culture Club.

Marilyn Manson

They're a bit reluctant to identify origins – convicted killer Charles Manson guards his name carefully, see the unrelated ▷ Mansun.

However, almost certainly a combination of Manson with screen star Marilyn Monroe. No relation to ▷ Marilyn either. Shocking name rip-off in best ▷ Dead Kennedys mode.

The Marine Girls
Because this British band recorded many songs which happened to be linked by the theme of the sea and sailing. Related: ▷ Grab Grab The Haddock, ▷ Everything But The Girl.

Marius And The Firebombers
Late 1970s British punk band from Oxford who took their name from the legend of Marius.

Mark-Almond
A band formed by former ▷ Bluesbreakers guitarist Jon Mark and sax man Johnny Almond. Unrelated to ▷ Marc Almond.

Bob Marley And The Wailers
Like an iron lion of Judah in Zion, he's also known as ▷ The King Of Reggae. There's ample evidence of his regal claims on *Legend*; even more on *Songs Of Freedom*. ▷ The Wailers.

The Marmalade
Chosen as a fruity name when the band decided to go all-out for commercial success in the mid-1960s. It was a wise move. Their earlier moniker was The Gaylords, soon tainted by sexual meanings which wouldn't help their popularity. Cf ▷ The Jam.

Marquee Moon
Berlin band named after the marathon title track of the 1977 ▷ Television album. Cf ▷ Friction, ▷ Elevation.

M/A/R/R/S
The prenomen initials of musicians who united to work on the 1978–88 hit *Pump Up The Volume*. (Martyn, Alex, Russell, Rudi and Steve.) Cf ▷ M.A.R.S.

M.A.R.S.
Simply the last name initials of the musicians: Macalpine, Aldridge, Rock and Sarzo. Cf ▷ M/A/R/R/S.

Marshall Tucker Band
No members of this country rock band, formed in South Carolina from the remnants of The Rants, had the name Marshall or Tucker. The name had nothing to do with their musical equipment either. Marshall Tucker was the owner of a hall they used for early jam sessions.

Martha And The Muffins
These Toronto funsters insisted they were just joking at vocalist Martha Johnson by including Muffin The Mule – they weren't poking pun at ▷ Martha And The Vandellas.

Martha And The Vandellas
Martha Reeves named her band in homage to Van Dyke Street near her Michigan home; and the vocalist ▷ Della Reese. She obviously decided against The Dykereeses. Cf ▷ The Supremes.

Martha's Vineyard
Because one of this quartet was called Martha. While they hail from Australia, the name was a bibulous reference to the exclusive U.S. holiday island off the coast of Massachusetts.

Hank B. Marvin
▷ The Shadows star Brian Rankin needed a U.S.-sounding handle as he modelled himself on ▷ The Crickets, right down to the ▷ Buddy Holly glasses and red Fender. Rankin became Hank; Brian abbreviated to an American initial and Marvin, from a friend called Martin, just sounded right.

The Mary Jane Girls
Mary Jane is slang for marijuana – as on leader ▷ Rick James's single *Mary Jane*.

Mason, Wood, Capaldi And Frog
Most supergroup monikers which list members' names are boring. This one is saved by the last – keyboardist Mick Weaver used the novelty name Wynder K. Frog. ▷ Traffic spin-off.

Massive Attack
This British band named from a newspaper splash. "Massive" and "attack" are common headline words, along with ▷ Clash. The choice was neither meant as phallic, nor was it a

statement of intent. They briefly abbreviated to the more tactful Massive during the 1991 Middle East conflict as the Allies bombed Iraqi forces, in a bid to avoid a radio ban. Among those to work with them: ▷ Tricky.

Masters Of Reality

They formed in 1980 in upstate New York and named after ▷ Black Sabbath's 1971 album *Master Of Reality* to turn off all the "punk snobs".

Matchbox

Britons dedicated to the revival of 1950s rock 'n' roll – 20 years later. They named after one of their favourite tunes, the ▷ Carl Perkins hit Matchbox, which became their theme.

Matching Mole

Founded by Robert Wyatt, ▷ Soft Machine drummer from 1966–71. At first glance meaningless or surreal, Matching Mole is a pun on the French for "soft machine", *machine molle*.

The Material Girl

Nickname for ▷ Madonna, based on her 1985 hit *Material Girl* and massive commercial success.

Matthews Southern Comfort

Ian Matthews McDonald, AKA Ian Matthews, late of ▷ Fairport Convention, wrote an LP of this name – from the well-known U.S. whisky blend – and recycled it as he formed a backing band. They became Southern Comfort after he left – fortunately, avoiding any legal action from the drink manufacturer. Related: ▷ Plainsong.

Matumbi

After an African word for revival.

Max Webster

There was nobody in this 1980s Canadian rock band called Max Webster. They thought it would give excessive prominence to an individual to call the group after him, so they chose a totally new name at random. They were sometimes asked "Which one's Max?" (like ▷ Pink Floyd being asked "Which one's Pink?") and amused themselves by kidding ignorant

journalists that Max existed: "he'll be along in a minute … " Other bands named after no member: ▷ Barclay James Harvest, ▷ Judas Priest, ▷ Marshall Tucker Band etc.

MC5

MC now means master of ceremonies: ▷ MC Hammer, ▷ Run DMC etc. Here it is Motor City: the five came together in "motor town" or ▷ Motown, Detroit in 1967. Spin-off: ▷ Destroy All Monsters. Inspired: ▷ Shakin' Street – although not ▷ Jefferson Starship, as sometimes suggested.

M.C. 900 Ft Jesus

American rapper Mark Griffin, from Dallas, took the name from a sermon by Oral Roberts.

MDC

This protest group from Austin, Texas, was originally Millions Of Dead Cops. But singer Davey got fed up of explaining this wasn't an advocation of mass murder. "The name is like everything else we do, it's supposed to make people turn around, think, do something." Hence they became MDC, which meant many other things, such as "Multi-Death Corporation".

Meatloaf

Texan schoolkid, meaty Marvin Lee Aday, weighed 240lbs in seventh grade. He was 13 when, loafing around as usual, he stumbled onto his football teacher's foot during a game. The Dallas teacher yelled in pain: "Gerroff me ya great hunka meatloaf!" A day later legally changed his name to Meatloaf and in 1993 was reported to have considered Nutloaf after going vegetarian.

The Meat Puppets

This American band explained they sometimes felt someone else was pulling the strings. They were slaves to computer-programmed instruments, promotional duties and concert tours.

Medicine Head

Because vocalist John Fiddler said music was therapeutic: "Like medicine for our heads."

023423

Mega City IV

From a cartoon strip featuring Judge Joe Dredd, the anti-hero who keeps law and order in Mega City. Dredd is a violent vigilante, a sort of cross between Dirty Harry and Mussolini … and the band said they liked him very much.

Megadeth

One of many "death rock" monikers, this was taken from the American army term for the impact of a large-scale nuclear conflagration with fatalities of one million people or more. The heavy metal act's albums include *Killing Is My Business*. Related band: ▷ Metallica. The band which became ▷ Pink Floyd had considered the similar Meggadeath.

The Mekons

There is only one mekon: an awesome and awful threat to the human race. The archetypal green man first appeared in a 1950 cartoon strip by Frank Hampson – and caught the imagination of the Manchester Mekon and the unrelated Mekons, from Leeds, who both sought world domination.

Mel And Kim

There have been two Mel And Kims. One was a U.K. vocal duo – Melanie Susan Appleby, who died aged 22 of cancer, and her sister Kim. The other was British comedian Mel Smith and ▷ Kim Wilde, making a charity record.

John Cougar Mellencamp

A story of an artist being renamed by management without his being consulted. (Cf ▷ Gary "U.S." Bonds, ▷ The Beach Boys.)

John Mellencamp from Seymour, Indiana, was signed by ▷ David Bowie's management company, where Tony De Fries thought his surname too long to write, say or remember. People had coped with names far worse (▷ Humperdinck, Garfunkel) yet he chose Johnny (after ▷ Chuck Berry's "Johnny B. Goode") and Cougar (another cat name – after an American puma: this was to be an all-American star). It was only when a bewildered Mellencamp was handed his first record in 1976 that he discovered the change: "Nobody's ever called me Johnny in my life," he complained.

Seven years later John Cougar became John Cougar Mellencamp and in 1989 John Mellencamp; longer names often indicate "maturity". His commercial standing increased as Mellencamp, suggesting the U.S. public had more intelligence than De Fries realised.

Members

This British group intended it primarily as an anatomical reference rather than to themselves or members of any other body. More punk two-level names: ▷ The Vibrators etc.

Memory

Because they revived old music: "We want people to recall these great tunes: they're memorable all right." And in 1979 they still had day jobs as insurance data processors in New Jersey: "It's our job to ensure the computers have memory."

Men At Work

As this 1980s Australian band got to work, they thought the standard pictorial roadworks sign of a man digging, used in many countries, would be widely understood.

Men In A Suitcase

British 1980s band recalling 1967–8 TV series *Man In A Suitcase*, about a former CIA agent.

The Men In Black

Tribute band named after ▷ The Stranglers' monochrome garb. The Stranglers album of 1981 was called *The Men In Black*. Cf ▷ Man In Black.

Menswear

The British 1990s hopefuls named because of their sartorial eloquence in a range of snappy neo-mod suits. The moniker was coined by ▷ Pulp bassist Steve Mackey's girlfriend. Singer Johnny Dean said: "I'm surprised no one's thought of it before. There are signs saying 'Menswear' everywhere!" It's sometimes written as MENSWE@R. Still, ▷ Paul Weller called the moniker "really 80s" – and within months guitarist Chris Gentry (as in Menswear to the Gentry of course) said he'd given his suit to a charity shop.

Mental As Anything

The Australian ▷ Madness – as nutty as ▷ The

Nutty Boys turned upside down – named after Oz slang and titled their 1985 album *Fundamental*.

The Men They Couldn't Hang

Folky British outfit named after the story of Victorian-era prisoner John Lee (1865–1933) who escaped the death penalty when the hanging machine failed to operate. Lee's story was the subject of a 1971 concept album by ▷ Fairport Convention.

Me Phi Me

This 1990s rapper from Michigan renamed after black college campus fraternities.

Freddie Mercury

This cosmopolitan singer's given name and origins are incorrectly given in every major encyclopedia and even book-length biographies. These say his parents were Persian. They were really Zoroastrian Parsees – who are of Persian extraction only back in the nineth century; most are now essentially Indian. The future star was born in 1946, when his parents were living in the British colony of Zanzibar off Africa.

His surname Bulsara was from the town of Bulsar north of Bombay. The star's first name, according to his family, was Farok, not Farookah or Farookh as many books have it. He became Freddie at boarding school. A recent biography has speculated that he may have played down his Indian origin to avoid discrimination, upsetting his family or make himself more exotic.

The Mercury came in 1970 after the messenger for the Gods. His brother-in-law Roger said it was Freddie's rising planet. "When he told me, I said it was a bloody good job it wasn't Uranus. Freddie never forgave me for that." It was only a coincidental reference to glam rock and sparkling stars (cf ▷ Quicksilver Messenger Service; Mercury's own ▷ Larry Lurex).

Ethel Merman

... fits the tradition of entertainers who anglicised, simplified and abbreviated their real name, particularly a Jewish moniker. The most celebrated lady of the Broadway musical was born Ethel Agnes Zimmermann. Cf Bob Zimmerman, ▷ Bob Dylan.

Merseybeats

Named after River Mersey which dominates this 1960s act's native city of Liverpool. It proved lucky – being picked before the success of ▷ The Beatles who popularised The Mersey Sound round the world.

Merton Parkas

Neo-mod band, named after their South London neighbourhood, Merton Park; and parkas, the anorak-style long coats which were essential mod garb. Keyboardist Mick Talbot joined ▷ Paul Weller, ex ▷ Jam – the biggest mod group of them all – in the ▷ The Style Council. Cf ▷ The Lambrettas.

The Metal Gurus

This 1990 U.K. band looked uncannily like ▷ The Mission in disguise, light-heartedly remaking 1970s records. "We agreed to name after one of the big hits of the time but The Amazing Graces didn't look that good on the bass drum," said guitarist Slick. They settled on ▷ T Rex's *Metal Guru* of 1972.

Metallica

Several articles had written of heavy metal generally as "metallica" about the time this L.A. band started to develop trash metal. Related to ▷ Megadeth.

Mezcla

It means "mix" in Spanish. This Cuban band put pop, reggae and samba into a blender and made a smooth musical cocktail.

Mezzoforte

These musicians, neither rockers nor balladeers, chose an Italian technical term for music mid-way between loud and soft.

MFSB

Officially: "Mother Father Sister Brother". Unofficially, there's loads of less respectable suggestions.

Miami Sound Machine

The all-male band adopted their first name,

Miami Latin Boys, from their base in Florida. After ▷ Gloria Estefan came on board, "sound machine" was taken, from a local disco.

George Michael
He was fat, had spots, glasses, and was called Georgios Kyriacos Panayiotou* at school. All that had to go. He made it big, at first with ▷ Wham!, choosing George Michael as an acceptable Anglicisation for public consumption of the Greek-Cypriot name.

* This spelling comes from Michael himself. Other reference books and papers have wrongly given the star's second name as Kyriacou and Kyriakou, his first as Georgiou, Gorgos, Yorgos, Yiorgos, Yorgios and Georgious – but is always pronounced "Gorgeous". Yog survives as a family nickname. U.K. public nickname: The Bubble With The Stubble (Cockney rhyming slang: bubble = bubble and squeak = Greek).

Middle Of The Road
European 1970s pop band were named after the phrase for moderacy in politics and music (often abbreviated to MOR). Their irritatingly catchy commercial confections must have caused many to wish they'd get run down while they were there.

Bette Midler
The Divine Miss M used her real name, the Bette being after actress Bette Davis.

Midnight Cowboys
A tribute to *Midnight Cowboy*, the 1969 John Schlesinger film starring Jon Voight and Dustin Hoffman.

Midnight Oil
Named from their late-night rehearsals. Inspired ▷ Candlebox. Their manager suggested the name ▷ INXS for another band.

The Midwich Cuckoos
U.K. hopefuls of the early 1990s. Named from English writer John Wyndham's 1957 book of the same name. Cf ▷ The Triffids.

The Mighty Ballistics Hipower
Named by Chris Maund after Tapper Zukie's

Ballistic Dub. (An entry which will read like code to those not in the know. Translation: another group named after another song.)

Mighty Lemon Drops
This Wolverhampton, U.K., band decided they preferred lemon drops to their original similar sweet soubriquet, The Sherbet Monsters.

The Mighty Wah!
▷ Wah!

Mike And The Mechanics
Studio mechanics, or sessionmen, led by ▷ Genesis guitarist Mike Rutherford.

Milk
After ▷ Swansway imploded, vocalist Maggie (DeMond) formed Milk – so named "because we're going to milk it to the max, and the music's cool as well".

Steve Miller
Aliases include The Space Cowboy and The Gangster Of Love, both inspired by 1973 hit *The Joker*.

The Million Dollar Quartet
Sun Studio's name for the 1956 Memphis jam session between ▷ Elvis Presley, ▷ Jerry "The Killer" Lee Lewis, ▷ Carl Perkins and ▷ Johnny Cash. "What else would you call them?" asked Sun's owner Sam Phillips.

Millions Like Us
"Spot the double meaning," they said. Does it mean millions adored their music? Or that there are millions of people similar to them? From the title of a 1943 British film about an ordinary family who, like millions of others, had to rise above the despair of war.

Milli Vanilli
A group, not an individual, name and therefore under "M" not "V". This German act named after a well-known New York discotheque but crashed to earth as it was revealed an award-winning single was recorded entirely by session musicians, not the credited duo.

Gordon Mills
U.K. pop businessman who named ▷ Engelbert

Humperdinck, ▷ Tom Jones and ▷ Gilbert O'Sullivan *inter alios*.

The Mindbenders

Originally The Jets, they were renamed by ▷ Wayne Fontana after a U.K. movie. By 1968, "mindbending" was a term applied to drugs, not something he'd intended, but by then he'd left the band. Spin-off: ▷ 10CC.

Zodiac Mindwarp And The Love Reaction

Fashion students making all the right moves; less of the right music. Leader Mark Manning hinted at a psychedelic revival; the rest managed some of the best monikers around. There was Trash D. Garbage; Flash Bastard; Cobalt Stargazer and Slam Thunderhide. Proof positive that a name isn't everything.

Ministry

From 1944 film *Ministry Of Fear*, a World War II tale loosely based on a Graham Greene novel.

Morris Minor And The Majors

U.K. comedy group who named after the much-loved Morris Minor car. A similar name was considered by the early ▷ Madness.

Minor Threat

From their song of the same name.

Mint Juleps

U.K. singing group who named for their fondness for the cocktail. Which is all very well if you like to drink Polo mints …

The Minutemen

That's "minute" spoken as in 60-to-an-hour time, not as in tiny. Because all of their early tracks clocked in at a minute or less – making for 45-song albums. Spin-off: ▷ fIREHOSE.

The Miracles

▷ Smokey Robinson said the name was chosen in a random, democratic way with each group member putting a name in a hat. They wanted an initial M like Matadors, their previous name. Other randomly chosen names include fellow ▷ Motown artists, ▷ The Commodores.

Miranda Sex Garden

The three original members of the madrigal-based rock band were busking at London's South Kensington Tube station in 1990 when they were spotted by promoter Eric Hands, who invited them to appear at a charity concert he was staging. The trio turned up, still without a name. Shortly before going on stage they were talking with American Tim Sheperd, singer with British grunge band Heisenberg. He suggested the name, having just invented it (contrary to some reports, it isn't a Shakespearean reference). They kept it as a talking point on signing to Mute records. Sometimes abbreviated to MSG (no relation to ▷ MSG).

The Misfits

Another self-disparaging name, another film reference. In this case, to the American 1961 film *The Misfits*, about cowboy loners.

The Mission

This British 1985-on goth-rock band, a break-away from ▷ Sisters Of Mercy, said they named after the Mission brand of speakers. They liked mission's extra devotional meaning. However, the original Sisters, led by ▷ Andrew Eldritch, disputed the origin, claiming the forthcoming Sisters album already had been given the working title *Left On A Mission Of Revenge*. What glorious revenge to filch it!

It's sometimes suggested – wrongly – that the moniker's a film reference. The band were referring to neither the Ennio Morricone-soundtracked 1968 movie nor to the De Niro Oscar-winner that emerged about the time they were forming. They were called "The Mish" by fans, who, predictably, were known as Missionaries. Spin-off: ▷ The Metal Gurus.

Mr Big

Two bands have used this name. One was a 1970s U.K. act; the other a U.S. metal group of 1989 on. The earlier took it from a ▷ Free song.

Mr Jelly Roll

▷ Jelly Roll Morton.

Mister Mister

Mr Mister was a character in a stage show they

had seen which also featured Lord Lord, Dr Doctor and Maj. Major.

Mr Mojo Risin'
Anagram for ▷ Jim Morrison (as J. Morrison) of ▷ The Doors; used on the title track of the group's 1971 album *L.A. Woman*. Also near-anagram Mr Mojo Riser.

Mister Partridge
"Group" of 1980 made up of Andy Partridge, Andy Partridge and Andy Partridge. The founder of ▷ XTC was on "a multi-tracking trip" at the time.

Mr Pitiful
Nickname for Otis Redding based on his singing style.

Mr Soul
▷ Sam Cooke.

Mr Wonderful
Actor-singer Sammy Davis Junior acquired this nickname from his role in the Jerry Bock-George Weiss show and film of the same name.

Joni Mitchell
Canadian Roberta Joan Anderson, always known as Joni, was first married to folk singer Chuck Mitchell. They became known for their joint concerts so she kept the surname when they separated after a year in 1966. Inspired: ▷ Clouds.

Mixed Company
The New Jersey singers got together in 1981 as The Street-Tones: "Because we spent more time rehearsing on the street than anywhere else. But deep down we knew we were a real mixed bunch."

The Mixers
Like ▷ Heaven 17, a band moniker of the future mentioned in 1962 novel *A Clockwork Orange* by Anthony Burgess. It's in the late punk tradition for names working on two levels. Cf ▷ Penetration etc.

MN8
The best thing about these 1990s teen idols was

their name, which they chose over ORIGIN8. Their street cred was wrecked when it was revealed Kule-T's mum calls him Terry and KG is not really a Kool Guy or a Krazy Geezer but a Kevin.

Mobile Freakout
Precursor of ▷ Hawkwind, this lot earn a separate entry purely for the madness of the seventies name: it was chosen because "we live our lives on the road, freaking out anywhere cool".

Moby
Time to trade on one's antecedents even if a little literary pandering won't mean much to the average rock punter. Richard Melville Hall was nicknamed Moby. He's at the end of the family line from novelist Herman Melville, who wrote 1851's *Moby Dick, Or, The Whale*. Unrelated: ▷ Moby Grape. For more blatant "celebutot" name-dropping: ▷ Wilson Phillips.

Moby Grape
This 1960s San Francisco troupe named after a joke. It made them laugh anyway. "Question: What's blue, large, round and lives in the sea? Answer: Moby Grape!!"

Regrettably, the overkill humour soon turned into overdone name hype. One of their many publicity stunts was the delivery of free bunches of grapes to journalists. After a 1974 re-formation they ran into legal problems and were known for a while as Maby Grope. Unrelated: ▷ Moby.

The Mock Turtles
They have the distinction of being the only band on earth to name after a rather disgusting broth, made from various ingredients in imitation of turtle. The name was lent to a mythical turtle-like figure created by Lewis Carroll. More excellent adventures with Carroll: ▷ Looking Glass etc.

The Modern Lovers
The sometimes irritating, sometimes child-like, sometimes brilliant, but always direct Jonathan Richman said the name was an apt description of his band's romantic ties.

M

The Modfather

The name should probably apply to members of ▷ The Small Faces and ▷ The Who, but it is most often spoken in reference to ▷ Paul Weller. The ▷ Godfathers-style appellation pays tribute to his mod-inspired image and music – especially during his time with ▷ The Jam and ▷ The Style Council.

Mojos

Mr Mojo; Mojos; Mojo Men. They have in common a word from African, meaning a good luck token or voodoo charm such as dried animal hands. Cf ▷ Muddy Waters, ▷ The Hoochie-Coochie Men.

Molly Hatchet

These Florida rockers named after a sweet little lady who ranks in the annals of criminal legend alongside Sweeny Todd and Jack The Ripper. The notorious Hatchet Molly was a Massachusetts whore, whose hobbies included robbery and axe dismemberment. Cf ▷ Lizzy Borden etc.

Moloko

Briton Roisin Murphy, the guilty party behind the nicely titled debut album *Do You Like My Tight Sweater?* said: "Moloko is a dark child. I suppose I wanted to be arty." (She started out in Stockport, singing with an art-punk outfit, Turquoise Car Crash, and confessed: "I think that's the worst name I ever heard.")

Therefore – for once – not a reference to *A Clockwork Orange* by Anthony Burgess. Moloko, milk laced with drugs, plays a central part in the book. Not related: ▷ Milk, Brian Molko from Placebo.

Monaco

The Mancunian origins of Peter Hook, of ▷ New Order fame, are the true root of this exotic name. 'Hooky' told *Vox* in June 1997: "Why Monaco? Well, it's a lot more interesting than Scunthorpe, innit?"

Monad

New York group headed by Phoebe Legere. Monad is defined in A.R. Lacey's *Dictionary of Philosophy* as "literally, a group of one … a unit which is essentially unitary and indivisible."

Zoot Money And His Big Roll Band

The British combo's name obviously suited its zoot-suited leader who was born in the money (real name George Money).

The Monkees

A manufactured group launched 1965 as America's answer to ▷ The Beatles, complete with custom-written records, pin-up looks and their own television show modelled on *A Hard Day's Night* and *Help!* Nearly all aspects of the band were calculated to achieve maximum appeal and humour, not least the name. Considerable brain storming in committees resulted in a short list which included The Boyz and The Monkeys, soon re-spelled in a Beatlesque manner. Cf The Beatles.

It fitted in with an early signing, Mickey Dolenz, who had monkeyed around in Mickey Monkey fashion in his child film roles.

The signing of another of the band members, Davy Jones, had a different effect on rock history – it turned a singer of the same name in London, U.K., into ▷ David Bowie.

Record producer Don Kirshner, who was heavily involved in the project, was later responsible for ▷ The Archies.

The Monkees soon proved more than monkeys prepared to play to the organ-grinder's tune, asserting their independence and rejecting everything bar the name. As their numbers fell away, an industry joke was that their next album would be credited to The Monkee.

Later, former band member Peter Tork – born Peter Thorkelson – called his band The New Monks, recalling The Monkees' name; a re-formed band in 1976 went under the less catchy name Jones, Dolenz, Boyce and Hart (the latter two being songwriters); and the Monkees proper finally reunited in 1996.

Earlier attempts to respond to the British invasion produced names such as ▷ The Beau Brummels and ▷ Sir Douglas Quintet.

Mike Nesmith's work could well have inspired ▷ The Tragically Hip.

Thelonious Monk

This jazz genius is an example of real names being stranger than their fictional equivalent. He inspired ▷ Thelonious Monster.

Nicknames: The High Priest Of Be-Bop and ▷ The Mad Monk.

Monochrome Set

This British band formed in the 1970s and named in reaction to "colourless music" and all-black-clothes bands of the time. (Cf ▷ Living Colour.) Black and white televisions were speedily being superseded. The moniker led to the 1983 compilation, superbly named from TV buttons: *Volume, Brilliance, Contrast*.

Matt Monroe

Just to show this book's boundaries extend beyond rock, a passing mention of Terry Parsons who renamed after pianist Winifred Atwell's father.

Chris Montez

Anglicisation and simplification of Christopher Montanez.

Montrose

Named after Colorado guitarist Ronnie Montrose.

Monty Python

... deserves a place in this book. The U.K. comedy troupe made records, had a successful musical spin-off in ▷ The Rutles and influenced bands such as ▷ Toad The Wet Sprocket.

The BBC show was nearly called *Gwen Dibley's Flying Circus* – the team simply wanted a curiosity-value title which might encourage people to tune in. Then "Monty" was suggested as an alternative by Eric Idle, after a drinking companion of his, and John Cleese offered "Python". Oh, and Cleese was born Cheese but decided it was too silly. Cue the cheese shop sketch.

The Moody Blues

This Birmingham, U.K., band enjoyed commercial success in the 1960s and 1970s in the face of critical reaction from indifference to contempt. Predecessors included John Lodge's El Riot And The Rebels (really).

The nucleus of the combo which was to become The Moodies – as they were called – agreed sponsorship with local brewer Mitchell & Butler in order to get pub work. Sitting around in one boozer, they studied the M&B beermats and became The M&B Five for billing purposes. On stage, they were the Moody Blues Five. This fitted their moody image and R&B, which they later notoriously broke away from in search of the lost chord, holy grail and perfect concept album. Spin-off: ▷ The Blue Jays.

Mookie Blaylock

From their favourite basketball player, the New Jersey nets guard. It was under this name that the group won a record contract, although they knew it was not the best choice. They became ▷ Pearl Jam. Blaylock's "Number Ten" shirt, sworn by Pearl Jam members, gave them the name of their first album in 1992. Related: ▷ Temple Of The Dog.

Moondog

There have been many Moondogs in popular music – usually howling at the stars. Kansas blind street musician Louis Hardin first took the name after an early song and successfully kept it despite a challenge by disc jockey Alan Freed, who started *Moondog's Rock 'n' Roll Party Show*. The moniker was used by an early version of ▷ The Beatles, Johnny And The Moondogs; and the mid-1990s saw new bands including Moondog and the unrelated Moondog Jnr.

Keith Moon

▷ The Who. His penchant for dressing up in Jester costumes and excess of the highest order led to his nickname: The Loon.

Martin Moon

Nickname for John Martin, from his lyrical obsession with the subject of the night sky.

Moors Murderers

A textbook example of how to get maximum U.K. tabloid coverage by naming offensiveness. In this case, call yourself after the notorious killers of children on the moors above Manchester and wait for incensed headlines about cashing in on misery. Several bands have followed this route, the most prominent being a short-lived duo consisting of ▷ Steve Strange and future ▷ Pretender Chrissie Hynde.

M

Johnny Moped

Punky Paul Halford released a string of comedy records under such tasteful names as Johnny Moped's Assault And Buggery, some featuring ▷ Captain Sensible. He said Moped was "the man you love to hate … everybody hates mopeds, don't they?"

Jim Morrison

▷ The Doors singer.

In typically rebellious form, Jim claimed his parents were both dead and further distanced himself from them by dropping one S from his last name (coincidentally leaving him with the same surname as ▷ Van Morrison and Sterling Morrison of ▷ The Velvet Underground).

His later *alter ego* The Lizard King grew out of his epic *Celebration Of The Lizard* fantasy composition. He said the title was chosen because lizards and snakes are identified with "unconscious forces of evil". The poem finally appeared on the 1970 Doors album *Absolutely Live* and its 1991 CD re-release *The Doors Live*.

For more: *No One Here Gets Out Alive* by Danny Sugarman and Jerry Hopkins, 1980.

He reportedly inspired the naming of ▷ Jamie Wednesday (incredibly enough).

Van Morrison

Born George Ivan Morrison: the middle name came from the Russian in his family. Nicknames: The Belfast Cowboy, Van The Man. ▷ Them.

Morrissey

The British vocalist/lyricist was born Steven Patrick Morrissey in May 1959, but became known by the surname during his Manchester schooldays. He used it in an apparent bid to stop excessive familiarity from others. Later Morrissey would blush at any journalists daring to call him Steven. (And doubtless a Steve would mean the immediate termination of the interview.) He would probably laugh at any fool who suggested he did it for the same reason as ▷ Sting or ▷ Madonna settled on single names.

Known to some fans as Moz/Mozzer. Unflattering nicknames: Moaner, Dorrissey (coined by former songwriting partner Johnny Marr). Before asserting his genius in ▷ The Smiths, he was in ▷ The Nosebleeds and ▷ Slaughter And The Dogs. No relation: Morrissey-Mullen.

Jelly Roll Morton

Ferdinand LaMenthe Morton wrote *Jelly Roll Blues* at the start of his career. It's a witty number about the perils of having a large jelly (jam) roll: something of a *double entendre*. Morton sang from experience: he started playing the seamier side of Los Angeles, including brothels, where he was known as Mr Jelly Roll.

Tex Morton

New Zealander Robert Lane was always getting in trouble with the police when busking. He came up with the name Tex Morton when stopped by an officer one day. It was taken from a nearby garage sign.

Mother Of The Blues

As opposed to ▷ Empress Of The Blues or ▷ Queen Of The Blues. Title for Ma Rainey, from her "big mama" size.

The Mothers (Of Invention)

▷ Frank Zappa's band was first called The Soul Giants, then The Muthers and later The Mothers. Zappa explained they were bringing into being "new things, new inventions, new life". But nervous record executives feared the all-male group could be seen as adopting a name short for "the oedipal compound word". Zappa, playing the innocent, raised a quizzical eyebrow at the suggestion … but was aware of its publicity value. MGM meanwhile suggested adapting the saying that "necessity is the mother of invention". Zappa solo projects sometimes flew as the Mothers; yet the term was rarely used from 1975 on.

Spin-off: ▷ Little Feat. Related: ▷ Captain Beefheart, ▷ Ruben And The Jets. Individual members included The Winged Eel Fingerling (also with Beefheart), Jim "Motorhead" Sherwood (a drugs reference – cf the unrelated ▷ Motörhead) and Arthur Dyre Trip III (more drugs).

The Mothers was also adopted by an act from Yorkshire, England. Such is the unshockable nature of our practical age that the choice produced concern not on moral but legal grounds: could the two combos be confused? Did Zappa have the copyright? Was it a registered trademark?

Mötley Crüe
Los Angeles heavy metal quartet whose name is based on their obnoxious image. More umlauts:▷ Blue Öyster Cult etc.

Motorhead/Motörhead
Former ▷ Jimi Hendrix roadie ▷ Lemmy misspent his youth becoming a veteran of bands including Opal Butterfly, Sam Gopal And His Dream, The Rockin' Vickers, The Motown Sect and The Rainmakers.

Motorhead is American slang for a speed freak, or amphetamine-user. (▷ The Mother's one-time saxophonist Jim Sherwood was Motorhead.) *Motorhead* was the last track Lemmy wrote for ▷ Hawkwind. The original version is on the B-side of the 1974 single *Kings Of Speed* and contains the classic lines: "Moving like a parallelogram/Yeah." No doubt parallelograms do move after an excessive intake of amphetamines: Lemmy should know. His drugs habit led to a 1975 on-tour bust in Canada and his sacking from the group. Bitterly down-and-out, he wanted revenge by calling his new act Bastard. (Cf the unrelated ▷ Bastard.) But this produced pleas from long-suffering manager Doug Smith, who thought it unviable. He accepted "Motorhead", thinking it something to do with Lemmy's many motorbiking fans.

The band is often credited as Motörhead, following the trend among heavy metal bands for excessive umlauts. The group's personnel includes excessive louts: Wurzel (Michael Burston – from his physical similarity to Worzel Gummidge, a scarecrow who comes to life in books by Barbara Euphan Todd, later televised); Animal (Phil Taylor's stage name came from his habits and nickname Philthy Animal); Eddie "Fast" Clarke (▷ Fastway) and Wizzo. Spin-off: ▷ Headgirl. Related: ▷ Thin Lizzy. Fan club: Motorheadbangers.

Motown
Because Detroit, the centre of the U.S.A.'s motor industry, was known as "Motor City" or "Motown". Hence Motown Records, ▷ Tamla Motown, ▷ MC5.

Motown Spinners
AKA Detroit Spinners; ▷ Spinners (U.S.A.)

Mott The Hoople
The Doc Thomas Band was given a makeover by A&R man Guy Stevens and renamed from an obscure 1967 story by writer Willard Manus. The group later split from then leader Ian Hunter to become Mott. Individual member: Ariel Bender (Luther James Grosvenor, ex ▷ Spooky Tooth). Related: ▷ Bad Company, ▷ British Lions.

Mountain
From the title of Leslie West's solo album of 1969, which featured members of the nascent band.

Mount Rushmore
Named after the well-known hill carved with U.S. presidents' heads, most famously parodied in a rock context by ▷ Deep Purple's 1970 album.

The Move
Roy Wood (born Ulysses Adrian Wood) lifted the 1960s dance word "move" as an expression of his desire to move on. Related: ▷ Wizzard and ▷ The Electric Light Orchestra.

Alison Moyet
Genevieve Alison Moyet: ▷ Alf.

M People
It originally stood for Mancunian leader Mike (Pickering). *Q* said in 1996: "Now it could stand for Money, Milan, Manchester City, Marketing or Mercury Prize. It might possibly refer to Muegler or the Masses." Tribute band: TheM People.

MSG
Michael Schenker Group, from the guitarist. Later McAuley-Schenker Group, adding vocalist Robin McAuley. Related: ▷ UFO.

Mu
The name of a lost sunken continent.

Mudcrutch
▷ Tom Petty.

Mudhoney
This Seattle act took the title of a 1965 Russ Meyer underground movie. Also named from Meyer films: ▷ Faster Pussycat etc.

The Mugwumps
These New York folkies were another band influenced by William S. Burroughs's tales of degeneracy, decadency, drugs and death. The mugwumps in *The Naked Lunch* are compulsive killers and ruthless rulers. In U.S. politics, mugwumps sit on the fence – with their mugs on one side, their wumps on the other. (See Partridge's *Dictionary Of Clichés*.) Related: ▷ The Lovin' Spoonful, ▷ The Mamas And The Papas. More Burroughs: ▷ Dead Fingers Talk etc.

The Mullanes
New Zealander Neil Finn formed this band as 1984's stopgap between his time in ▷ Split Enz and ▷ Crowded House.
    Mullane was the middle name of both Neil and mother Mary.

Münchener Freiheit
Means "Munich Freedom" in German.

Murder Inc.
This ▷ Killing Joke spin-off chose a similar name, borrowing the British title of a U.S. 1950 film elsewhere called *The Enforcer*.

MUSE
The muse that led to the creation of the album *No Nukes*. It stands for Musicians United For Safe Energy.

Musical Youth
Because their average age of 15. Band from Birmingham, U.K., who had hits on both sides of the Atlantic.

The Music Students
▷ Ian Dury.

Muswell Hillbillies
Alter ego for ▷ The Kinks after signing to RCA

in 1971. It led to an album recalling characters from Ray and Dave Davies's youth in Muswell Hill, London. The name is partially derived from U.S. TV show *The Beverly Hillbillies*. The show also inspired the naming of ▷ The Bodines, ▷ The Notting Hillbillies and ▷ The Stamford Hillbillies – Notting Hill and Stamford Hill are other areas of the British capital.

Mute Drivers
Not a reference to being unable to speak; this U.K. duo – Steve Wright and David Rogers – used to work as couriers for the Mute organisation.

Mwandishi
Swahili for "composer". ▷ Herbie Hancock pseudonym, also the title of his 1970 LP.

My Bloody Valentine
Buzzsaw bass, cutting lyrics about love, grating axe guitars … there was always going to be blood on the tracks when this Irish combo played. The name combines a story of genocide and *My Funny Valentine*, covered by ▷ Frank Sinatra, ▷ Elvis Costello and many others.

The Mynah Birds
▷ Rick James and ▷ Neil Young, making reference to their relatively unknown status at the time compared to ▷ The Byrds.

The Mystery Girls
This late 1970s Liverpool band consisted only of blokes, of course. It was the gender-bender activities of frontman (frontwoman?) Pete Burns, later of ▷ Dead Or Alive, which suggested the namecheck of ▷ New York Dolls' track *Who Are The Mystery Girls?* Related: ▷ The Teardrop Explodes, ▷ Wah!

Mystery Trend
This Californian band named after a mis-hearing of the ▷ Bob Dylan song *Like A Rolling Stone* which refers to "a mystery tramp". The word isn't terribly clear, even on CD, but the context makes it clear and anyway there are plenty of lyric books available.

The Nabob Of Sob

▷ Johnnie Ray.

The Naked Lunch

This act named after William S. Burroughs's most famous novel, 1959's *The Naked Lunch*. His masterpiece of cut-up prose documents the life of a drug addict in horrible and surreal detail. The book's title was suggested by fellow writer Jack Kerouac: Burroughs's handwriting *The Naked Lust* was misread by Allen Ginsberg. More Burroughs: ▷ Dead Fingers Talk. More Kerouac: ▷ Dharma Bums.

Napalm Death

Napalm, blazing jellied petrol, was used extensively in the Vietnam War and caused horrific injuries. The name was chosen to offend: something that singer-guitarist Bill Steer achieved admirably with his next band, ▷ Carcass. Cf ▷ Death.

National Health

Non-British readers may need to be told that this band named after the U.K.'s public medical provision system set up by the 1945 Labour government.

Nazareth

This combo came from Dunfermline, Scotland, not Jesus Christ's home village. Their alias was inspired by ▷ The Band's 1968 song *The Weight*, about the trials and tribulations of Joseph and Mary.

The Nazz

The word "naz" was part of the street-talk of the New York black community. It meant "Jesus-of-Nazareth-like" or "very good". It was adopted by musicians and comedians such as ▷ Lord Buckley, whose *Sermon On The Mount* was delivered by a Jesus-like character called The Naz, giving deranged and strangely contemporary directions to his followers.

There were two bands of this moniker: first, a nascent version of ▷ Alice Cooper named in tribute to Buckley. Second, the young ▷ Todd Rundgren formed a group in Philadelphia and nuncupated them after ▷ Yardbirds track *The Nazz Are Blue*. Rundgren said that they spent some considerable time trying to work out what the title meant.

Neck

Not so much a noun, more a verb. "It sounds like ▷ Kiss." Snog was out of the question. "And that's like Smog or Smeg or something." A typical short 1990s name, cf ▷ Blur.

Ned's Atomic Dustbin

The BBC radio comedy show *The Goons* was a big hit in the 1950s and revived in the 1980s. One of the central characters was Neddy, played by (Sir) Harry Secombe. *Ned's Atomic Dustbin* was the title of a show dating from 1959 and involving some irradiated jolly japes at Ned's expense.

This band, from the English Midlands, thought the choice good, obscure and oddball.

N

Vocalist Jonn Penney said it was "his fault" because his mother read him Goons scripts when he was a child. He didn't even have the excuse of planning it as a nuclear protest. In a 1995 *NME* interview with Mark Sutherland he said: "If we'd ever thought we were going to have a career out of it, we'd have called ourselves something succinct. We can't even shorten it to NAD. We all lose sleep over the fact that we're in a band with a horrendously bad name."

See also: *The Eight Legged Atomic Dustbin Will Eat Itself*, by Martin Roach, 1990. It's about Stourbridge bands Ned's, ▷ Pop Will Eat Itself – almost a worst tag – and ▷ The Wonder Stuff, also known as The Eight Legged Groove Machine.

Les Negresses Vertes
A somewhat misleading name, on a par with ▷ The Fat Lady Sings. This mixed French group got their moniker from racist abuse thrown at them by drunken bikers at an early gig.

Nelson
Either you can play down your dad's name or you can trade on it. Identical twins Gunner and Mathew chose the latter. They are sons of ▷ Rick(y) Nelson.

Rick Nelson
His name was Eric Hilliard Nelson and his family changed it to Ricky Nelson when he became a teenage TV star. He later (1960) became Rick Nelson. Related: ▷ Nelson.

Neu!
German for New!. This spin-off from ▷ Kraftwerk didn't really have a name, though the cover of their untitled first album sported a big NEU! sticker, made to look like a new improved soap powder.

Neutral Blue
The name came because the group's guitarist used it as the way of remembering how to wire a plug. Scottish band formed by Roddy Frame prior to his success in ▷ Aztec Camera.

Alexander Nevermind
▷ Prince, when composing *Sugar Walls* for ▷

Sheena Easton. He said the words were too dirty for him to look at so they needed to go through an *alter ego* first to clean them up.

New Christy Minstrels
U.S. folk group who spelled out their desire to revive the aims of the original popular-harmony outfit The Christy Minstrels a century before.

New Edition
Manager Maurice Starr named this band because he was trying to mould them into a new edition of ▷ The Jackson Five, ▷ New Kids On The Block.

New FADS
Nothing to do with fads and fashion: AKA New Fast Automatic Daffodils. This British act took it from the title of a poem which is a cut-up of Wordsworth's "Daffodils" and a Dutch advertising leaflet promoting the DAF (Daffodil) motor car. "I wandered lonely as THE NEW, FAST DAFFODIL" etc. It's by Liverpudlian writer Adrian Henri, **not** Brian Patten as sometimes reported. Unrelated: ▷ DAF.

New Kids On The Block
Manager Maurice Starr was on course to moulding ▷ New Edition – into ▷ The Jackson Five when he decided to try the same with a bunch of white kids too. He started with a song called *New Kids On The (Showbiz) Block* to introduce them. He said the moniker was "pretty obvious when you know the story".

Randy Newman
His prenomen has been the target for amusement in the U.K. where to be randy translates as to be horny in American English. He was born Gary Randolph, *hence the name*. Cf Randy Jackson of ▷ The Jackson Five.

New Model Army
This British troupe liked the name of the 1645 model Roundhead army which was victorious against Royalists. Vocalist: Slade The Leveller. Similar origin, unrelated band: ▷ The Levellers.

New Order
▷ Joy Division were doomed after the suicide

of Ian Curtis. Some time before the band had agreed to abandon the name if any member "left". Curtis's wife Deborah wondered at the time if the others had expected something to happen to the epileptic singer – or if they were planning to kick him out.

The new moniker revived allegations of fascist connotations. Journalist Biba Kopf wrote in the *NME*: "It is a stupid choice of name for a group previously steeped in gloomy, magnificent Gothic romanticism." Joy Division was a Nazi term. Hitler had spoken of "a New Order", his plan for the world, in *Mein Kampf*. Certainly the use of *two* Nazi-linked names seemed more than coincidental.

Since Hitler's time, however, New Order has become a common term for any new regime. Factory Records boss Tony Wilson said the appellation was chosen by the act's manager Rob Gretton after seeing a report on ITN's *News At Ten* saying the Khmer Rouge had renamed as The New Order of Kampuchean Liberation. Renaming after Pol Pot's genocidal reign of terror and death lightened things up a bit after the horrors of Joy Division.

The musicians have vehemently denied allegations of right-wing bias, and say the suggested handle was accepted because they were making a fresh start after a tragic death. The new vocalist, born Bernard Dicken, who sometimes had been known as Bernard Albrecht in Joy Division, emphasised the break by becoming Barney Sumner. He claims he personally was so naïve he didn't even understand the terms "left wing" and "right wing". Wilson added: "I am convinced it never dawned on the band until they started reading about it in the papers." Peter Hook, also quoted in Mick Middles's 1996 book *From Joy Division To New Order: The Factory Story*, further confirms this.

The picture was obscured by Gretton, who had taken great pleasure in stirring up the rock press with false leads to generate publicity. Videos were said to have "Nazi chic" while New Order sleeves recalled German less-is-more design.

Name notes: No relation to short-lived The New Order, a U.S. band formed of ex ▷ MC5 and ▷ Stooges members, related to ▷ Destroy All Monsters. Spin-offs: ▷ Electronic,

Revenge, ▷ The Other Two, ▷ Monaco. Their *Blue Monday* is thought to have led to the naming of ▷ Happy Mondays.

New Riders Of The Purple Sage
▷ Grateful Dead spin-off, named after Zane Grey's adventure novel.

Newtown Neurotics
U.K. group named after their native postwar new town of Harlow, Essex, the influences of which "make people neurotic", they say. Unrelated: ▷ Harlow.

New York Dolls
The New Yorkers' name was lifted from the 1970 Russ Meyer film *Beyond The Valley Of The Dolls* – his first for a major studio and with no direct connection to *Valley Of The Dolls*. In both cases "doll" is narcotics slang for an amphetamine or barbiturate drug in capsule form. It carried an extra meaning for the doll-like all-male band with a strongly transvestite dress sense.

Name notes: Individual member Sylvain Sylvain inspired ▷ David Sylvian of ▷ Japan (note differing spellings). They inspired ▷ The Mystery Girls; Meyer inspired ▷ Faster Pussycat and ▷ Mudhoney. Cf ▷ Valley Of The Dolls.

Nigel And The Crosses
▷ R.E.M.'s 1989 Green world tour included a part-time band called Worst Case Scenario featuring Peter Buck. They renamed at one point in honour of Nigel Cross, the original editor of the magazine called *Bucketfull Of Brains*.

The Nightingales
The post-punk band took its avian inspiration from *Luscinia megarhynchos*, noted for the rich love song of the male heard mainly at night.

Nihilistics
Hardcore band from Long Island, New York who were self-confessed anarchists, systematically rejecting all beliefs and institutions.

Nilsson

Born Harry Edward Nelson III, the singer-songwriter changed the spelling to avoid associations with ▷ Rick(y) Nelson.

999

From their theme *Emergency*. For non-U.K. readers: 999 is the British number for police calls, equivalent to ▷ 911 in the U.S.

911

From the U.S. emergency number, coincidentally echoing ▷ Public Enemy's *911 Is A Joke*.

The Nipple Erectors

Offensive U.K. punk band led by Shane MacGowan, later of ▷ The Pogues. The name's orgasmic reference led to its abbreviation to The Nips.

Nirvana

There have been at least three professional bands of this name ... one is credited with being the most influential of the 1990s, popularising grunge and featuring Kurt Cobain (1967–94) who shot from nothing to superstardom – then shot himself.

He and Chris Novoselic started in 1987 as ▷ Skid Row. While they weren't the first to use the name, it was apt given their destitute state. Cobain said it referred to a part of Seattle where logs were skidded downhill on to barges. In fact many towns have a skid row; the term, originally from lumberjacking, refers to any poverty-stricken or seedy district.

Within weeks they'd played as: Ted Ed Fred, Pen Cap Chew, Throat Oyster, Windowpane, Bliss and Nirvana. Only the last two fitted Cobain's criteria: "I wanted a name that is beautiful and nice and pretty instead of a mean, raunchy punk name like the Angry Samoans. I wanted something different." (See Michael Azerrad's book *Come As You Are*, 1993.) Nirvana originally meant Buddhist beatitude or blessedness. Its origin is Sanskrit for extinction: here, the breaking down of individuality and its absorption into a supreme spirit. It has come to have a meaning wider than the purely religious, applying to any state of ecstasy.

Hence the name. Hence the ripped jeans.

However the heavenly moniker suggests reflective folk, trance-like ambient music or soothing mantras rather than Cobain's vocals-from-hell, Dave Grohl's machine-gun drumming and Novoselic's guitar assault on titles such as *Territorial Pissings*. You have only to listen to Cobain's pain on these tracks to understand his suicide: this is the very antitheses of pleasure.

Most acts have apparently accepted that their appellation will be taken as describing their music or image in some way – whether intended or not. Those groups who have got away from this have chosen vague or misleading handles. Nirvana show how an identifier can be almost anything once a band has become ultra-successful: it becomes a label with meaning removed.

Still, the more successful the star, the more likely someone else will try to establish a previous right to their designation. In 1991 a religious-rock act called Nirvana issued ceased-and-desist orders against television and radio stations playing *Nevermind*. The suit was settled in 1992 for $50,000.

Another Nirvana was a 1960s-on British group led by Patrick Campbell-Lyons, who took legal action. This ended with a $100,000 payment to him and his partner, minus a 30 per cent lawyer's fee, according to reports. The names stayed while Cobain agreed not to perform psychedelic rock. Still, Cobain's miserable drug-ravaged appearance on *Top Of The Tops* could hardly be confused with happy Campbell-Lyons in hippy gear 20 years before. After Cobain's death the British Nirvana recorded a version of *Lithium*.

Name notes: Cobain's widow is ▷ Courtney Love of ▷ Hole. ▷ Todd Rundgren considered Nirvana as an alternative name to ▷ Utopia. See also Christopher Sandford's 1995 book *Kurt Cobain*. Spin-off ▷ Foo Fighters. Pronunciation guide: It's Kurt CO-bane, not C'bane, according to the BBC and his family.

Nitty Gritty Dirt Band

U.S. outfit named because of their down-to-earth aim of wanting to get back to the basics of country music. They also considered The Illegitimate Jug Band, because they didn't have a jug player. After a 1976 split the remnants became The Dirt Band.

NKOTB

▷ New Kids On The Block, abbreviated to New Kids and NKOTB. As one U.S. disc jockey asked: "When did they move in?"

Nobs

Aristocratic nose-thumbing from ▷ Led Zeppelin to the Zeppelin family.

Nokemono

Highly popular and much-loved Japanese rockers who named ironically. *Nokemono* means a misfit or pariah, disliked by everybody.

Nomad

Leader Damon Rochefort knew he had a prenomen seen by some in Britain as having as little appeal as Darren (▷ Dare). He reversed its letters to make himself into a wanderer.

No Means No

This Canadian hardcore male trio borrowed the anti-rape slogan to show feminists they understood – and remind men: "No doesn't really mean Yes or Maybe! It means No."

The Nosebleeds

Never a true heavy metal band, they jested about fans' nosebleeds which are sometimes produced by head-banging and standing too close to rock speakers. Among those to work with the group after the departure of ▷ Ed Banger: ▷ Morrissey.

Notes From The Underground

Indeed an underground band, this American hippy group were more spoken of than listened to. The name came from Russian writer Fyodor Dostoevsky's *Notes From Underground*. They later kept the literary influence under their new name Prince Bakaradi.

The Notting Hillbillies

Like ▷ The Traveling Wilburys, an attempt to get back to their roots, basics and small clubs while burying star status (they were led by Mark Knopfler of ▷ Dire Straits). The name is a reference to their hillbilly-cowboy sound, but:
1. U.S. fans should know Notting Hill is an area of west-central London where Knopfler had a home and where he first asked Steve Phillips if he could join the band. They had worked together as ▷ The Duolian String Pickers.
2. British fans may just need to know it is also a reference to the U.S. TV series *The Beverly Hillbillies*; the series also inspired the naming of ▷ The Bodines, ▷ The Stamford Hillbillies and ▷ The Muswell Hillbillies.

Nova Mob

This mob named from U.S. writer William S. Burroughs's story *Nova Express*. More Burroughs: ▷ Dead Fingers Talk etc.

No Way Sis

Mid-1990s U.K. tribute band named in punning reference to ▷ Oasis. "Oasis don't play in Scotland much so we're the next best thing," they said. Cf ▷ The Gallaghers.

NRBQ

Formed in Florida in the 1960s, they've always used this abbreviation and became reluctant to reveal what it stands for. Perhaps because the truth, sadly, is prosaic. It means "New Rhythm And Blues Quintet".

NTM

Offensiveness alert. French rap group whose name means *nique ta mere* or "fuck your mother". Cf ▷ LHOOQ.

Ted Nugent

▷ The Amboy Dukes, ▷ Damned Yankees.

Nugerte

Anagram of Atlantic Records boss Ahmet Ertegun – used as a credit when composing music.

Gary Numan

Apart from a short spell with ▷ The Lasers, Numan was solo, although he disguised this under ▷ Tubeway Army for a time. He was born as Gary Anthony James Webb, but like ▷ Cliff Richard (born Harry Webb) thought the name had little stage appeal. Numan reflected futuristic electronic music. Fans called: Numanoids, unbelievably.

The Nurk Twins

Unkind nickname for Lennon and McCartney,

sometimes spelled Nerk Twins. Largely self-bestowed for an appearance at Caversham. Cf ▷ The Glimmer Twins, ▷ The Toxic Twins.

The Nutty Boys

▷ Madness spin-off by Chris Foreman and Lee Thompson – with the Madness ska sound, Madness madness and Madness nutty boy nickname. Album title: *Crunch!*

NWA

Like ▷ The Beatnigs, this Californian rap band wanted a name which expressed their positive response to being black and their fight against prejudice. They wanted to be called Niggers With Attitude. The U.S. slang is now worldwide: "attitude" = to have a strong manner; pugnacity. They abbreviated to NWA after much misunderstanding by ignorant radio disc jockeys, who couldn't comprehend how "nigger" could be used in any way but pejoratively.

The Nymphs

Singer Inger Lorre, who first worked with The Healing Dream, said: "Believe it or not, I picked the name out of the dictionary at random. A nymph is a bug lava and I joke that one day we'll grow into ▷ The Beatles."

Laura Nyro

She was born Laura Nigro and renamed to avoid possible racist "negro" confusion. The New York singer-songwriter also worked with ▷ LaBelle.

Oak Ridge Boys

U.S. gospel singers who came together in Tennessee and used to perform regularly at a place called Oak Ridge.

Oasis

The story of the band described as "the most important pop act of the 1990s" and "the best in Britain since ▷ The Smiths and ▷ The Stone Roses" – or "the biggest hype of all time", depending on your point of view – opens on 29 May 1967, the day ▷ The Beatles were giving a press conference to announce the release of *Sgt Pepper* ... and Noel Gallagher, who is now Oasis's lead guitarist and songwriter, was born. His singer brother Liam was born on 21 September 1972. They both grew up in Burnage – and in love with the music of ▷ The Beatles.

By 1991, The Roses were working fitfully on a second album, the Smiths had long since split and Manchester's finest were ▷ The Inspiral Carpets. At that time, Noel was a roadie for the Inspirals, a job he had had since 1988; he failed to become the act's singer but was writing songs. The Inspirals called him "Monobrow" after his thick eyebrows which almost joined in the middle. Meanwhile Liam formed his first group with Bonehead – the rhythm guitarist was named after his thinning hair – Tony McCarroll and bassist Guigsy; they were called Rain. There was a relatively obscure Beatles track of this name – the B-side of *Paperback Writer* and for years not available on album.

Noel tells of Oasis's naming in a 1996 BBC Radio One documentary, *What's The Story?* "My particular story, which isn't the true one but which sounds better than anybody else's, is that there was a clothes shop in Manchester called Oasis where you could buy these decent trainers and is where all the football hooligans used to go. And a lot of people say it is the name of the local taxi firm in Burnage, and a lot of people say it is the name of the local curry house around the corner from Bonehead. The real story is when I was roadie-ing with Inspirals, they did a gig at a place called the Swindon Oasis and Liam thought it was a good name for a group. Everybody else thinks we sound like a reggae band."

This explanation has been gleefully accepted by the Wiltshire Council, whose literature proudly plays up the superstar link.

Another theory Noel didn't mention is that the handle came from a ▷ Happy Mondays record. The fellow Mancunians included the track *Oasis* on their lengthily titled debut album, 1986's *Squirrel & G-Man Twenty Four Hour Party People Plastic Face Carnt Smile (White Out)* (sic). Even if there is any truth in this being the origin, Oasis could well be reluctant to admit it. Confidently, if not arrogantly, they've always seen themselves as the best and certainly wouldn't want to acknowledge a nuncupation debt to anyone else. Perhaps this is what Noel means when he talked about his account not being the true one.

On the *Definitely Maybe Singles* box set interview CD, there's yet another version: "It's on a poster on me bedroom wall just sitting there, and I saw the word Oasis and I just thought: That's very nice. I thought: I'd have a bit of that. It's better than being called ▷ Ned's Atomic Dustbin, innit? What kind of name's that. You've got to love yourself mate, or no one else will love you."

Liam's combo played their first gig as Oasis on 18 August 1991, watched by Noel and The Inspirals. Bonehead says Noel thought it was terrible. They asked him to be their manager; he joined as leader after they heard his song *Live Forever*. Some magazines said the Swindon theory is wrong because Oasis was adopted before Noel joined. This last is correct, but that doesn't rule out him having originated the name.

Hence the name. Hence millionaire Noel's Rolls-Royce.

As Oasis became massively successful, with their gigs sold out and demand huge, tribute groups came into being quickly: Blurasis, ▷ The Gallaghers, ▷ No Way Sis and Oasisn't.

A trawl through the growing mountain of press cuttings reveals that critics have variously seen Oasis as a brilliant and an awful choice for a band. Either way it is an obvious one. It's a short word – always good for a name. It has a pleasant original meaning, a watering hole in the desert or any haven of refreshment and relaxation. Hence the widespread use of Oasis as a trading name. Perhaps most famously it applies to a clothes shop, not just in Manchester but part of a U.K. chain. Also, it was used for an indoor market in Birmingham Bull Ring shopping centre, where Martin Degville of ▷ Sigue Sigue Sputnik had a stall; for a make of wet and dry flower-holders used for arrangements; a range of exotic fruit soft drinks; a holiday resort in the Lake District National Park; and an international equity fund for savers.

Oasis have escaped serious challenges, settling out of court in June 1995 with the clothing chain over the use of Oasis on clothing and tee-shirts. The Gallaghers agreed to pay a once-only amount to the shop. A spokesman at the time told the *NME*: "It's not a big deal. We came to an amicable arrangement for what will be a nominal sum."

Lesser stars have been taken on by lawyers in the past and lost: cf ▷ Chicago, ▷ Yazoo etc. Although some have got away unscathed by arguing that only an idiot would confuse a music act with a different commercial product: ▷ Thomas Dolby is one such who lived to tell the tale of legal threats. Legislation is tougher in the States yet judicial opinion suggests that other users of the Oasis name would only succeed if the band started encroaching on their territory by making flower-arranging kits or selling soft drinks, for example.

The name Oasis has also been used in a musical context before, by a very different and short-lived trio: ▷ Oasis of the 1980s. There was also a pub duo in Leeds, Yorkshire, called Oasis; the first time the Gallagher brothers played at The Duchess of York in the city, there were only about 12 people there because everyone thought it was the other Oasis.

An organisation called The National Band Register was established some years ago in Britain in a bid to avoid potentially costly disputes over duplicating names between rival acts, although legal opinion is divided on copyright of handles and titles of songs as opposed to trademarks. In any case, a legal report in *The Times* of London suggested that defunct groups lose many rights to identifiers. It would be absurd for them to prevent everyone else from using the name for the rest of time, especially when they no longer have records in the shops, are no longer performing and the later musicians are totally unaware of their existence.

Oasis on the Internet: Try a search on Ultimate Band List; or http://www.oasisnet.com. Related: ▷ The Smoking Mojo Filters.

Oasis (1980s)

Everyone has heard of 1990s stars ▷ Oasis. Not many people know Oasis was also used by a short-lived 1984 supergroup – formed by Mary Hopkin, Peter Skellern and Julian Lloyd Webber – aiming to be "an oasis in a desert".

Dr Winston O'Boogie

▷ John Lennon referred to himself as this on a number of occasions and used it as a credit when working with ▷ Elton John in the 1970s. The "Winston" is his own original middle name, earlier legally replaced with "Ono".

Ocean Colour Scene

Coming together from Birmingham, U.K., bands The Fanatics and The Boys, they secured a deal with a local label. Contrary to some reports, the record company was called ▷ !Phfft, not the group. Ocean Colour Scene was chosen as "three words we liked which sounded good together". Cf ▷ Living Colour.

Sinéad O'Connor

Unflattering derivative – based on her shaven-head period of course: Skinhead O'Connor. Pronunciation guide: "Shin-aid" not "Sigh-need".

Odetta

Another single-name artist. Born Odetta Holmes Felonius Gorden.

Odyssey

Odyssey as in a long strange journey. This band took it as a unusual description rather than because of its links to Homer, James Joyce or *2001: A Space Odyssey*.

Oedipus Wrecks

Formed by ▷ Wah! star Pete Wylie who managed a pun on Greek tragedy *Oedipus Rex* and manic-depressives with oedipal complexes (pretty much the subject of Sophocles' play).

O.G.

"Original Gangster": nickname for ▷ Ice T.

Ohio Express

Because they came from Ohio. Perhaps other bands from the U.S. state can be more imaginative …

Ohio Players

… or perhaps not. Because they came from Ohio.

Oingo Boingo

Named after an L.A. comedy revue which evolved into their musical act.

O'Jays

This fledgling Ohio band surprisingly didn't call themselves The Ohio … Somethings. They received advice on their sound and image from local Cleveland DJ Eddie O'Jay. "Eddie helped us tons," Eddie Levert said. "We were the Mascots … then we thought the best way of thanking Eddie, naming after him."

Ol' Blue Eyes

Nickname for ▷ Frank Sinatra.

The Old Groaner

Or The Groaner. ▷ Bing Crosby nickname, because of his singing style on ballads.

Ollie And Jerry

Ollie Brown and Jerry Knight. Nothing to do with Ben And Jerry, the ice-cream company behind Cherry Garcia (▷ Jerry Garcia).

Omar

Omar Hammer became a single-name artist on stage and in 1991 changed his surname by deed poll to Lyfehook, his mother's maiden name – reportedly because he hated being compared to ▷ MC Hammer.

OMD

Or O.M.D./O.M.I.T.D. ▷ Orchestral Manoeuvres In The Dark.

One Dove

This 1990s band started as The Doves. They ran into trouble with the already existing Thrashing Doves, who were frequently referred to as The Doves and soon became formally known as such. This group became One Dove, not a reference to the ▷ Bob Marley reggae song *One Love* but to an ecstasy tablet.

One-Eyed Jacks

Reportedly an appropriated film title. True enough, there was a 1961 outlaw movie which fits the bill. But the band winked as they mentioned this … Were they aware "one-eyed Jack/Joe" is a slang term for male genitalia? Of course they were.

101'ers

An R&B-style outfit starring ▷ Joe Strummer,

later of ▷ The Clash, and Don Kelleher, later of ▷ Public Image Ltd. The usual story is that they named after the rat torture room in George Orwell's 1949 novel *Nineteen Eighty-Four*. The truth is more prosaic. It was the address of a London squat, 101 Walterton Terrace, home of Strummer and the rest of the band. They had a residency at a local pub, The Chippenham.

13111

Spin-off project from ▷ R.E.M., one of many. This was a one-off release by Bill Berry. The name came from the record's matrix number.

The Only Ones

Formed 1976. The *NME* reported in 1991 that vocalist Peter Perrett said it came from a fantasy about the end of the world, with the band the only ones left. Related: ▷ England's Glory.

Open Road

Named in 1970 from the song *Open Road* by ▷ Donovan, dating from the same year.

The Opium Eaters

Promising Liverpool, U.K., band of 1978, whose members went on into ▷ Frankie Goes To Hollywood, ▷ The Slits and ▷ Wah!. They were encouraged by Mick Jones of ▷ The Clash, who suggested the name from *Confessions Of An English Opium-Eater*, the 1822 book by essayist Thomas De Quincey.

Orange Juice

Absolutely no relation to Oran "Juice" Jones! They adopted their off-beat name as a refreshing change amid rancid punk.

Roy Orbison

Born Roy Kelton Orbison. The Big O joined the 1988 superstar aggregation ▷ The Traveling Wilburys as Lefty Orbison, a studio leg-pull based on a political discussion. Their next album was dedicated to the late Lefty.

Orbital

This band play spacey music so you might expect this to be a reference to high-flying satellites. Their inspiration was firmly earth-based. They named after the British capital's main orbital road, the M25 motorway, the

quickest way of getting to warehouse parties at which they performed in the late 1980s.

Orchestral Manoeuvres In The Dark

Liverpudlian keyboard players Andy McCluskey and Paul Humphreys have a musical curriculum vitae which opens in the 1970s with groups with radically different names, none of them successful or known outside their home city. They first worked together in their school band, Equinox, and moved on into ▷ The Id and ▷ VCL XI. The duo were also part of an archetypal pubescent prototype punk pairing, perversely called Hitlerz Underpantz – a name reflecting punk fascination with Nazis and guaranteeing commercial failure.

McCluskey then went on into ▷ Dalek I until he and Humphreys decided to become a partnership. Other members of their combo were Paul Collister and a tape recorder which was dubbed Winston. One of Winston's first "songs" featured tank sounds and explosions off a sound effects record. Aptly, it was to be entitled *Orchestral Manoeuvres In The Dark*. The act, and the appellation, became permanent as more members were recruited and Winston – like his non-human counterpart ▷ Echo, of the Bunnymen – was retired.

The Orchestral handle was liked because it stood out amid a wealth of short punk monikers – their music was emphatically never punk – but it was soon abbreviated to O.M.I.T.D., O.M.D. and OMD. The band told *Melody Maker* in 1982 that embarrassing similarities with ▷ ELP and ▷ ELO were coincidental. The designation was meant to be over the top – as in World War I trenches presumably – and was designed "to make people listen". Which it certainly did.

Hence the name. Hence the junk culture.

The long identifier also sparked a misconception that it was an anagram. *Q* magazine was asked by one of its readers in 1994 what anagrams could be made from it. Suggestions included: "Dr Kevin loathes carthorse manure", "Unrehearsed shamrock ventilator" – neither of which make sense – and "R.E.M. – horrendous theatrical knaves". The latter is particularly unlikely to have been an origin – ▷ R.E.M. didn't then exist. More interesting is the anagram "Uncontroversial Remarketed Hash".

Humphreys left OMD to form the Listening Pool.

The Orioles
One of the first of a large number of "bird" bands, they came from Baltimore, Maryland, U.S.A., and named after the mascot associated with various sports teams from the city.

The Orlons
This Philadelphia vocal group began supporting The Cashmeres and chose the textile name as meaning something similar. Cashmere is from goats' hair; orlon is synthetic.

Orpheus
This U.S. band read a book about Greek legends and named after Orpheus, who could enchant the beasts and trees with his lyre, a gift from Apollo.

Ozzy Osbourne
Born 1948, widely known as Ozzy. Journalists interviewing him at his Buckinghamshire mansion have been told to call him by his proper name. "I'm bleedin' John Michael Osbourne here, y'know." ▷ Black Sabbath, ▷ Blizzard Of Oz. No relation to the rock bands Oz or Ozz.

Osibisa
African-tinged rock band formed by Teddy Osei which played bisaba, the West African native music, in a rock style.

Gilbert O'Sullivan
The Irish singer-songwriter was born Raymond O'Sullivan. Gordon Mills, manager (and namer) of both ▷ Tom Jones and ▷ Engelbert Humperdinck thought his prodigious songwriting ability matched some of the greats of the past. The fledgling star became Gilbert, while retaining his surname in reference to the popular British composers Sir William Gilbert and Sir Arthur Sullivan.

The Other Two
It was 1990, and two ▷ New Order members were going their own separate ways with spin-offs … First there was Peter Hook's band Revenge, then Barney Sumner's ▷ Electronic. This left the quieter couple of the band, Stephen Morris and Gillian Gilbert, to step reluctantly into the spotlight. They've offered two explanations: that the moniker had "plenty of ironies" and that "it was getting late and we're crap at names". There's nothing like honesty.

Johnny Otis
Legendary U.S. pop talent scout and recording artist, the Otis came from his real (Greek) surname, Veliotes, given an anglicised touch. ▷ The Godfather of R&B (Rhythm And Blues).

Ox
▷ Who bassist John Entwistle formed this band after ▷ Rigor Mortis. The moniker is his own nickname, given for his taciturn nature and large, unmoving stature on stage. A remark probably by Entwistle inspired the naming of ▷ Led Zeppelin.

The Ozark Mountain Daredevils
Mountain range in Oklahoma and Arkansas. The band's 1975 *The Car Over The Lake Album* illustrated the name with a daredevil automobile in mid-flight over an Ozark valley.

Ozric Tentacles
This British band formed in 1983 at a Stonehenge Free Festival and light-heartedly cultivated a long-haired Somerset crusty image, complete with lentil and ley-line references. Unfortunately, most people thought they were serious.

Few people got the name either: not surprising, because it was an in-joke. Keyboardist Joie Hinton tried to convince a friend for an April Fool's joke that the tentacles were a new type of breakfast food with a hallucinogenic effect. He also considered calling the imaginary cereal – and the group – the Desmond Whisps or the Malcolm Segments.

Paddy Goes To Holyhead
Pub-rock band whose name makes fun of ▷ Frankie Goes To Hollywood, whose lead singer was ▷ Holly Johnson.

Holyhead is a seaport in Wales, best known for its ferries to Ireland, *hence the name*.

Also worked with ▷ The Sweet.

Larry Page
British singer Leonard Davies renamed in honour of the *Jolson Story* star. It also allowed the phrase "Larry Page, the teenage rage". He later became a manager and was instrumental in christening ▷ The Kinks, ▷ The Troggs and ▷ Reg Presley.

Pandora's Box
There have been two groups of this name, both with different reasons for selecting it.

The better known, from the U.S., named in honour of the mythical figure Pandora, with her magical box of tricks.

The other Pandora's Box, from the English Midlands, were making a risqué reference to the posh Pandora in writer Sue Townsend's *Adrian Mole* comic novels. "Box" is a slang word for female genitals in both the U.S. and U.K.

Cf ▷ The Box.

Trivia note: ▷ Aerosmith separately entitled their 3-CD set of 1991 *Pandora's Box*. The title was also a single for ▷ OMD.

Pan's People
Dancers on BBC show *Top Of The Pops*

1968–76. Choreographer-leader Flick Colby said they had wanted to be Dionysus's Darlings but went for a shorter alliterative-cum-mythological version.

Pansy Division
In the 1960s bands named after gays for a joke: ▷ The Kinks, ▷ The Pink Fairies. By the 1990s gays were openly and more seriously choosing their own names such as ▷ Sister George and this lot, who were a little tongue-in-cheek with their Nazi Panzer reference.

Pantera
Spanish for panther.

Paper Lace
Because many of their friends worked in a British Midlands factory which made lace paper. No relation to Black Lace.

Paradise Lost
Heavy metal gets literary. It is open to dispute quite how many fans of this lot knew it was a name shared with a classic poem. English author John Milton (1608–74) wrote *Paradise Lost* and a later sequel, *Paradise Regained* (1671).

The poem opens with "man's first disobedience" and expulsion from paradise, the Garden of Eden . Cf ▷ East Of Eden.

Parasites Of The Western World
Oregon, U.S.A., band adapting Irish playwright

J.M. Synge's 1907 title *The Playboy Of The Western World*.

Charlie Bird Parker
▷ Bird.

Colonel Tom Parker
Eminence grise behind ▷ Elvis Presley. The manager was born Andreas Cornelius van Kuijk in the Dutch town of Breda. The respectable all-American name was assumed as he arrived as an illegal immigrant while the military "rank" was an honorary title bestowed on him by the Tennessee Militia. He died in 1997.

Parliament(s)
Young ▷ George Clinton was looking for a name for the vocal group he was forming in the 1950s ... and found it in his pocket. Where he had a packet of Parliament cigarettes. It therefore had nothing to do with politics in Clinton's case.

A legal dispute with his record company over the rights to the name forced Clinton to turn to ▷ Funkadelic, combining Parliaments with their backing group. After winning the name case in the 1970s, he revived the vocal band as Parliament and ran it in conjunction with Funkadelic.

Larry Parnes
U.K. manager who named, among others: ▷ Vince Eager, ▷ Georgie Fame, ▷ Billy Fury, ▷ Johnny Gentle (!), ▷ Duffy Power (!!), ▷ Dickie Pride (!!!), ▷ Tommy Steele and ▷ Marty Wilde.

The Alan Parsons Project
Initially this was a code name used by London's Abbey Road Studios for bookings made by resident engineer Alan Parsons (whose credits included ▷ The Beatles) as he recorded with partner Eric Woolfson in a then unnamed group.

Bill Parsons
Singer Bobby Bare got a shock when his record came out. It was mistakenly credited to Bill Parsons, who was another artist on the same record label. The song, 1958's *All-American Boy*, was a hit under this name.

Gram Parsons
He was born Cecil Ingram Connor. At 13 he was given the second name of his mother's second husband, who also called him Gram, from Ingram. He worked with ▷ The Byrds and ▷ The Flying Burrito Brothers, and inspired ▷ Angelband.

Partners In Crime
A trade paper survey a few years ago revealed that this was the most common name for amateur bands in Britain, with at least seven acts using the name. None has yet been successful (which might prove that crime never pays). The best-known Partners In Crime was a 1980s spin-off from ▷ Status Quo.

Billy Paul
He was born Paul Williams but reversed the names to William Paul, then Billy Paul, because there were already two famous people called Paul Williams – one was in ▷ The Temptations and the other was an actor.

Pavlov's Dog
Named after experiments using dogs by Russian psychologist Ivan Petrovich Pavlov (1849–1936). Dogs salivate when given food, and he rang a bell every time his laboratory dogs were fed. Finally he discovered the dogs would salivate just on hearing the ringing of the bell without any food being present. This might all sound obvious, or a waste of time, but was apparently invaluable for those studying conditioned responses.

This U.S. band, formed 1973, is said to be a tribute to The Rolling Stones, whose 1971 song *Bitch*, on the LP *Sticky Fingers*, includes the line "when you call my name I come running like a Pavlov dog."

Albums include their second, dating from 1976, called *At The Sound Of The Bell*. Ugh.

Peaches And Herb
Herbert Feemster formed this duo with Francine Hurd, whose Peaches childhood nickname came from her friendly disposition. After she left Linda Greene became Peaches – although she didn't have the same peachy cheeks ...

P

Pearl

Nickname for Janis Joplin and name of her posthumous album. Cf also ▷ Big Brother And The Holding Company.

Pearl Harbor And The Explosions

▷ Pearl Harbor.

Pearl Jam

Bass guitarist Jeff Ament gives a truncated early history: "Green River: three records, three tours ... the Seattle sound, sup-pop, long hair ... etc. Mainly etc. One thing didn't lead to another and they left. Mother Love Bone: two records, one tour. Love rock ... Mookie Blaylock ... Reeenk Roink ... Pearl Jam ... The coming together of *Ten*."

If this looks like gobbledegook, here's a translation. Pearl Jam are from Seattle, Washington, U.S.A. They came together mainly from two other bands, called ▷ Green River and Mother Love Bone. The latter contained drummer Gary Gilmour (no relation to the more infamous murderer Gilmour) and a promising vocalist, Andrew Wood, who died of a heroin overdose in 1990. They first played under their new line-up as ▷ Mookie Blaylock and were offered a recording contract.

They knew they needed a new moniker. Mookie was cute yet an in-joke that would not be understood (see separate entry on this). They replaced it with another in-joke, yet one that sounded better and more "profound". Publicists at record company Epic said the name was something to do with music (cf ▷ The Jam) – they were wrong.

What they didn't know was that it was taken from new vocalist Eddie Vedder's American Indian great-grandmother, Pearl, and her finest recipe, a fearsome jam which supposedly had hallucinogenic properties. Vedder said it used a Mexican cactus yielding mescalin, carefully boiled and distilled with the spines removed ... he urged kids not to try this at home. By the way, the name's origin isn't an either-or choice between grandmother and jam: it came from both.

Pearl Jam, from their first album *Ten* onwards, have played a key part in the 1990s grunge movement and are associated with fellow Seattle band ▷ Nirvana, although in truth their links with ▷ Soundgarden were stronger (▷ Temple Of The Dog).

For more, see Brad Morrell's 1993 biography *Pearl Jam*.

Pearls Before Swine

The name comes from the old proverb, adapted from the Bible – Matthew 7:6: "Do not throw your pearls before swine, lest they trample them under foot and turn to attack you." It was an indirect statement on how this U.S. band regarded their work – pearls - though, they said, not how they regarded their audience. Unrelated: ▷ Blodwyn Pig.

John Peel

The U.K. disc jockey and one-time pop entrepreneur was born John Robert Parker Ravenscroft. The name change to the old Lakeside hunting character (as in 'd'ya ken John Peel') was suggested by a secretary at Radio London where he was working in the 1960s. It was "less unwieldy", he explained.

The Pelvis

Nickname rhyming with ▷ Elvis (Presley), from his provocative hip thrusts which were judged too racy to be shown on U.S. television in the staid 1950s.

Penetration

Late 1970s Durham, U.K., punksters, whom the *NME* reported as playing "penetrating music". Any resemblance to a term used in advertising was purely accidental ... and any coincidence with sex purely deliberate.

There were many other two-level punk names: perhaps the best known being ▷ The Members.

Pentangle

... because there were five people in this group. The name, they said, "seems to cover all the angles."

Percy

So you want to know the origin of ▷ Led Zeppelin star Robert Plant's nickname. Percy was born during the band's tour to promote their first album. It was an in-joke because he was a plant and the most famous English gardener at the time was Percy Thrower, of Shrewsbury Flower Show repute.

Disregard reports that the tight-trousered one's appellation came from the film *Percy* about, ahem, a man who has a penis transplant. The film was made in 1971; the nickname dates from 1969. Those were in the days before pop stars whammed shuttlecocks down their shorts (▷ Wham!) and Planty was followed by fans on account of the bulge in his pants (and that wasn't his wallet).

Pere Ubu

The always undeservedly obscure, progressive band from Cleveland, Ohio, U.S.A., aptly chose their name from the anti-hero of an undeservedly obscure, futuristic play by Alfred Jarry entitled *Ubu Roi*.

The rotund rockers came across the play when it was made into a film by animator Jan Lenica in 1976. They liked the surreal plot and instantly hated Peru Ubu, who is one of the most dislikeable title characters ever – self-centred, stupid, sadistic – but they liked his name.

Leader Dave Thomas said the choice was much better than their earlier Foggy And The Shrimps and was nicely vague.

Spin-off: ▷ Friction.

Carl Perkins

The rock 'n' roll singer corrected his birth certificate, which misspelled his name as Perkings. Inspired: ▷ Matchbox. No relation to jazz musician called Carl Perkins.

Peter, Paul And Mary

Wisely chosen in preference to their surnames Yarrow, Stookey and Travers, which one record company said sounded like a firm of undertakers. Stookey's first name was actually Noel but he renamed because it went better with Peter and Mary.

Petra

If you're going to do a rock pun, aim for class. Petra is the Greek word for rock, as in stone. (As in "petrified", meaning to turn to stone etc.) There is also a Jordanian city called Petra. Petra the band come from America and they are a Christian outfit whose albums include *Petra Means Rock* and *The Rock Cries Out*.

Pet Shop Boys

A name with a simple explanation, a darker alternative – fiercely denied – and unintentional controversy. In 1981, London-based Neil Tennant and Chris Lowe (a journalist and architecture apprentice respectively) were *habitués* of clubs in the smart West End of the British capital city. They struck up a conversation in a King's Road hi-fi shop and were soon writing songs together, forming a duo called West End. The title was continued through their PSB single *West End Girls*.

Tennant reckons "everybody knows" how the new moniker originated. They worked with record producer Bobby O (Robert Orlando) who knew three lads who worked in an Ealing pet shop. Tennant suggested the trio should start a band, possibly playing *How Much Is That Doggie In The Window*. It sounded like a rap group, "American", like The Peech Boys: "just silly, a bit twee and camp".

Still, there is an urban myth suggesting that some gays, called "pet shop boys", indulge in a sado-masochistic sexual ritual. A *Guardian* article describes this as "a practice among Hollywood decadents of anally inserting (doctored or) tortured small animals to induce a sado-masochistic masturbatory high."

In Chris Heath's 1990 biography *The Pet Shop Boys, Literally*, Tennant claims not to have known of this S&M reference until about 1986. Music journalist Betty Page admonished him: "We all know what the name means." When Tennant was told he was "absolutely horrified". The duo realised it was too late to change, while Tennant believes the hamster angle to be apocryphal, having spoken to "some people in New York who might know".

Appearing at the Oxford Union in the 1990s, he was asked point blank about the origin. He obliquely answered: "You know, it's funny to think that people are looking at you and thinking: There goes a man who puts hamsters up his bottom." He brought the house down. Whatever you say about the Pet Shop Boys, they're never *Being Boring*.

The legend has been helped by three traits. First, Tennant says it has been "endlessly referred to" by many including journalist Fiona Russell Powell and comedian Stephen Fry, when introducing them. Second, the PSB affect

P

an air of knowing satire at all times, which suggests that things are not what they seem. Third, there's their sexuality. There's some confusion of issues here. It's obvious that someone can be gay without knowing of, or condoning in any way, animal torture. Unfortunately, it isn't obvious to some tabloid journalists.

Hence the name. Hence the Boy baseball caps. Unrelated: The Farmers' Boys.

Tom Petty
Petty might have never made it if he had stayed as a member of the unpleasantly named Mudcrutch, a homage to Florida's muddy alligator swamps. Fortunately, he moved to a new outfit more sensibly called The Heartbreakers. (Cf ▷ The Heartbreakers.) ▷ The Travelling Wilburys.

P.F.M.
Italian band formed 1971, with a name that stands for Premiata Forneria Marconi.

PhD
Chosen as a variation of the rock 'n' roll doctors theme. University degree for Doctor of Philosophy, sometimes abbreviated as D.Phil.

Cf ▷ Doctor Feelgood, ▷ Doctor Hook etc. No relation to ▷ The Three Degrees.

The Pheasant Pluckers
Ceilidh group who chose a tongue-twister, hoping to trip up announcers. Related: ▷ Fairport Convention.

!Phfft
Birmingham independent record label perhaps best known for its links with ▷ Ocean Colour Scene. The unfortunate onomatopoeic name is meant to represent the sound of a lager can being opened, although, inevitably, less savoury theories are rife.

Little Ester Phillips
The blues singer was born Ester Mae Jones in Texas, U.S.A. She took her name after seeing a poster advertising Phillips Gasoline.

Phoenix
Recalling the mythical bird that burnt itself on a funeral pyre and rose from the ashes. The most famous Phoenix came from the ashes of ▷ Argent.

The Photos
The Photos begun life as a deadbeat punk band from Evesham, Worcestershire, U.K., called Satan's Rats (who had one small hit on ▷ DJM Records with *You Make Me Sick*, a cult classic of the genre).

The group were then re-formed, Wendy Wu was brought in and sources close to the band say The Photos name was meant to be a little obscure and dual-meaning and because the photogenic members wanted to be photographed a lot on their way to stardom. Seems fair enough. Their debut single, appropriately, was *I'm So Attractive*.

Wu, later as Wendy Cruise, joined with ▷ Steve Strange in ▷ Strange Cruise.

More punky dual-meanings: ▷ The Mixers, ▷ Penetration.

Edith Piaf
France's greatest cabaret star was born Edith Gassion but started her career at 15 as La Môme Piaf – the child/waif sparrow/songbird – an affectionate reference to her slight frail appearance and seemingly fragile sound.

Piano Red
Pianist William "Willie" Perryman's albino condition and pink eyes gave rise to the nickname. His songs were instrumental in naming ▷ Doctor Feelgood.

Pickettywitch
If you thought ▷ Planxty or ▷ Pyewackett sound like silly names for folk or pop bands then consider this one, which was picked purely because it was an unusual word. This band said they found it in an old book of maps of England. The village does not feature in even authoritative modern gazetteers which include tiny hamlets such as Picklescott, Leebotwood. (Now there's an interesting band name ...)

Pigbag
Mishearing of ▷ James Brown's song *Papa's Got A Brand New Bag*, a track which they covered.

The Piglets

▷ Jonathan King chose the name for this studio session group based on the song he'd written for them, *Johnny Reggae*. This one-hit-wonder tune was about a skinhead with a schoolgirl friend whom King envisaged as having "a beaming, polished little face that looked like a piglet. *Hence the name*."

PiL

▷ Public Image Ltd.

Piltdown Men

The Piltdown skull (1912) was accepted as conclusive proof of the existence of new kind of early form of mankind when it was first put on show, but it was later proved as an elaborate fake. This early 1960s U.S. band chose it to fit in with their cavemen image and records such as *Goodnight Mrs Flintstone*.

Absolutely no relation to British band Hotlegs (precursor of ▷ 10CC), who made *Neanderthal Man*.

More Stone Age inspiration: The Cavemen, ▷ The Cro-Mags, ▷ The Dinosaurs, ▷ Dinosaur Junior.

The Pink Fairies

A tongue-in-cheek name some people did not know whether to take seriously or not. It was meant to be a joke. As you can tell with albums which have titles like: *Oh, What A Bunch of Sweeties.*

It came from the name of a group of friends in Notting Hill, London, who formed what has has been described as "a drinking club-cum-terrorist organisation". The club was also called The Social Deviants and spawned a band which later evolved into The Pink Fairies. It may have been a reference to the fairy stories of J.R.R. Tolkien (who also inspired ▷ Cirith Ungol and ▷ Marillion).

The drummer (John Alder) became known as Twink because of his tightly curly hair "and people used to joke I used Twink setting lotion".

Cf ▷ The Pretty Things.

Pink Floyd

The British band formed from the wreckage of Sigma 6, also called The T-Set, Meggadeath (cf ▷ Megadeth), the Architectural Abdabs and The Screaming Abdabs. All failed to find a record deal and they became The Pink Floyd Sound, in typical sixties fashion when everyone had the definite article.

The most popular explanation is that Syd Barrett, (ex Hollering Blues), namechecked two music heroes. Pink Anderson (1900–74) and Floyd Council (1911–76) had jointly made a record which he happened to have in his collection, according to one report.

But the London *Evening Standard* reported: "Roger Waters shared a flat in 1967 in Earls Court with artist Duggie Fields and someone called Mick Steadman. They had two cats called Pink and Floyd. Although the name is widely believed to derive from a synthesis of two Georgia bluesers' monikers ... we think it came from the cats."

One *New Musical Express* report suggested the group was christened "after dead boxer Floyd Paterson and a jazz singer named Pink" but this account seems to win favour with nobody else.

The main problem with the blues version is that Anderson is very obscure and Council came from North Carolina; he made only a handful of records. The erratic Barrett became a recluse and now refuses the interview that might clear up the case once and for all. After all, this world-famous act might have been Anderson Council. Barrett inspired ▷ Gigolo Aunts.

At Pink Floyd's first meeting with record company EMI, an ignorant executive is said to have asked: "Which one's Pink?" This was recalled in *Have A Cigar* on 1975's *Wish You Were Here*; the 1982 film *The Wall* featured a character called Pink. "Which one's Pink" tee-shirts were sold at Roger Waters concerts after he left and legal disputes developed.

Hence the name. Hence the box set.

For another story involving a cat and some mystery: ▷ Procol Harem. Good reference: the Pink Floyd fanzine, *The Amazing Pudding*.

Pink Kross

All-female trio described by *NME* as: "Glasgow's foremost purveyors of Day-Glo fuzzy punk." They named after ▷ Redd Kross. The latter returned the compliment by giving them a support spot.

Pink Military

Ex ▷ Big In Japan vocalist Jayne Casey, from Liverpool, who was wearing military gear, was reportedly first seen by a talent scout while she was standing near a pink wall in a pub. *Hence the name.*

Pink Moon

One of those poetic names that lingers, stays in the memory, hangs in the sky like a big beautiful balloon. Taken from Nick Drake's 1972 album *Pink Moon.*

The Pips

They were named after a cousin of leader Gladys Knight, Pip Woods. It swiftly became an acronym for Perfection In Performance.

Unflattering derivative: Gladys And Her Pips.

The Pirates

Leader ▷ Johnny Kidd needed to wear an eye patch ... so they dressed as pirates ... therefore were called The Pirates ... life used to be simple. This entry is included to illustrate how names were basic fancy dress – while it's now possible to call a band anything clever, unusual, obscure and downright pretentious. Perhaps it's time for a new Pirates?

Pixies

This hard-rocking American band has made it big in the 1990s on the back of a name which says almost nothing about their heavy guitar fuzz. It was found from the pages of a dictionary by guitarist Joey Santiago, according to the *Q Encyclopedia Of Rock Stars.*

The Ps also yielded "panoply" so they were initially Pixies In Panoply, which sounded like a fairy tale from a mythical country. Arguably, the Pixies is more misleading than meaningless – it sounds like the name for a fey folk-rock band in the early ▷ Tyrannosaurus Rex style. They described their early influence as everything from ▷ Peter Paul And Mary to ▷ Hüsker Dü.

Like their fellow Bostonians the Throwing Muses, they eschew the definite article.

Individual members included Charles Michael Kitteridge Thompson IV, more pithily known as Black Francis.

Offshoot: ▷ The Breeders.

P.J. Harvey

Name of Polly Jean ▷ Harvey's backing band – while, to all intents and purposes, she is the sole star.

Plainsong

Ian Matthews, late of ▷ Matthews Southern Comfort, adopted this term for medieval music using a single line of vocal melody as he got back to folk basics.

Planxty

This Irish folky band named after a Gaelic word for a greeting, or a piece of music written for someone else. One of their tracks was an "in memory" tune and therefore a *planxty. Planxty* is principally an expression of goodwill, approximating to "best health".

Plastic Ono Band

▷ John Lennon.

Plethyn

Welsh vocal group whose name means "plaited". The voices are supposed to blend together like hair in a plait.

Plimsouls

This soul band gets an entry simply to remark on the terribleness of their punning moniker, beaten only by The Jive Bombers and ▷ Eire Apparent.

PM Dawn

From the duo's stage names, Prince B and Minute Mix – respectively brothers Attrell and Jarrett Cordes.

Poco

The band formed after the 1968 breakup of ▷ Buffalo Springfield as Pogo, recalling a U.S. newspaper comic strip by Walt Kelly, because their manager looked like Pogo himself. They encountered legal difficulties with the cartoon's owners and changed it as little as possible. *Poco* is a musical term – from Italian

– meaning "slightly". Cf similar minimal name change to avert legal action: Red Cross to Redd Kross.

Several books on ▷ The Beatles mention Poco. One suggests, and another explicitly states, that ▷ John Lennon named the band. Poco members have replied these accounts are incorrect: "The name was picked long before we met John – though it would have been an honour if he'd picked it."

The Pogues

Shane MacGowan – he with the teeth like sharks', skin like shrapnel, voice like tearing sandpaper and drunk set eyes – was a member of lost punks ▷ The Nipple Erectors before forming this riotous Irish band in the early 1980s. Again, he chose a saucy name and was forced to abbreviate it. This one came from Irish *póg ma thón*, which translates as "kiss my arse". (Cf ▷ Kiss.) The pronunciation of the Gaelic – the T is silent – is Pogue Mahone, which was the name of the record label. When bosses at BBC Radio One found out, they refused to play the band's first recordings. *Pogue Mahone* was a 1995 album title.

MacGowan says in his autobiography the choice was "no big deal". They played in the 1987 film *Straight To Hell* as The McMahon Gang. Later recruit: ▷ Joe Strummer.

Poi Dog Pondering

This American band's logo recalled the ▷ HMV sign which inspired ▷ Bow Wow Wow. Except the dog in question is a "poi" or non-pedigree – which, they explained, was like their music. The mutt was indeed "pondering", a word added for alliterative effect.

Polecats

More rockabilly-revival feline names. ▷ The Stray Cats.

The Police

Chosen because the word is internationally known as Police/Polizei etc.

It also fitted in well with similarly named enterprises by manager Miles Copeland, brother of drummer Stewart Copeland (ex ▷ Curved Air; the man behind ▷ Klark Kent). These included CIA, FBI, the Illegal record label and the later Outlandos (i.e., outlaws) Charity Trust. The names were inspired by their father, who was a former executive with the Central Intelligence Agency.

▷ KGB (similar name, not related).

When Copeland and ▷ Sting first joined with Andy Summers they played briefly (with Mike Howlett) as ▷ Strontium 90.

Summers (ex ▷ (New) Animals, ▷ Soft Machine, ▷ Zoot Money and just about everything else) was born Andrew Somers and changed his name to avoid spelling confusion.

Miles also played a part in naming ▷ Lords Of The New Church.

Tribute band: The Secret Police.

The Poni-Tails

This 1950s vocal group did not disappoint salivating punters expecting schoolgirls with pony-tails. More hairstyle names: ▷ The B52s, ▷ The Marcels etc.

Pooh Sticks

A joke reference to the ever-popular 1920s children's books by A.A. Milne about Winnie-the-Pooh, Piglet, Tigger *et al*. Pooh and his pals got many hours of happiness by dropping sticks from bridges to see which would move fastest downstream. Sad. As the band put it: "I mean, get a *life!*"

Cf ▷ Edward Bear.

Pooka

Pooka is Gaelic for a rare type of Irish leprechaun who brings bad luck. There's always one, isn't there?

The Poozies

No, not "the pussies". A female quintet – later reduced to a quartet – featuring varied rock, jazz and folk backgrounds. The silly-sounding name is in honour of Poosie Nancies, an Ayrshire pub once favoured by Robert Burns in which they had first discussed forming a band.

The Pop Group

It can be argued The (Highly-Experimental And Strictly Non-Radio-Friendly) Punk Group would have been a better name for this lot. The name can be seen as refreshingly modest or one with all the commendable

P

arrogance of ▷ The Band (*The* Pop Group, as if no other matters). It was *meant* to be an antidote to overstated and pretentious names, an anti-name in a similar way that ▷ Public Image Ltd and ▷ The Smiths did later.

Offshoots include ▷ Rip Rig + Panic.

Iggy Pop

Michigan-born James Newell "Jewel" Osterberg took the Iggy from his time as a member of failed Detroit punk band The Iguanas (1964). With ▷ The Stooges (to the 1970s), he became Iggy Stooge. The Pop, honouring local personality and well-known drop-out Jim Popp, was symbolically added as he moved for the pop market under the guidance of ▷ David Bowie (early 1970s on).

The Popinjays

A search through the dictionary for poppy puns showed that most of them had been done. There was always "popinjay" of course. This has nothing to do with "popping in". The word, probably in imitation of a bird's cry, originally meant a woodpecker or other bird with conspicuously bright plumage. Now it means "a conceited young dandy" – and this struck the band as suitably self-mocking and ironic. (Cf ▷ The Immaculate Fools etc.)

Poppy Factory

A boastful reference to the band's production-line ability to turn out pop music, while hinting at opium making.

Popticians

Punning name for ▷ John Peel-played band *c.* 1984–5 who never had the success they deserve for wonderful pop concoctions such as *The Old Scout Master*. A case of pop not always paying.

Popul Vuh

… eh?, you may ask. This little-known yet long-lasting and highly influential German band named from a Mayan sacred book much read among the hippy fraternity of the late 1960s. *The Rough Guide To Rock* notes there was a Norwegian variant that came into being about the same time.

Pop Will Eat Itself

This British band started in "grebo rock" mode as Wild And Wandering. They said the phrase "Pop Will Eat Itself" came from *NME* reporter David Quantick when interviewing ▷ Jamie Wednesday. Quantick confirms he had used the phrase. It's abbreviated to PWEI and The Poppies.

Jeremy J. Beadle has an interesting addendum in his 1993 book *Will Pop Eat Itself? Pop Music In The Soundbite Era*. He writes: "In one of those stories which sounds suspiciously 'after the event' the group claim they sent the same tape to three different record companies, using a different name with each (the other names were 'The Pop Tarts' and 'Grrr'), intending to adopt the name for the demo which proved successful."

It's indeed unlikely any band would want to name after the breakfast toaster food and risk wrath from a certain cereal company – although it's a great pun. It's even more unlikely Grrr would be successful – not an easy one for disc jockeys to introduce – although this didn't stop ▷ Riot Grrrl. Both do fit the Poppies' spirit of anarchism, but more plausibly they told the present writer they liked the final name because it best combined this with their poppy sound.

Porno For Pyros

Pornography for pyromaniacs. In other words, more shock-rock from ▷ Perry Farrell, the man who brought the world Lollapalooza and Jane's Addiction with an album cover of full-frontal naked bodies in flames.

Tedham Porterhouse

One of many incognito names used by ▷ Bob Dylan.

Portishead

From their home, a coastal town near Bristol, England. Bristol is known for its attractiveness in parts yet Portishead has little to commend it in the same way, making the place-name choice, like the unrelated ▷ St Etienne, possibly slightly perverse. Still, it fitted in with Portishead's unassuming music.

Portsmouth Sinfonia

▷ Eno-associated project; ironically named to sound professional, they were all amateurs of minimal experience who played in an off-key sub school-orchestra way and had a hit with the deliberately dreadful *Classical Mudley*.

Powderfinger

West Coast rock from Britain's Kensal Green. The American 1960s revised and celebrated in the mid-1990s. The name is a tribute to ▷ Neil Young. His song *Powderfinger*, about a tragic 22-year-old left in charge of a remote riverpost with only a gun and his naïf wit, opens the second side of the 1979 classic album *Rust Never Sleeps*, arguably his best. There's plenty of pages on the Net of Young fans giving their interpretation of the song's meaning.

Duffy Power

He was originally Ray Howard. Power came about as Svengali ▷ Larry Parnes misheard his surname.

The Power Station

From The Power Station, the name of the New York recording studio where they rehearsed in 1985. Also a reference to the power of their *Get It On* single.

▷ Duran Duran spin-off (Andy and John Taylor, with a little help from Robert Palmer, Michael Des Barres etc). If they had translated the name into German, they would have got ▷ Kraftwerk.

Another Duran spin-off: ▷ Arcadia.

Will Powers

… was actually not a man but a woman photographer, Lynne Goldsmith. "The name and the records are to encourage people to maximise their potential by using their will powers."

Andy Pratt

This book is mainly the story of people who changed their names. By way of exception, this American singer refused to change his surname and so, despite critically successful LPs, was never was taken seriously. The word "prat" or "pratt" has been synonymous with "the buttocks" or "a person of no account" for

centuries. Sorry to Pratts everywhere, but it takes a Pratt to show the importance of a name.

Praying Mantis

They liked the famous story of how the female of this insect species first mates with the smaller male – then promptly eats him alive. Yet another band to name after bugs: it's all the more amazing when psychological polls show that most people detest or fear insects.

Prefab Four

British comedy quartet from London, pulling the legs of the real ▷ Fab Four, ▷ The Beatles.

Prefab Sprout

Leader Paddy MacAloon found the name in 1973 from a mishearing of the words "pepper sprout" in Nancy Sinatra (▷ Boots) and Lee Hazelwood's 1967 song *Jackson*. They sing about their love for each other being hotter than the aforesaid sprout. MacAloon saved the phrase away for years: he'd come up with hundreds of possibilities, often with allied titles for potential songs and albums. It was first choice when he formed a group in Newcastle in 1982. "It was worth the wait." Bored with this, he later told reporters it was an attempt to put forward two unrelated words: "The second choice was Chrysalis Cognos."

The appellation was as surreal as ▷ The Electric Prunes from the 1960s, and ▷ Aztec Camera in the 1980s. And MacAloon admits to having been inspired by deliberately strange progressive monikers of the 1970s: "You hear it and think, what does that mean?" The intent was always serious, not silly. Prefabs were quickly built prefabricated houses built in large numbers in Britain to replace blitz-damaged property after World War II. They were "homes for heroes". How a naturally growing brussels sprout can be prefabricated is never explained. "Work it out for yourself," MacAloon told the writer.

So, ladies and gentleman, I give you … Prefab Sprout! As the man says: "What *does* that mean?"

The Prefects

British punks, counterparts to ▷ The Cortinas.

In this case named not after the Ford Prefect but school pupils. Unflattering derivative: The Defects.

Pregnant Pause

An apposite name for an all-female band. They admit it was chosen as a protest: "But we were more inspired by being women than feminists."

The Presidents Of The United States of America

The Seattle, Washington, group started as the perversely named supergroup: "We wanted to be satirical, different." The current moniker evolved for similar reasons in 1993. "We looked for the most significant, most important name we could choose in America. And this was it." It was guitarist Chris Ballew's suggestion. The Presidents play some non-serious music which borders on comedy. Their appellation is seen as the perfect antidote to excessive seriousness.

Elvis Presley

He was born Elvis Aron – note original spelling – Presley in Tupelo, Mississippi. He had no need of stage names – at first, as a modest kid, later, as perhaps the greatest of all stars. Elvis was his father's middle name and fortunately was a unique choice in showbusiness. It was uncommon except against poor white southerners in the U.S. who imported it from the English Helwiss. To many he was simply Elvis, El, ▷ (Elvis) The Pelvis or ▷ The King. He was also known as the Mississippi/Memphis Flash and The Hillbilly Cat.

Vernon and Gladys Presley had named their son Aron. The doctor respelled the middle name – the more normal way – as Aaron on the birth certificate. The star's gravestone bears the name Aaron.

Notes: Elvis's backing bands included The Blue Moon Boys – from his early song *The Blue Moon of Kentucky*; he was part of the 1956 ▷ Million Dollar Quartet. His name and work inspired ▷ Elvis Costello and ▷ Vince Everett (seriously), ▷ The Sid Presley Experience and ▷ Death In Vegas (less seriously), ▷ The Troggs, ▷ Reg Presley and

▷ Dread Zeppelin's Tortelvis (not very serious at all).

Elvis also inspired the spoof band Liberty Mountain.

One of his songs inspired ▷ The Heartbreakers; Elvis's drummer D.J. Fontana inspired the naming of ▷ Wayne Fontana. ▷ Kid Creole was named partly in tribute to *King Creole*, one of Presley's films.

His movie role names were usually all-American or butch sounding. Here's a selection: Clint Reno, Vince Everett (which inspired ▷ Everett), Tulsa McLean, Lucky Jackson, Rusty Wells, Pacer Burton, Rick Richards, Johnny, Dr John Carpenter, Joe Lightcloud and Deke Rivers.

Reg Presley

The story so far: the singer of ▷ The Troggs has an unsuitable name. He's managed by ▷ Larry Page, who's since gone down in history as the man who renamed ▷ The Kinks. Page is searching for a new name for his new protégé, who is an apprentice bricklayer-builder with a yokel accent – bound to be seen as a joke in sophisticated London. Page calls his friend Keith Altham, *New Musical Express* journalist and PR man extraordinaire.

Keith takes up the story in a 1996 television documentary: "Larry phoned me up. He said, 'I'm a bit worried about the lead singer. His name is Reginald Maurice Ball. Now what can I call him?' I said: 'Presley!' for a joke on the phone. He said, 'That's great!' I said, 'No, I was only kidding.'"

Reg said: "I thought, Oh my God ... couldn't they have thought of a less well-known name, like Crosby or Sinatra?" Journalist Charles Shaar Murray added: "For someone called Reg, who looked like that, to be called Presley was as splendid an act of defiance as a geek in glasses to call himself Elvis." ▷ Elvis Costello later also named after the king of rock, sex symbol and American cultural icon supreme, ▷ Elvis Presley (for it is he). It was indeed absurd for the bloke next door to take on songs such as the sexy *I Can't Control Myself* and for him to be called Reg ... Presley made it all the more interesting.

The Pretenders

Taken from ▷ Sam Cooke's version of The Platters' 1956 hit *The Great Pretender*. The track was revived in 1987 by ▷ Freddie Mercury. Leader Chrissie Hynde admired the song; subsequent changes meant that she was effectively The Pretender(s). Her previous experience was with the less auspiciously named Frenchies, Jack Rabbit, ▷ Moors Murderers and early ▷ Damned. Inspired: ▷ Tattooed Love Boys. Tribute band: The Pretend Pretenders.

Pretty Boy Floyd

First, there was Kansas gangster Charles Floyd. Second, there was an admiring prostitute who gave him his nickname. Third, there were two groups – from L.A. and Canada – who named after him. Fourth, there was ▷ Ugly Kid Joe, who named after the Californians. Not related: ▷ Pink Floyd.

The Pretty Things

Dick Taylor, founder-bassist of the ▷ Rolling Stones, left them on the brink of their turning professional in 1962. His new band played R&B – showing their liking for ▷ Bo Diddley and naming from his just-released 1963 composition *Pretty Thing*. They performed the song on their first LP.

"Pretty" was meant ironically – most were pug-ugly with long, unkempt hair. Vocalist Phil May claimed to have the longest locks on any British male. Their drummer later joined ▷ The Pink Fairies, whose name showed similar thinking.

Dory Previn

Née Langdon, she kept her name from her brief marriage to composer André Previn.

Dickie Pride

▷ Larry Parnes expanded his stable of stars with commendable speed, if not haste, as each seemed to hit gold.

One young hopeful named Knellar was picked for his voice and promptly told that from then on his surname was Pride. First name? Richard? Make that Dickie.

This was 1958, when naïvety was normal, but even a cursory consideration should have told Parnes that he was saddling his new creation with a name which would produce plenty of phallic-size sniggers. Which, of course, it did. Possibly Parnes's worst name in his U.K. star stable.

Primal Scream

Formed by ex ▷ The Jesus And Mary Chain drummer Bobby Gillespie, named after Arthur Janov's seminal essay *The Primal Scream*.

The psychologist advocates the vocal release of tension and anxieties, returning to the emotional freedom of babyhood.

Janov's books have influenced many hippies – and other rock acts. It is he who is responsible for the naming of ▷ Tears For Fears. And his instruction also accounts for all the yelling on early ▷ John Lennon solo records: "Mama don't go … ooOOooOOOAAAHHH!"

A Primal Scream song was taken as a name by spin-off band ▷ Spirea X.

The Primitives

U.K. indie group inspired by style guru ▷ Lou Reed from 20 years before. In his 1963 pre- ▷ Velvet Underground days, he played in a garage band named after their basic playing skills.

Prince

The star's story starts in Minneapolis, Minnesota, where his pianist father John Nelson, using the stage name Prince Rogers or Roger Prince, led a jazz band called the Prince Roger Trio. John's wife, singer Mattie Nelson, also got into the act. They called their son Prince Rogers Nelson after the family concern, though he was known in the family as Skipper.

Hence the name. Hence "My Name Is Prince".
Later Prince used a hieroglyph:

P

The androgynous sign was first seen in the early 1990s and explained by fanzines as covering the masculine and feminine sides of his personality. The circle represented unity, while the cross-over meant music. Prince himself offered few clues. (▷ Led Zeppelin had gone under runes years before.) Andrew Smith, writing in the *Sunday Times* in 1996, said the doodle was "the kind of thing your dog might accidentally create while lying on the floor chewing a pen".

From the start, nobody knew how to pronounce the symbol – and some magazines could not reproduce it. He became "The Artist Formerly Known As Prince" or TAFKAP. The renaming, and his year-long habit of scrawling "Slave" over his face, was seen as linked with a long-running dispute with his record company at the time, Warner Bros. He hoped it might, like the scarf he wore round his face, allow him to work outside his contract. David Rowntree of ▷ Blur replied at a Brit Award ceremony by writing Dave on his visage.

The formal renaming came on 7 June 1993, Prince's 35th birthday – after a period when he had reportedly been very ill and afraid for his sanity. The move was meant to mean new-found stability. Prince also became known as "retired", briefly threatening to release vaulted material only. In a late 1996 American interview, TAFKAP said that, contrary to near-universal reports, he'd decided to change his appellation long before the Warner row.

It was reported in 1995 that thousands of Sydney people joined a poll by Triple J radio to find a new moniker. The winning entry, widely used in Australia, was Davo. The *Sun* in Britain organised a similar phone-poll that year, offering readers five possible tags: TAFKAP, Prince, Symbol, Prize Prat and Sharon. The latter won.

In late 1996, TAFKAP signed a record deal with EMI and was reported to be considering reverting to his old handle. Publicists at the label called him The Artist publicly, reverting to Prince in private conversations. Still, in an interview with Liz Jones, he said: "Changing my name made perfect sense to me. I'm not Nel's son, Nelson, that's a slave name. I was ridiculed for that, but they did the same to Mohammed Ali and Malcolm X. A lot of people call me sir now. They never did **that** before."

Name notes:
1. Nicknames and unflattering derivatives: His Royal Badness, His Royal Purpleness, Prance, Ponce, Princess (the latter from school contemporaries); Squiggle (after his renaming). Also the Imp of Perverse. The last was coined by British biographer Barney Hoskyns in reference to lyrical obsessions and stature. The renaming coincided with a decline in the quality of Prince's music in the view of critics. The former Prince was variously dubbed The Artist Formally Known As Sane, The Artist Formally Known As Talented and The Artist People Formally Cared About (the last by American shock jock Howard Stern).
2. Unrelated: ▷ Rick Nelson and ▷ Nilsson. Inspired: ▷ The Lightning Seeds.
3. Pseudonyms: ▷ Camille, Christopher (writing for ▷ The Bangles), ▷ Joey Coco, ▷ Alexander Nevermind, ▷ Spooky Electric, Jamie Starr (producing Time and other bands), Christopher Tracy, ▷ Victor, and Tora Tora. His bands include: Grand Central, Champagne, The Revolution, The Royal Family, Time and Vanity 6, later Apollonia 6.
4. ▷ Michael Jackson was reportedly annoyed when Prince rejected an invitation to duet on *Bad*. Jackson's son Prince was **not** nuncupated after Prince.

Prince Buster
It came from his real name Colin Bustamente Campbell when he started out as a disc jockey in Jamaica. His parents were paying tribute to politician Alexander Bustamente. The Prince became a ska star and inspired ▷ Judge Dread and ▷ Madness.

The Prince Of Wails
Nicknames for ▷ Tom Jones, ▷ Johnnie Ray.

The Prisoners
They harked back to a cult television series, *The Prisoner*. The nameless hero, Number Six, awakes to find himself a prisoner in what seems like a luxury holiday camp and he makes repeated unsuccessful bids to escape. The reason for his incarceration is unclear, giving the whole a Kafkaesque feel.

The original adventure series ran in 1967–8 and starred Patrick McGoohan.

Cf ▷ Josef K.

Procol Harem

They met in 1959 as The Paramounts, backing ▷ Sandie Shaw, and re-formed in 1967 as an outlet for compositions by pianist-singer Gary Brooker and Keith Reid, the lyricist. The duo said a mutual friend had a long-haired Burmese cat, which had a birth certificate including its name: Procul Harem. Whoops! Feline experts say it was probably a related-pedigree name.

As far as the duo knew it was meaningless. The "harem", particularly, just sounded right. Their record came out crediting Procol Harem. Whoops!! They discovered they'd accidentally misspelled it. Whoops!!! They were also told that it actually meant something. *Procul harem* is Latin. It means "at a distance / far from here".

Given the slip-ups in this comedy of errors, it isn't surprising that few past accounts have been correct. The cat is said to have been owned by Brooker and the Latin bit was said to be coincidence. The confusion resembles that over ▷ Jefferson Airplane – named after a dog – and ▷ Pink Floyd – named after either two bluesmen – or, alternatively, two cats.

The author has tried, unsuccessfully, to establish what the cat's real name was: few owners use pedigree or breeder's names. *Cherchez le chat.*

Prong

They said it recalled an electrical device, sounded like an electric guitar's chord and was "ultimately phallic".

Psychedelic Furs

Before leader Richard Butler got fed up of questions about it, he admitted he was influenced by ▷ The Velvet Underground – "we were never a pop band" – and the name came from their 1967 cut *Venus In Furs*. This song also led to the naming of ▷ Siouxsie sidekick ▷ Steve Severin. They were at the forefront of 1981's psychedelic revival attempt in Britain. Critics wondered if they were wholeheartedly accepting the past or sarcastically snubbing it: 1960s references were *passé* after the punk revolution. The band didn't wear psychedelic clothes and

didn't condone the fur trade, yet their moniker turned people off – they should have waited ten years. Later they abbreviated to The Furs ... by which time, ironically, psychedelia was coming back into fashion.

Butler was sometimes called Rep Butler in reference to his name's similarity to Rhett Butler, a character from American writer Margaret Mitchell's only novel, 1936's *Gone With The Wind* (filmed 1939). The Furs take this book's Albatross Around Neck runner's up prize: the overall winners are ▷ Gaye Bykers On Acid. Influenced ▷ Inspiral Carpets' first name, The Furs.

Psychic TV

Their first album expounds a faith called "The Temple of Psychic Youth", while the musicians wanted to use the most powerful medium of today – television – to advance their case (one came from a group called Alternative TV). It was explained in mind-numbing detail by leader, ex ▷ Throbbing Gristle vocalist Genesis P. Orridge.

Psychotic Pineapple

Jokingly poking fun at fruity hippy names such as Colossal Pomegranate, Ballpoint Banana and ▷ The Strawberry Alarm Clock. This lot were 1980s comedians. The rest were deadly serious 1960s musicians who seemed unaware of the comedy of their surreal monikers.

Public Enemy

The phrase "public enemy number one" emerged in America in the early part of this century. F.B.I. director J. Edgar Hoover used it to refer to bank robbers like ▷ Pretty Boy Floyd and George "Babyface" Nelson.

The criminals had inspired the naming of Jamaican reggae artists such as ▷ Dennis Alcapone and ▷ Dillinger. By 1982 it was the turn of the New York rappers: Chuck D. used the term "public enemy" to challenge the perception of young black men as criminal by inclination and definition.

His strident politics shone through not just in the name but in albums such as 1990s militant *Fear Of A Black Planet*.

P

Individual band members have included: Chuck D, Flavor Flav, Professor Griff (Minister Of Information) and DJ Terminator X.

One of their songs, by Chuck D, inspired the naming of ▷ Follow 4 Now.

Public Image Ltd

Ex ▷ Sex Pistol Johnny Rotten reverted to his real name John Lydon in 1978 and chose this band moniker as a reaction against mainstream rock, which he felt was based on media-led hype and public image. After the LP *Public Image Ltd* the band became known as PiL. In the early days, it was conceived as one of a consortium of companies with similarly faceless names. Chief among these were P.E.P. – Public Enterprise Productions, handling production – and M.I.C. – Multi Image Corporation, for video projects. On some releases, public relations and business advisers were credited as if part of the "anti-corporate-culture corporation".

PiL members have included ▷ Jah Wobble and graduates of ▷ Magazine, ▷ Rip Rig + Panic and ▷ Siouxsie And The Banshees. Spin-off: ▷ Time Zone. Inspired: ▷ Flowers Of Romance.

Gary Puckett And The Union Gap

Gary Puckett was born in Hibbing, Minnesota, in 1942 but was brought up in the historic town of ▷ Union Gap. He chose it as the name for his band and extended its famous association to their Civil War togs. The image was already *passé*: groups in uniforms were being swept away by the British invasion and the rising tide of hippiedom – as the similar ▷ Paul Revere And The Raiders discovered.

Pulp

Pulp is typical of the 1990s vogue for short names: ▷ Blur etc. The moniker gained fashionability with Quintin Tarantino's 1994 film *Pulp Fiction* which parodied and celebrated kitsch, camp and violence. Meanwhile the band were on their way to the top with *Different Class*.

In fact the appellation's far from new – and wasn't always so short. Leader Jarvis Cocker (who isn't related to singer ▷ Joe Cocker, also from Sheffield) said it was originally Arabicus Pulp, taken from a coffee bean commodity. He uncovered the term during a lesson in 1978 while studying at Sheffield City Comprehensive, South Yorkshire. He told author Paul Lester: "We were in economics and someone had the *Financial Times*. That's how it happened. Everyone hated it. People thought you'd coughed – "pulp" – and it was frequently spelled wrong. We've been billed as Pope and The Pulps. I like the idea that it means ephemeral material that gets thrown away, like the cheap novels printed on crap paper. People collect those books now. Things that are meaningless and throwaway often survive to define a period."

Punk Funk Chorus

Critics called ▷ Rick James's music "punk funk" – so he gave this to his backing singers.

Pure Prairie League

This U.S. band recalled a film starring Errol Flynn. It combined ecological concern with a suitable collective term.

The Purple Hearts

British band who intended this name as an oblique reference to hearts etc, assuming few would spot the 1960s drugs link. In fact many people did so, immediately. For those that don't know, purple hearts – so called because the originals were purple – are tablets containing barbiturate and, often, morphine. Some counterfeits were sold, with white painkillers dyed with purple ink.

While they were very famous, they have now been replaced by drugs said to be safer and more effective.

The name is the sort of thing that one might expect of purple fanatic ▷ Prince.

Pussy Galore

U.K. author Ian Fleming and later scriptwriters chose the names of the molls in James Bond thrillers for their laugh value. (Typical dialogue: Doll: "I'm Plenty." Bond: "Of course you are.") This American quintet stole this one for its sexual pun. Honor Blackman played Pussy Galore in *Goldfinger*.

PWEI
$\triangleright$ Pop Will Eat Itself.

Pyewackett
This band playing updated traditional folk chose an old English name meaning "intimate of witches".

Pylon
Named from 1935 novel *Pylon* by U.S. writer William Faulkner (1897–1962). The book paints a depressing picture of the American south. "And we should know," said the close neighbours of $\triangleright$ R.E.M.

P

Q Magazine

... was going to be called "Cue", as in "cue the music". There were fears this sounded like a snooker publication and they went for a minimalist pun.

Q Tips

Q Tips are cotton ear buds used to clean out dirty lobes. Use them to better appreciate harmonious soul bands like Paul Young's early outfit. Or, he said, use them to block out noise from louder acts.

Quantum Jump

"We wanted to jump into the future," they said. "We want to be the future." Rather than making history, this band now is history – leaving some records and the name which comes from a term in physics for a fundamental change in matter.

Quarterflash

This U.S.A. AOR band named after the Antipodean colloquialism, "a quarter flash and three parts foolish". They admitted: "It sums us up well."

Quatermass

This heavy rock band with an interest in science fiction named after Nigel Kneale's story of a secret research base. It was made into a highly successful BBC TV serial and spawned films (1955, 1957, 1967), the best known of which is *The Quatermass Xperiment*.

Queen

John Deacon played with The Opposition; Brian May was in 1984 (after George Orwell's book) and The Left-Handed Marriage (from an early song). Drummer Roger Meddows-Taylor, who dropped the Meddows for added brevity and street-cred, had played with Cousin Jacks (colloquial term for Cornish tin miners – he's from Truro); the Reaction; and Smile. It was under this last name they first played with ▷ Ibex singer ▷ Freddie Mercury – who separately auditioned for ▷ Sour Milk Sea. They considered two other choices: The Grand Dance (from C.S. Lewis's *Out Of The Silent Planet* books: both May and Taylor had read the trilogy) and ▷ The Rich Kids (which recalled Cocteau; later used by another band).

The queenly title was chosen by Mercury during a visit to Cornwall, while sitting in the Taylors' kitchen. Taylor's mother recalled: "He kept saying how regal it sounded." It was also simple and short, with endless visual possibilities "and it's *so* much better than king, darling."

In the early 1970s "queen" was more commonly used than "gay" as a British euphemism for homosexual. The other band members were heterosexual and knew Mercury wasn't referring to the House of Windsor. It was an appropriate parody of his outrageous flamboyancy – before anyone else made fun of it. His idea was accepted by the end of April 1970.

Hence the name. Hence the I Want To Break Free video.

Name notes: ▷ Larry Lurex, ▷ Hair, Nose And Teeth. Spoof bands showing the sincerest form of flattery: Africa (African Queen, geddit?), ▷ Kween, Magic, The Royal Family. There's more in Mark Hodkinson's book *Queen: The Early Years*, published in 1995.

Queen Latifah

... was plain New Yorker Dana Owens, until she drew on her roots. *Latifah* is an Arabic word meaning sensitive or delicate.

The Queen Of Country (and Western)

There are those who think ▷ Patsy Cline should top this list. Country's Leading Cowgirl carved a special place in C&W hearts, but her career was short and the nickname only came later. The following dubbed themselves "The Queen Of Country Music": Muriel Deason, ▷ Loretta Lynn, Dolly Parton and Kitty Wells. That leaves Tammy "Stand By Your Man" Wynette as The Queen Of Country And Western and Minnie Pearl, The Queen Of Country Comedy.

The Queen Of Disco

▷ Donna Summer: from her run of disco dance smash hits in the late 1970s including *Love To Love You Baby* and *I Feel Love*.

Queen Of Flash

▷ Cher. Flash, as in flash trash: showy. And flash, especially, as in to teasingly display. With an exposed tatooed buttock here, a bellybutton diamond there. Hence ▷ The Great American Navel.

The Queen Of Soul

Billing name usually applied to Aretha Franklin – a 1968 album was called *Lady Soul*. A highly contested tag claimed by a number of others.

Queen Of The Blues

Dinah Washington and, especially, Bessie Smith. The latter's also ▷ Empress Of The Blues. Ma Rainey's ▷ Mother Of The Blues.

The Queen Of The Pops

▷ Madonna by any other name.

Queensrÿche

U.S. heavy rock band of the 1980s on – known for their ▷ Queen-like sound and name. Their name's German for "Queen's country" and they decorated it with an umlaut in ▷ Blue Öyster Cult style.

? And The Mysterians

Like ▷ The Guess Who, a naïve attempt to create interest by giving the impression they were a major band moonlighting under another name. The Mysterians was taken from a Japanese film about a race who wanted to take over the world. The lead singer, ?, wore sunglasses constantly – even in dark clubs – shunned interviewers and legally changed his name to Question Mark. People weren't sure whether they should call him Question or Mr Mark. This book can reveal his real name was Rudy Martinez.

The gimmick generated publicity as reporters tried to find out the prosaic truth behind those shades. It didn't last long: the group formed in 1963, had one huge hit – *96 Tears* – in 1966 and folded two years later as reporters lost interest.

The Quick

A Biblical reference to "the quick [i.e., the living] and the dead," not to this 1980s act's fast guitar-playing abilities.

Tommy Quickly

A protégé of ▷ The Beatles, his stage name is a simplification of Thomas Quigley. He stands alongside ▷ Dickie Pride in the pantheon of British 1960s badly named stars.

Quicksilver Messenger Service

As they started, U.K. acts were everywhere: it was unfashionable to be American. Accordingly, they were The Brogues. Like the early ▷ Byrds – who were The Beefeaters – this was an attempt to sound British.

As John Tobler explains in the liner notes to the CD re-issue of *Happy Trails*, all four founders shared the same birth sign, Virgo: two were born on 24 August, the others on 4 September. Astrology buff and bassist David Freiberg said they also had in common Mercury – their joint ruling planet. "Mercury was not

Q

only a term for liquid metal (quicksilver in thermometers) but also the messenger in Greek mythology." Therefore it wasn't taken from the name of a U.S. wild west telegraph and delivery service, as sometimes reported. Later they became Quicksilver. ▷ Spin-off ▷ Dinosaurs.

The Quiet One

▷ George Harrison nickname, even used as the title of a biography.

Quiet Riot

This bunch of blokes initially wanted the misleading Little Women after Louisa May Alcott's 1868 book; an offshoot of ▷ Traffic had also considered it. Like ▷ Alice Cooper, they thought it would be fun to have a "dainty, feminine" label for a raucous rock band. Still, you couldn't get much louder than this lot, said ▷ Status Quo's Rick Parfitt: "I had been saving up 'Quite Right' or something for some time but I hadn't found any suitable chance to use it. I met the guys and gave it to them for free. They loved it."

Quintessence

This progressive jazzy band explained the beautiful name meant a pure form and came from their eastern philosophies.

The Quireboys

The musicians formed in the mid-1980s and considered the name The Choirboys – the world's least angelic band. According to *Q* magazine, they worked on a building site – arriving in worn eyeliner and hair gel after clubbing the night away – and their foreman's blunt reaction to the projected moniker was to retort "Queer Boys, more like!"

So they went on the college circuit as the Queerboys – figuring it would have an impact. Still the response wasn't all good: after "gay soc" protests and bans they reluctantly compromised before playing the 1987 Reading Festival. Unflattering derivative: Not The Hoople. Cf ▷ Mott The Hoople.

Quiver

Medieval arsenal pun to rival the more modern ▷ Magazine. A shiver or a tube for carrying arrows? "It meant whatever you want it to mean," said the band, who worked with The Sutherland Brothers. "It's got multi-meanings."

Eddie Rabbitt
His real Gaelic name. No relation to Jimmy Rabbitte, Irish manager of ▷ The Commitments.

Radiohead
Oxford's most-likely-to named as a tribute to ▷ Talking Heads. They took it from a track title on the 1986 album *True Stories*.

Rage Against The Machine
From the 1960s anarcho-hippy slogan of the San Francisco "tune in, turn on, drop out" rallies: "Rage, rage against the machine" – from Dylan Thomas's "rage, rage against the dying of the light" in *Do Not Go Gentle Into That Good Night*.

This 1990s band shared this political bumper-sticker consciousness. The same soundbite sloganeering permeated their tracks such as *Settle For Nothing*. Revolutionaries by nature, revolutionaries by name … but still signed to Sony.

RAH Band
Nothing to do with rah-rah, hurrah or ra-ra skirts. From founder Richard A. Hewson.

The Raiders
▷ Paul Revere And The Raiders.

The Railway Children
Wigan band named from the "enchanting" – so they say – children's story by Edith Nesbitt. It was made into a movie starring a young Jenny Agutter and a not-so-young Bernard Cribbins. ▷ I Start Counting named after another Agutter film of the period.

Rainbow
The trendy Los Angeles Rainbow Bar was visited by ▷ Deep Purple guitarist Ritchie Blackmore and inspired a song and album title, cut with New York band Elf. He renamed the musicians later, saying the label was more colourful than his previous group. No relation to the famous Herbert Stothart song *Somewhere Over The Rainbow*. Cf naming of fellow heavy metal act ▷ Whitesnake. Related: ▷ Wild Horses. Not related: Rainbow, a precursor of ▷ Kiss.

The Raincoats
The group formed in London in 1977 at the height of the punk era, influenced by the likes of ▷ The Slits, which founder-member Palmolive went on to join. Gina Birch told author Amy Raphael that the name came about because "Ana's [da Silva] from Madeira and she was fascinated by London and rain and dreary old days. It was never my ideal name but she was so keen that I went along with it."

Rain Tree Crow
Effectively a one-off-album reunion of ▷ Japan in 1991 under the leadership of ▷ David Sylvian – who refused the reincarnation of the earlier name. He offered as an explanation of

R

sorts the fact that the crow name was a symbol of his work over four years – "a dark period" – with music as a healing process.

Marvin Rainwater

Marvin Percy was of an American Indian origin and the Rainwater was from his mother's original Cherokee name.

RAK Records

Because its albums were sold from racks set up in locations outside of conventional music outlets, such as filling stations.

Ramones

▷ Paul McCartney was briefly Paul Ramon in the days when he was still a rocker. A decade later, another bassist, New Yorker Douglas Colvin, became Dee Dee Ramone. His fledgling group shared a love of ▷ The Beatles, although their music has little in common with the ▷ Fab Four's. They agreed with McCartney the name was different and glamorous. Macca apparently intended it to be pronounced "Raay-mon". This band made it "Rah-moan". Recruits to the group all adopted the image – ripped jeans, rancid sneakers, pinhead stares – and pretended to be brothers: Joey, Johnny, Tommy, Marky, Richie, CJ.

Name notes: They inspired the naming of ▷ Bad Brains and ▷ Exploding White Mice. They also influenced the music of ▷ The Runaways, though not their naming, as is sometimes reported.

Shabba Ranks

The common explanation is that this Jamaican named from the Queen of Sheba. In fact Shabba means "African king" and was apt for a performer originally called Rexton Gordon – his first three letters already made him a king.

It's sometimes suggested his surname came from notorious local bandit, Trevor Ranks. This sounds credible: this book includes many stars of the "slacking" scene, as it was known, who named after gangsters: ▷ Dillinger etc. However, "Ranks" was Kingston slang for top stars, as in *Up Town Top Rankin'*, and it was directly from there that Shabba, other aspiring stars and the criminal took their aliases.

Rapeman

Another misunderstood choice by Chicago musician Steve Albini, ex ▷ Big Black. This 1980s name was intended as an anti-rape comment (cf ▷ No Means No, ▷ Nirvana's *Rape Me*). Albini was fascinated by Japanese comics with favoured "gokan" rapes – for long accepted in Asia, although now attracting wider criticism.

Rare Earth

There are cases of a record label being named after a group: for examples ▷ Harvest and ▷ Barclay James Harvest. This is the reverse and taken from a ▷ Motown subsidiary.

The Rascals

Later name for ▷ The Young Rascals.

Sun Ra

Alabama boy Herman Sonny Blount's fascination with mythology led to his claim to come from outer space as the son of Ra, the Ancient Egyptian sun god. Hence also the name of his band Solar Arkestra.

Ratt

This American heavy metal band liked the sound of cartoon rodent Mickey Rat's name, and selected this as their first choice. When the artist objected, they became Ratt, adding an extra t to make it sound more like a surname.

Rattlesnake Annie

Named because she wore a rattlesnake's tail in her right ear.

The Ravens

Another of the earliest "bird" bands, dating from the 1940s. They joked fans were "ravin'" about them. The name was also used by the early ▷ Kinks and by a 1990s heavy metal band.

Ravishing Beauties

Two-thirds of this female trio say it's ironic self-description; the third says it's an immodest statement of their talents.

Raw Power

Powerful rock combo, aptly named after the 1973 album by their proto-punk heroes ▷ The Stooges.

Raydio

Lots of groups have gone for a radio-friendly name to guarantee airplay and this is about as close as you can get to naming after the medium itself. Having said this, Raydio remains a terrible pun on band leader Ray Parker Junior.

Johnnie Ray

Because of his tendency to cry during emotionally fraught numbers, he acquired the nicknames The Cry Guy, The Howling Success, The Nabob Of Sob and the Prince of Wails/ Wales (the last shared with Welsh ballad king ▷ Tom Jones).

RCA

Stands for Radio Corporation of America.

The Real Black Moses

Reply by nickname-collector ▷ James Brown to his soul rival Isaac Hayes's title ▷ Black Moses.

The Real Roxanne

New York radio was flooded in 1984–5 with rap records raving about a girl called Roxanne. First there was ▷ UTFO's *Roxanne, Roxanne*, followed by *Roxanne's Mother, Roxanne's Doctor* etc. This swiftly produced singers claiming to be Roxanne herself – and this one did better than most, hitting at rival Roxanne Shante and hitting the charts with *Bang Zoom Let's Go*.

Real Westway

The Westway is a main road west out of London, from Paddington towards the Oxford M40: a commuter endurance test past shabby towerblocks. It was in one of these apartments that early ▷ The Clash songs were written – the Westway is mentioned in *London's Burning*. Guitarist Mick Jones chose it after the Clash broke up, indicating a return to his original values. ▷ Big Audio Dynamite.

Re-Animator

1985: *Re-Animator* the film. Plot: rehashed science fiction – boffin reinvigorates corpses. Reviews: mixed. **1987**: Re-Animator the band. Sound: thrash metal. Inspiration: above film. Reviews: as above. **1989**: *Re-Animator 2* the film. Plot: as above. Reviews: "recycled rubbish." There's no new ideas, only recycled ones.

The Rebel Rousers

Formed 1959 by ▷ Cliff Bennett in Drayton, U.K., in tribute to Duane Eddy single hit of the year before, *Rebel Rouser*.

The Reclines

▷ k.d. lang's first band, playing country music and with a name paying tribute to country star ▷ Patsy Cline.

Red

Nickname for Mick Hucknall. ▷ Simply Red.

The Red And The Black

Former English student Mike Scott of ▷ The Waterboys is known for his literary references and lifted the title of French writer Stendhal's novel of 1830, *Le Rouge Et Le Noir*.

Redbeards From Texas

Lookalikes/soundalikes in take-off and tribute to that well-known trio ▷ ZZ Top, who have reddish beards (two of them) or are called Beard (the other) and come from Texas.

Redbone

Los Angeles 1960s act formed by American Indians; "rehbon", pronounced "redbone", is slang for half-breed. Their music fused their ethnic style with traditional U.S. pop. Compare to ▷ Cher, who recorded an album called *Half Breed* in 1973. Not related to Leon Redbone. Drummer Peter DePoe also used his Indian name, Last Walking Bear.

(The) Red Crayola

For a few years this Texas-based outfit became Red Krayola after legal mutterings from Crayola, the U.S. manufacturer of children's drawing equipment. Cf ▷ Redd Kross dispute.

Redd Kross

These Californians tore up their first choice The Tourists (not related: ▷ The Tourists) after seeing a re-run of the 1973 film *The Exorcist*, which features a masturbatory scene in which a cross is covered in blood. The name was well known, included an internationally known symbol and "worked on many levels".

The International Committee of the Red Cross was red-faced and cross at the hijacking of its charitable symbol – saying any misuse could endanger lives. Idiosyncratic re-spelling of the ▷ Red Crayola/Krayola sort followed. It's now one of the most frequently misspelled of all band monikers. Inspired ▷ Pink Kross.

The Red Hot Chili Peppers

This American 1980s-on rap-funk-punk band first had the mock hippy name The Miraculously Majestic Masters Of The Universe: surely one of the worst original choices of all time.

The Red Hot Chili Peppers was considered "a perfect hatstand name" and apt given their chilling penchant for wearing just strategically placed socks for their encores. Not related: ▷ Chilli Willi And The Red Hot Peppers. Individual names include: Antwan The Swan – born Anthony Kiedis – and Flea – originally Mike Balzary.

The Red House Painters

Californian band of the 1990s, reminding us of the casual greatness of ▷ Jimi Hendrix's blues workout, *Red House*.

Red Lorry Yellow Lorry

The playground-tongue-twister was an attempt to make announcers slow down, so the name was absorbed by listeners. It posed particular potential problems in Japan, where locals have difficulty differentiating between western Ls and Rs. "Led Lolly Yellow Lolly? Led Rolly Yerrow Rolly?" Drummer Mick Brown, who later joined ▷ The Mission, was coincidentally a former lorry driver. Cf another twister: ▷ The Pheasant Pluckers.

The Redskins

Punk acts, and the Oi! bands which followed, were often awash with Nazism: the prime example being ▷ 4 Skins, who combined sexist, racist and political slurs. The reply came from a Northern English group called No Swastikas – a comment on Nazi insignia misguidedly worn as fashion accessories. The more-innocent-sounding "American Indian" rename took "red" from their left-wing views and "skins" because of their near-shaven heads – a deliberate challenge at a time when such a hairstyle implied membership of a right-wing organisation.

Red Sky At Night

After the old English rhyme: "Red sky at night, shepherds' delight. Red sky in the morning, shepherds' warning." They have denied it was a reference to songs by ▷ Bob Dylan, ▷ The The or ▷ U2.

Jimmy Reed

The Mississippi singer's full name was Mathis James Reed Leland. He chose the middle names as the most marketable and memorable.

Lou Reed

Lou Reed has produced some music of remarkable sensitivity – but he can be insensitive and awkward. He rebuffed attempts to secure an interview: the author figured he might like to put the record straight after many contradictory accounts. Maybe he doesn't care, wants to forget, preserve the mystery, protect his family or protect his private life – but he's been in the public eye for years and many of his songs are autobiographical.

His birthdate is also a mystery: in the early 1970s RCA's press department reportedly said they were too nervous to ask. The consensus is 2 March 1942. Some encyclopedias give the year as 1943 or 1944. On the location, the consensus is Beth El Hospital, Brooklyn, while some books name Freeport, Long Island. This was his home.

He's been the subject of many biographies such as *Lou Reed: Growing Up In Public*, by Peter Doggett from 1992 and Victor Bockris's 1994 *Lou Reed – The Biography*. The majority of articles give his real name as Lewis Allan Reed, while others claim he was born Louis Allan Firbank. His father was legal accountant Sidney George Reed, while his mother was former beauty queen Toby Futterman. Drummer Mo Tucker has denied Lou changed his name, while Bockris says Lou's father had switched from Rabinowitz some time before. It still leaves the possibility that Lou wishes to erase the past: his self-made parents had hoped he would go into their business and gave him electro-shock therapy at 17 because of concern about his sexuality.

He was once a member of Pasha And The Prophets; The Shades (wore sunglasses – which he has done a lot in his later career too); The

Jades (wore sequins); LA And The Eldorados (stood for Louis Allan); the Roughnecks; and surfers The Beach Nuts. He also worked with Three Screaming Niggers, believe it or not. This inauspicious start at school, Syracuse University and as a contract songwriter for Pickwick Records also included work with ▷ The Primitives, a name borrowed two decades later by another ensemble. During his time with Pickwick, he was a "member" of scores of "bands". The label would put out cheap albums, apparently compilations of up-and-coming acts – whereas in fact they'd all be the Pickwick staffers using different aliases for each track.

Reed then launched ▷ The Velvet Underground. The dark prince of songs like *Heroin* might have been laughed off the stage if it was thought this "decadent low-life druggie" was actually Louis Firbank, son of middle-class millionaires. His lyrics helped name ▷ Holly Johnson, ▷ Sid Vicious and ▷ The Waterboys. Cf also ▷ Drella, ▷ The Godfather Of Punk.

Reef
Widely reported to be an anagram for "Free". This is denied by singer Gary Stringer. "But I think ▷ Free are rad." This didn't stop Paul Rodgers sending them a message: "He thought our record was ace." Another theory which the band deny is that it's an abbreviation of "reefer". Stringer says the name "just emerged" after they decided to ditch their previous moniker Naked. He told *Vox*: "We wanted to be living rock animals, ha ha!"

Reel 2 Real
Reel-to-reel, or open spool, tape recorders were used domestically before the advent of cassettes and are still common in professional studios. This band specifically denied any link to the 1984 album *Real To Reel* by ▷ Marillion.

Della Reese
Based on her real name, Dellareese Taliaferro. Inspired: ▷ Martha And The Vandellas.

Martha Reeves
▷ Martha And The Vandellas.

Vic Reeves
"Jim Moir is not a showbiz name," says the British musician-comedian of his birth moniker – which in addition he later found he shared with a BBC executive. Vic Reeves was "the first name to come into my head".

Regular Music
This British group played "systems music", developed by Philip Glass and Michael Nyman, which relies on regularly-repeated elements and interwoven melodies.

R.E.M.
Perhaps the most critically acclaimed band of the 1980s and 1990s. Their ambiguous, sometimes mumbled, lyrics and strange album titles are dissected by students worldwide. Their name, and its many offshoots, has produced as many myths, legends and false trails as the often oblique and obscure song references.

Singer-lyric writer Michael Stipe (born John Michael Stipe) recalls the early amateur group needed a moniker after being offered a gig in 1980. At the time they were living in a near-derelict church in Athens, Georgia, U.S.A. His account comes in *It Crawled From The South* by Marcus Gray (1992, updated 1996). "We sat up one night and we just got completely drunk. We had all this chalk, and we took every name someone could think of and wrote it on the wall in the living room." By morning, the top choices were R.E.M., Negro Eyes – which they knew would provoke racist allegations – plus the punky Slut Bank, Cans Of Piss and Twisted Kites. According to some reports, they played the first concert as Twisted Kites, although others deny this.

Guitarist Peter Buck said: "We just wanted something that was kinda short and concise and wouldn't typecast us." Quite a few acts have chosen handle for similar reasons: cf ▷ ABC etc. (How Cans Of Piss was even considered is a mystery.) He added many of the "good names had been taken" – he loved the surreal ▷ Strawberry Alarm Clock. (Though again this isn't the vaguest or shortest of choices.)

Michael said: "We just like the dots." According to legend, R.E.M. came from forming random sequences of letters and was almost meaningless. The fact that it fitted several abbreviations is said to be coincidental,

R

particularly the scientific term Rapid Eye Movement: a phenomenon in sleep during dreaming when eyeballs move rapidly in jerky movements as an indication of the dreamer looking around at the visual events in his dream world. According to dictionaries of abbreviations, R.E.M. is also used – in English – for: Rontgen Equivalent in Man – to do with X-Rays; Remote Magnetics: Radio and Electronics Measurement; Research of European Migration; and Railway Engineering Maintenance. Their early posters featured eyes prominently, again suggesting R.E.M. once stood for something. They later called a record Rapid Ear Movement.

It was only later they found there had been at least four other short-lived groups called R.E.M. or Rapid Eye Movement. All the others were commercially unsuccessful, so it's not surprising others had unwittingly adopted the same identity. R.E.M. were soon well known – to be sure, they trademarked the title to prevent further problems. A few other combos have used name trademarks (cf ▷ The Human League) – while name copyrights are hard to enforce and many are also trademarking their logos now, which is important for the production of tee-shirts and other items. They are obviously no relation to REM Inc., a company supplying disabled people. So far, the legal feathers have yet to fly on this one.

R.E.M.'s members had previously played projects including ▷ Shadowfax, ▷ The Back Door Band, ▷ The Frustrations, ▷ 1066 Gaggle Of Sound, and Gangster – the last featured an embarrassed Stipe under the *alter ego* Michael Valentine.

Aliases considered by the aspiring stars included ▷ Hornets Attack Victor Mature, Worst Case Scenario, Fat Drunk & Stupid and ▷ It Crawled From The South – all rejected as too bizarre but used for one-off events later, along with others such as Bingo Handjob, William, Pink Pyjamas and Plateshot. Such appellations have allowed them to play intimate venues for true fans only without attracting massive crowds.

Individual projects have featured handles such as Tanzplagen, ▷ Adolf And The Casuals, ▷ Nigel And The Crosses, The Corn Cob Webs, The Southern Gentlemen and ▷ 13111.

Spin-off: ▷ Hindu Love Gods. Stipe worked with ▷ H.E.A.L. and ▷ Hetchy Hetchy and also christened ▷ Concrete Blonde. R.E.M. also chose ▷ Let's Active's designation. They also worked with ▷ The Troggs in one of rock's surprise alliances. Unflattering nickname: Boffin, Bongo, Beardy and Weirdy.

Renaissance
Formed from graduates of ▷ The Yardbirds in 1969, they were fusing classical, folk, jazz, blues and rock to create a renaissance.

REO Speedwagon
You can name a band after anything. ▷ Buffalo Springfield chose an old steamroller, and this Illinois outfit chose a type of antique fire truck. It was the suggestion of keyboardist Neil Doughty, who was a student in Champaign, Illinois (cf ▷ Champaign). He came across a truck made in about 1920 by Ransom E. Olds, the father of the Oldsmobile, and thought its name "kinda sexy". The rest of the group were less impressed when he put it to them, thinking it was a reference to Rio de Janeiro, Brazil. "So we made it capitals – it's R then E, O – okay? The capitals looked great too. It was like at the start of Olds's career, so that was right for us too."

Reparata And The Del-Rons
▷ The Del-Rons.

The Replacements
▷ The Impediments' impediment was booze. Inevitably, the American group turned up to play their first professional concert in their home town of Minneapolis so drunk they could hardly stand. After this fiasco, owners of clubs in the town threatened to place a blanket ban on the immaculately named act. They got round this after sobering up by an immediate change – to a similarly apt moniker.

The Residents
The minimalist band achieved what ▷ ? And the Mysterians failed to do by maintaining total anonymity, wearing masks at all times. An amusing story has now been confirmed as authentic, not apocryphal as sometimes suggested. In 1971 the fledgling combo, based in California, sent off four demo tapes. The

packages included their San Mateo address and no names. One company returned the tape addressed to The Residents.

They later channelled contact with the media through a P.R. company called The Cryptic Corporation, with even that was headed by a pseudonymous John Kennedy. *Hence the name, hence the strange eyeball heads.*

Return To Forever

Massachusetts-born keyboard whiz Chick Corea chose this as the far-out title of his 1972 album. It was liked so much by the jazz musicians gathered around him that it became their own band name the following year.

Paul Revere And The Raiders

The original Paul Revere (1735–1818) was an American patriot who is said to have ridden from Charlestown to Lexington in 1775 to warn colonists of the approach of British troops. There are doubts he made the journey in the way described, but folklore doesn't let facts get in the way of a good story. The legendary feat was immortalised in a Longfellow poem and echoes through U.S. culture right up to ▷ Bob Dylan's 1965 *Tombstone Blues*.

His modern namesake was born in 1942 in Idaho and named by his parents Paul Revere Dick. His backing musicians were known as The Night Riders and adopted eighteenth-century stage outfits. He wasn't the only star to, erm, cut off his Dick. ▷ Fish shares the potentially embarrassing surname, as does ▷ Byrds drummer Michael Clarke, born Michael Dick.

Revillos

The remains of ▷ The Rezillos after a split. They wanted a similar name to their previous band.

Revolution 9

English *avant-garde* trio of the 1990s who recall the long, experimental John Lennon track on ▷ The Beatles 1968 double album.

Revolver

British band of the 1990s with various 1960s influences, including most notably ▷ The Beatles. Their name comes from the Fabs' 1966 album title.

The Rezillos

Scottish punky band, named after an Edinburgh club. They divided into Shake and ▷ The Revillos after a 1978 split. Jo Callis went on into ▷ The Human League.

RIB

Leader of Euro band Quadrophenia, rapper RIB Master explains his handle means Rootless Intelligent Being, taken from science fiction jargon for UFOs.

Cliff Richard

He was born Harry Rodger Webb, October 1940, in Lucknow, India. No relation to the poet Harry Webb or another famous Webb: ▷ Gary Numan. Gary also thought the surname fine for "a solicitor, scrap metal dealer, shop assistant or a soldier but not a star".

Harry first played with the Dick Teague Skiffle Group in London pubs, then formed Harry Webb And The Drifters. They were offered more work by promoter Bob Greatorex – if the singer renamed. The matter was discussed at a Soho pub and the names Russ Clifford, Cliff Russord and Cliff Russard were suggested. This in turn became Cliff Richards. Some reports said Greatorex had a cousin called Richard Cliff, although this version is now disputed.

Guitarist Ian Samwell suggested dropping the final S of the surname, so Richard could correct reporters when they got it wrong, so ensuring it was mentioned twice. Cliff said in an interview: "The name paid tribute to ▷ Little Richard. It was two Christian names which was good and unusual." He later showed he was a committed Christian, although this is by the way.

Compare to ▷ Rolling Stone ▷ Keith Richards, as different a musician as you could wish to find, but whose change was inspired by Cliff. However, down the years the surname has become redundant, in Britain at least: like Elvis, Bruce and Jesus, Cliff is enough. Or perhaps Sir Cliff after the sword of knighthood fell on his shoulders.

Hence the name. Hence "I'm Nearly Famous".

Name notes: Richard changed his appellation by deed poll after encountering customs problems with an alias: plane tickets were booked in one name and his passport was in another. Unflattering derivative: Riff Pilchard. The Drifters changed to ▷ The Shadows to end confusion with U.S. band ▷ The Drifters. For more, see his own books *Questions: Cliff Answering Reader and Fan Queries* (1970) and *Which One's Cliff?* (1977, with Bill Latham).

Keith Richard(s)

Born Keith Richards, in Dartford, Kent, U.K., he dropped the last letter from his surname on leaving home – a change inspired by ▷ Cliff Richard, then with his rocker credibility still intact. The two rapidly became chalk and cheese, Keith's demonic drug Mr Dirty image contrasting with Cliff's Christian Mr Clean. Still, journalists persisted in spelling his surname Richards. He gave in to the inevitable in 1977 and after a reconciliation with his father reverted to Richards.

The ▷ Rolling Stones' nicknames include The Walking Laboratory, The Living Skull, The Human Riff, The World's Most Elegantly Wasted Human Being, half of ▷ The Glimmer Twins etc; his bands include ▷ The Ex-Pensive Winos. He is commonly referred to by fans and music papers alike as simply Keith – or, frequently, ▷ Keef.

Rich Kids

A name considered by early ▷ Queen and used by a ▷ Sex Pistols spin-off joined by ▷ Midge Ure. From French writer Jean Cocteau's *Les Enfants Terribles*. Cf ▷ The Cocteau Twins.

Harry Richman

This 1930s star anglicised his real name Harry Reichman so he had something to live up to. He went on to own mansions, planes and limousines, while he tipped with legendary generosity.

Jonathan Richman

▷ The Modern Lovers.

Ricky And The Red Streaks

▷ The Beatles dallied with the *alter ego* Long John And The Silver Beetles in their early days, in tune with the "and the" trend of rock 'n' roll names. This didn't last long.

By 1969 they were thinking of going full circle. Paul in particular wanted to rehearse the

band, revive songs they were doing years ago – a *Besame Mucho* cover, the self-penned *One After 909* – and go back on the road. They planned an album called *Get Back and 12 Other Songs* with a cover resembling *Please Please Me, Love Me Do And 12 Other Songs*. The cover was used for the Blue Album, *1967–70*; the songs found their way into *Let It Be*. The only thing they needed was a moniker for their on-the-road act in order to play medium-sized venues. Their choice was the "very retro" Ricky And The Red Streaks. The tour never happened and the tag's only reference now comes in a track on the 1996 album *Anthology 3*. Cf ▷ Sgt Pepper, which was apparently first considered as an anonymous tag for touring.

Ricky Cool And The Icebergs

"Because we're the coolest." One of the best collective names, on a par with Telephone Bill And The Smooth Operators and Sweaty Betty And The Perspirations.

Riff Raff

A short-lived New York band of this name recalled the Butler in *The Rocky Horror Picture Show*. Briton Billy Bragg also used it for an early group, referring to scruffy punks and musical riffs.

The Righteous Brothers

These Californians weren't brothers. Nor were they terribly religious. Nor were they black, as listeners initially assumed. Billy Hatfield and Bill Medley started in 1962 as The Paramours – not the Paramounts, as they were sometimes wrongly billed. They made an immediate impact with their gospel voices, getting dubbed: "The Jesus Boots Duo", "Blued-Eyed Soul Brothers", and "The Righteous Brothers".

"Righteous" meant "the best" in ethnic argot. However, according to several semiotic histories of American philology, it was also used to mean "typical of whites or white society" so it may not have been so complimentary. After a split in 1968, Hatfield kept the name and forged a short-lived partnership with Billy Walker but the original "brothers" later reunited.

Right Said Fred

The perpetrators of the 1991 British hit *I'm Too*

Sexy named after a much earlier novelty single, recorded in 1962 by Bernard Cribbins. The phrase was an in-joke: one of the band was called Fred.

Rigor Mortis
▷ Who bassist John Entwistle, ▷ The Ox, formed the band to promote his 1973 concept album, *Rigor Mortis Sets In*, which said rock had died, becoming stiff and contrived.

Terry Riley
Cult composer whose smaller claims to fame include inspiring ▷ Curved Air, although not ▷ Anthrax as sometimes thought.

Riot Act
British 1980s act named from the document that police were supposed to read out loud to warn those participating in civil disturbances they faced immediate arrest if they didn't disperse. Officers have now been released from this onerous Victorian requirement. Concert promoters feared it meant trouble and refused to book the group. Unrelated: ▷ Riot Squad.

Riot Grrrl
A musical movement including the likes of ▷ Babes In Toyland, ▷ Hole, ▷ L7 and others defining femininity. Chris of ▷ Huggy Bear said the name was chosen to express "snarrrling" aggression.

Riot Squad
From the British police unit assembled to deal with civil disturbances. Cf ▷ Riot Act.

Rip Rig + Panic
An offshoot of ▷ The Pop Group, named after a ▷ Rahsaan Roland Kirk album in the collection of jazz trumpeter Don Cherry: his daughter Neneh was in the band before solo success.

Rising Sons
Simply named by two of the U.S. West Coast's finest rising musicians, Ry Cooder and ▷ Taj Mahal.

Johnny Rivers
Louisianan John Ramistella was brought up in Baton Rouge and renamed after its bayou by the man who gave rock 'n' roll its name, DJ Alan Freed.

Roachford
Named after leader Andrew Roachford.

The Roadrunners
British popsters named from the 1960 ▷ Bo Diddley single, *Road Runner.*

The Roaring Boys
Roaring boys, according to *The Oxford English Dictionary*, are *habitués* of ale houses described in works by Foote, Rowley and Scott. They were – in some respects – forerunners of the Mods, Rockers and many youth cults of today.

Roaring Jelly
Long-running British comedy band named after the traditional Irish jig with a humorously absurdist title.

Smokey Robinson
Detroit boy William Robinson was known as Smokey from an early age. His band The Matadors became ▷ The Miracles, which forced a name change for ▷ The Temptations. His name forced U.K. band Smokey to become Smokie. Daughter: Tamla Robinson.

The Roches
All the members of this all-girl family stubbornly kept their surname Roche – despite people thinking it a revolting reference to cockroaches or roach clips for smoking cannabis. Similar refusal to rename: ▷ Andy Pratt.

Rock Lobsters
Like Rock Salmon, a pun that has been done several times. The best-known Rock Lobsters mimic ▷ The B-52s, who had a hit with a song of the same name.

Rockpile
Dave Edmunds named a 1972 album, and this band with ▷ Basher (AKA Nick Lowe), after a Welsh studio in which he had invested.

The Rolling Stones
Rolling stones may gather no moss, but rock has

R

been littered with them: The Temptations' *Papa Was A Rolling Stone*, ▷ Bob Dylan's *Like A Rolling Stone*, ▷ Muddy Waters' *Rollin' Stone*. The Rollin' Stones took their name in 1962 from the last, the blues star's Chess debut issued 12 years before. In 1963 manager Andrew Loog Oldham added the G – although the members, of course, are often called The Stones.

Hence the name, hence the 1995 cover of the Dylan song. Dylan's lyric was written in 1965 – about any rolling stone but with the Britons in mind.

It's allowed many jokes down the years, with records including *Heart Of Stone*, *Stone Age* and *Hot Rocks*. It hints at rock 'n' roll, getting stoned and rolling down the road – all essential elements of their style.

The beginning of the "Greatest Rock Band In The World" can be traced to 1960 when one Michael Philip Jagger met one Keith Richards on a train. They first worked in an R&B outfit called Little Boy Blue And the Boy Blues, fronted by Jagger, then graduated via Alexis Korner's Blues Incorporated. J. & R., whose songwriting has sometimes gone under the tag Nanker Phelge, also acquired the nickname ▷ The Glimmer Twins and have used it as a production credit. J. seems less happy about his own tag Ol' Rubberlips. A 1960s joke said his mother used to wet his lips at night and stick him up on the wall. R. swiftly dropped the last letter from his surname on leaving home but later reinstated it ▷ Keith Richard(s), ▷ Keef.

The early Stones, playing blues material, also featured Dick Taylor, later of ▷ The Pretty Things, and Brian Jones, from The Ramrods. Jones gave himself the suitably authentic handle Elmo Lewis when he played blues. (An appellation shared with the father of ▷ Jerry "Killer" Lee Lewis.) He was born Lewis Brian Hopkin-Jones but like ▷ Queen's Roger Taylor, he decided a double-barrelled surname wrecked working-class rock credibility. On the other hand, new bassist Bill Perks went upmarket to become Bill Wyman. The Stones later included Ron Wood, ex ▷ Faces and ▷ Birds.

Name notes: Unflattering derivative: ▷ The Strolling Bones. Spoof acts: The Rolling Clones and ▷ The Counterfeit Stones. Spin-offs include ▷ The Ex-Pensive Winos and ▷ Willie

And The Poorboys. The Stones' music inspired the naming of ▷ The Stone Roses. Tracks on the album *Sticky Fingers* inspired ▷ Pavlov's Dog and ▷ Wild Horses. Plenty of combos have nuncupated partly because of the ease of abbreviating their identity Stones-style: such as ▷ The Boomtown Rats – to the Rats – and ▷ The Black Crowes – to The Crowes.

Sprog notes: Jagger's daughter was called Jade, Richards's was Dandelion; the latter, unhappy at being christened after a weed, later chose the less conspicuous Angela. She's not the only rock star offspring to discard an headline-grabbing prenomen: ▷ David Bowie's son Zowie became Joe.

At least 100 books have been written on the Stones. Most are rubbish, some reasonable and a few excellent. For more on the naming start with Philip Norman's 1984 book *The Stones* and Nik Cohn's 1975 *The Rolling Stones – A Celebration*.

Roman Holliday

The band from unexotic Harlow, Essex, went for a touch of Italian romance and showed they couldn't spell, recalling the Oscar-winning *Roman Holiday*. The movie boosted Audrey Hepburn's career – and sales of 1950s sunglasses, headscarves, silk suits, scooters, cappuccinos and ice-creams.

Ronettes

Their leader was Veronica Bennett, known by her family as Ronnie. She said the band name fitted in with the popularity of similar-sounding groups such as the Marvelettes. "-ettes" as a suffix means "small", as in kitchenette, cigarette, wagonette, serviette or maisonette.

Rosebud

"Rosebud" was the dying word of the anti-hero of Orson Welles's *Citizen Kane*. A reporter spends his time trying to uncover the significance of this remark – it only becomes clear in the final seconds. The film also inspired ▷ The Kane Gang and ▷ Eden Kane. More roses: ▷ Guns N' Roses, ▷ Madder Rose, ▷ Rose Royce, ▷ Rose Tattoo, ▷ The Stone Roses.

Rose Royce

Car and aero-engine maker Rolls-Royce is

fiercely protective of its name. This band came as close as it could to R.R. and lived to tell the tale. The former ▷ Temptations backing band were renamed in 1976 by Motown producer Norman Whitfield, who wanted something to fit his musical *Car Wash*. More trademark stories: ▷ Chicago, ▷ Poco, ▷ Band Aid, ▷ Yazoo etc.

Rose Tattoo

The Rose Tattoo was a classic song of American Grand Ole Opry. It became the title of a 1951 Tennessee Williams drama as well as inspiring this Australian band with its symbol of permanent love.

W. Axl Rose

... was born in Lafayette, Indiana, on 6 February 1962. He was – so he thought – William Bailey, the eldest son of L. Stephen and Sharon E. Bailey. It was only when he was 17 that he discovered his real father was William Rose, a local hellraiser whom his mother had divorced long before. The teenager decided to revert to Rose, while abbreviating his formal first name to W., to distance himself from his real father who "was an asshole". Still, the star-to-be later tracked him to a graveyard in Illinois – he'd been murdered in 1984.

W. naughtily made his name into an anagram of "oral sex" by adding A.X.L. – the name of his first band. Others thought W.A.R. was an apt set of initials given his temper. This led in turn to ▷ Guns N' Roses. There's more in Mark Putterford's 1993 book *Over The Top: The True Story of Guns N' Roses*.

Rossington Collins Band

From founders Gary Rossington and Allen Collins, survivors of the plane crash which curtailed ▷ Lynyrd Skynyrd's career.

Johnny Rotten

▷ Sex Pistols Svengali Malcolm McLaren liked the idea of his charges having stage identities. In a manifesto he urged them to announce themselves in the most dramatic way possible. Johnny Lydon was so mistrustful he hadn't told anyone his surname. He was always spitting, blowing his nose and inspecting his rotting teeth. Guitarist Steve Jones found this repulsive and his catchphrase became: "You look rotten/you sound rotten/your teeth are rotten/you're rotten, you are."

McLaren liked the name, coined in 1975, because it was the opposite of the pop entrepreneur choices of the past. In the 1960s ▷ Larry Parnes had come up with appealing adjectives for his fledgling stars: Fame, Gentle, Pride, Power, Wilde. In the 1970s stars were being "more honest".

▷ Neil Young reminded the world in 1979 that Elvis was dead – the king was gone yet not forgotten. Punk rock had made it the story of Johnny Rotten. In reality, this handle had already been confined to the dustbin of musical history; ▷ Public Image Ltd was led by one John Lydon.

Rough Diamond

This term for an ill-mannered but well-meaning person has been used by several bands, one of which took legal action when a supergroup was formed. In this case, the newer outfit won.

Rough Trade

Cambridge graduate Geoff Travis founded Rough Trade, initially as a record shop and later as a label best known for ▷ The Smiths. The name comes from gay slang about rent-boys, although it can apply to any business.

Roxy Music

▷ Bryan Ferry first sung with The Banshees (no relation to ▷ Siouxsie And The Banshees) and The Gas Board (from the English public utility and fashionable phrase "it's a gas"). He chose Roxy in honour of a favourite cinema and rock music, and to indicate old-style Ritzy glamour. The "Music" distinguished them from another act with the same handle. The moniker was originally in ironic inverted commas.

Hence the name. Hence Bryan's cream tuxedo.

Ferry, a humble miner's son from Sunderland, aspired to the upper class and married a genuine "lady", while the others played down middle-class origins. ▷ Eno abbreviated his name while guitarist Phil Manzanera trimmed from Phillip Targett-Adams. ▷ Queen's Roger Taylor and Brian

Jones of ▷ The Rolling Stones also cut double-barrelled surnames. Inspired: ▷ Bananarama, ▷ Diamond Head. Related: ▷ 801, ▷ Warm Jets. ▷ Byron Ferrari.

Ruben And The Jets

▷ Frank Zappa 1968 project named for a "nice 1950s feel" with a pastiche of doo-wop with appropriately Zappesque lyrics.

The Rubinoos

From their leader, Jon Rubin.

Harry Ruby

Anglicisation of Harry Rubinstein.

Rufus

The soul-funk group named from *Ask Rufus*, a write-in question column in magazine *Mechanics Illustrated*.

Rumblefish

Spin-off from ▷ The Police. From *Rumble Fish*, a 1983 Francis Ford Coppola film about a boy who draws parallels between fishing aquarium fish and urban unrest around him.

The Runaways

They said it was neither a reference to ▷ Del Shannon's massive 1961 hit *Runaway*, nor to ▷ The Ramones. The latter's *Leave Home* was recorded in 1977 – the Runaways were going two years before that. It was more "a rebellious dare to … romance and adventure". Related: ▷ The Blackhearts.

Todd Rundgren

▷ The Nazz, ▷ Runt, ▷ Utopia.

Run DMC

From the New York vocalists' nicknames: Joe "Run" Simmons and 'DMC' Darryl McDaniels. Related: ▷ H.E.A.L. Nickname: ▷ The Kings From Queens.

Runrig

They started in bucolic mode as The Run-Rig Dance Band – the name referred to ploughing furrows – playing Scottish Highland ceilidh with Gaelic lyrics.

Runt

It was affectionately applied by Patti Smith to ▷ Todd Rundgren, combining his surname with a term of mild abuse. His 1973 album *A Wizzard, A True Star* was dedicated to her in return.

The Rutles

British television series ▷ *Monty Python's Flying Circus* led to a spin-off, *Rutland Weekend Television*. This band's name is a combination of the show title and ▷ The Beatles, whom they parodied.

Bobby Rydell

This early 1960s U.S. star simplified his name, Robert Ridarelli, and later provided the name of the college in hit musical *Grease*.

Mitch Ryder

Singer William Levise Jnr, AKA Billy Lee, was urged by his record company to find a more inspiring name before his first major release. They told him: "Any name's better than yours." He took them at their word, walked to the nearest phone booth and opened a Detroit directory at random. His finger stabbed on the name "Mitch Ryder".

Several Mitch Ryders have claimed the entry was theirs, although the star wasn't sure which address he picked. One real Ryder was quoted in a local newspaper as saying: "Good luck to him. It's a fine name." Another said: "He stole my name without asking … he didn't even call. And his music sucks." ▷ The Detroit Wheels.

Sabri Brothers

Sabri is a Sufist term for followers of the religion.

Sad Café

Members of this British band liked the evocative *The Ballad Of The Sad Café* by U.S. writer Carson McCullers (1917–1967), a tale about unrequited love first published in the 1950s. The title of their 1979 album, *Façades*, was an anagram of their name.

Sade

The singer was born in Nigeria as Helen Folasade Adu and abbreviated to Sade Adu. It's pronounced "Shar-day" and not "Said", "Sayeed", "Sadie" or "Sad". Her four-strong group sans Sade herself call themselves Sweetback.

Sadistic Mika Band

Japanese band named after the Ono-esque screeches of female vocalist Mika Katoh, wife of guitarist Kazuhiko Katoh.

S.A.H.B.

Short for Sensational Alex Harvey Band.

Sailor

From their 1974 debut, a concept album about a life on the ocean wave, complete with a self-conscious vaudeville image. Misunderstandings ahoy!

Saint Bob

Call him Saint Bob, ▷ Sir Bob, Modest Bob. Call him ▷ Bob Geldof. The "beatification" was inspired by his saint-like status while tirelessly campaigning for the Live Aid charity.

St Etienne

This U.K. band started as Next Projected Sound but possibly ill-advisedly chose their next appellation in tribute to a French town. Challenged by *Melody Maker* as to why they named after "a crap soccer team", the group said that they thought it "sounded good". It didn't mean they supported the club.

St Vitus Dance

This dance act referred to a nervous disorder causing uncontrolled convulsive movements – named from a saint, martyred with his nurse. More medical bad taste: ▷ The DTs etc.

Soupy Sales

The U.S. comedian, associated with musical acts such as ▷ The Archies, got his stage name from his real name Milton Hines Supman (Heinz Soup-man).

Salt 'N' Pepa

Cheryl "Salt" James and Sandra "Pepa" Denton, from Brooklyn and Jamaica respectively, were named from their appearance by producer Hurby Aznor, using the title of a 1969 Sammy Davis Junior film. (Cf ▷ A Man Called Adam.)

S

Sam And Dave

American vocalists Sam Moore and Dave Prater. Unrelated: ▷ Chas And Dave.

Sam Apple Pie

An all-American name for these U.S. music-loving Britons, combining the symbols of Apple Pie and Uncle Sam. Cf some all-American names: ▷ America; ▷ Damned Yankees; ▷ The Presidents Of The United States of America; ▷ Gary Puckett And The Union Gap; ▷ Paul Revere And The Raiders. Cf some Britons pretending to be Yanks: ▷ Cherokees; ▷ Ivy League; ▷ Billy J. Kramer And The Dakotas. Cf Americans playing at being Brits: ▷ Sir Douglas Quintet etc.

Samson

… were formed by guitarist Paul Sampson, *hence the name*. No relation to the Biblical strong man. Vocalist Bruce Bruce went on into ▷ Iron Maiden under his real name Bruce Dickinson.

Sam The Sham

Domingo Samudio, known from his last name as Sam, borrowed the 1960s jargon for simultaneous dancing and singing.

Sanctuary

Chosen not from literature (such as William Faulkner's 1931 novel) but in ironic reference to their eardrum-splitting grunge. From Seattle, Washington, and the same musical school as ▷ Nirvana, ▷ Pearl Jam and ▷ Soundgarden.

The Sandpipers

They renamed when an unrelated group became successful under their first choice: ▷ The Four Seasons. The trend for bird names was at its height and they chose this species for its musical reference.

Santana

Originally Santana Bluesband, from the name of Mexican-born Carlos Santana. The name applied as much to the guitarist as to the band and soon became effectively just him with whatever session musicians he was working with at the time.

Fortunately, the group remained Santana while he flirted with a new name. He became enamoured of the teachings of Bengal mystic Sri Chinmoy at the instigation of friend John McLaughlin, AKA ▷ Mahavishu, and said he wanted to be called Devadip. This wasn't the most elegant name for a band: it translates more poetically as "The enlightenment of the lamp of the Lord". The dilemma resolved itself when the musician abandoned Chinmoy. Similar religious renaming: ▷ Roger McGuinn of ▷ The Byrds. Spin-offs: ▷ Abraxas Pool, ▷ Journey. Unflattering derivative: Sultana.

Satan's Rats

Cult band from Evesham, Worcestershire, who had a classic punk name (although not much else going for them). They evolved into the so-attractive ▷ Photos.

Satchmo

Nickname for Louis Armstrong, from his cheeks when playing a long passage: "satchel mouth". Cf ▷ Dippermouth.

The Saw Doctors

The latest in a long line of musical "doctors" – and one of the few without curing qualities of the highest order. These quack medical hacks' surgical solution is to roughly remove any offending organ. Cf: ▷ The Charlatans.

saXon

These U.K. rockers started as Son Of A Bitch and renamed after the Germanic race in the 1970s as their music veered closer to heavy metal, with its near-obligatory Teutonic references. Sprog notes: Sky Saxon called his child Dog.

Leo Sayer

It grew from Jackie, wife of manager ▷ Adam Faith, who named Gerard Sayer "little Leo lion" on account of his mane of hair and 5 ft 4 ins height.

Scorpio Rising

The 1963 short film took its subject matter from cult to commercial success in Harley-Davidson supercharged form. It's hard to get on video – yet rated by this band, 30 years on, as one of the best biker movies ever.

Scritti Politti

It was taken from Italian for political writing, *scritti politichi*, used in a work by Communist leader and theoretician Antonio Gramsci (1891–1937). The re-spelling recalled ▷ Little Richard's single *Tutti Frutti*. The name tied in with the early left-wing political leanings of Welshman, Cardiff-born Green Strohmeyer-Gartside, later Green Gartside and finally (the environmentally friendly) Green. Influenced: ▷ Wet Wet Wet.

S.D.M.

Short-lived band formed by rock gypsy ▷ Ric Grech with singer Claire Hamill. Not Sado Masochism but Square Dance Machine; Grech was dabbling in country music at the time.

Seal

Disregard reports that he was born Bernard Young and the single moniker came from his collection of porcelain seals – stories which find their way into otherwise excellent reference books. Seal told *Q* magazine in 1995 his birth name is Sealhenry Samuel. His grandparents come from Brazil and it's a common appellation there. He has a small collection of seals, mainly sent in by fans – long after he became famous as Seal.

Seals And Crofts

Texans Jim Seals and Dash Crofts. Nothing to do with Scotland.

The Searchers

The Liverpool combo ended their search when they took the title of John Wayne's 1956 western.

The Secret Goldfish

Taken from the title of a fictional book mentioned on the first page of J.D. Salinger's 1951 novel *The Catcher In The Rye* about a little boy's pet.

The Secret Lemonade Drinkers

The phrase "secret lemonade drinker" inspired British writer Guy Bellamy's 1977 novel, an advertising campaign by R. Whites and this 1980s British band, who saw it as a riposte to "boozy" acts such as ▷ Serious Drinking.

Section 25

It was intended as a humorous reference to Britain's Mental Health Act under which patients are confined to asylums. Section 25 later become controversial as patients released for Care in the Community staged a series of violent attacks.

See For Miles

From ▷ The Who's 1967 hit *I Can See For Miles*.

The Selecter

The Special AKA lacked the money to record a B-side for their 1979 single *Gangsters*. Instead they let a guitar, drum and trombone group use the flip side for an instrumental ska track called *The Selecter* (sic). The track was hastily credited to The Selecter. The spelling error was retained, while they said it had many political, mechanical, sexual and racial connotations. ▷ The Specials.

Captain Sensible

AKA Ray Burns of ▷ The Damned.

Sepultura

Latin Americans who showed commitment to "death rock". The *All-Music Guide To Rock* says it's Portugese for "grave", while the band has moved on to address issues such as social conditions in their native Brazil.

Sgt Pepper's Lonely Hearts Club Band

▷ The Beatles came up with this in 1967 as they contemplated touring again, according to artist Peter Blake – the man responsible for the packaging of their landmark album with this title. He said a "smokescreen" name would allow them to play smaller venues without the ballyhoo which had made their last tour unpleasant. In the event, the Fabs never went back on the road (discounting the *Magical Mystery Tour*).

Their summer of love album was formally credited to The Beatles yet purported to be a show by Sgt Pepper's merry men. The original *Dr Pepper's Lonely Hearts Club Band* was dropped because of fears of legal action by the well-known soft-drinks maker. The record company bosses were still unhappy at the world's biggest group associating themselves in any way with something as sad as a lonely hearts club, but that stayed. The Fabs had after all already recorded *Eleanor Rigby*. Cf ▷ Ricky And The Red Streaks.

Serious Drinking

British band with a not-very-serious name and a love for lager. "Serious" as an adjective in the 1980s came to mean heavy, excessive or large: drinking to get drunk.

Set The Tone

British popsters/poseurs named from the inside sleeve of Andy Warhol's *Popism*, seen by art/design expert Kenny Hyslop (ex ▷ Simple Minds).

Steve Severin

A naughty nineteenth-century novel by Leopold von Sacher-Masoch called *Venus In Furs* is narrated by pervy Severin, who is in love with Wanda – and her whip. Like his fictional protagonist, Sacher-Masoch had given himself to Baroness Bogdanoff as a sex slave. Masoch was a name borrowed later by psychologist Krafft-Ebing to describe the condition of enjoying pain.

In the 1960s Masoch's title was recycled; first by Piero Heliczer for a film in the New York artistic community which included ▷ Lou Reed; then for a track on the 1967 ▷ The Velvet Underground album which included Reed, one of the first punks.

Punk rock exploded in England a decade later. Young Steve Bailey was part of the infamous ▷ Bromley Contingent, going under the punkish moniker Steve Havoc, until he renamed on hearing the 1967 song. The track also inspired ▷ The Psychedelic Furs. Cf ▷ The Glove, ▷ Siouxsie And The Banshees.

Sex Gang Children

▷ Boy George's version in *Take It Like A Man* says: "I came up with pretentious names: In Praise Of Lemmings and The Sex Gang Children, a line stolen from a ▷ Bow Wow Wow song." He had sung with the latter as ▷ Lieutenant Lush. Other books say it was ▷ Malcolm McLaren's idea, on a list passed to George, and taken from William Burroughs's

work (cf ▷ Dead Fingers Talk etc). The appellation certainly got in a free advert for McLaren's clothes shop Sex – the same thinking in part explains ▷ Sex Pistols.

Either way it was a good attempt to annoy the radio censors – while Boy George subsequently settled on ▷ Culture Club. Sex Gang Children later regrouped and achieved success without him.

The Sex Pistols

The musical equivalent of an advert which starts: "SEX!!!" And continues: "Now we have your attention." The Pistols would have probably grabbed attention anyway, given the music, lyrics, publicity stunts and outrage. But the name kick-started their career – which has veered from rejection of capitalism to its embrace, from "do you ever feel you've been cheated?" to "getcha money's worth" on the Filthy Lucre Reunion Tour in 1996.

They began in 1974 as The Swankers. This is a swanky choice sometimes said with a silent S; if anything almost better than The Sex Pistols, which was created by punk guru ▷ Malcolm McLaren in the autumn of that year. In November 1975 the group, with a new line-up, had rehearsed for a month and had to agree with his decision as concert venues were booked.

"Sex" came from the name of McLaren's clothes shop at the time at 430 King's Road, Chelsea. The boutique had also been called Let It Rock and Too Fast To Live, Too Young To Die. He said it was too short and provocative on its own to get airplay. Cf ▷ Sex Gang Children. So "pistols" was added – a misspelling of Sex Pistils, a botanical term meaning the male sexual parts of flowers. The whole was about as close as he dared go to The Penises. He said it had associations of "pistols ... guns ... assassins ... young, vicious, sex" – some explored by Shakespeare's *Henry IV* and *V.*

There are differing accounts of the idea's popularity in Jon Savage's 1991 book *England's Dreaming*. ▷ Johnny Rotten (Lydon) says: "The word 'Sex' had never been used in that blatant way before. I thought it was perfect to offend old ladies." McLaren recalls: "Rotten just wanted to be called 'Sex'. It was only Jones that loved it. Cook wanted something more normal-sounding. Matlock sided with John. I was in control and I wasn't going to waste my time with a bunch of herberts going out with a name like Sex. I was out to sell lots of trousers."

Hence the name. Hence the safety pins.

Name notes: Because of legal problems and concert venue bans, they completed a 1977 tour under the names Acne Rabble – cf ▷ Cockney Rebel – and – continuing the skin problem theme – ▷ SPOTS, which meant "Sex Pistols On Tour Secretly". Related: ▷ Public Image Ltd, ▷ Rich Kids, ▷ The Flowers Of Romance. Anagram: Sexist Slop. They inspired ▷ The Buzzcocks, ▷ The Celibate Rifles and ▷ The Tex Pistols; ▷ Sid Vicious inspired ▷ The Sid Presley Experience. McLaren played a part in forming ▷ The Damned, who might conceivably have been called The Sex Pistols – but only if they had met him before Rotten and his crew.

S'Express

The only band in the world to "sexpress themselves" by naming after minicab company Essex Express.

Seymour

This relatively unknown British indie group took their "see more" name from a sympathetic character dreamt up by singer Damon Albarn. They became better known as ▷ Blur.

Shabby Tiger

One of many tiger bands, this 1970s combo named from their theme song.

Shadowfax

Another debt to J.R.R. Tolkien, from Gandalf's horse in *The Lord Of The Rings*. The name has been used by two U.S. outfits: a band from Chicago and a short-lived hobby group dating from 1975 in Macon, Georgia, featuring Bill Berry and Mike Mills, who later joined ▷ R.E.M. More Tolkien: ▷ Marillion etc.

The Shadows

They started backing ▷ Cliff Richard as The Drifters, a romantic name in the 1960s when drifting was okay. They faced legal action from a U.S. black group of the same moniker when they moved to release a single in the States in 1959

and hurriedly became The Four Jets – the track was called *Jet Black* and the band included Jet Harris. Still, he and ▷ Hank B. Marvin remained unhappy and later that year met at a pub in Ruislip, Middlesex, where they decided on The Shadows, partly because of their role shadowing Richard. There was considerable public interest in The Shads yet backing bands in those days were supposed to be anonymous.

Shaft

The 1990s band tipped their hats to 1970s movie *Shaft*, and its score by ▷ Black Moses himself, Isaac Hayes.

Shag

One of many names created by ▷ Jonathan King. If asked whether this was anything to do with the British slang for a popular activity involving an interchange of bodily fluids, King would nod – while saying: "It's after the seabird." Make your own mind up on this one.

Shakespears Sister

English author Virginia Woolf (1882–1941) had written a feminist essay asking what would have happened if England's greatest writer William Shakespeare had been a woman. ▷ Morrissey of ▷ The Smiths lifted this for a 1985 song called *Shakespeare's Sister*. In 1989, Marcella Detroit and Siobhan Fahey (born Siobhan Marie Deidre Fahey-Stewart), ex ▷ Bananarama, formed a band named after The Smiths' song. They claimed mistakes on their first record cover, omitting an E and an apostrophe, were the fault of a graphic designer – adding the choice was right, however spelled, because: "It says something poetic about women and it's a great name."

Shakin' Street

Taken from the name of a song by ▷ MC5. It's on their 1970 album *Back In The U.S.A.*

Shalamar

Suitably upmarket-sounding tag chosen by California record producer Dick Griffey for a collection of studio musicians. He took it from a travel brochure which pictured the Shalamar park in Lahore.

Shamen

The word often turns up in a rock concept, being notably applied to ▷ Jim Morrison. Shamen perform wild or emotional rites – like early concerts by this British group which evolved from ▷ Alone Again Or.

Sham 69

In 1969 the hippy apotheosis in America meant the slogan "love and peace". By 1979 the punk ascendancy in Britain led to the reversal "hate and war", as recorded by ▷ The Clash. This band summed up the attitude, saying the 1969 ethos was a sham.

Sha Na Na

From the singing phrase, specifically as in the lyrics of The Silhouettes' 1957 single *Get A Job* but also in many other tunes of the same era. Cf ▷ Showaddywaddy.

The Shangri-Las

This all-female group named after the area which has become a byword for any paradise: James Hilton set his novel *The Lost Horizon* in the Tibetan Shangri-La lamasery. So another "heavenly" tag along the lines of ▷ Ambrosia, ▷ Nirvana and ▷ Utopia, plus a vocal line reference like ▷ The La's later.

Del Shannon

Born Charles Westover. The new prenomen was an adaptation of his favourite car, the Coup De Ville L or "Coup Del". The surname thanked his helper, Mark Shannon. Cf ▷ The Runaways.

Artie Shaw

The U.S. jazz star simplified his real name, Arthur Jacob Arshawsky.

Sandie Shaw

Dagenham-born Sandra (Sandy) Goodrich leapt to fame after having the chutzpah to blag her way into meeting ▷ Adam Faith, kick off her shoes and sing. She often appeared barefoot on stage, as if walking on a shoreline: the name suggested by manager Eve Taylor. She later worked with ▷ The Smiths.

Sheila E

Sheila Escovedo, a protégée of ▷ Prince.

Shelleyan Orphan

Unlike ▷ Pete Shelley, this band named in tribute to the English poet Percy Bysshe Shelley. The source was *Rebel Of Islam*, where one stanza starts: "An orphan in my parents' house."

Pete Shelley

Peter Campbell McNeish wasn't paying homage to the English poet (Percy Bysshe Shelley 1792–1822). It was simply what his parents would have called their child had he been a girl. He renamed on Saturday, 21 February 1976 immediately after seeing ▷ The Sex Pistols and naming ▷ Howard Devoto and ▷ The Buzzcocks. He changed by deed poll on Friday 16 February 1979.

Shinehead

Edmund Carl Aiken had a very full head of hair: the name came when he contemplated shaving it off one hot day.

The Shirelles

From lead singer Shirley Owens. They later became Shirley And The Shirelles.

Michelle Shocked

The singer of *Short Sharp Shocked* won't reveal her real name: "I've always been shocking!" The author replied that the "me shell-shocked" pun was too contrived to be a baptismal name. A little research and this book fearlessly reveals the shocking truth: the camp-fire revolutionary was born plain Karen Johnson.

The Shondells

Tommy James's backing band, named from singer Troy Shondell.

Shonen Knife

This Japanese female pop band noted that Bowie – after a Bowie knife – had been done. Cf ▷ David Bowie. Hence this near alternative: *shonen* means "boy" in Japanese.

Showaddywaddy

Many barber-shop groups, rockabilly and doo-wop bands used this backing line in songs: Showaddywaddy had most in mind Maurice Williams's composition *Little Darlin'*. Cf ▷ Sha Na Na.

Shredded Tweet

This came from the punchline of a joke: "What do you get when you cross a bird with a lawnmower?" Cf ▷ Lawnmower Deth. More jokes: ▷ The Cranberries, ▷ Moby Grape.

Shusha

Shusha Guppy, from Iran, is known now for her writing and son Darius; she found fame under her first name as a folk-singer.

The Sid Presley Experience

This South London act aimed to combine the energy of ▷ Sid Vicious of ▷ The Sex Pistols with the excitement of ▷ Elvis Presley and the exhilaration of ▷ The Jimi Hendrix Experience. Related: ▷ The Godfathers.

Sigue Sigue Sputnik

This 1980s British band were described as "the fifth generation of rock 'n' roll" and "the biggest hype of all time".

S.S.S. mastermind Tony James told the author it was inspired by a Moscow street ruffian gang he'd read about in *The International Herald Tribune*. "Russia's the place. It sounded like *A Clockwork Orange*." Subsequent perusals of the *Herald Trib* files have failed to find it. They rapidly became known as The Sputniks (artificial unmanned satellites launched by the U.S.S.R.). Related: ▷ The Sisters of Mercy. *A Clockwork Orange* inspired ▷ The Droogs and others.

The Silencers

The source was a 1966 film, intended as a spoof on James Bond. The ▷ Magazine-like ammunition reference was intended to "leave fans speechless".

Silverfish

Many acts have named after fish and insects. Silver fish are a colourless variety of goldfish, silverfish are bugs found living in mouldy places.

Simon And Garfunkel

Paul Frederic Simon and Art (short for Arthur) Garfunkel. Their earliest recordings (1957) were as the cartoon-like ▷ Tom and Jerry. Simon released material as Jerry Landis, Paul Kane, True Taylor and part of Tico And The Triumphs while Garfunkel tried Artie Garr before they reunited in 1964. At this stage Simon had some folk success of his own and they decided to risk record company fears about Garfunkel being too long to pronounce; they figured it was unusual enough to remember.

The decision was nearly overridden by record bosses, who preferred Simon And Garfield as the credit for the 1964 LP *Wednesday Morning, 3am*. This would now provide associations with another cartoon cat, Garfield. Simon recalled: "I was frightened people might think that we were comedians or something, but at least we were honest. I always thought it was a big shock to people when ▷ Bob Dylan turned out to be Bob Zimmerman." Cf ▷ Kris Kristofferson.

Nina Simone

She was born in North Carolina as Eunice Waymon; the simplification was made early in her career "after my name had been misheard one too many times".

Simple Minds

Their success would have been inconceivable under their original punk name ▷ Johnny And The Self-Abusers. However, it was chosen as a similarly self-depreciating laddish moniker. The source was ▷ David Bowie's *The Jean Genie*, about an astronaut "so simple-minded" he cannot drive his module.

The choice recalls many other bands who apparently don't take themselves too seriously: ▷ The Animals, ▷ Bad Brains, ▷ Barmy Army, ▷ The Blockheads, ▷ The Electric Prunes, The Emptyheads, ▷ The Immaculate Fools, ▷ Madness, ▷ Mental As Anything, The Vacuous Poseurs, ▷ The Zombies and many more ... Simple Minds rapidly became known as The Minds, while the rest of The Self-Abusers became ▷ The Cuban Heels. Also related: ▷ Set The Tone.

Simply Red

Mancunian vocalist Mick Hucknall's juvenilia bands were: Purple Haze, named after a ▷ Jimi Hendrix song; Joe Stalin's Red Star Radio Band, from guitarist Mark Reeder's fascination with the Soviet Union; Four Day Creep, after a

▷ Humble Pie number and ▷ The Frantic Elevators.

He soon insisted on being called Red: his most striking feature was unruly ginger hair, the butt of "ginger nut" school jests. It was an attempt to accentuate the positive; many tall, short or plump entertainers have defused criticism by becoming "long John", "shorty", "chubby" or "fats". "Red" had been used by many stars, including jazzmen Henry Allen and George Callender and actor Richard Skelton. It seemed amazingly uninventive – until Hucknall pointed out it's also a reference to colours of Manchester United and the U.K. Labour Party, whom he supported; and to the dominant hue in many paintings by his favourite artist Henri Matisse.

Hucknall was by now the star, employing former members of ▷ Durutti Column to back him, and coming up with names to reflect his leading role. There was Red And The Dancing Dead – used for their first gig – Just Red – for their second – All Red and Simply Red, punning on "simply read".

Hence the name. Hence the ruby in the tooth.

Some magazines have printed the apocryphal, amusing but wrong, story that Hucknall turned up at a noisy club and asked to sing solo. The owner asked for a billing. "Call me Red," said Mick. "What?" "Call me simply, Red." He was billed as Simply Red.

Robin McGibbon and Rob McGibbon add details in their 1993 biography *Simply Mick*.

Frank Sinatra
He was born Francis Albert Sinatra on 12 December 1915, the only child of Italian parents. At the christening the priest got confused and nuncupated the baby after godfather Frank Garrick. The child was supposed to share his father's prenomen Martin. Bandleader Harry James employed the young star in 1939 and wanted to call him Frankie Satin ... but thought again after he was giving a severe talking-to by Sinatra's forthright mother Dolly.

Name notes: Inspired: ▷ Danny Wilson, ▷ The Trash Can Sinatras. Daughter: Nancy Sinatra (▷ Boots). A headline said to be about Sinatra led to ▷ Frankie Goes To Hollywood. Nicknames: The Guv'nor, ▷ The Hoboken Canary, Ol' Blue Eyes and The Voice. Tribute band: Come Fly With Me (from a 1957 album title).

Single Bullet Theory
This 1990s band recalled an event which rocked the world years before: the assassination of President John F. Kennedy (1917–63). The "single bullet theory", accepted by the Warren Commission of inquiry, said alleged killer Lee Harvey Oswald was the only person involved; subsequent research cast doubt on this, while never disproving it. The name is "an invitation to think about official explanations". Cf ▷ The Dead Kennedys.

Siouxsie And The Banshees
▷ Bromley Contingent punkette Susan Janet Dallion, born 1957, was always known as Susy, although this came to be creatively spelled the American Indian way. She took the rest of the name from a 1970 horror film about a sixteenth-century magistrate and the ghosts of his past. Their early tunelessness resembled the howl of the Irish legendary banshees.

Name notes:
1. More American Indian influence: cf ▷ Cochise, ▷ Crazy Horse etc.
2. Related: ▷ Big In Japan, ▷ The Glove, ▷ The Opium Eaters, ▷ Steve Severin, ▷ The Slits.

Sir Bob
Tabloid-speak for Bob Geldof. As an Irish citizen he isn't strictly allowed to call himself Sir Robert Geldof; the knighthood is honorary.

Sir Douglas Quintet
Texan Doug Sahm was the original Southern Gentleman, but decided that U.S. groups looked outdated at the height of the British Invasion. He therefore became Sir Douglas and cultivated across the Atlantic music. Still, his strong southern accent quickly revealed his true origins. Similar motives explained the naming of ▷ Harpers Bizarre and many others.

Sirone
Norris Jones: a close anagram of his prenomen.

Sister George

An uncompromisingly lesbian stance is reflected in their name, from 1968 film *The Killing Of Sister George*. They said: "The symbolism was good and the plot breaks your heart." Cf ▷ Pansy Division.

Sister Ray

▷ Velvet Underground 1968 song covered by many bands including ▷ Joy Division and inspirational behind the naming of fellow Mancunians Sister Ray, a precursor to ▷ The Smiths.

Sister Sledge

This band from Pennsylvania chose this in preference to The Sledge Sisters. More real sisters: The Beverly Sisters, Fontane Sisters, Jones Girls, The King Sisters, The Lennon Sisters, The Lucas Sisters, McGuire Sisters, Paris Sisters, The Peters Sisters, The Pointer Sisters, Shepherd Sisters, and The Sinclair Sisters. Sisters only in name: The Coyote Sisters, The Davis Sisters, ▷ The Kaye Sisters, ▷ The Sisters of Mercy, Sisters Unlimited, and ▷ The Vernon Girls.

Sisters Of Mercy

The 1980 princes of darkness nuncupated from a doom-laden song about whoredom by Leonard Cohen. He was also thinking of the Catholic order of nuns of the same name – who have nothing in common with the goth-rock authors of *Vision Thing* with its "25 whores in the room next door". Founder ▷ Andrew Eldritch liked the contrast between sisters of sin and sanctity.

After a break-up in 1985, both halves toyed with the name The Sisterhood. The row was won by Eldritch, who released a record under this name – with a sleeve decked out in familiar Sisters black – then carried on under the original name. The other half became ▷ The Mission. Record company called: Merciful Release. Related: ▷ Sigue Sigue Sputnik. Like ▷ Echo And The Bunnymen, their first drummer was a machine, which was retained for far longer than Echo and called Doktor Avalanche.

Skatalites

... because they played ska music; an inexcusably dreadful pun.

Skid Row

The word skidroad was used in lumberjacking to refer to slippery or steep tracks for rolling logs to saw-mills. It has come to mean any disreputable district frequented by drifters.

Like ▷ Dire Straits, it describes the penniless state of many fledgling bands and has been used at least three times. The first started in Eire in 1968 and worked with Gary Moore; the second formed in New Jersey in 1986 and received help from ▷ Jon Bon Jovi; the third – unaware of the others – was a short-lived group from Seattle in September 1987 who found grunge fame as ▷ Nirvana.

The Skids

The uninitiated may see this vague moniker as a reference to skid row, car accidents, or moving fast. In fact (sometimes ignorance is best) it's a shock-punk reference to underpants stains. (Sorry, blame Richard Jobson.) More tastefully named spin-offs: ▷ The Armoury Show and ▷ Big Country.

Skinny Puppy

"In solidarity with animals treated cruelly and oppressed people everywhere. One day even a skinny puppy will grow up to be well fed and happy."

S-K-O

Made up of writers with the surnames Schuyler, Knobloch and Overstreet.

Skunk Anansie

Named from the skunk and spider characters in Jamaican fairy stories.

The Skyliners

They admired the Charlie Barnett song of the same name.

Slade

At a time when many other bands were long-haired sandal-wearers, this British Midlands act adopted the bovver boots and razored skulls of skinheads as a publicity stunt, calling themselves Ambrose Slade. "Slade" was from the name of a heath five miles north of their Wolverhampton base. Manager Chas Chandler abbreviated the name. Titles include *Slayed?* and *Slayed Alive*. Unrelated: ▷ Greenslade.

Slash

The ▷ Guns N' Roses guitarist was born Saul Hudson in Stoke-on-Trent, Staffordshire. The nickname Slash was bestowed by a family friend. "It wasn't because I had a problem going to the bathroom. It wasn't a bladder thing," insists Slash. It was because he was always dashing around.

Slaughter And The Dogs

British punk band with a canine obsession and harking back to ▷ their major influence David Bowie's *Diamond Dogs* album. Among those to have worked with them: ▷ Morrissey.

Sleeper

The outspoken Louise Wener says her band took the name from the title of a Woody Allen film. Their second choice was Starsky.

Slim Chance

▷ Led Zeppelin named because of a comment that such a band would go down like a lead balloon. The shambolic ▷ Faces star Ronnie Lane latched on to similar remarks. "I had high hopes. Nobody else had. They didn't think we had a chance," he told the *NME*.

The Slits

Billed as "the female equivalent of ▷ The Sex Pistols", this British all-girl bunch of minimalist punk rockers chose a feminist equivalent of the phallic name. Cf ▷ Hole. Related: ▷ The Raincoats.

Slowhand

Nickname for ▷ Eric Clapton, based on his measured guitar style on ballads. In response, his 1977 album was named *Slowhand* and includes the slower number *Wonderful Tonight* written for his wife Patti.

Sly And Robbie

Noel Dunbar, known as Sly after ▷ Sly And The Family Stone, and Robbie Shakespeare.

Sly And The Family Stone

Sylvester Stewart was first in The Stoners and known as Sly Stone, before coming together with other members of his family living in a Hollywood commune. Spin-offs: ▷ Graham Central Station, Little Sister Stone. Inspired: ▷ Sly Dunbar.

The Small Faces

The fashion leaders of the 1960s London mod scene were called "faces". Founders Steve Marriott and Ronnie Lane realised ▷ The Who – musicians trying to be mods – were the undisputed "faces" revered by West London mods. The Small Faces were mods trying to be musicians and hailed by East Londoners. They were "small" because they were less well-known – and from their physical stature. Related: ▷ The Faces, ▷ Foreigner, ▷ Humble Pie, ▷ The Rolling Stones, ▷ Slim Chance.

S*M*A*S*H

Dubbed "the punks most likely to" by the *Sunday Times*. Most likely to do what: revive punk maybe? The name and logo recalled the U.S. television series *S*M*A*S*H*, although they were keener to point out its similarity to their idols ▷ The Clash.

Smashing Pumpkins

Their contemporaries Smashing Orange recalled the slogan for Jaffa Cakes: "Love the smashing orange bit inside." There have been many reports that this band named after a remark about the fate of fruit hollowed out for Halloween jack-o-lantern candles. Still, in a rare early interview with *The Chicago Tribune*, songwriter Billy Corgan played down the surrealism: "It just came to me. It means absolutely nothing. It's the most ambiguous name I could think of."

Smiley Culture

Because Smiley, AKA David Emmanuel, used to chat up girls by asking them for a smile.

The Smithereens

This American band formed in 1980, so pre-dating the similarly named but musically different ▷ The Smiths in the U.K. "We heard the word on television and loved it."

Hurricane Smith

Musician Norman Smith, ▷ Beatles engineer and ▷ Pink Floyd producer, renamed before his 1972 solo success *Oh Babe, What Would You*

Say? He used a favourite film, the 1952 Nat Holt release *Hurricane Smith*.

The Smiths

The story begins and ends with ▷ Morrissey, lyricist and vocalist extraordinaire – he's avoided the description "singer". He was reacting against flashy fifteen-syllable concept names, searching instead for something as short and normal as possible – selecting the most common English patronym to put the spotlight on the words and music, not individual members.

Author Johnny Rogan recounts in *Morrissey And Marr – The Severed Alliance* that Morrissey met potential members Gary Farrell and Johnny Marr (born John Maher) in 1982 and produced a postcard on which he'd scrawled suggestions: "Smiths", "Smithdom" and "Smiths' Family". They all liked the first.

Rogan explains: "The name ... was an antidote to all those portentously grandiloquent group names such as ▷ Orchestral Manoeuvres In The Dark and ▷ Blue Rondo A La Turk. The Smiths implied a back-to-basics approach and unexotic Englishness that promised songs about real people in real situations, rather than some fantasy-island romance or techno-crazed incoherence."

There are many secondary "Smiths" associations, most coincidental or unconscious. For example, the suggestion is sometimes advanced it's a tribute to the victims of the Moors Murderers near the bands' Manchester homes. Sick sadistic killers Myra Hindley and Ian Brady were turned in to the police in the 1960s by David Smith, Hindley's brother-in-law. Morrissey wrote the song *Suffer Little Children* about the horrific tape-recorded killings. It closes the group's 1984 debut album. Stewart Copeland, later of ▷ The Police, was cited as a member of a totally unrelated 1978 band which was to be called ▷ The Moors Murderers; this would have been in keeping with determined-to-shock punk names such as ▷ Joy Division.

A second suggestion is that it's a tribute to fellow Mancunian Mark E. Smith of ▷ The Fall. Morrissey has denied the direct link. Thirdly, it recalled the famous 1960s Manchester club Mr Smiths in Brazil Street. Fourthly, it nicely summed up the Morrissey-Marr mutual admiration for punk poetess Patti Smith. Only the last of these is seen as being relevant.

The humdrum handle also had its bad points. It was prosaically boring, in contrast to Morrissey's poetic and Marr's musical brilliance. It concealed the Irish extraction of the act under an English tone. And even Morrissey's literary hero Oscar Wilde had observed: "Surely everyone prefers Hamilton and Buckingham to Jones or *Smith* ... " It was in line with other everyday indie-act names such as ▷ The Birthday Party and ▷ The Wedding Present, yet The Smiths' sound was unique.

Name notes: Morrissey asserted his genius after playing a small role in ▷ The Nosebleeds and ▷ Slaughter And The Dogs. The band's other members earlier worked with The Paris Valentinos, Freaky Party, White Dice, The Hoax, Victim and ▷ Sister Ray. Marr later played with Billy Bragg under the pseudonym Duane Tremelo and then formed ▷ Electronic. Spin-off: ▷ The Adult Net, ▷ Rough Trade.

Smokie

.. started as Kindness, became Smokey and changed spelling to avoid links with ▷ Smokey Robinson. The band's reluctance to say much on their appellation has reinforced suggestions that it's something to do with illicit substances.

The Smoking Mojo Filters

Taken from the lyric of ▷ Beatles song *Come Together*. This one-off September 1995 band contained the trio of ▷ Paul McCartney, Noel Gallagher of ▷ Oasis and ▷ Paul Weller, who performed the track for the *Help!* charity album.

Snafu

From World War II forces slang. "Snafu" is the standard response to questions on how things are going. It an acronym for "Situation Normal, All Fouled/Fucked Up". They insisted it meant "All Funked Up". Cf ▷ Fugazi.

Sniff 'N' The Tears

Ranks as one of the best collective names, with ▷ Telephone Bill And The Smooth Operators. Great album covers too; shame about the sub-▷ Dire Straits music.

S

Sniff The Glove

This was inspired by ▷ Spinal Tap's legendary LP *Smell The Glove*. As manifestly silly a command as the names Poke It With A Stick or Pass The Butter, You Bastard (- yes, two bands really used these). Unrelated: ▷ The Glove.

Snoop Doggy Dogg

When still a baby, Calvin Broadus was called Snoopy by his mother. As a stage name this could have led to problems with the Charles M. Schulz *Peanuts* series. He became Snoopy Doggy Dogg, after his cousin Tate Dogg.

Soft Boys

A dual reference to the late William Burroughs's experimental works *Soft Machine* – from 1961 – and *Wild Boys* – from 1962. It was intended as a comment on modern wimps but spawned unwelcome Mr Flopsy sexual jokes. Related: ▷ The Egyptians. More Burroughs: ▷ Dead Fingers Talk.

Soft Cell

Rolling into one "soft sell" and "padded cell". Fan club: Cell Mates. ▷ Marc Almond.

The Soft Machine

The title of a disturbing 1961 novel by William Burroughs, sequel to 1959's *The Naked Lunch*. It is about the effect of drugs on the soft machine of the body and brain. Leader Daevid Allen had worked with Burroughs in 1961 and decided to ask permission to lift the name. "I arranged to meet him on a street corner in Paddington. He [Burroughs] appeared and said: 'Can't see whaa not.'" Related: ▷ Caravan, ▷ Elton Dean, ▷ Matching Mole, ▷ Whole World. More Burroughs: ▷ Dead Fingers Talk etc.

The Soft Watches

Like ▷ Dali's Car, a reference to painter Salvador Dali (1904–89), whose dreamlike landscape at one stage had a leitmotif of melting clocks.

Soft White Underbelly

Early name for ▷ Blue Öyster Cult. Special award for one of the most revolting names of all time. According to one report inspired by Smorg the dragon in Tolkien's *The Hobbit*.

Soma

Named after the miracle pleasure-inducing drug named in Aldous Huxley's *Brave New World*. More bands with a Huxley influence: ▷ The Doors (with William Blake); ▷ Eyeless In Gaza (with Milton); and ▷ The Feelies (*Brave New World* and a children's game).

Sonic Youth

This New York band were named by Thurston Moore, who explained it was an amalgam of reggae act Big Youth and Sonic's Rendezvous Band, the post ▷ MC5 outfit led by Fred "Sonic" Smith from 1977 to 1979. Bassist Kim Gordon said it gave them the idea of first marrying reggae "toasting" with discordant rock, although their direction's always changing. Related: ▷ Ciccone Youth. Anagram: Touch Noisy.

Sonny And Cher

▷ Cher.

Sons Of Champlin

Not actually related. From a 1966 San Francisco underground paper's reference to veteran leader Bill Champlin and his "sons and younger disciples".

Sopwith Camel

A plane not an animal, although they titled one album *The Miraculous Hump*. Unrelated: ▷ Camel.

David Soul

Anglicisation of David Solberg. He became a musical star after his role as Ken Hutchinson in 1970s TV series *Starsky And Hutch*. The series inspired ▷ Lovebug Starski and ▷ Huggy Bear.

Soul II Soul

Selected by disc jockey Jazzie B (born Beresford Romeo), as the name of his audio company serving mobile discos. His shows became increasingly based on him rapping over records; it's impossible to say where the group began and the disc jockey ended. He said the choice was "spiritual" and based on the rap: "I gonna put my soul into your soul." Later it applied to enterprises covering fashion, records, management and videos. Cf ▷ Boyz II Men, ▷ Reel 2 Real.

Soundgarden

Named after a sculpture in Magnuson Park, Seattle, U.S.A. Douglas Hollis's art work *A Sound Garden*, dedicated in 1983, features wind turbines to make a constantly changing sound. Guitarist Kim Thayil said they named in 1984 after the "bleak and sublime" aeolian sculpture. "We thought of tougher and scarier names, like Bat Skull Fuck Dick." Soundgarden wasn't obvious. "It sounds like Pure Joy or Rain Parade. It fools people."

The Soup Dragons

These Britons – also known as The Soupies – quirkily named after the BBC series *The Clangers*, fondly remembered from childhood. It starred anteater-like creatures whose enemy was the wicked Soup Dragon.

SOUR

Means "Sound Of The Underground Records".

Sour Milk Sea

Sour Milk Sea was a Jackie Lomax song, released on ▷ The Beatles label ▷ Apple and written by ▷ George Harrison. This Oxford band were earlier called Tomato City (!) and worked with the young ▷ Freddie Mercury. Not a lot of people know that.

Southern Comfort

▷ Matthews Southern Comfort.

Southern Death Cult

▷ The Cult.

Southside Johnny And The Asbury Jukes

Singer Johnny Lyon started working with the then unknown ▷ Bruce Springsteen and future members of ▷ The E. Street Band. Like them, he was a kid from Asbury, New Jersey – but loved the blues style which began in the drinking dens on Chicago's South Side. Origins include the delightfully named Dr Zoom & The Sonic Boom and the Blackberry Booze Band.

Bob B. Soxx (And The Blue Jeans)

A bobby-soxer was any adolescent girl following in the 1930s-40s fashion of wearing bobby socks (white cotton, worn below the knee). Pop producer extraordinaire Phil Spector chose it to fit this vocal group's leader, previously Bobby Sheen.

The Space Cowboy

▷ Steve Miller.

Spandau Ballet

The members of Gentry and The Makers had become part of the London club scene recorded by writer and style guru Robert Elms. To cut a long story short, he'd seen "Spandau Ballet" written on a wall in the still-divided city of Berlin and offered it to them. Spandau is a suburb famous for its prison which housed former Nazi leader Rudolf Hess until his death.

Gary Kemp's group were criticised for abandoning their homeland to peddle fascist chic, but they said the new romantic image was a refreshing break from drab recession – and Islington Ballet didn't sound right.

Spanky And Our Gang

Movie producer Hal Roach gathered child actors for a series of slapstick routines under the series title *Our Gang* in the 1920s. These continued into the 1940s with new actors including the Billy Bunter-like George "Spanky" McFarland. Cut to the 1960s. Scene: Chicago. Elaine McFarlane was called Spanky because her name was like the film star and, secondly, she too was plump, later even joining ▷ The Mamas And The Papas as a replacement for the late Mama Cass. The films also inspired ▷ The (Young) Rascals.

Sparks

Idiosyncratic brothers Ron and Russell Mael were Halfnelson – until their zany records were likened to The Marx Brothers films.

Spearhead

Michael Franti, from San Francisco, was inspired by his hero King Shaka's redesign of Zulu weaponry. Related: ▷ The Disposable Heroes Of Hiphoprisy. Spear names: ▷ Burning Spear, ▷ Spear Of Destiny etc. Head names: ▷ Diamond Head, ▷ Motörhead etc.

Spear Of Destiny

The Spear of Destiny is a warhead with Biblical associations which was later supposedly owned by a string of dictators and despots. Leader Kirk Brandon said: "The name came about on a Scandinavian tour. Trevor Ravenscroft saw it in the papers. It's said that whoever holds the 'spear' holds the destiny of the world in his hands." Unflattering derivatives: SOD, Spear of Broccoli. Related: ▷ Theatre Of Hate. Cf ▷ Burning Spear.

The Specials

Coventry, once Britain's equivalent of motor city, produced this band which took up motoring inspiration as The Coventry Automatics. Their ska music brought them into contact with special one-off records manufactured for toasters and DJs – so suggesting the new name. Related: ▷ The Selecter, ▷ General Public and ▷ The Fun Boy Three.

Spice Girls

This U.K. all-girl band made up a power-pop phenomenon from 1996. Yet the five reportedly couldn't sing or dance when they first met Ian Lee, who ran charity-funded Trinity Studios in Woking, Surrey. At least that's Lee's account. He claims recent reports have all but "airbrushed out of existence" the group's early helpers in favour of emphasising the stars' own abilities. On the other hand, the feisty five, asserting their trademark "girl power", have insisted they were always talented and firmly in control of their destinies.

Lee said the idea was to form a female act to rival boy attractions ▷ Take That and ▷ East 17. The girls were chosen from 400 hopefuls and their combo was provisionally called Touch, though this wasn't liked much.

Lee said: "They got their name from Tim Hawes, who co-wrote a song with them and titled it *Sugar and Spice*. They were sitting around afterwards and he said: 'There's your name. It's perfect because you're a bunch of spicy bints.' They loved it." The band were already projecting an unblushing "sassy and sexy" image. It's interesting though, that in line with the title – about little girls being made of "sugar and spice and all things nice" – they could have been The Sugar Girls.

In fact Touch became, simply, Spice, and they were to launch as this. But just before *Wannabe* was released a rap artist called Spice 1 had a hit in the U.S.A. Record A&R Ashley Newton recalled: "It was an instant decision on their part. They say: 'You lot always call us the girls, so we'll be The Spice Girls.'"

By mid-1997 U.K. success for the Spices had reached the point that even Prime Minister-to-be Tony Blair was being asked on election phone-ins if he could name all the girls. They quickly acquired nicknames in tabloid coverage: Baby Spice (Emma Bunton – her innocent air, youth and pigtails), Posh Spice (Victoria Addams – her accent), Scary Spice (Mel B., or Melanie Brown – her spiky hair and outgoing manner), Sporty/Athletic Spice (Mel C., or Melanie Chisholm – keep-fit interests and gear) and Ginger Spice (Geri, Geraldine Halliwell – her hair colour). By the end of 1997, the five were busy trying to ditch the nicknames and "cartoon" image , according to reports.

They have inspired many lookalike tribute bands, including All Spice, Nice N' Spicey, Old Spice (grannies recalling the aftershave lotion), The Spiced Girls, The Spiceish Girls, The Spicey Girls and Wannabe Spice Girls. *If you wannabe my soundalike …*

Spinal Tap

A 1984 fictional rock satire film of this title led to its heroes becoming reality. It reveals their earlier names include: The Lovely Lads, The Originals, The Thamesmen, The Doppel Gang, Waffles and The Mud Below … but it fails to make much sense of spinal tap, the name of a medical operation. However, it's intimated The Lobotomies might have been preferable. Inspired: ▷ Sniff The Glove. Cf similar HM spoof ▷ Bad News.

The Spin Doctors

The idea came from a music tutor of guitarist Eric Schenkman, who said a political spindoctor distorts a newsworthy story; a cricket spin doctor tampers with the ball. The American pop act said it linked with records "spinning", "doctors" as in scores of other musical "medics" and the 1988 U.S. presidential election, during the course of which they formed.

The Spinners

This Liverpool folk group seemed to have named less from the spinning of records than their granny fans knitting in time to their bland harmony. Included here mainly to note their clash with ▷ The (Detroit) Spinners.

The Spinners (U.S.A.)

From the spinning of records (and nowadays CDs) of course; disco polished to perfection. A band worthy of the name: but they had to be known as The Detroit or Motown Spinners in Britain because of ▷ The Spinners.

Spirea X

Spin-off from ▷ Primal Scream, named after a B-side by the parent group.

Spirit

They started as Spirits Rebellious, after a book by Kahlil Gibran – the guru quoted by ▷ David Bowie and others. Related: ▷ Jo Jo Gunne.

SPK

Australian band whose name stood for System Planning Korporation. Later they added Sozialistisches Patienten Kollektiv and even Surgical Penis Klinik.

Split Enz

One early article said they first named Split Ends after a friend, who was always complaining about her hair. When they moved to Australia they included a reference to their New Zealand homeland by becoming E*nz*. Spin offs: ▷ The Mullanes, ▷ Crowded House, ▷ ALT.

Splodgenessabounds

Their comedian leader rejoiced in the moniker Max Splodge. "Explanation? We just are." He was aided and abetted by the improbably named Donkey Gut, Baby Greensleeves, Smacked Arse O'Reardon, Poodle, and Tone Tone The Garden Gnome.

Spooky Electric

▷ Prince maintained he had a dark side which showed itself on the electro-funk of *The Black Album* as Spooky Electric. The good side was ▷ Camille as shown on *Lovesexy* and elsewhere.

Spooky Tooth

A nonsense Scrabble combination (like ▷ Foghat) which Gary Wright preferred to earlier name Art. Related: ▷ Humble Pie, ▷ Mott The Hoople, ▷ The VIPs.

SPOTS

▷ The Sex Pistols trying to keep a discreetly low profile, for once. Spotty acronym for: "Sex Pistols On Tour Secretly".

Dusty Springfield

She was born Mary O'Brien in Hampstead, London. Dusty was reportedly from her cat, Springfield her mother's maiden name. She was first in the Springfields with her brother Tom.

Bruce Springsteen

Yup, the U.S. superstar's name, hair and teeth are his own. He was born Bruce Frederick Joseph Springsteen. Nicknames include ▷ The Boss and ▷ Brooce. Groups include The Castiles, Earth, Child, Steel Mill, Dr Zoom & The Sonic Boom, The E Street Band and ▷ MUSE. ▷ Southside Johnny also sent greetings from Asbury Park.

Squeeze

These Britons picked their name from a hat – and nobody admitted making the suggestion. Several were ▷ The Velvet Underground fans so the commonest theory is that it's a reference to the 1972 LP cut by an ersatz Underground kept going by Doug and Billy Yule after the departure of ▷ Lou Reed and others. Still, "squeeze" is sometimes used by Cockney types as slang for "sweetheart".

Stamford Hillbillies

Another hilly part of London seizing on the *Beverly Hillbillies* joke. Cf ▷ Notting Hillbillies, ▷ Muswell Hillbillies. Related: ▷ Guns 'N' Moses.

Alvin Stardust

The British singer was born Bernard Jewry but failed to make it big as the leader of the American-sounding Shane Fenton And The Fentones. A ▷ Gary Glitter-like calculated change of image – with leather trousers, silly shades and stuck-on sideburns – was inspired by ▷ David Bowie's Ziggy Stardust. The strategic name switch shot him to stardom.

Ziggy Stardust

Ziggy was the hero of ▷ David Bowie's 1972 album *The Rise And Fall Of Ziggy Stardust And The Spiders Of Mars*. "The ultimate rock creation", he's a plastic, disposable, self-destructive shooting star who lives fast and dies young in a world which knows it has only five years left.

"Ziggy" came from a clothes shop Bowie passed on the train one day. It also reminded him of his friend ▷ Iggy Pop. "Stardust" came from The Legendary Stardust Cowboy who was on Mercury Records at the same time as Bowie. It did not come from a Hoagy Carmichael song, as some music papers have wrongly reported: the author has this direct from Mr Bowie himself.

The character and creator inevitably became confused – Ziggy's hopes for stardom were Bowie's too. So when Bowie announced the character had played his "last show" many thought he was announcing his own retirement. Inspired: ▷ Alvin Stardust.

Jamie Starr

One of many *alter egos* used by ▷ Prince.

Ringo Starr

The ▷ Beatles' grandfather had the patronym Parkin but renamed on impulse. Richard "Ritchie" Starkey found the new surname useful because it would abbreviate easily to give him a stage name in Rory Storm And The Hurricanes: his drum solos were introduced as "Star Time". But he was usually called Rings/Ringo because of his fondness for ostentatious finger jewellery. Hence the tortuous plot of 1965 film *Help!*

Name notes: He was introduced as Billy Shears on *A Little Help From My Friends*. Ringo sounds like "apple" in Japanese (▷ Apple). Sprog note: son called Zak Starkey.

Starry Eyed And Laughing

This British act – with stars in their eyes – reverentially named from a phrase in ▷ Bob Dylan's 1964 long lyric *Chimes Of Freedom*.

Starship

▷ Jefferson Airplane, ▷ Jefferson Starship.

Lovebug Starski

New Yorker Keven Smith renamed after the *Starsky And Hutch* TV show as it became popular – and ten years later went on to have hits as Lovebug Starski. The 1970s cops-and-robbers programme, starring ▷ David Soul, also inspired ▷ Huggy Bear.

Status Quo

In 1967 this British band considered The Spectres (dropped over confusion with producer Phil Spector) and Traffic (soon overtaken by another act) before their manager found Status Quo, Latin for "the present position". The unpretentious group saw it as a label without special significance and nearly truncated it to The Quo when they ditched 1960s psychedelia for 1970s three-chord rock. Spin-off: ▷ Partners In Crime. Inspired: ▷ Quiet Riot. Tribute band: Fake Us Quo.

Tommy Steele

Another of the stable of 1950s/1960s U.K. pop stars groomed by promoter and entrepreneur ▷ Larry "Shillings And Pence" Parnes. Steele was born Thomas Hicks. It is usually said the hard surname was suggested by PR man John Kennedy and Parnes.

Steeleye Span

Ashley Hutchings, ex ▷ Fairport Convention, took the suggestion of his friend Martin Carthy, who remembered a wagoner's name in the traditional song *Horkston Grange*. Spin-off: ▷ The Albion Band.

The Steel Magnolias

The term describes any woman with a hard disposition concealed under a soft appearance. It was famously applied to the wife of U.S. President Jimmy Carter. *The Steel Magnolias* was also a play and a 1989 film – both written by Robert Harling. This band liked its contradictory feel, echoing ▷ Iron Butterfly.

Steely Dan

Another *recherché* reference to William Burroughs. New Yorker singer-songwriters

Donald Fagen and Walter Becker chose it for a musical project which consisted of themselves plus a constantly changing set of session players. The Steely Dan is mentioned in the 1959 novel *The Naked Lunch*. It's a steam-powered, milk-squirting, extra-large dildo – used by revengeful lesbians to bugger males. The subject is surprising given that Steely Dan made tastefully sophisticated music.

Name notes: in their formative years, they were Leather Canary, used the superbly modest name The Bad Rock Group and backed the clean-cut ▷ Jay And The Americans. Inspired: ▷ Deacon Blue. More Burroughs: ▷ Dead Fingers Talk etc.

Steppenwolf

Der Steppenwolf was a novel by Hermann Hesse (1877–1962). This band thought it fitted the East European background of vocalist John Kay, who was born Joachim Krauledat and escaped from East Germany while still a child. And they could have hardly recorded *Born To Be Wild* under their previous name, The Sparrows.

Stereolab

By 1990, when this band formed, we'd already had enough tracks sampling: "This is a journey into stereophonic sound." Stereolab was a name taken from 1960s test records, particularly those by the hifi section of Vanguard Records.

Cat Stevens

Of Greek extraction, London born Steven Georgiou combined his first name with Cat, a fashionable 1960s term. His conversion to the Muslim faith resulted in his retirement from western pop and a change to Yusef Islam.

Rod Stewart

… was born Roderick David Stewart. At 20 he became known as Rod The Mod, after appearing in a TV documentary of the same name about the life of "a typical mod". Anagram: Rated Worst. Cf ▷ The Faces, ▷ Hair Nose And Teeth.

Stiff Little Fingers

Band from Belfast, Ireland, who started the Rigid Digit label. It wasn't a reference to aliens in 1960s TV science fiction series *The Invaders*, as sometimes reported. They were inspired by an obscure B-side by ▷ The Vibrators, which included the lyric: "If it wasn't for your stiff little fingers nobody would know you are dead."

Stiltskin

One-hit wonder 1990s rock band named after the fairy talk of wicked Rumplestiltskin, who is undone when his name is guessed. Trivia note: Rumpled Foreskin was used by two punk bands, one in America and one in Britain.

Sting

Meeting this superstar, the author found he could happily give a full answer to questions from journalists about his name. But I'm told that more recently he simply suggests reporters haven't done their homework before daring to interview him and could we now get back on to discussing the brilliant new album, please?

Turn to the dictionary and what do you get? "STING, noun, verb. 1. Sharp-pointed section of insect etc used for defence or attack …" Relevance to 1970s-90s rock?

The answer we gain from the man himself is this. Twenty-one-year-old British primary school teacher Gordon Sumner, born in Newcastle, found his stage moniker during his time as a part-time jazz bassist/singer for various local bands.

"It was just a joke," he says. "An accident." The young Gordon habitually used to wear a horizontally striped yellow and black jumper: it was all he could afford. This made him look like a bee or a wasp, and the nickname was suggested by local jazz player Gordon Soloman.

This might come as a surprise to those journalists who have speculated that the pseudonym must be profound and deep-meaning given Sting's serious tone. Among the incorrect but amusing theories peddled in explanation are the following:
1. It's a reference to Scott Joplin and *The Sting*;
2. It was picked as an insect tag like ▷ The Crickets and ▷ The Beatles;
3. It's a comment on being stung by cupid's arrows or love, as in Elvis Presley's *I Got Stung*;
4. It's a "criminal" reference, with a "sting" meaning a bank robbery.

▷ The Police, ▷ The Blue Turtles. Unflattering derivative: Stink.

S

The Stone Poneys

Linda Ronstadt-led folk trio named after veteran U.S. blues singer Charley Patton's *(Stone) Pony Blues*.

The Stone Roses

Great pop questions of the 1980s: What is an ▷ Aztec Camera? A ▷ Prefab Sprout? And just *what* is a stone rose?

Here's the answer.

Their long evolution started in 1979–80 when Manchester acts The Patrol and The Mill started operations. Four years later they evolved into English Rose, which was the title of their favourite song – an acoustic track on ▷ The Jam's 1978 album *All Mod Cons*. Another two years passed and they became The Stone Roses, inspired by ▷ The Rolling Stones. The Roses later refused to play warm-up gigs for Jagger's cohorts on tour: "They should be supporting us!" The whole had a light-heavy/ surreal/ ▷ Led Zeppelin/ ▷ Iron Butterfly quality.

By 1989 they had recorded an acclaimed debut album. Its follow up arrived in 1994 and the Roses were history by 1997: rare and slow-flowering blooms.

Stone Temple Pilots

Or how the record label signed a band with a logo that resembled the STP oil company's.

"Hey guys, we're a bit worried about the logo: STP might not like it. Say, what does it stand for? Maybe we could use that instead."

"Oh yeah. Forgot to tell ya. It means Shirley Temple's Pussy." Cue mass corporate heart attacks.

Much to publicists' relief all round, the group became Stone Temple Pilots. Scott Weiland's tones reminded some people of ▷ Peal Jam's Eddie Vedder, leading to some unflattering derivatives: Clone Temple Pilots and Stone Temple Pirates.

Stone The Crows

The exclamation gained a secondary meaning as "stoned" came to mean intoxicated. This Scottish band was first called Power, but reportedly renamed after a very short review which read simply: "-less". (There was an even shorter review for ▷ Yes, which was simply: "No".)

The Stooges

The name was suggested while the band, in suitably stoned disarray, watched a programme by the Three Stooges American comedy troupe. Their lead singer therefore became Iggy Stooge, and, later, ▷ Iggy Pop. Related: ▷ Destroy All Monsters, ▷ Tin Machine. Inspired: ▷ Raw Power.

Stormbringer

Switzerland has brotherly love, 500 years of democracy and peace and what does it produce? The cuckoo clock – oh, and ▷ Yello, plus this hard rock band with a name filched from their greatest influence, ▷ Deep Purple. The Purps recorded a 1974 album of this name. "It was a hard choice between this and other Purple titles," they told *Soundcheck* magazine. "We also liked Machine Head." Cf ▷ Machine Head.

The Stormsville Shakers

British rock band whose name was inspired by Americans Johnny And The Hurricanes.

Stormy Weather

The quintet from Indiana formed at the end of the 1960s. They admired The Spaniels, another local act, and named after one of their songs because "it's a title of action".

Strange Cruise

After ▷ Steve Strange's time in ▷ Visage he attempted a comeback in Strange Cruise. This was named because he was working with Wendy Wu, ex ▷ The Photos, and by then renamed Wendy Cruise.

The Strangeloves

The cue for the headline-grabbing name came from the controversial 1963 film *Dr Strangelove (Or How I Learned To Stop Worrying And Love The Bomb)*. The band created three characters to tie in with this: Giles, Miles and Niles Strange. In the Stanley Kubrick film, the star Peter Sellers also played three parts.

Steve Strange

Welshman Steve Harrington got his name after moving to London where his behaviour and way-out clothes made him one of the leaders of the New Romantic movement. ("My dear, I look strange because I am on stage 24 hours a day ... ") The name recalls Doctor Stephen Strange, a Marvel Comic figure who starred in the 1978 TV film *Doctor Strange*. ▷ Moors Murderers, ▷ Strange Cruise, ▷ Visage. Unflattering derivative: Nobby Normal.

The Stranglers

This U.K. band originally called themselves The Guildford Stranglers in a typical let's-be-controversial move. It was a reference to the notorious serial killer who struck many times in the Surrey area. The group was formed near Guildford in 1974. Spoof band: ▷ The Men In Black.

Strawberry Alarm Clock

U.S. West Coast band who left behind them one massive hit – the anthem *Incense And Peppermints* and their appellation, one of the best relics of the psychedelic era.

They started as Three Sixpence – like many other American bands of the time trying to pretend they were English. As for the later moniker, strawberries were big in the summers of love in the 1960s. It wasn't a tribute to ▷ The Beatles' 1967 single *Strawberry Fields Forever*, which came later. The rest was caused by an alarm going off as they discussed a new name. It sounded better than ▷ The Soft Watches.

Strawberry Switchblade

Glaswegian glamour dolls with a colourful image recalling psychedelia of ▷ The Strawberry Alarm Clock for their 1980s success.

Strawbs

One encyclopedia wrongly says this was a reference to *Strawberry Fields Forever* by ▷ The Beatles. The strawberries on their record covers give the clue. It was short for The Strawberry Hill Boys, after the area near London where they first worked.

The Stray Cats

Another variant on the popular "cat" name. There have in fact been at least two groups with this moniker. One, a 1970s outfit, featured Keith Moon of ▷ The Who and David Essex; the other was the 1980s U.S. rockabilly act – Lee Rocker, Brian Setzer and Slim Jim Phantom. Both Stray Cats have one thing in common: production by ▷ Dave Edmunds, who also produced ▷ The Pole Cats.

Streetwalkers

Former ▷ Family men Roger Chapman and Charlie Whitney unimaginatively named Chapman Whitney to record an LP more interestingly entitled *Streetwalkers*. They soon reconsidered.

The Strolling Bones

Nickname for the veteran ▷ Rolling Stones based on their touring and thin visages – especially those of ▷ The Glimmer Twins.

Strontium 90

This band is famous mainly as a precursor to ▷ The Police containing ▷ Sting. Strontium 90 is a dangerous chemical which can collect in bones because of fall-out. Several years later, they joined with ▷ Hawkwind under the name The Radio Actors to record a protest song *Nuclear Waste* featuring the refrain: "Strontium 90, I wanna live till 1990."

Strumboli

▷ Joe Strummer's volcanic temper, which could produce explosions to rival Italy's Mount Stromboli, led to the nickname by the time he joined ▷ The Pogues. ▷ The Clash.

Joe Strummer

Born John Mellors, he got his name from a combination of "Joe Cool" and his ukulele playing as a London busker. ▷ The Clash, ▷ Strumboli.

The Style Council

Paul Weller's band after ▷ The Jam, formed with ex ▷ Merton Parka member Mick Talbot. The moniker reflected an interest both in style and democracy – Weller had moved to the left and early gigs were called Council Meetings. The politically conscious 1984 single *Soul Deep* was recorded with an amalgam of other musicians, including Jimmy Ruffin and Junior, and therefore credited to The Council Collective.

Poly Styrene

She was plain Marion Elliot until she became a

punk icon – complete with braces on her teeth and the freshly minted name. The ▷ X-Ray Spex vocalist said it was a protest against "plastic artificial living". Society was turning people into "pieces of styroform".

Styx

This is not a mis-spelling of "sticks" but a reference to *The Inferno* by Dante Alighieri (1265–1321). This is part of *La Divina Commedia*, which also inspired the band ▷ The Divine Comedy later.

The Italian's epic poem mentions the mythical River Styx, one of the dark waterways of the underworld Hades. The story reflected the band's music, ranging from ambitiousness to pretentiousness. Spin-off: ▷ Damned Yankees.

The Subterraneans

Their name recalls underground movements and trains, the underworld, darkened clubs and ▷ The Velvet Underground. It actually came from the same source as ▷ The Dharma Bums and ▷ Elmerhassell. That is, Jack Kerouac (1922–1969), described as "the new Buddha of American prose". His books include *The Subterraneans* as well as his influential *On The Road*.

Suede

British band of the 1990s whose name: follows the 1990s fashion for short monikers; ties in with tradition of "fabric" names seen by dozens of groups (▷ The Chiffons, ▷ Felt etc); sums up singer Brett Anderson's slightly "swayed" appearance and androgynous covers. Unflattering derivative: Pseud. They have had to be known as London Suede in the U.S.A. because of another band called Suede.

The Sugarcubes

The first album by ▷ The Jesus And Mary Chain was described by one reviewer as "an innocent little sugarcube just waiting for the tongue." So this band's name sounds innocent, suggesting sweet music, but as many drug users know, LSD is often taken soaked up into sugarcubes. They included the later solo star ▷ Björk.

The Sugarhill Gang

Collection of U.S. rap artists assembled by Sylvia Robinson and named after her label Sugarhill Records. This was in turn taken from the Sugar Hill area of New York.

Suicide

… It might have ruled out much of the airplay this U.S. new wave band deserved, but they reasoned it was more interesting than life. Not "death rock" from the ▷ Megadeth school, as the name suggests.

Sultans Of Ping FC

According to *The Big Issue*, a combination of the Subbuteo soccer game and part-reference to *Sultans Of Swing*, a track by ▷ Dire Straits. Pop music put in the blender, with a smattering of ▷ Stray Cats, ▷ The Buzzcocks and ▷ Happy Mondays.

Donna Summer

Née LaDonna Gaines, she became LaDonna Sommer after her marriage to Austrian actor Helmut Sommer (which later ended in divorce). She simplified this before shooting to fame. ▷ The Queen Of Disco.

Sundance Kids

They loved *Butch Cassidy And The Sundance Kid*, the 1969 film starring Paul Newman and Robert Redford.

Super Furry Animals

Welsh rock 1990s-style. Frontman Gruff (pronounced Griff) Rhys says enigmatically: "The name came out of something in a comic."

Supergrass

The hairy Oxford would-be superhero trio of the 1990s started under the misleading moniker The Jennifers. They've claimed Supergrass came from a newspaper headline about big-time criminal informers who get lighter sentences in return for information on their former buddies. However, this may be just a smokescreen: many fans assume it to be a coded reference to cannabis.

Supertramp

They came together under patronage of Dutch millionaire sugar daddy Stan Miesegaes and so began as Daddy. Supertramp was suggested by sax-playing recruit Dave Winthrop to suit their initially super-scruffy image. In 1969, Tramp was a fashionable word for everything from clothes shops to clubs. It was also a reference to a 1910 autobiography by British writer W.H. Davies, *The Autobiography of A Supertramp*, relating his experiences of abandoning wealth and roaming the U.S.A. incognito as a down-and-out. Cf ▷ The Trammps.

The Supremes

This female group called themselves The Primettes, after The Primes, whom they backed. After The Primes went solo in 1960, record company Motown ordered a name change. In fact The Primes soon became ▷ The Temptations, so it could have stayed. About that time the "-ettes" suffix was used by many contemporary female singing acts, the "ette" meaning small. Cf ▷ The Ronettes etc.

All of the trio had doubts about Motown's suggestion of The Supremes. Rapid success ensured it stayed even though Ballard didn't, quitting in 1967 to be replaced by the splendidly named Cindy Birdsong from ▷ LaBelle. After Diana Ross became the new boss they became Diana Ross and the Supremes. Ross's parents had wanted her to be called Diane; she was incorrectly called Diana on her birth certificate.

Screaming Lord Sutch

Plain David Sutch, a British commoner but never a common man, claims "screaming" came about from his singing style – which has reminded many of American star ▷ Screamin' Jay Hawkins. Lord was added in 1968 on account of his trademark top hat. He told the author: "I didn't see anything wrong with making myself a Lord. I later tried to change my name to Margaret Thatcher, but I was told it would be too confusing when I am elected a member of parliament." His band The Savages featured future stars of ▷ Deep Purple and ▷ Led Zeppelin.

SVT

Former ▷ Hot Tuna and ▷ Jefferson Airplane member Jack Casady wanted to play music which would "get hearts racing and blood pressure raised". He therefore named after supra ventricular tachycardia – and only discovered later it was an undesirable medical condition. "By then it was too late."

Swan Arcade

Northern English band who named after a lost and much-missed landmark in Bradford.

Swansway

This Brummie band named from the novel sequence *A La Recherche Du Temps Perdu*, best translated as *In Search Of Lost Time* rather than *Remembrance Of Times Past*. It was written by Frenchman Marcel Proust (1871–1922) and published between 1913 and 1927. The first volume is 1913's *Du Côté de Chez Swann*, translated as *Swann's Way*. Spin-off: ▷ Milk.

SWAPO Singers

An offshoot of the political movement. Stands for "South West Africa People's Organisation".

Sweet

Wainwright's Gentlemen became Sweetshop became Sweet. No relation to Bitter Sweet. Later re-formed as The New Sweet, Brian Connolly's Sweet etc – with legal action to prevent some other ex-members using the name. Also worked with ▷ Paddy Goes To Holyhead. They said they wanted to appeal to young people like sweets or candy. "Bubblegum pop – with fruity lyrics," said one advert.

Sweethearts Of The Rodeo

From the influential countryish album by ▷ The Byrds called *Sweetheart Of The Rodeo*. ▷ Flying Burrito Brothers.

The Swinging Blue Jeans

In the beginning, there were the Genes, who gave their name to cotton jeans. The denim clothing became fashionable and his group added the trendy swinging sixties tag while dressing the part to win commercial endorsements.

David Sylvian

Chosen during his early ▷ Japan days as more exotic than his own name, David Batt – hardly suitable for someone dubbed "the world's most beautiful man". It was a tribute to Sylvain Sylvain (note spellings) of ▷ The New York Dolls. His work with Ryuichi Sakamoto was credited to Sylvian Sakamoto. His brother Steve, also in Japan, became Steve Jansen. ▷ Rain Tree Crow.

S

Tad

Not from "tad" as in "slightly" for example "a tad loud". "Tad" as in guitarist "Tad Doyle".

TAFKAP

The Artist Formerly Known As ▷ Prince.

Take That

The teen idols fitted the pattern of ▷ Boyzone, ▷ Bros, ▷ News Kids On The Block and ▷ East 17 by being critically reviled while saying "take that" to the media by enjoying considerable commercial success. The men didn't know but the little girls understood.

Their air-brushed image carefully concealed any potentially embarrassing facts such as the other names they used: the group's publicists merely said they went through "a telephone book's worth of suggestions". Gary Barlow met Mark Owen in 1987 and three years later formed a group called The Cutest Rush. Jason Orange and Howard Donald were break-dancers in a troupe called Street Beat.

The appellation's source was ▷ Madonna. The official version says "someone caught sight" of a tabloid newspaper headline: "Take That And Party". Owen said: "We all really liked it, so we called ourselves Take That And Party, but we dropped the Party bit when we heard about the American group The Party." It sounded as if it was lifted from a cartoon or a *Tom And Jerry* show. Cf ▷ Wham! a decade before. The full phrase was finally used as the title of their first album, released in August

1992. This "nice" account is given in the Oliver Books 1994 biography *Take That*.

The less polite account is given by Keith Manning of British agency PA News: "The name comes from a Madonna video, where she grabs at her crotch and shouts at the audience: Take That. It might have been an unlikely choice for five clean-cut working class lads but the band's young audiences would not have guessed its inspiration." The five-man group was down to four by 1995 and it was all over the following year.

Talking Heads

This American act – makers of exceptional music in the 1980s – said a fellow graduate of the Rhode Island School of Design, Wayne Zieve, saw "talking heads" in New York's *TV Guide*. It's televisionspeak for a close-up of an onscreen speaker. David Byrne liked it for a myriad of reasons, including his hope the group would communicate – while, ironically, such shows are among the cheapest forms of conventional televised entertainment.

Byrne rejected other contemporary collective appellations, such as The Portable Crushers, The Vague Dots, The Tunnel Tones, Bizardi, The Artistics, The Artistic Blocks – and even The Autistics. He also considered The Beans and The Human Beans. (Unrelated to a Dave Edmunds group or 1960s U.S.A. garage act The Human Beanz.)

Like other "serious" artists, they wanted something which didn't tie them down to one kind of music. Years later, Chris Frantz said in the liner notes to a Talking Heads retrospective album that when he had a Talking Heads tee-shirt made, the first person he met on New York's trendy Bleecker Street said: "That's a terrible name!" This strong reaction convinced him it was right.

Hence the name. Hence "The Name Of This Band Is Talking Heads".

The combo, colloquially called The Heads, disbanded in 1991 as Byrne went solo. In 1996 a re-formed version was billed as ▷ The Heads, after some reported disagreements on ownership.

Name notes: Spin-offs: ▷ Bonzo Goes To Washington, ▷ Tom Tom Club. Inspired: ▷ Radiohead. ▷ Brian Eno released a solo record called *King's Lead Hat* during his time working with them – the title's an anagram of Talking Heads.

Talk Talk

Mark Hollis's first efforts were with his band The Reaction who recorded a rough track, *Talk Talk* which became their "theme tune". He later came to regret the double name which reinforced unwelcome comparisons with ▷ Duran Duran, who initially shared the same label and producer.

Talulah Gosh

This name is based on a *NME* headline about Clare Grogan of ▷ Altered Images. Clare was sometimes known as Talulah, a name shared with Tallulah Bankhead – although note spelling.

Tamla Motown

America's hit-making record label of the 1960s began as two separate companies. Tamla was originally to be called Tammy, after the Ray Evans song from the 1957 movie *Tammy And The Bachelor*. Oscar Brodney was already writing more Tammy films, so this was scuppered. See also ▷ Motown.

The Tams

They were on a budget and couldn't afford stage clothes; inexpensive tam hats seen in a thrift store provided them with an image and name.

Tannahill Weavers

Named after the textile community in the Scottish town where they lived. Cf ▷ Paper Lace. Unrelated: ▷ The Weavers.

A Taste Of Honey

From this band's "sweet music"; the original idiom, based on a Biblical quote, has come to mean to sample anything appealing, especially sexual: as in English writer Shelagh Delaney's play of the same name.

Tattooed Love Boys

From the title of a 1980 ▷ Pretenders song. Its Chrissie Hynde lyric includes the put-down: "Stop snivelling/You're gonna make some plastic surgeon a rich man."

Bernie Taupin

The man who writes the words for ▷ Elton John. ▷ The Brown Dirt Cowboy.

Tea And Symphony

British Midlands act with a dubious play on "tea and sympathy", chosen in part as a tribute to their close neighbours ▷ ELO.

The Teardrop Explodes

Julian Cope was looking for a name for his psychedelic group A Shallow Madness when he chanced upon an old D.C. Marvel comic, *Prince Namor*, number 77, June 1971, to be exact. The cartoon says : "Filling the wintered glades of Central Park with an unearthly whine ... painting the leaf-bare branches with golden fire ... THE TEARDROP EXPLODES!! ... for echoing seconds the sky is filled with silver webs of lightning – and, with the glow's fading, a new menace is revealed!"

Very poetic for a comic that was originally intended to be read, thrown away and forgotten. In an interview, Cope said most hip bands of the time had "cold" names and it was "warmer, more colourful, emotional." Related: ▷ Dalek I, ▷ Echo And The Bunnymen, ▷ The Mystery Girls, ▷ Wah! May have inspired ▷ Aztec Camera.

Tears For Fears

U.S. psychologist Arthur Janov was the pioneer of Primal Therapy, a technique set out in

T

Prisoners Of Pain. It suggests using "tears for fears" – releasing emotion to relieve depression. The strong emotions of these British new-wavers are thus supposed to help the anxieties of the performers – and listeners. It was more than just a name, reflecting their lyrical interest. Their 1983 debut LP was called *The Hurting* while their second, 1985's *Songs From The Big Chair*, is a reference to a girl with 16 different personalities sitting in a psychiatrist's chair.

Roland Orzabal, the songwriting psychobabble buff, was born Orzabal de la Quintana. Janov also influenced ▷ Primal Scream.

Teenage Fanclub

This Scottish band started as The Boy Hairdressers, then chose to make a barbed comment on the great teen idols of the past.

Teenage Heads

Toronto quartet named after 1971 album by ▷ The Flamin' Groovies.

Telephone Bill And The Smooth Operators

The better-than-average collective name came from the song *Ring Your Bell Well*.

Television

This New York group started in 1971 as The Neon Boys, revamping in 1973 as guitarist Thomas Miller reinvented himself as ▷ Tom Verlaine. At a meeting to discuss renaming, they quickly rejected Goo Goo and The Liberteens. Television was ▷ Richard Hell's suggestion and Verlaine backed it with great enthusiasm. It was only later that the others realised it fitted his new initials. Verlaine was inspired by literature but was moving away from serious poetry, which he had reluctantly decided that "hardly anyone read", to the mass media.

Meanwhile second guitarist Richard Lloyd told Clinton Heylin, in *From The Velvets To The Voidoids*: "We wanted something that was really tinkly and mechanical and always there ... So you lose your consciousness about it. Television's in every home in America. It's so obtrusive, its unobtrusive."

Name notes: Inspired ▷ Elevation, ▷ The Frantic Elevators, ▷ Friction and ▷ Marquee Moon. Related: ▷ The Heartbreakers, ▷ The Voidoids and ▷ The Waitresses. Cf ▷ The Box, ▷ Monochrome Set and ▷ Terrorvision.

Temple Of The Dog

A one-off album project involving members of ▷ Mookie Blaylock and ▷ Soundgarden. It was tribute to the late Andrew Wood, vocalist with Mookie predecessors Mother Love Bone. His death was drug-related. The name's a line in his song *Man Of Golden Words*.

The Temptations

This massively successful band from Michigan was made up of members of The Distants, The Questions and The Primes. They rejected The Elegants when they heard of a white act of the same appellation. Some reports say that another possibility was ▷ The Miracles; but the ▷ Motown label had already signed an act of this name – ▷ Smokey Robinson's band.

The final choice was arrived at during a brain storming session. According to Jay Warner's *Billboard Book Of American Singing Groups* Otis Williams hit on the word while standing on the porch of Motown's Hitsville office with label employee Billy Mitchell.

One of their backing bands became ▷ Rose Royce; another – previously the Primettes – became ▷ The Supremes.

10CC

Many people probably have bought 10CC records without knowing what this refers to: a small car engine? The combined size of their brains? The answer is it originally referred to nothing at all as dreamt up – literally – by ▷ Jonathan King. The bustling businessman told a music paper that he had gone to bed, perchance to dream, slept on the subject, and woke up with a very firm idea. This account led to suggestions that 10CC is a reference to the average amount of sperm ejaculated during orgasm. It is said that King chose to make the figure up to a round ten, slightly more than the usually accepted nine cubic centimetres. The conceit of it.

This theory is credible because King is a man not known for his modesty. The band included one Lol Creme; similar references had come from ▷ Cream and ▷ The Lovin' Spoonful.

Still, King later said it was simply short and meaningless.

Related: ▷ Frabjoy and Runcible, ▷ Godley Creme. ▷ The Mindbenders and ▷ Wax.

1066 Gaggle O'Sound

Michael Stipe solo project in the early days of ▷ R.E.M.; named because 1066 is his "favourite year in history".

10,000 Maniacs

Several articles have incorrectly cited the name's source. It was not from a B-movie called *Ten Thousand Clowns*. It was actually mis-remembered from another flick called *2,000 Maniacs*.

Ten Years After

Even those people who remember Alvin Lee's mind-blowing solo on *Goin' Home* at 1969's Woodstock may not be able to explain the name. Lee gives 1956 as the date "when rock became the dominant form of popular music". While this is arguable, it was the time of ▷ Elvis Presley's first big successes which inspired Lee to form The Jaybirds then Quickmire. By 1966, a decade on, his sound had moved from blues to straight rock: *hence the name*. The band re-formed in the 1970s as Ten Years Later.

Terrorvision

Taken from the title of a 1960s horror film; the flip-side of ▷ Television, a protest against the violence of the small screen, and wry comment on how it rules the lives of many.

Tesla

These Californians paid tribute to unjustly neglected Yugoslav-American electrical engineer Nikola Tesla (1856–91), saying his ideas "changed the world as we know it".

Test Department

From the experimental sound of these British post-punk artists, echoing contemporaries ▷ Einstürzende Neubauten.

Texas

... were nearly called Paris ... and they were from neither Dallas nor France but Glasgow.

They thought it a good description of their music and "gave us room to grow". (Cf another Scottish group, ▷ Big Country, named for identical reasons.) In particular it paid homage to the film *Paris, Texas*: they loved Ry Cooder's soundtrack. Similar place misnomers include ▷ Berlin Blondes, also from Glasgow.

Joe Tex

Joseph Arrington was known as Joe Tex from his Texan origin.

The Tex Pistols

Spoof Texan version of ▷ The Sex Pistols.

That Petrol Emotion

This Northern Ireland band took their name from a line in one of their early songs, speaking of explosive emotion. Conflict in the province has been punctuated by petrol and drogue bombs, shootings and armalite attacks.

The The

The moniker for projects which have generally consisted of back-up players hired by British studio master Matt Johnson, from East London. Therefore, a group in name only (cf ▷ Aztec Camera, ▷ The Lightning Seeds etc) – which is all it needed to be, the singer-songwriter said in an interview: "The purpose of a band's name is to be remembered, which is why I chose this one, and everybody remembers it."

It's also vague, he said – a common prerequisite of thinking stars. (Choices such as ▷ R.E.M., ▷ The Smiths and ▷ Talking Heads also avoid pigeonholing.) So this is a very definite article, even if it sounds like it's selected by someone with a stutter, or short of ideas. Johnson had plenty of alternatives yet thought it a good swipe at contemporary punks – ▷ *The* Sex Pistols, ▷ *The* Damned, ▷ *The* Clash – obsessed with the "The". In fact many 1950s combos prefixed with Del, meaning the, and The was also common in the 1960s, as in ▷ The Pink Floyd.

Theatre Of Hate

The original Theatre of Hate derived from French director Antonin Artaud (1896–1948), who called for emotional involvement from the audience. Singer Kirk Brandon borrowed the thespian term because he was trying to do the same. Related: ▷ Spear Of Destiny.

Thelonious Monster
Rockers of the 1990s who spawned a monster hybrid of jazzman ▷ Thelonious Monk and ▷ Dinosaur Jnr.

Them
▷ Van Morrison's first major band lifted it from a film released nine years before, in the mid-1950s. The "them" of the title referred to a race of invaders – so terrible that nobody dared to speak about them by name: "them" was enough.

Then Jerico
This band from southern England liked the sound of the Jordanian city which they heard on a news bulletin. Unfortunately they spelled it incorrectly.

Therapy?
Named after the possible healing power of music. The question mark came about because of an error in spacing in an early home made poster advertising a concert which they decided to fill with a ? to make it symmetrical. No relation to ▷ Group Therapy, or British 1970s band Therapy.

They Might Be Giants
This zany American duo took their moniker from a play and film by James Goldman. Many fans thought it a statement of ambition to make it big, although this was denied. TMBG was picked mainly for its zaniness – and because it was a complete sentence. Even then, a quick flick through any movie guide suggests some even more off-the-wall possibilities. (Random examples: *They Go Boom*; *Are We All Murderers?*; *Hallelujah, I'm A Bum*; and *Angels Who Pawned Their Harps*.) Cf ▷ I Start Counting, ▷ It Crawled From The South.

Thin Lizzy
The Irish group came together in 1970, naming from British comic *The Beano* which featured a robot cartoon strip called Tin Lizzie. The band re-spelled both words, pointing out the Irish don't pronounce the H. These changes helped avoid any lawsuits, although the name was itself adapted from a Model T Ford motor car. Spin-offs: ▷ Dare, ▷ Wild Horses. Cf ▷ Johnny The Fox.

The Thin White Duke
The opening words of ▷ David Bowie's 1976 album title track *Station To Station* refer to "the return of the Thin White Duke". It became an apposite nickname for Bowie in his pale, emaciated mid-1970s phase – looking drugs-worn but still with the almost aristocratic hauteur of an artist making impressive music despite it all.

Thin White Rope
A reference to male ejaculate; blame the late William Burroughs, who first used it. The American writer has inspired more than his fair share of monikers: cf ▷ Dead Fingers Talk.

Third Stone
▷ Jimi Hendrix named a song *Third Stone From The Sun*, describing the earth. It inspired ▷ Kinky Machine and this group.

Third World
A reflection of their concern for world issues and Rastafarian faith – also seen in their *Journey To Addis* (Ababa, in their spiritual home Ethiopia).

The 13th Floor Elevators
Going Up. This 1960s Texas band is remembered as being the apogee of hippiedom.

Elevators. Because they were making psychedelic music which they hoped would be uplifting/help people to get high. They weren't the only artists to use lifts to hint at "black and blues" status: ▷ Otis "Elevator" Gilmore.

13th Floor. While many developers missed the 13th floor in buildings for superstitious reasons, this is a drug reference: 13th letter = M = marijuana. The band's advocacy of drug use produced concern from police who accused them of encouraging criminality.

Going Down. Guitarist Stacy Sutherland was later imprisoned and then shot dead by his wife.
Inspired: ▷ The Fire Engines.

.38 Special

An early rehearsal of this U.S. band, playing blow-you-away rock, generated a noise complaint and a visit from police wielding .38 calibre handguns – among the most powerful of their kind. The name paralleled their double-barrelled-attacking music which resembled the *Saturday Night Special* twin guitars of the late Ronnie Van Zant's ▷ Lynyrd Skynyrd – .38 Special singer Donnie is his brother. Amid anti-gun lobby complaints, he strenuously denied advocacy of dangerous firearms.

This Machine Kills

From the scrawled inscription on an acoustic guitar used by U.S. folk singer Woodie Guthrie. The motto was later adopted by ▷ Donovan.

This Mortal Coil

From the famous speech in Shakespeare, the "to be or not to be" soliloquy in which Hamlet talks of dying: "when we have shuffled off this mortal coil". More Shakespeare: ▷ The Darling Buds. Related: ▷ The Cocteau Twins.

Thompson Twins

None of the band is a twin; none called Thompson; and there were three, not two, members during their most successful period in the 1980s. There were four when founder Tom Bailey took the name from Hergé's famous Belgian comic strip *The Adventures of Tin-Tin*, which featured The Thompson Twins, bungling and bumbling sleuths, identical in appearance (handlebar moustaches), dress (suits, bowler hats) and catchphrases ("You're under arrest" etc).

Hence the name. Hence the 1983 hit "We Are Detective" (sic).

▷ Stephen "Tin Tin" Duffy ran into legal problems from Hergé. Presumably the publisher thought it had more to protect in the prominent Tin-Tin character, used on books, videos, posters and even tee-shirts. The Thompson Twins are a peculiarity of English-speaking countries; elsewhere they have other names.

Thousand Yard Stare

U.K. indie hopefuls of the early 1990s. They borrowed a term of military origin meaning someone suffering from shellshock and having a tendency to distractedly stare into the distance.

The Three Chuckles

New York promoter Charlie Bush heard the yet-unnamed trio sing and was keen to sign them. He sent them away to look for a name. His next interview was with a mother-and-son act. The child wasn't interested in performing, just chomping on a Chuckles candy bar. Bush told the woman: "Congratulations! You haven't got the job ... but your boy's just given me a great idea." Perhaps the choice wasn't so great. Many people expected a comedy act and the Chuckles sang serious ballads.

3 Colours Red

Polish director Krzysztof Kieslowski finished his career with a 1993 trilogy of films inspired by the French revolution: *Three Colours Blue*, *Three Colours White* and *Three Colours Red*. Each had its own tricolour theme and subject: equality, freedom, fraternity. This band played down art-house expectations: they came, they said, not to praise Brit-pop but bury it in an avalanche of feedback.

The Three Degrees

This Philadelphia act named not in reference to qualifications but third degree – brutal questioning, especially by gangsters or police. A light-hearted reference to their being a trio.

Three Dog Night

Californian musician Danny Hutton came up with the idea of a group with three lead singers and wanted a name to reflect this. He turned to a dictionary where he found a little-known expression from Australia – where aborigines used to keep warm at night by sleeping alongside their dogs. One dog night, chilly. Two dog night, colder. Three dog night, freezing.

The Three Johns

This Leeds trio was indeed composed of three chaps called Jo(h)n. They started as Three Johns And A Michael but the latter left. It's also a crack at the London habit of calling everyone John as in Alexei Sayle's *Ullo John Gotta New Motor?* Related: The Mekons.

T

Three Mustaphas Three

There were originally six of them, all based in London yet with with Balkan origins and all bearing the Mustapha name.

Percy Thrills Thrillington

This "thrilling" tag was ▷ Paul McCartney's idea of a joke – a half-baked muzak version of the 1971 *Ram* LP by ▷ Wings.

Throbbing Gristle

This British electropop band said their name meant "not just any old gristle throbbing on the dance-floor". It was Northern English slang for an erection. They chose it for its embarrassment value – despite the risk of losing sales. Individual names include Christine Newby's rechristening Cosey Fanni Tutti, a pun on Mozart's opera *Così fan tutte*, and Neil Megson's Genesis P. Orridge. Related: ▷ Chris and Cosey, ▷ CTI, ▷ Psychic TV.

Thumper

Nickname for ▷ Phil Collins of ▷ Genesis because of his tub-thumping skills as a drummer. The name recalls the Disney character Thumper and is no relation to the similarly violent sounding ▷ Basher.

Thunderbyrds

▷ The Byrds.

Thunderclap Newman

Named as a joke on jazz pianist Andy Newman. The producer who thought of the name was one Bijou Drains – better known to the world as Pete Townshend of ▷ The Who. He'd known Newman for years.

Thurman

Oxfordshire hopefuls of the mid-1990s, named after *Pulp Fiction* actress Uma Thurman.

Ice-T

Entry under ▷ Ice.

Tiffany

She was born Tiffany Renee Darwish in California. So another real single name, like ▷ Madonna and ▷ Prince. Absolutely no relation to the U.K. *Eastenders* TV character.

Timbuk 3

They didn't come from the desert settlement of Timbuktu; nor were there three of them. This U.S. duo were being humorously perverse.

The Timelords

Their name matched the hit *Doctorin' The Tardis* about British television series *Doctor Who*. The title character of course is a Time Lord, custodian of the Tardis time machine. Related: ▷ The Justified Ancients Of Mu Mu, ▷ The KLF. Cf ▷ Dalek I.

Time Zone

A teaming of ▷ Afrika Bambaataa and ▷ Public Image Ltd singer John Lydon; they named from a line in their 1985 single *World Destruction*.

Tin Machine

▷ David Bowie's band named after the grinding feedback they made on *Tin Machine*. They took the phrase: "Hey hey we're ▷ The Monkees" and made it into: "Hey hey we're Tin Machine." This was because they had a "Davy Jones" in the band. This was Bowie's original name, changed because the Monkees man became famous first.

He was trying to recapture the lighter heavy metal sound of ▷ Iggy Pop, using the rhythm section of ▷ The Stooges, Hunt and Tony Sales. One critic had described the power of their *Fun House* as "like a metal machine crashing into top gear". Bowie thinly mixed The Stooges 1973 *Raw Power* album to give a tinny cheap-transistor sound.

Still, their first choice was Four Divorced Men, followed by Alimony Inc., building on their own admission: "We're all of a certain age and all divorcés." But then guitarist Reeves Gabrels remarried and they reconsidered.

Tin Tin

▷ Stephen "Tin Tin" Duffy.

Tiny Tim

New Yorker Herbert Boutros Khaury (1925–96) hated his real name, even claiming the initial B stood for Buckingham. During his desperate drive for recognition, he was Darry Dover, Larry Love, Texarkana Tex, Juditch Foxglove,

Vernon Castle and Emmet Swink. Then one of his many transient managers remarked the lumbering 6 ft 3 in giant was "about a foot less than the Empire State building". Herbert was 1,466 ft shorter than the city landmark, which ironically reminded him of a minor character out of Charles Dickens – the youngster son of Bob Cratchit, Scrooge's clerk in 1843's *A Christmas Carol*.

Sprog note: his daughter was named Tulip (after his hit *Tiptoe Though The Tulips* of course).

TLC

The familiar abbreviation meaning "tender loving care" fitted their prenomens to produce an ▷ Abba-style acronym: T = Tionne "T-Boz" Watkins; L = Lisa "Left-Eye" Lopez and C = Rozonda "Chilli" Thomas.

Toad The Wet Sprocket

Californians who named from a sketch by the U.K. ▷ Monty Python troupe. *The Contractural Obligation Album* reports that Rex Stardust, lead triangle for Toad The Wet Sprocket, needed an operation after an unfortunate accident.

To Damascus

From Los Angeles, formed by keyboardist Sylvia Juncosa. ▷ Damascus (no relation) had nothing to do with Damascus either. Cf ▷ Then Jerico.

Nick Todd

... was born Nicholas Boone, the brother of the more famous Pat. Todd came from the reverse spelling of his record label Dot.

Toe Fat

At the start of the 1960s, groups were severely constrained in naming. By the decade's end, anything was feasible – and this nasty choice was an attempt to explore boundaries of the possible. It tied in with their first album, which featured a medical photograph of people with very fat toes. Related: ▷ Uriah Heep.

The Tokens

Brooklyn boys Neil Sedaka and Henry "Hank" Medress named not from New York subway coins but from the phrase "token of affection".

Tolpuddle Martyrs

This British band with political ties recalled six Victorian farm workers who were deported to Australia for starting a trade union, and later pardoned after a public outcry.

Tom And Jerry

When they first met in a school play, Art Garfunkel was playing a Cheshire cat so he became Tom (Graph) and the more diminutive ▷ Paul Simon became Jerry (Landis). The name recalled the cartoon cat and mouse characters produced by Fred Quimby. Many stars have run into trouble by alluding to such names. They escaped, probably because their single *Hey Schoolgirl* was unsuccessful, so the media moguls didn't notice.

Tom Tom Club

▷ Talking Heads bassist Tina Weymouth and drummer Chris Frantz first applied Tom Tom to a new studio in the Bahamas, because of their interest in native drum rhythms. Other artists dropped in on the sessions and so joined the fledgling club.

Tonto's Expanding Headband

While feathered-hat-wearing Tonto was the companion of fictional hero The Lone Ranger, in this context it stood for "The Original New Tibrel Orchestra". Unrelated to Shiva's Headband.

Steve Peregrine Took

Peregrine was from a character in J.R.R. Tolkien's *The Lord Of The Rings*. The word for a type of falcon was apt because it also means "unusual" or "a traveller". He played drums with the early ▷ Tyrannosaurus Rex at London club The Middle Earth, named after the Tolkien's imaginary setting; their early songs were populated by Tolkienesque creatures. Cf ▷ Marillion etc. Took later joined ▷ The Pink Fairies.

Tools You Can Trust

From a slogan by a firm making saws, planes, drills etc. Cf ▷ Kitchens Of Distinction.

The Tortilla Flats

From John Steinbeck's 1935 novel, *Tortilla Flat*. Cf ▷ East Of Eden, ▷ The Grapes Of Wrath.

T

Peter Tosh

The ▷ Wailer was born Peter McIntosh and has recorded as Tosh and Touch (how it's pronounced in a Jamaican accent).

The Toss Pots

British 1960s band forgotten apart from their name, a textbook example of a lamentable choice. "We're a load of Brummie toss pots so why not?"

Toto

This Los Angeles MOR band named after Dorothy's dog in the musical *The Wizard Of Oz*. It was "short and simple, cute and memorable". Fearing this explanation to be embarrassing, singer Robert Kimball took to claiming falsely he was born Robert Toteaux, pronounced Toto. This joke is perpetuated by many reference books and articles, which get the origin wrong. Cf ▷ Jefferson Airplane – also named after a dog but widely believed otherwise.

Toure Kunda

"Kunda" means family. The African founders were all named Toure – sometimes said to mean "elephant".

The Tourists

These itinerant, British backdated hippies wanted to be The Spheres Of Celestial Influence; their record company thought better. Later ▷ Eurythmics. Cf ▷ Redd Kross.

The Toxic Twins

Nickname for Joe Perry and Steven Tyler of ▷ Aerosmith. A counterpart to Lennon/McCartney, ▷ The Nurk Twins, and Jagger/Richard(s), ▷ The Glimmer Twins.

Toyah

The exotic British princess of Punk was born Toyah Ann Willcox in the less-than-exotic King's Heath area of Birmingham. Mother Barbara said: "I found it while reading a book about a ballerina – named Toyah." As a rock star, she used her prenomen only. As a serious actress, she's Toyah Willcox. She's married to Robert Fripp of ▷ King Crimson.

T'Pau

British couple Carol Decker and Ronnie Rogers, from Shrewsbury, took it from the *Star Trek* TV series. T'Pau was a stateswoman from the planet Vulcan, home of Second Officer Mr Spock, who appeared in the episode *Amok Time*. The duo thought it was an interestingly different name, sounding like a comic book Pow! or ▷ Wham! More Trekkies: ▷ Caretaker Race.

Traffic

One of the most pivotal British combos of the late 1960s named when they had a hard time crossing the road one day because of the volume of traffic. Not a reference to ▷ Jimi Hendrix's *Crosstown Traffic* – which came a year later. The name was also considered by ▷ Status Quo. Related: ▷ Blind Faith, ▷ The Crickets, ▷ Derek And The Dominos, ▷ Family, ▷ Ric Grech, ▷ Mason, Wood, Capaldi And Frog, ▷ S.D.M., The Spencer Davis Group.

The Tragically Hip

The band, formed in 1986, said the name comes from former ▷ Monkee Michael Nesmith's produced film *Elephant Parts*. In 1982, ▷ Elvis Costello wrote a song called *Town Cryer* which featured the words: "Other boys use the splendour of their trembling lip/ They're so teddy boy tender and so tragically hip." This is often, wrongly, quoted as the source.

The Trammps

This U.S. group named from their humble origins. They were fed up of being told they would never amount to anything: "all you'll ever be is tramps!" They made the prediction come true.

The Transformers

Punks inspired by ▷ Lou Reed, whose 1972 LP was called *Transformer*. The album featured a classic song about sexual transformation, *Walk On The Wild Side*, and an "is-he-or-isn't-she" picture on the back. Cf ▷ Penetration etc.

The Transmitters

Another name working on two levels. The Transmitters were strictly post-punk, more like ▷ Pere Ubu.

The Transporters
"Transport" as in to move physically and emotionally. Cf above two entries.

Transvision Vamp
Blonde bombshell Wendy James, always a bit of a vamp, formed the British band with her boyfriend, Nick Christian Sayer. The name, made up in their bedroom, was supposed to suggest "worldwide excitement – revamping the musical scene". She later worked with ▷ Elvis Costello.

Trash
... started off as White Trash, from one of their songs. They pointed out they were white – what was wrong with calling themselves trash? How was this racist? (Cf: ▷ Average White Band.) By the late 1960s they were simply Trash.

The Trash Can Sinatras
Named for the 1990s after ▷ Frank Sinatra and his daughter Nancy (▷ Boots.) They wanted to reflect "the two sides of music ... tinsel and trash; stardom and shit; the glitter and the gutter"; gold and garbage; riches and rags ... but by now you have the picture. Other trash-rock, as opposed to thrash-rock, tags: Garbage, ▷ Ned's Atomic Dustbin, ▷ Trash.

Traveling Wilburys
The band billed as "the ultimate superstar aggregation" began as a fantasy by two Englishmen in America, ▷ George Harrison and Jeff Lynne, of ▷ Electric Light Orchestra fame, who wanted to include the people they most admired. They thought of the "homely" name – initially Trembling Wilburys, which suggested a non-pro family outfit who toured despite incurable stagefright. (Similar incognito motives belied the naming of ▷ The Notting Hillbillies, ▷ Derek And The Dominos, ▷ The Blue Ridge Rangers etc).

For their first LP ▷ Harrison was Nelson Wilbury, Lynne rechristened Otis, ▷ Bob Dylan was reborn as Lucky, ▷ Tom Petty chose to be Charlie T. Jnr and ▷ Roy Orbison turned into Lefty. Their second album was dedicated to the late Lefty as ▷ Del Shannon nearly joined them. Harrison changed to Spike, Lynne renamed Clayton, Dylan became Boo and Petty was Muddy: the latter had once been in a band called ▷ Mudcrutch.

The Tremeloes
From the musical term meaning a succession of up and down pitches. The band accepted by ▷ DECCA Records instead of ▷ The Beatles.

T Rex
The British band started in 1968 as Tyrannosaurus Rex, after a prehistoric dinosaur. Leader ▷ Marc Bolan said: "Tyrannosaurus Rex is extinct ... but it's the largest animal that ever lived. That's rather nice isn't it?" Manager Simon Napier-Bell added that Bolan chose it "because he was going to be that big too". However producer Tony Visconti commented the first word was impracticably long for posters and often misspelled. Bolan initially resisted a cut but knew it was more commercial and the change was made in October 1970 – despite fears of legal action by household cooking fat firm Trex. Note no full stop in name: T Rex not T. Rex.

This move coincided with a move from acoustic to electric; the departure of ▷ Steve Peregrine Took and arrival of Micky Finn – real name, no relation to the drink – and an abbreviation of titles from whimsies like *My People Were Fair And Had Sky In Their Hair But Now They're Content To Wear Stars On Their Brows* to *Tanx*. The ▷ Beatle-mania style reception that followed was called T-Rextasy Inspired: ▷ The Metal Gurus. Cf ▷ Dinosaurs, ▷ Dinosaur Jr.

A Tribe Called Quest
Many early 1990s rappers were in posses or tribes: cf ▷ Boo-Yaa T.R.I.B.E. This bunch were named by The Jungle Brothers after their leader Q-Tip: no relation to ▷ Q Tips.

Tricky
Briton Adrian Thaws was raised in Bristol and was nicknamed Tricky Kid as a teenager because of his delinquent behaviour. His career illustrates that petty crime doesn't always pay: he was jailed briefly for handling forged banknotes. Related: ▷ Massive Attack. Unrelated: ▷ Dodgy.

T

The Triffids

Australian band named from John Wyndham's (1903–69) most famous novel, 1951's *The Day Of The Triffids*, about nasty alien plants, walking on three roots and with lethal stings. For more Wyndham fun: ▷ The Chrysalids, ▷ The Midwich Cuckoos.

Trip Hazard

This short-lived 1980s group operated a fierce anti-drug policy and named from a sign at Bank Station on the London Underground, advising passengers of an uneven floor surface during repairs. More Tube influences: ▷ Bakerloo, ▷ Central Line, ▷ Way Out.

Troggs

British act Ten Foot Five were searching for a better name when they heard "trogg", a 1960s abbreviation of troglodyte or cave-dweller, meaning any moronic person. Their 1967 album was entitled *Trogglodynamite*; members included ▷ Reg Presley and drummer Ronald Bultis, renamed Ronnie Bond because of his liking for James Bond films. Their music has been championed by ▷ R.E.M. and ▷ Wet Wet Wet.

Truth

British 1960s pop band named from their favourite song, *Tell The Truth* by ▷ Ray Charles. They also considered Plain Truth but decided that truth is rarely plain or straightforward. Unrelated: ▷ The Truth.

The Truth

British 1980s act led by Dennis Greaves, who explained: "Truth is a strong word, but stands for honesty ... within the band, honesty in the music, honesty in every way possible." Unrelated: ▷ Truth.

TSOL

... The Sound Of Liberty.

The Tubes

They chose the word – from a key part of the human ear – because of its many alternative meanings: televisions, trains etc.

Tubeway Army

This was chosen to sound right about the time of punk but was also ironic; the act was essentially ▷ Gary Numan, with a few shadowy cohorts.

Tina Turner

She had a star's voice, looks and charisma, but Nutbush, Tennessee, girl Annie Mae Bullock knew she hadn't the name. That came with her marriage to Ike Turner: he chose Tina because it fitted in alliteratively. ▷ The Ikettes. Nickname: Duchess.

The Turtles

Their record company suggested The Tyrtles – the spelling from the then-breaking act ▷ The Byrds, who also made their name with ▷ Bob Dylan covers. They baulked at the spelling but allowed titles such as *Turtle Soup* and *Shell Shock*.

TV21

Scottish 1980s quintet named after the 1960s fantasy comic.

23 Skidoo

This post-punk band named after reading Aleister Crowley's *Book Of Lies*. More Crowley: ▷ Golden Dawn, ▷ The MacGregors.

Conway Twitty

It seems natural to assume this was chosen for a joke – like ▷ Engelbert Humperdinck. In fact Harold Lloyd Jenkins was deadly serious when he chose the names respectively from towns in Arkansas and Texas, after a day leafing through the atlas and considering various combinations. The Mississippi boy's original name was a tribute to silent film star Harold Lloyd.

2 Men, A Drum Machine And A Trumpet

Andy Cox and David Steele of ▷ Fine Young Cannibals made the infectious 1988 single *Tired Of Getting Pushed Around*. David said: "We used a pseudonym because we didn't want people to associate it with FYC and if it bombed, well, no harm done. It went straight to the top of the charts." An amusing, unpretentious choice which beats many carefully crafted, elaborate appellations.

2Pac
From leader Tupac Amuru Shakur (1971–96). His real name was Lesane Crooks; his mother, Black Panther activist Afini Shakur.

2.13.61
Harry Rollins-led projects named after his birthdate.

The Tycoon Of Teen
American producer Phil Spector; nickname from his success with a string of hit records in the 1960s.

The Tygers of Pan Tang
The sexual tiger imagery – the feline power and roaring danger – has attracted many bands. This 1980s Northern England band took their name from characters in a science fiction novel by British writer Michael Moorcock (cf ▷ Hawkwind).

Tyrannosaurus Rex
▷ Marc Bolan, ▷ Steve Peregrine Took, ▷ T Rex.

The Tyrell Corporation
This bland, official-sounding name conceals dark secrets known to this 1980s-on U.K. dance act but presumably few else. The Tyrell Corporation makes robots featured in the film *Blade Runner*, which is a cult classic both in its original and 1991 director's cut versions.

T

UB40

Fledgling musicians of the reggae band, from Birmingham, U.K., were unemployed when they began, in 1979. Legend has it that they met in a dole queue. In fact, they told the author that several knew each other before. It's true they took the number of the unemployment benefit card UB40 issued by the Department of Health and Social Security. Their first album, in 1980, was *Signing Off* and featured a reproduction of the hated UB40. In an interview, a DHSS spokesman denied the form number was later changed in response to UB40's political records such as 1981's *One In Ten*, a barbed comment on British unemployment rates.

The name became more of a label in time, like ▷ U2. Memories of the UB40 form faded after its abolition, and their lyrical range expanded to rats in the kitchen, red red wine and much else. Ali Campbell said: "The name summed up where we were and where we'd been. We didn't want to go back. We just wanted to get away from all that. A lot of people understood – at once. It seemed *obvious*."

UFO

An abbreviation used by various bands. The *Sunday Times* revealed the full meaning of a jazzy outfit: "The sharpest suits and the coolest coifs in Tokyo belong to the United Future Organisation ..." However, the best-known UFO inflicted hard rock on the world. "It means Unidentified Flying Objects," they said.

"What else?" Suggestions have included Utterly Fuckin' 'Orrible and Unbelievably Fantastic Operators. Related: ▷ Fastway, ▷ MSG, ▷ Waysted.

Ugly Kid Joe

Chosen as a riposte to ▷ Pretty Boy Floyd.

U.K.

From the people who brought you ▷ Asia, another boring name. These Britons wanted a tag which said something about their origins, so after much head-scratching, creative barnstorming sessions and sleepless nights they came up with this ...

Ultramarine

From *Ultramarine*, the 1933 debut novel by Malcolm Lowry.

Ultravox

From the Latin *ultra*, meaning "beyond", now widely seen as meaning "better than" or "best". And *vox*, meaning "voice". Therefore translated "the ultimate voice" or more accurately "the voice from beyond". The early guiding light was Dennis Leigh, better known as John Foxx. Ultravox! (exclamation soon dropped) went with this nicely and probably came from Vox speakers.

The band flirted with Tiger Lily – one of a few to use this – The Zips, The Innocents, Fire of London and London Soundtrack. Later vocalist: ▷ Midge Ure. No relations: ▷ Bono

Vox, ▷ Christopher Cross (the band contained Chris Cross); ▷ The Stone Roses (Leigh's first band was Stoned Rose).

Undercover
Because they played covers. End.

The Undertakers
This 1960s British act were originally called The Vegas Five but this was misunderstood when they placed a local newspaper advert for a concert which came out as The Undertakers. The gig was a success so they retained their grim name and added black frock coats as stage wear.

The Union Gap
The name completed the image for ▷ Gary Puckett. It was a reference to the U.S.A. as a whole as much as his own town.

Unit 4 + 2
It sounds like an item of trendy 1960s furniture. This group started as Unit 4, a quartet, and renamed as they grew to six. Their success led to the similarly named Four Plus One, a quintet, becoming ▷ The In Crowd.

Unleded
Jimmy Page and Robert Plant vowed never to re-form ▷ Led Zeppelin after the death of John Bonham. When they reunited they resorted to this pun. ▷ Percy, ▷ Bonzo, ▷ Dread Zeppelin etc.

Upsetters
Lee Perry's groups were named after his 1960s hit *The Upsetter*.

Midge Ure
Born James Ure in Glasgow, Scotland, the nickname was a dig at his diminutive stature. His bands include ▷ Visage, Slik, ▷ The Rich Kids and ▷ Ultravox.

Urge Overkill
This Chicago band's appellation paid tribute to a song by ▷ Funkadelic, an early influence.

Uriah Heep
Heep is a character in Charles Dickens's 1850

masterwork *David Copperfield*. Obsequious, toadying and full of false "'umbleness", he tries to blackmail his saintly employer Mr Wickfield. Related: ▷ Rough Diamond, ▷ Toe Fat. Another band recalling a dislikeable character with an unusual name. Cf ▷ Pere Ubu.

UTFO
Brooklyn rappers, or Un-Touchable Force Organisation. Their *Roxanne, Roxanne* inspired ▷ The Real Roxanne.

Utopia
In his strive for perfection, ▷ Todd Rundgren christened this occasional backing band after an imaginary ideal state. The similar meaning ▷ Nirvana was an alternative name under consideration. The word "utopia" is from the Greek for "no place", cynically suggesting perfection is impossible.

U2
This Irish band rose to world domination after starting life in 1976–77 as ▷ Feedback and ▷ The Hype.

Bassist Adam Clayton, seeking advice on the music business, had approached Dublin musician Steve Averill, AKA Steve Rapid of The Radiators. Punk was everywhere but both thought the name should be mysterious and not pin the act down to any one style or time. This had been the trouble with tags such as ▷ The Beach Boys, while some of the best bywords were vague. Adam liked ▷ XTC's pun and Steve came up with U2 as being on the same lines. It was "you too" or "you two", with the implication every fan could share the music, success and excitement. At the time this pun was novel; it later became less so thanks to ▷ Prince's influence, with titles like *Nothing Compares 2U*. The likes of Sinéad O'Connor spelled things similarly.

Hence the name. Hence the audience singalongs.
U2 had many meanings, some of which they discovered only later:
1. A size of battery, Ever Ready's best-selling model.
2. A famous railway in Berlin.
3. A type of submarine.
4. An American plane, used for intelligence gathering. One of these was shot down over

U

the U.S.S.R. in May 1960 and its pilot, Gary Powers, was put on show in Moscow in what was called The U2 Incident. Lead singer ▷ Bono was born four days after this event.

Adam had to work hard to convince Bono and ▷ The Edge about the choice, with them playing one gig in the first half as The Hype – with Dick Evans, later of The Virgin Prunes – and the second as U2.

The best account is Eamon Dunphy's 1987 book *Unforgettable Fire: The Story of U2*. The worst accounts get the facts wrong. One says the combo were christened from a list that manager Paul McGuinness obtained from a friend. This not only fails to take into account their creativity and their unlikelihood of accepting an alias from anyone else. It also gets the sequence of events wrong because the identity was in place before McGuinness took them on. Another incorrect story suggests they were originally V2, a reference to The Virgin Prunes. Bono's lot were billed at one early concert as V2, but only after a mishearing, and they were never officially that.

The V2 was a German rocket-propelled bomb used in World War II. The random doodlebugs would fly over Britain and land erratically as they ran out of fuel, exploding on impact. There is obviously no link, either, to Richard Branson's record label ▷ V2, which he only set up in the 1990s after his involvement with ▷ Virgin.

Name notes:

1. They became acquainted with the Berlin U2 main underground Ruhleben-Pankow while recording the album *Achtung Baby*. Some Berliners thought it more a symbol than the Wall and considered the city only reunited at the end of 1993 with its reopening after 32 years.

2. U2 patronage has helped ▷ Cactus World News, ▷ Clannad and ▷ The Hothouse Flowers.

3. Spoof acts: Doppelganger, ▷ The Joshua Trio.

4. The appellation hasn't been said as "u-two" everywhere; in the early days it was spoken as "u-dos", "u-deux" and so on by misinformed European fans.

Ritchie Valens
Born Richard Valenzuela of Indian-Mexican parents in Los Angeles, his patronym was shortened just before the release of his first single in 1958.

Valley Of The Dolls
This British band of the 1980s and 1990s named after the 1967 film about a naïve actress who is lured into a life of lust, drink and dolls – or drugs. In was based on the best-selling Jacqueline Susann novel. Cf ▷ The New York Dolls.

Frankie Valli
Anglicisation of Francis Castelluccio.

The Vandellas
▷ Martha And The Vandellas.

Vandenburg
Dutch heavy metal act, named from guitarist Adrian Vandenburg.

Van Der Graaf Generator
This British band recalled U.S. scientist Dr Robert J. Van de Graaff (1901–67) who built a generator at M.I.T. in the 1930s and later produced a scaled-down version to demonstrate static electricity. They saw a newspaper headline "Death of a Boffin" – and thought his name "really original".

Vangelis
He was born Evangelos Odyssey Papathanassiou, in Valos. His record company rebirth christened him simply Vangelis – they knew the problems people had already had with Greek names like Nana Mouskouri. ▷ Aphrodite's Child.

Van Halen
They started under the "pukeworthy" punky name Rat Salade then thought better of it and named after guitarist, Dutch-born Eddie Van Halen, and his drummer brother Alex Van Halen. Yet David Lee Roth was from the first the primary attraction for many fans. *Kerrang!* magazine said the choice was "amazing ... given the size of Lee Roth's ego".

Vanilla Fudge
This U.S. band started as The Vagrants and described themselves as "white guys doing black music". Cf ▷ Average White Band. This prompted one fan to say their sound was like "tasty fudge in a white colour". The "contradiction in terms" idea was shared by hippy surrealists: ▷ The Soft Watches etc ... and plenty of heavy metal bands – most famously ▷ Led Zeppelin. Spin-off: ▷ BBA.

Vanilla Ice
Solo star, so entry under ▷ Ice. Like ▷ Vanilla Fudge, another white musician to use "vanilla" as a name.

Vanity Fare
They recalled the *Vanity Fair* by British novelist William Makepeace Thackeray (1811–63) and the later magazine; cf ▷ Harpers Bizarre.

Vardis

A slight reworking of Tardis, the machine in which BBC TV series character Doctor Who travelled through time and space. Cf ▷ Dalek I, ▷ The Timelords.

VCL XI

▷ Orchestral Manoeuvres In The Dark in an earlier guise. The name was from a valve number on the back cover of ▷ Kraftwerk's 1975 album *Radio Aktivitat*.

Bobby Vee

Simplification of Robert Velline. He reverted for an attempted "serious" 1970s comeback.

Vee Jay

U.S. record company named from its founders: Vivian Vee Carter and James Jay Bracken.

The Velvet Underground

– a shorthand way to convey the group's interest in dark, fetishist, and underground matters. ▷ Lou Reed took it from *The Velvet Underground*, a book by Michael Leigh. A friend, Tony Conrad, had literally picked up from the gutter a battered copy of the sexual exposé – and brought it to Ludlow Street, where he had been living. He kept a friendship with John Cale through their work in ▷ The Dream Syndicate. The pulp paperback – with sado-masochistic cover showing a whip, mask and kinky high-heeled thigh boots – would have quickly been forgotten. Because of Reed's interest, it's been republished many times; its themes explored in his song *Venus In Furs*.

Reed, quoted in Victor Bockris's biography, says the name was simply "swiped". He's also on record as claiming to have met Leigh's daughter soon after the name was adopted: Leigh had just died. Another band member, Sterling Morrison, said it tied in with a CBS News report about "underground" art in which they played a role. He's quoted in *Up-tight: The Velvet Underground Story* by Bockris and Gerard Malanga.

Hence the name. Hence the black nail varnish.
Name notes:
1. Directly or indirectly inspired ▷ Dream Academy, ▷ Loop, ▷ The Primitives, ▷ The Psychedelic Furs, ▷ Sister Ray, ▷ Squeeze,

▷ Steve Severin and ▷ Verve; Reed inspired ▷ Berlin, ▷ Holly Johnson, ▷ Sid Vicious and ▷ The Waterboys. Also: ▷ Drella.
2. One of their early names was The Warlocks, a name shared with the early ▷ Grateful Dead. The West Coast band renamed after they heard of their eastern namesakes.
3. They also considered The Falling Spikes – entertainingly in view of their song *Heroin*.
4. Sometimes abbreviated to V.U. – also the title of one of their albums. Absolutely no relation to Texas R&B group The Velvets.

The Ventures

Bands from Seattle, Washington, didn't always play grunge. Go back to 1960 and they played pop under bland tags such as The Versatones – the first name for this outfit. The renaming came because they hoped they were embarking on a new venture with their single *Walk Don't Run*. It was a top 10 hit. Cf ▷ The Adventures.

Tom Verlaine

Born Thomas Miller in New Jersey, the vocalist-guitarist renamed after French Romantic poet Paul Verlaine (1844–96), friend of Arthur Rimbaud. The French symbolists had initially inspired him to write poetry before turning to lyrics. It is fitting a man with the initials T.V. should lead a band called ▷ Television.

Apollo C. Vermouth

▷ Paul McCartney pseudonym used while producing ▷ The Bonzo Dog Doo-Dah Band.

Vernon Girls

There were up to 70 of them at one stage, so not surprisingly they were not related. The name came rather from the U.K. football pools company which sponsored and organised their early performances.

Veruca Salt

This American 1990s band named from the spoilt, rich, precocious brat who screams: "I want the world and I want it now" in Roald Dahl's *Charlie And The Chocolate Factory*. British listeners who were unaware of Dahl thought it a revolting name: the group had to be told "verruca" is an English word for an unpleasant boil-type lump on the foot. They retaliated by calling their music "wart-core" as opposed to "hard-core". Anagram: Veruca Salt = A Vast Ulcer.

Verve

Verve means a special talent, as in artistic or intellectual vigour. Perfectly fitting the 1990s trend for short names – cf ▷ Blur *et al* – this U.K. group named after the U.S. Verve record label, best known for being the home of ▷ The Velvet Underground. Legal problems of the ▷ (London) Suede kind followed and they became known as The Verve in the States. They helped influence ▷ Mansun's name.

The Vibrators

Another attempt at punkoid phallicism/ gratuitous rudeness, even though the new wave Vibes, like ▷ The Stranglers, were considerably older than other bands comprising the London scene in 1977. Cf ▷ The Mixers. Inspired: ▷ Stiff Little Fingers.

Vice Squad

Because of their scatological lyrics, the sort of stuff Scotland Yard's Vice Squad was set up to hunt out and eliminate. The squad's tactics generated adverse publicity in the 1970s, with civil liberty groups – and this band – complaining it was no business of the police to investigate personal sexual morality. ▷ Beki Bondage.

Sid Vicious

London schoolboy John Simon Ritchie was also known as John Beverley, from his mother's second husband. Friends called him John; family addressed him as Simon or Sime; John Lydon (later ▷ Johnny Rotten) met him in the early 1970s and christened him Sid after his pet hamster. The name Vicious first came up about 1973, echoing ▷ Lou Reed's *Vicious*, the opening track of his just-released album *Transformer*. Later Ritchie formed ▷ The Flowers of Romance – confirming the aptness of his vicious *alter ego* by being involved in violence at early ▷ Sex Pistol gigs before joining himself. Rarely has a casually assumed identity predicted so much. Vicious lived up to his name. And died too. He was charged with murder after stabbing to death his girlfriend Nancy Spungen. While on bail he suffered a fatal heroin overdose.

"Be the star, sing the songs, be the name, walk the walk, talk the talk, live the life, live fast, die young." And, like ▷ Frank Sinatra, Vicious did it his way. But a lot less tunefully.

He was one of the inspirations behind ▷ the Sid Presley Experience.

Victor

▷ Prince suggested in the early 1990s that this could be a possible new name. He later decided on an indecipherable, androgynous symbol instead as "The Artist Formally Known As Prince" or TAFKAP.

Village People

U.S. producer Jacques Morali based the band on gay cult nightclubs in Greenwich Village, New York frequented by macho-men types. Each member humorously fitted one of the stereotypes: GIs, policemen, leathermen, cowboys or building-site workers.

Gene Vincent

Virginian Vincent Eugene Craddock shortened his real names. Partly inspired: ▷ Gene, ▷ Gene Loves Jezebel.

Vinegar Joe

An early star vehicle for joint vocalists – and sometime lovers – Robert Palmer and ▷ Elkie Brooks. The name sounds a mystery at first: none of the members was Joe, although some reporters addressed Palmer as such because he was the front man. It referred to one of the U.S.'s greatest wartime commanders, General Joseph Warren Stilwell (1883–1946), who commanded American forces in Burma and China. According to *Harrap's Book Of Nicknames* he got the soubriquet from his sour temperament.

The Violent Femmes

The spur-of-the-moment choice was contradictory and counter-productive. The violent bit led some promoters to fear possible riots. (Cf ▷ Riot Act, ▷ Quiet Riot.) The "femmes" raised questions as all the members are male, producing allegations of homophobia: "femme" is lesbian slang for a passive partner.

It's also sparked suggestions – hotly denied – that it's a comment on "husband-bashing" or female sexual violence against men. Still, like ▷ The Pixies, it matches this act's confusing blend of styles.

The VIPs

As in "very important person"; from the 1963 Richard Burton-Elizabeth Taylor film of the same name. The band went on to become ▷ Spooky Tooth.

Virgin

Richard Branson chose it for his company, at first distributing records, because he was a business virgin and it had a subversive sound. His runner-up choice: Slipped Disc Records. The early label issued singles in a saucy "deflower me" styled sleeve with an open-legged virgin who needed to be strategically torn to be opened. ▷ V2.

Virginals

They collapsed under sustained questioning. "It's after the instrument. Like a harpsichord. Erm, no, we don't play one. Okay, it's more to do with wanting virgins. *Like A Virginal* by ▷ Madonna."

Visage

This British 1980s studio band chose French for "face" "because it sounded classy". The Face had been a mod buzz-word years before (▷ Small Faces) and was title of the 1980s magazine that chronicled the rise of London club culture championed by media *eminence grise* ▷ Steve Strange.

The Voice

Nickname for ▷ Frank Sinatra.

The Voice Of The Beehive

Two American sisters who moved to England, they named after an Italian movie. So not a beehive hairstyle-name like ▷ The B–52s. Albums called *Let It Bee* and *Honey Lingers*.

The Voidoids

Clinton Heylin's 1993 book *From The Velvets To The Voidoids* says American punk ▷ Richard Hell named the band after an unfinished novel he had written in 1973, "though only after dispensing with alternatives like the Savage Statues, the Junkyard, the Morons, the Dogbites and the Beauticians."

The Voidoid novel was finally published later in the 1990s, with Hell at last explaining. He'd blended "void" and "android" to mean "an empty future": twentieth-century non-personalities with all originality sucked out by the media. Hence the 1977 EP *Blank Generation* with its *Pretty Vacant*-style cover defining the moronic sneer. Related: ▷ The Heartbreakers, ▷ Television.

Voodoo Chile

Band of the nineties inspired by a child of the sixties: ▷ Jimi Hendrix, known as Voodoo Chile after his two songs of the same name. More voodoo: ▷ The Hoodoo Gurus, ▷ Wall Of Voodoo.

V2

Record company founded by Richard Branson in the mid-1990s after moving away from his ▷ Virgin label. He left people wondering to what extent the new company was Virgin Two or a reference to the V2 rocket. Cf ▷ U2.

The Wackers

Outfit with a ▷ Beatles fixation. They had read that "wack(er)" was a popular term in the ▷ Fab Four's native city Liverpool. In fact, the word had been on the way out for years – cf ▷ The La's. The band therefore faced questions about whether it was anything to do with spanking, while some cruel wits made subtle alterations to the spelling on posters.

Wacko Jacko

Unflattering derivative for ▷ Michael Jackson. Long known as Jacko, he became "wacko" as tabloid reports grew about his eccentric behaviour, plastic surgery, skin colour changes, sleeping in an oxygen tent, funky monkey Bubbles, and so on. The fact that some reports were exaggerated or false didn't stop the Wacko tag from gaining near-universal currency. As we've seen, nothing, except scandal, spreads faster than a good nickname. Michael's comment (in every song): "Ohhh!"

Wah!

Said by some to be a reference to New York's Café Wah?, which was the starting point for many folk acts including ▷ Bob Dylan. Began as Wah! Heat; also known as The Mighty Wah! and Shambeko Say Wah!, after a group of Nazi-fighters. Similar slightly changed names include the various incarnations of ▷ Foetus. Founder Pete Wylie also played in ▷ The Mystery Girls, ▷ The Opium Eaters and ▷ Oedipus Wrecks.

The Wailers

Like ▷ Siouxsie And The Banshees, their sound gave them the name; the Wailing Wailers was first coined by their Jamaican manager ▷ Clement Sir Coxsone Dodd.

Loudon Wainwright III

The American folkie says his name has been misspelled so many times that he's gone past the point of worrying – or thinking about changing it. ▷ Virgin even managed to spell it wrong – Wainright on his 1992 album *History*. His prenomen has appeared as Louden, Ludin, Lowdown and Gordondon. Unflattering derivative: Loudmouth Wainwright.

Waitresses

Ohio lyricist Chris Butler wanted to write some songs from a woman's viewpoint. (Most astute effort: *I Know What Boys Like*.) He explained: "The waitress character is always an ordinary woman put upon by difficult circumstances and has to grapple with it."

Walker Brothers

Actors Noel Scott Engel – who also recorded as Scotty Engel – and John Maus were cast as the Walker brothers in a 1964 TV play and kept the sibling illusion when they started making records. More bogus brothers: ▷ The Chemical Brothers, ▷ The Doobie Brothers, ▷ Flying Burrito Brothers, ▷ The Righteous Brothers. Real brothers: ▷ The Allman Brothers, ▷ Bros etc.

239

Junior Walker And The All-Stars

Walker, called Junior by his family, claimed an ecstatic punter at their first gig cried out: "These guys are all stars." The name, and story, might be an exaggeration but – poetic licence – what the hell.

Wall Of Voodoo

This weird name for a weird group came about in a weird way, according to their weird leader Stan(ard) Ridgway. He had been playing in Los Angeles country bands but became unemployed in 1975 and set out to be a businessman.

He tried to produce horror film music with his partner Marc Moreland under the name ACME Soundtracks. One dark and stormy night they were trying to create a Phil Spectre "wall of sound" effect in their tiny rented Hollywood Boulevard office but the tape recorders kept fusing and power mysteriously failing. Marc leaned over to whisper: "Stan, this is no longer like a Wall Of Sound." He got the reply: "Yeah, it's creepy … more like a Wall Of Voodoo." Ridgway woke up the next day with a brainwave, tore down the ACME sign and put up "Wall Of Voodoo". He was already interested in faith healing, and had pinned up some paranormal photos – which duly found their way on to their record sleeves.

The Waltons

Named after a U.S. television drama about a Virginian family during the Depression and World War II.

Wang Chung

▷ Huang Chung.

Hank Wangford

Sam Hutt's day job: Harley Street gynaecology. After his girlfriend married his best friend, he drank off his sorrows in a pub near Wangford, Suffolk. The American prenomen was because "all the best country singers are Hank" (e.g. ▷ Hank Williams).

War

This black funk band from Long Beach, California, had been known as Señor Soul, The Romeos, Night Shift and The Creators before former ▷ Animal, Briton Eric Burdon, joined them in 1969. They suggested War as a contrast to the love-and-peace preoccupations of the time. Burdon was less sure after his recent hippy phase which produced the *Love Is* album. Vietnam was a major issue and he didn't want to capitalise on the misery of others. The others convinced him the *nom de noise* made something bad into good. It was "easy to remember and hard to forget".

Robin Ward

Session singer Jackie Ward took the name of her baby daughter Robin while recording the hit *Wonderful Summer*.

The Warm Jets

The Warm Jets were effectively ▷ Roxy Music minus ▷ Bryan Ferry and used for Eno's *Here Come The Warm Jets* January 1974 album. He said it sounded like a 1950s rock or high-tech name. However, he was fully aware that it a sexual reference to what is euphemistically called "watersports". Another Warm Jets surfaced in London in 1996. They told *NME* they took the title because "it sounded good – we're not paying homage to Bryan or anything".

Warsaw

Early ▷ Joy Division, from the experimental track *Warszawa* on ▷ David Bowie's 1977 album *Low*. The choice was dropped after they heard of a London band called Warsaw Pakt, named after the old defence alliance.

Dionne Warwick

Marie Dionne Warrick changed her surname in a bid to end spelling confusion (it's pronounced War-wick; the English town Warwick is said Worrick). She tried briefly adding an E for luck, inspired by ▷ Sam Cooke and on the suggestion of astrologer Linda Goodman but Dionne Warwicke's records were less successful.

Was (Not Was)

The enigmatic studio wizards and "brothers" Don and David Was preferred to leave their name clouded in mystery for years. Was or not Was, that was the question? David was born Weiss, sometimes incorrectly spoken as Was or Wass although it should be said Vice. Don was never Was and was born Don Fagenson. So the one was Vice Not Was and the other was always Not Was. Pronounced: Wass (Not Was).

Wasp Factory
Taken from a 1984 novel title by British writer Iain Banks.

The Waterboys
Critic Robert Christgau, reviewing the 1973 album *Berlin*, castigated ▷ Lou Reed for the song *The Kids*, which repeats: "I am the waterboy." Christgau asked: "What is a waterboy anyway?" Mike Scott, of this British 1980s-on band, said he didn't know either and wanted to provide an answer. He earlier considered Funhouse – from an album by ▷ The Stooges. Related: ▷ The Red And The Black.

Muddy Waters
One of the greatest U.S. blues stars, he had an inauspicious start. For little McKinley Morganfield was born in poor surroundings on the Mississippi delta in 1915. The river itself is called Old Muddy. One of his favourite play areas was a dirty creek near his Rolling Fork home and his long-suffering grandmother – who had the unenviable job of constantly cleaning him up – called him Muddy. The nickname stuck, in the same way mud sticks …

He inspired and influenced many including ▷ The Rolling Stones (in name and early repertoire), ▷ David Bowie (▷The Mannish Boys), and all bands called ▷ Mojos.

Watts 103rd Street Rhythm Band
Named after the Watts area of L.A., California.

Wax
U.K. songwriter Graham Gouldman first used this in 1967 before ▷ 10CC. In 1980 he formed Common Knowledge with Andrew Gold and in 1985 they became Wax. In the intervening years the old waxy method of mastering vinyl was falling into disuse, while it could still mean "waxing lyrical".

Way Out
This British band took it from an an exit sign seen on the London Underground, resembling the hippy compliment meaning "freaky" or "impressively unusual". (More Tube notices: ▷ Trip Hazard.)

Waysted
British heavy metal band namechecking their leader (cf the related ▷ Fastway). In this case, Pete Way, ex ▷ UFO. He laboriously explained this one in an interview with the author in case it wasn't clear (you know, Pete Way so, like, Waysted, good eh?). Not as elegantly wasted as ▷ Ex-Pensive Wino, ▷ Keith Richards.

The Weathergirls
Originally Two Tons Of Fun, these larger than-life-singers renamed to suit their hit *It's Raining Men*.

The Weathermen
Tribute to ▷ Bob Dylan, whose 1965 *Subterranean Homesick Blues* includes the lines: "You don't need a weather man / To know which way the wind blows." The simplest interpretation is: "Before smoking illegal substances, check there are no policemen downwind." Other interpretations refer to the breeze of political and social change: Dylan had said the answer was blowing in the wind. The same song inspired ▷ fIREHOSE.

The Weavers
Political folk band named after a 1892 play about working-class suffering by German Gerhart Hauptmann (1862–1946). *Die Weber* gained a new audience in the U.S. in 1965 after it was translated.

The Wedding Present
Guitarist-singer David Gedge explains this Northern England band chose this moniker – over The Lost Pandas – because it sounded "deep and classy, like a play or a film". Fans call them The Weddoes. Cf "everyday name" ▷ The Birthday Party.

Weddings Parties Anything
These Australians named after an early advert offering their musical services for hire. They joked: "Available for concerts at a bar mitzvah near you. Purveyors of folk music to the gentry. … or anyone who'll pay. Ceilidhs a speciality."

Wednesday Week

Los Angeles band named after a 1980 Undertones song, not the ▷ Elvis Costello B-side.

Weekend

Jazzy British ensemble who named because "everyone looks forward to the weekend". Spin-off: ▷ Working Week.

Paul Weller

▷ The Jam, ▷ The Style Council, ▷ The Cappuccino Kid, ▷ The Modfather, ▷ The Smoking Mojo Milters.

Westworld

This vocal combo named after a Yul Brynner movie about a holiday complex recreating the old wild west. They said the best things about the picture were "its title – and a crazy badman robot" which goes berserk. Cf the film-inspired ▷ Go West.

Wet Willy

The makers of *The Wetter The Better* had backing vocalists called The Williettes and confessed: "We did it to get noticed."

Wet Wet Wet

This Scottish pop band faced derision for the name – yet it hasn't stopped a run of hit singles, including the multi-million-selling *Love Is All Around*, originally by ▷ The Troggs. A ▷ Scritti Politti song they adored, 1982's *Gettin', Havin' and Holdin'*, says "his face is wet, wet with tears". They're widely known as The Wets – an abbreviation seen as inevitable and not uncomplimentary.

We've Got A Fuzzbox And We're Going To Use It

▷ Fuzzbox.

Wham!

▷ George Michael and Andy Ridgeley started in 1979 with an unsuccessful ska act, The Executive. Their starting point as a duo was a Michael song with a "Wham bam thank you ma'am" line. (*Hence the name.*) It evolved into 1982's *Wham! Rap (Enjoy What You Do)*. This parody backed a life on benefit but annoyed officials, who feared it encouraged "scrounging" – while some on the dole said they couldn't get work despite trying desperately hard. Cf ▷ UB40. The punchy name quite coincidentally recalled comics such as *Batman* and especially American artist Roy Lichtenstein's 1963 two-canvas picture *Whaam* showing a pilot destroying an enemy fighter.

Name notes: Their backing singers included ▷ Dee C. Lee. Wham! inspired the answer-naming of Plop!, the band which later became ▷ Frazier Chorus. Tribute act: Club Tropicana. Note the exclamation mark, cf ▷ Wah!

Whippersnapper

Dave Swarbrick was long regarded by many as "the finest folk fiddler in England". He formed Whippersnapper in mid-1984 during a break from ▷ Fairport Convention reunions. Swarbrick told the author another choice was Morgan after the make of car, because it had "an old-English feel to it". "One of our songs is about *Hard Times In Old England*, so it would have been right. There were a few names about. Whippersnapper won in the end, it's a good cheeky word."

Whirlwind

U.K. rock 'n' roll revivalists named from an old Charlie Rich song.

Whitesnake

Ex ▷ Deep Purple star David Coverdale named his band after the title of his first "solo" LP. Inspired: ▷ Copperhead. Unflattering derivative: ▷ Robert "Percy" Plant used to call Coverdale "David Coverversion".

White Zombie

American movie buff Robert Straker named himself Rob Zombie, and his 1990s band after the title of a 1931 Bela Lugosi film. No relation to ▷ The Zombies. More Lugosi: ▷ Bodysnatchers.

The Who

They started at school in Acton, London, backing a certain Roger Harold Daltrey as The Detours. This lasted for some time until U.K. television show *Thank Your Lucky Stars* featured a nine-piece Irish combo also called The Detours.

Guitarist Peter Dennis Blandford Townshend – yes, those really are Pete "Beaky" Townshend's middle names – and friend Richard Barnes suggested No One, The Group or The Who. The aim was to curtail the Detour jokes of the smarmy MC at the Oldfield Tavern, their regular concert venue. "On stage next we have ... The Who." "Who?" Or: "Please give a big hand for – No One!"

There was a diversion at this point because Townshend also liked the Hair, which was becoming a major moral issue: older people were concerned about decadency, dirtiness and sexual confusion. The younger generation said it wasn't the hair length but the mind that mattered. However, the act didn't have especially long hair. Townshend's compromise The Hair and The Who was rejected as too complex by Daltrey, who said: "The Who's short enough to print big on posters." (The band were heroes of ▷ The Jam later, who used much the same "keep it short" thinking in deciding on their moniker.)

The Who were taken on by publicist Peter Meaden, who decided the name was "airy-fairy". He decided to cash in on growing youth culture by moulding them into an archetypal mod outfit, The High Numbers. This was mod lingo for a flash, fashionable person. (In the late 1970s there was a spoof 1960s combo called ▷ The Low Numbers.) Their debut was the Meaden-penned I'm The Face. (Cf ▷The Faces and ▷ The Small Faces.) The musicians weren't happy, the single flopped and they gained a new manager, Kit Lambert. He thought a change might shake off their rapidly acquired, unwelcome reputation for wrecking concert venues and make them sound less like a housey-housey session. So they reverted to The Who. Bingo!

Lambert told author Dave Marsh The Who was a gimmick which could provoke confusion and even fights. Still it was "easy to remember, made good conversation fuel, provided ready-made gags for disc jockeys. It was so corny it had to be good." There's more in Marsh's 1993 book *Before I Get Old: The Story Of The Who.*
Hence the name. Hence the smashed guitars.
Name notes: Compare ▷ The Guess Who – there were minor disagreements between the two outfits because of possible confusion.

Townshend (AKA Towser) produced his protégés ▷ Thunderclap Newman under the superbly absurd appellation Bijou Drains. Drummer Keith Moon, who died in 1978, was called The Loon because of his manic antics. Bassist John Entwistle formed ▷ Ox and ▷ Rigor Mortis. A remark by Entwistle – probably, although it may have been Moon – led to ▷ Led Zeppelin. Also inspired: ▷ See For Miles.

Whole Oates
▷ Hall And Oates.

The Whole World
Kevin Ayers, ex ▷ Soft Machine, named this band in reference more to its size than to any universal message. The large personnel included David Bedford and Mike Oldfield.

Widowmaker
From American slang for anything that is lethally dangerous. Lumberjacks used it to describe falling boughs; southerners applied it to tornadoes.

Wigan's Chosen Few
The stomping hit, 1975's *Footsie*, had a misleading group credit. It featured chanting by thousands of fans – not a chosen few – and wasn't made anywhere near Wigan. It was originally by Canada Chosen Few and remixed in Britain as Sounds Of Soul. It was a northern dance-floor hit but when it was taken up for national airplay, a change was needed for copyright reasons. Wigan was added by way of thanks for the area's support. Cf overstated: ▷ 10,000 Maniacs, ▷The Whole World.

Wild Cherry
Not directly from the fruit. Accident victim Rob Parissi woke up in hospital and looked at his bedside table ... and saw a box of cherry-flavoured cough drops. Called Wild Cherry.

Kim Wilde
Born Kim Smith, the daughter of ▷ Marty Wilde and sister of Ricky Wilde. She continued the patronym first given to her father by ▷ Larry Parnes. ▷ Mel And Kim.

243

Marty Wilde

Singer Reginald Smith had already moved to Reg Patterson when ▷ Larry Parnes saw him, renaming after his wild act. His backing band was The Wilde Cats and his daughter ▷ Kim Wilde.

Wild Horses

Spin-off from ▷ Rainbow and ▷ Thin Lizzy; named after a ▷ Rolling Stones track on the 1971 album *Sticky Fingers*. Cf ▷ Crazy Horse.

Hank Williams

The Alabaman country singer was born Hiram Williams, although it was incorrectly spelled Hiriam on his birth certificate. He hated the prenomen – however written – and preferred the more authentic American Hank. As such, a star was born.

Willie And The Poorboys

Mid-1980s group fronted and formed by ▷ Rolling Stone Bill Wyman, who named them with conscious irony; he is not one of this world's paupers but the project was designed to raise cash for charity. Equally a tribute to ▷ Creedence Clearwater Revival's 1969 LP *Willie And The Poorboys* and the song *Willie And The Hand Jive*.

Wilson Phillips

Some progeny of famous parents try to play down their parent's links. An increasing number – Arlo Guthrie, Julian Lennon, Zak Starkey, and Jeff Buckley to name a few – are open about it. Some are shameless …

▷ Beach Boy Brian Wilson's daughters Wendy and Carnie were two-thirds of the trio. Chynna (China, geddit?) Phillips was the daughter of John and Michelle Phillips of ▷ The Mamas And The Papas.

Windbreakers

After much misunderstanding and humour, let's be clear it's a reference to their trademark warm jackets, not flatulence.

Wind In The Willows

This folky New York outfit purloined the title of *The Wind In The Willows*, the 1908 children's novel by Briton Kenneth Grahame (1859–1932). Included Debby Harry, soon to form ▷ Blondie.

Wings

If it's hard thinking of a moniker, consider the problems facing ▷ Paul McCartney as he pondered what to call his outfit after what is widely regarded as the greatest-ever group. How do you top ▷ the Beatles?

The Fabs' name was not as brilliant as their music – but Macca's choices are hardly the greatest to be found in this book. First he thought of The Turpentines (unusual); then McCartney And The Dazzlers (a bit retro); finally Wings. Reports at the time said it indicated the star's desire to travel after years in the studio. Macca told British newspapers the name was "futuristic", "optimistic" and "hopeful". It was also a stork-wings message to his wife Linda, who was expecting a baby any day soon.

Wire

This arty quartet survived and outgrew their punky origins as The Geezers. They wanted a minimalist name to reflect their minimalist songs, which they described as "not short, just not long". Guitarist Bruce Gilbert had suggested The Wires or Wire. They chose the latter because there were many other plural monikers around. It could refer to guitar strings, electric flex or much else. They later briefly became Wir after founder drummer Robert Gotobed left.

Witchfinder General

British heavy metal group named after Matthew Hopkins, who toured England in the seventeenth century in a Spanish Inquisition style search for witches. He caused 4,000 people to be hanged and was later pronounced a fraud.

Wizzard

Leader Roy Wood – born Ulysses Wood – adopted the visual image of a crazed wizard. Later called Wizzo Band; like ▷ The Electric Light Orchestra, a spin-off from ▷ The Move.

Jah Wobble

From a misunderstanding about his real name, John Wardle. Bassist with ▷ Public Image Ltd, later solo.

Wolfking Of L.A.

Nickname for John Phillips of ▷ The Mamas And The Papas. He used it as the title of his 1970 album.

WOMAD

Stands for World Of Music, Arts And Dance. Created in large part by Peter Gabriel, ex ▷ Genesis, the foundation has presented music and arts festivals worldwide.

Stevie Wonder

His prenomen's Steveland. ▷ Motown billed the blind star as Little Stevie Wonder on the release of his first LP at the age of 12. His father's name was Judkins and Little Stevie's early songwriting credits were to S. Judkins. Stevie however insists his birth certificate says Morris, which he's long preferred: it was his mother's married name. He later played one record as Eivets Rednow (Stevie Wonder backwards).

The Wonder Stuff

The band, formed in the 1980s and with a large following 10 years on, are informally known as The Stuffies. Strangely, not The Wonders ...

Vocalist Miles Hunt had for a long time claimed the name "doesn't mean anything". However, recently he said his uncle Bill Hunt, keyboard player with ▷ Wizzard, knew ▷ John Lennon. The former ▷ Beatle supposedly met the energetic young Miles and remarked the boy had "the wonder stuff". Hunt said Lennon used to visit when he returned to England from New York. Lennonologists are still picking over this story. They point out that while Lennon visited The Big Apple several times before settling there, he left Britain on 3 September 1971, and never returned. The jury may be out, but it is remarkable that Lennon could be having an effect on music in quite this way.

Wonder Who

▷ The Four Seasons in disguise for a 1966 single designed to prove to their record company that they could have hits without the prop of their famous name. The group's members were proved right as the song reached the top five. Perhaps the point would have been even better proved with a totally anonymous name. Wonder Who, like ▷ The Guess Who, suggested somebody famous was involved.

Brenton Wood

Alfred Jesse Smith wanted to make enough money to live in the Hollywood suburb of Brentwood. *Hence the name, hence the hits.*

Woodentops

This 1980s British group named from the 1955–58 BBC television serial *The Woodentops*. It was repeated many times in the 1960s as part of the *Watch With Mother* series. Cf ▷ The Flowerpot Men, ▷ The Soup Dragons.

Woodworm Records

Literally, a cottage industry this one, set up by Dave Pegg, of ▷ Fairport Convention and ▷ Jethro Tull. It was named after his home in an Oxfordshire village. When he first acquired it, the black and white building suffered from severe woodworm. The beams have now all been treated and the cottage known as Woodworms Hilton. Cf ▷ The Cocktail Cowboys, ▷ The Pheasant Pluckers.

Working Week

Formed by members of ▷ Weekend as the band broke in two amid musical differences. They chose a name which is the exact opposite of their previous moniker.

Johnny Worth

Songwriter Les Van Dyke renamed after his local telephone exchange area in London.

WOT

What? Wot? Stands for World Of Twist.

X

From singer Exene Cervenka. Another single-letter-moniker: ▷ M. There's plenty of letters left, although there's been one group named A Band Called A.

X-Clan

New York band "fighting for the black cause", named after activist Malcolm X. One of his civil rights campaigner colleagues was Sonny Carson, whose son Lamumba founded this act. Lamumba met Malcolm X as a child and remained inspired by him.

The X-Pensive Winos

▷ The Ex-Pensive Winos (either spelling is correct).

X-Ray Spex

Brilliant name recalling the punk enthusiasm for toy spectacles which can "see through" things – even more brilliant name for their singer, ▷ Poly Styrene (born Marion Elliot). The glasses were advertised on the back of *True Detective* magazine.

XTC

This British band started in 1977 as The Helium Kidz. The name is obviously "ecstasy". That's happiness, not the drug, which wasn't known when they started and only became sadly fashionable at raves about a decade later. Spin-off: ▷ Mister Partridge.

Xymox

This Dutch band named from the English word "zymotic," meaning the fermentation of germs. It was the last entry in a dictionary they had.

Stomu Yamash'ta

The Japanese percussionist abbreviated his real name Tsutomu Yamashita.

Yanni

Yanni Chryssomallis to his bank manager. A ▷ Vangelis-style abbreviation for a fellow Greek keyboard star who comes on like a cross between Vangelis, Jean Michel Jarre, Ennio Morricone and Mantovani.

Yardbirds

These British 1960s little red roosters who liked doing purist versions of old songs were paying a tribute to ▷ Charlie "Bird" Parker, whose name came from his fondness for chickens – or, more accurately, eating them; he called them "yardbirds".

They later became New Yardbirds, managing to peacefully co-exist, without any flurries of feathers, with the similarly named ▷ Byrds. Related: ▷ BBA, ▷ Eric Clapton, ▷ Led Zeppelin, ▷ Renaissance. Inspired: ▷ The Nazz.

Yazoo

Vince Clarke's first band after ▷ Depeche Mode, with vocalist ▷ Alf. The suggestion has been made that Yazoo came from ▷ Bob Dylan's *Basement Tapes* track, *Yazoo Street Scandal*. However, Dylan's wordy folk-rock has little in common with Yazoo's electronic pop. The name was later abbreviated to the somewhat regrettable Yaz in the U.S.A., because a small record company had already registered the Yazoo title. The name later was appropriated by a drink. No relation: ▷ Yazz.

Yazz

The British singer, who made her name working with The Plastic Population and Coldcut in the 1980s, shortened her full name, Yasmin Evans.

Yeah Yeah Yeah

From ▷ The Beatles. Specifically *She Loves You (Yeah Yeah Yeah)*.

Yello

Means "a yelled hello" rather than being a Germanic misspelling of "yellow". Singer-lyricist and former artist Dieter Meier, from Switzerland, is much too well educated to do a thing like that.

Yes

The zenith – or nadir, depending on where you stand – of British art-rock in the 1970s. The act evolved from the less-satisfactorily-named Mabel Greer's Toyshop. Singer Jon Anderson wanted a change; while guitarist Peter Banks admitted the old moniker was "silly".

The name was chosen – like the final word of Irish writer James Joyce's magnum opus *Ulysses* – because: "It's the most positive word that can be conceived, and one of the shortest – so it prints up bigger on posters, like ▷ The Who." But it also inspired one of the shortest record reviews ever: "No."

Later the band splintered, with the re-formed original outfit considering (Spock-like) becoming The Affirmative. Legal problems meant they had to be known as ▷ AWBH or Anderson Bruford Wakeman Howe (AKA Anderson Wakeman Bruford Howe). Related: ▷ Asia, ▷ Buggles.

Yesterday's News

New York 1980s *a capella* act. They were looking for details of a forthcoming gig in the *Daily News*. After going through the news section without success, they found the answer in … "yesterday's news". *Hence the name.*

Yo La Tengo

Spanish for "I've got it". It is roughly the same as "Eureka!" in Greek and represents this band's joy at finding a name.

It is used as a cry by Spanish-speaking outfielders in baseball. Ira Kaplan took it in honour of a Latin ballplayer for the New York Mets, the favourite team. He's shortstop Elio Chacon.

Kaplan hoped it would be meaningless enough to avoid distracting questions. In fact, it's provoked many, with its dance-band connotations leading to the band's records often being misfiled alongside the Gipsy Kings.

The Youngbloods

These 1960s American hit-makers were named to fit in with star member ▷ Jesse Colin Young.
… Talking of whom …

Jesse Colin Young

Perry Miller said that he renamed in tribute to:
1. *Jesse* James, the legendary American Robin-Hood style criminal;
2. *Colin* Chapman, the racing driver;
3. Cole *Younger*, a cowboy hero.

His new stage name led to the naming of ▷ The Youngbloods, which he formed and led.

Neil Young

▷ Buffalo Springfield, ▷ Crazy Horse, ▷ The Godfather Of Grunge, ▷ The Mynah Birds. Inspired: ▷ Powderfinger.

The Young Ones

U.K. comedians, professing to be fans of ▷ Cliff Richard, named their TV series about students after his 1962 film and song. They later joined Richard on a charity remake of his 1959 hit *Living Doll*. Spin-off: ▷ Bad News.

The Young Rascals

The story opens in 1920, when producer Hal Roach produces a series of single-reel movies called *Our Gang*. Cut to the 1950s when the long-running children's comedy show is revived on TV as *The Little Rascals*. Then watch the slapstick shorts inspire ▷ Spanky And Our Gang; gasp as the idea is passed to a New York soul band; be amazed as they become The Young Rascals; laugh at their silly kid image; cry as they age, become The Rascals and disappear from public view.

The Zantees

Named after characters in the *Outer Limits* television show.

Frank Zappa

Francis Vincent Zappa Jnr to his friends, he was born to Greek parents. So Zappa has always been Zappa (apart from his brief time as ▷ Ruben And The Jets). Father of the band ▷ The Mothers of Invention and valley girl Moon Unit Zappa. She went on to form ▷ Fred Zeppelin with the equally-extraordinarily-named brothers Dweezil and Ahmet Rodin. Other Zappa child: little Diva – no relation to ▷ Little Eva.

Zeitgeist

At least two British bands took their names from this German historical term. *Zeit* means time, *geist* is spirit, and together they are (roughly translated) "the spirit of the age". The better Zeitgeist's version of ▷ The Temptations' hit *Ball Of Confusion* was a little-known 1980s classic.

Zodiac Mindwarp And The Love Reaction

The full entry – including names worthy of ▷ Captain Beefheart's Magic Band – is under ▷ Mindwarp.

Zombies

An intellectual British pop band who were photographed reading university set-text books and even playing chess together. Their original bassist, Paul Arnold, later qualified as a doctor.

The appellation was thus ironic: the word "zombie" has come to mean a brain-dead individual. For more "we're thick" names, see the entry on ▷ Simple Minds. Rod Argent later formed ▷ Argent. Not related: ▷ White Zombie.

Zoso

The alphabetic rendering of the runic symbol for Jimmy Page of ▷ Led Zeppelin. Also used by some as the name of Led Zep's fourth album (which actually has no real title, although it is often catalogue-listed as *Led Zeppelin 4* or *Four Symbols*).

ZTT

British record company and production force, best known for work with ▷ Frankie Goes To Hollywood. Formed by Trevor Horn, ex ▷ Buggles and ▷ Yes. ZTT should be said as "Zang Tumb Tuum", which is the onomatopoeic version of the sound of a machine gun as written by Italian futurist Luigi Russolo. Russolo's works also inspired the naming of ▷ Art of Noise, a band on the label.

Zucchero

The Italian pop star was born Adelmo Fornaciari but got the nickname Zucchero ("sugar") in early childhood.

ZZ Top

Final notes to note for names aficionados:
1. Pronunciation guide for English fans: the Zs

are said U.S.A.-style: it's "Zee Zee Top", not "Zed Zed Top".

2. The Texas-raised trio, who started at the end of the 1960s, achieved their greatest success after frontmen (Billy) Gibbons and (Dusty) Hill grew long beards. Note that the clean-shaven one is called (Frank) Beard. Names, as we have seen throughout this book, can be misleading things.

3. They inspired a spoof band, ▷ Redbeards From Texas.

4. They were formed after the break-up of The Warlocks – a name also considered separately by ▷ The Grateful Dead and ▷ The Velvet Underground – and the similar demise of the psychedelia-influenced Moving Sidewalks. Far out, right?

And why ZZ Top?

The *Q Encyclopedia Of Rock Stars* says it came from an open pair of hay-loft doors on a barn with Z beams seen by Gibbons. The band told the current author it was an attempted parody of venerable blues players like ▷ B.B. King and Z.Z. Hill. "We wanted to be like a crusty bluesman". Z.Z. was always going to make their records easy to find in record shops – and their entry easy to find in books like this.

Many accounts give the origin of Top from cigarette rolling papers: Top, Zig Zag or Rizla brands, which share some similarities with the band's ZZ logo. Gibbons says it just came to him one day to fit the ZZ. "It was a top name." So there we have it.

"*… hence the name!*"